'The Mediterranean, so eternally young, the very symbol of youth!'
D. H. Lawrence

Since the eighteenth century, the warm south of the Mediterranean has attracted countless British visitors. Among these travellers were many painters, writers, collectors and architects, from Byron and Turner to Virginia Woolf, Robert Graves and Patrick Leigh Fermor. They went seeking beauty, fulfilment and inspiration of a kind that they often failed to find in their grey, insular northern home. The effect on their art would go on to definitively shape British culture.

From the 1700s, Great Britain was successful in war, conquest and trade, but far less so in cultural achievement. To help forge a national aesthetic, the British turned to the Mediterranean to supply romance, grandeur and a fresh sense of light. An emerging 'Britishness' was indelibly marked by this search for an idealized beauty that Europe's South – that 'Magick Land' – came to represent.

Robert Holland, one of the world's leading historians of the region, traces how the Mediterranean came to be the prime theatre of British sensibilities beyond the homeland, from the Grand Tour through to the twenty-first century. This is the story of how a persisting Mediterranean tradition, in which a glorious Graeco-Roman past interacted with jarring modernity, shaped British literature, painting and the other arts.

Invitingly panoramic and richly persuasive, **The Warm South** shows how every movement, from Romanticism to modernism and the postmodern, was refracted through this imagined world of colour, carnival and sensual self-discovery.

THE WARM SOUTH

The Warm South

HOW THE MEDITERRANEAN
SHAPED THE BRITISH IMAGINATION

ROBERT HOLLAND

YALE UNIVERSITY PRESS
NEW HAVEN AND LONDON

Jacket illustration: James Dickson Innes, *The Town of Collioure, c.* 1908. Bradford Art Galleries and Museums, West Yorkshire, UK / Bridgeman Images.

For information about this and other Yale University Press publications, please contact:
U.S. Office: sales.press@yale.edu   yalebooks.com
Europe Office: sales@yaleup.co.uk   yalebooks.co.uk

Set in Adobe Garamond Pro by IDSUK (DataConnection) Ltd
Printed in Great Britain by Gomer Press Ltd, Llandysul, Ceredigion, Wales

Library of Congress Control Number: 2018947137

ISBN 978-0-300-23592-0

A catalogue record for this book is available from the British Library.

10 9 8 7 6 5 4 3 2 1

To Hillia, again

O, for a draught of vintage! that hath been
Cool'd a long age in the deep-delved earth,
Tasting of Flora and the country green,
Dance, and Provençal song, and sunburnt mirth!
O for a beaker full of the warm South.

John Keats, 'Ode to a Nightingale', 1819

CONTENTS

List of Illustrations   viii

Acknowledgements   xiii

1   Shelley Burning: The Mediterranean and British Culture   1

2   The Antique, the Noble and the Stupendous: The Turn   23
to the Mediterranean, 1740–1800

3   The Distorted Mirror: The South in British Culture during   65
the Age of Byron, 1800–30

4   Blue Solitudes: The Mediterranean and the Shaping of   109
Victorian Britain, 1830–60

5   An Enchanted Garden: The Mediterranean and the Aesthetics   157
of High Victorianism, 1860–90

6   The Cult of Beauty: The Mediterranean and British   192
Modernism, 1890–1918

7   That Splendid Enclosure: Meanings of the Mediterranean   225
from Rupert Brooke to Damien Hirst

Notes   263

Select Bibliography   297

Index   306

ILLUSTRATIONS

Plate Section

Between pages 82–3

1   John Ruskin, *St Mark's, Venice. Sketch After Rain* (1846).

2   David Allan, *Sir William Hamilton and the First Lady Hamilton in their Villa in Naples* (1770). Compton Verney, Warwickshire, UK / Bridgeman Images.

3   Katharine Read, *British Gentlemen in Rome* (*c.* 1750). Yale Center for British Art, Paul Mellon Collection.

4   Thomas Patch, *British Gentlemen at Sir Horace Mann's Home in Florence* (*c.* 1763–5). Yale Center for British Art, Paul Mellon Collection.

5   Pietro Fabris, *The Bay of Naples from Posillipo* (1770). Compton Verney, Warwickshire, UK / Bridgeman Images.

6   Joseph Wright, *Vesuvius in Eruption, with a View over the Islands in the Bay of Naples* (*c.* 1776–80). © Tate / CC-BY-NC-ND 3.0 (Unported) / http://www.tate.org.uk/

7   Thomas Jones, *The Garden of the Villa Borghese* (*c.* 1776). Yale Center for British Art, Paul Mellon Collection.

8   Francis Towne, *St Peter's at Sunset, from above the Arco Oscuro* (1781). © The Trustees of the British Museum.

9 David Roberts, *Old Buildings on the Darro, Granada* (1834). © Victoria and Albert Museum, London.

10 John Phillip, *The Antonia* (1863). Photo © Tate / CC-BY-NC-ND 3.0 (Unported) / http://www.tate.org.uk/

11 Robert Smirke, *Kalamata, Greece* (1802–4). Yale Center for British Art, Paul Mellon Collection.

12 Edward Lear, *Town and Harbour of Gaio, Paxo*. Plate IX in Edward Lear, *Views in the Seven Ionian Islands* (1863).

13 Hiram Powers, *The Greek Slave* (1844). Yale University Art Gallery.

14 Archibald Archer, depiction of the Elgin Marbles in the British Museum (1819). © The Trustees of the British Museum.

15 Edward Burne-Jones, *Cupid and Psyche* (*c.* 1870). Yale Center for British Art, Yale Art Gallery Collection, Mary Gertrude Abbey Fund.

Between pages 178–9

16 John Singer Sargent, *Breakfast in the Loggia* (1910). Freer Gallery of Art and Arthur M. Sackler Gallery, Smithsonian Institution, Washington, D.C.: Gift of Charles Lang Freer, F1917.182a-b.

17 Winifred Knights, *Italian Landscape* (1922). Photo © Tate / CC-BY-NC-ND 3.0 (Unported) / http://www.tate.org.uk/

18 Walter Sickert, *Palazzo Eleanora Duse, Venice* (*c.* 1901). Amgueddfa Genedlaethol Cymru National Museum of Wales.

19 Arthur Melville, *A Barber's Shop, Spain* (*c.* 1890–5). © The Trustees of the British Museum.

20 Roger Fry, *Le Petit Port, St Tropez* (1922). Private Collection / Photo © The Bloomsbury Workshop, London / Bridgeman Images.

21 Charles Rennie Mackintosh, *Port Vendres* (1926–7). © The Trustees of the British Museum.

22 Poster for Famagusta, Cyprus (1940). © Costas and Ritas Severis Collections, Centre of Visual Arts and Research.

23 Lady Mary Evelyn Chenevix Trench, *Kyrenia Harbour* (*c.* 1935). © Costas and Ritas Severis Collections, Centre of Visual Arts and Research.

24 Meredith Frampton, *Still Life* (1932). © Royal Academy of Arts, London / John Hammond.

25 John Armstrong, *Pro Patria* (1938). Private Collection / Photo © Peter Nahum at The Leicester Galleries, London / Bridgeman Images.

26 John Craxton, *Galatas* (1947). © Estate of John Craxton. All Rights Reserved, DACS 2018.

27 Elizabeth David, *A Book of Mediterranean Food* (1950), cover illustration by John Minton. John Minton © The Estate of John Minton / Royal College of Art, London.

28 John Minton, *The Road to Valencia* (1949). Arts Council Collection, Southbank Centre, London / Estate of John Minton / Bridgeman Images.

29 Susan Hawker, *Pine Tree, Italy* (1979). Susan Hawker.

30 The Italian Chapel on Lamb Holm, Orkney (1940s). Kevin George / Alamy Stock Photo.

31 Damien Hirst, *Hydra and Kali Discovered by Four Divers*. Photographed by Christoph Gerigk. © Damien Hirst and Science Ltd. All rights reserved, DACS / Artimage 2018.

Illustrations in the Text

Louis Édouard Fournier, *The Cremation of Shelley* (1889).   2
Liverpool, Walker Art Gallery.

Emma Hamilton as 'The Muse of Dance', engraving by   25
Friedrich Rehberg (1794). National Maritime Museum,
Greenwich, London.

William Watts, *Chiswick House in Middlesex, the Seat of the*   27
Duke of Devonshire (1781). Yale Center for British Art,
Paul Mellon Collection.

George Frideric Handel, *Giulio Cesare*, first edition manuscript   30
published by Cluer (1724).

Charles Turner, mezzotint after Sir Joshua Reynolds, *The*   34
Dilettanti Society (early nineteenth century). © Victoria and
Albert Museum, London.

Frontispiece to Richard Payne Knight, *An Account of the*   45
Remains of the Worship of Priapus (1786).

James Bruce, *No. 7 The Interior Part of the 3rd Temple Looking*   46
from the West Front (1762–3). Yale Center for British Art,
Paul Mellon Collection.

Paul Sandby, *The Opening of the Carnival at Rome* (*c.* 1781). 58
  Yale Center for British Art, Paul Mellon Collection.

Sir Robert Smirke, *Temple of Concordia* (1802–4). Yale Center 70
  for British Art, Paul Mellon Collection.

Thomas Landseer, etching of horses from the Elgin Marbles 73
  (1816). © The Trustees of the British Museum.

Illustration from Madame de Staël, *Corinne ou l'Italie* (1857). 82
  G. Staal.

Illustration of the Hall of the Abencerrajes of the Alhambra 105
  from James Cavanagh Murphy, *Arabian Antiquities of Spain*
  (1812–16).

Elizabeth Barrett Browning, albumen *carte-de-visite* by 125
  Elliott & Fry, after Macaire (1858). © National Portrait
  Gallery, London.

John Ruskin, *The Palazzo Contarini-Fasan, Venice* (1841). 136
  John Ruskin.

Edward Lear, *Campagna of Rome from the Villa Mattei* (1841). 144
  Yale Center for British Art, Gift of Donald C. Gallup,
  Yale BA 1934, PhD 1939.

The Alhambra Court in the Crystal Palace at Sydenham, 151
  photograph by Philip Henry Delamotte (1854). © Victoria
  and Albert Museum, London.

British volunteers fighting with Garibaldi in Italy during the 154
  struggle for Italian unification (1860). World History
  Archive / Alamy Stock Photo.

Grand Canal, Venice, photograph by Robert MacPherson 156
  (1860s). Yale Center for British Art, transfer from the
  Yale University Art Gallery.

Garibaldi received by a crowd in Trafalgar Square, *Illustrated* 162
  London News (23 April 1864).

Sir Edward Burne-Jones at work in his studio, photograph 170
  by Frederick Hollyer (1890). © Victoria and Albert Museum,
  London.

The British School at Athens, 1892. Reproduced with the 182
  Permission of the British School at Athens. BSA Photographic
  Archive: BSAA8–3 (SPHS–5028).

Trial of the Greek brigands in Athens, Greece, *Illustrated London*   184
    News (11 June 1870).

Portrait of Edward Lear (1867).   191

Oscar Wilde, photograph by Napoleon Sarony (1882).   195

Portait of Aubrey Beardsley (*c.* 1895). Library of Congress,   196
    Prints & Photographs Division, LC-USZ62–112699.

Aubrey Beardsley, *Lysistrata Her Coynte* (1896). © Victoria   196
    and Albert Museum, London.

Harry Fenn, *Keats' Home in Rome* (1894–5). Gift of   219
    Sarah Cooper Hewitt; 1931–66–94.

Muirhead Bone, *A Spanish Good Friday (Ronda)* (1925).   237
    © Estate of Sir Muirhead Bone. All Rights Reserved,
    DACS 2018.

Leonard Woolf, Virginia Woolf, Roger Fry and Joan Fry   239
    in Athens, May 1932. Houghton Library, Harvard University.

John Craxton and Margot Fonteyn on Bourtzi, 1951.   255
    © John Craxton Estate.

ACKNOWLEDGEMENTS

Writing this book would have been impossible without access to the indispensable collection of the London Library, a jewel in the crown of the city's cultural institutions. I am grateful for the assistance of the librarians and other staff there. The Centre for Hellenic Studies at King's College, London has provided a congenial and stimulating academic home during the period. This is the first book I have set out to write without having arranged a publisher, when access to the latter seems nowadays to require a bevy of intermediaries. I was fortunate that at a vital juncture Julian Loose, Editorial Director at Yale University Press, took the book under his wing and helped shape its final form. The anonymous expert readers for the Press provided invaluable critical scrutiny. At the Press, Marika Lysandrou efficiently oversaw the publishing schedule, and the copy-editing supervised by Rachael Lonsdale brought to bear wide-ranging knowledge and scrupulous accuracy. Charlotte Chapman contributed an eagle eye to the process. Thanks go to the Library and Archive of the British School at Athens for making available the photograph of the School appearing in Chapter 5, and to Ian Collins and the John Craxton Estate for providing the lovely photograph of the artist and Margot Fonteyn in Chapter 7. The two colour plates of Cyprus were kindly made available by Dr. Rita Severis at the excellent Centre for Visual Arts and Research (CVAR) in Nicosia. Amongst many Mediterranean locations appearing in these pages, Cyprus is mentioned only sporadically, but it is that island which has been to me what Henry Miller once wrote Greece had afforded him – 'a world of light'. My gratitude goes to friends there who have given me their generosity, warmth and love over many years. This book is dedicated to my wife, Hillia, for her constant support.

Robert Holland
30 April 2017

Chapter One

SHELLEY BURNING

THE MEDITERRANEAN AND BRITISH CULTURE

Every scene seemed anticipated in some dream – it appeared Magick Land.

Thomas Jones in Rome, 1776

The Mediterranean, so eternally young, the very symbol of youth!

D. H. Lawrence, 1927

On 16 August 1822, it took Lord George Byron, his friend Edward Trelawny, a gaggle of Tuscan soldiers and a local health official an hour to find the spot on the beach near Viareggio where Percy Bysshe Shelley's corpse had been left two weeks before in the burning yellow sand.[1] They started to dig it out. It was the dull thud of a mattock on the skull that first uncovered the body, a dark indigo blue from the lime that had been spread during the temporary burial to arrest decomposition. The limbs and the trunk were still in one entire piece, and the whole was lifted into the iron-furnace, specially ordered for the occasion by Trelawny in Leghorn (today's Livorno), and could then be manoeuvred into position rather awkwardly on its poles.

The improvised pyre was made from the timber of wrecks left on the beach and pine from the local forest. Once the fire was applied, the wine, oil and salt with which they had coated Shelley's remains, and the pine resin, made the flames quiver in the wavy glare of the heat. Because the head was resting on the red-hot iron at the base, the brains, Trelawny wrote in his description, 'literally seethed, bubbled and boiled'.[2] But as the body fell open he was able to snatch the heart from the fire undamaged. For Byron it was all too much. He often wrote about agonizing scenes in his poetry, but the actuality always reduced him to an abject pity that he was not always successful at controlling or hiding.[3] On this, the most famous of all such incidents, he took himself into the sea and swam away from the shoreline, as he had once swum across the Bosphorus, with large, powerful strokes and the club foot that moved better in the water than on the land, while watching the gleaming outline of the Apennines in the distance. It was a searing-hot day.

Relics from the burning of Shelley's corpse later became a cause célèbre, with claims attached to locks of hair and splinters of bone; the cremation became a source of mythology in its own right.[4] But the heart was naturally the most discussed item. Byron had taken it to the widow, Mary Shelley, wrapped in black silk, and many wrongly believed that it was included in the long-delayed interment along with the ashes in Rome's Cimitero degli inglesi

The Cremation of Shelley
Louis Édouard Fournier (1889)

in January 1823 (all such non-Catholic ceremonies had, by local regulation, to take place in time of darkness).[5] In fact Mary Shelley had taken the heart back to England with her when, the previous July, she had departed Italy after the tragedy, 'truly iced', as she put it, in her own heart.[6] One story went that once at home she would take the organ around with her.

What happened to the heart in the end nobody knows, though there was a rumour that it disappeared when Mary's home in Chelsea was burgled.[7] She and her son certainly did not have it with them when they made their only visit to Percy's grave in 1843. By then the site had already become a place of cultural pilgrimage, especially for British and American travellers in Rome who were pleased, as one writer remarks, to have a respite from all the classicism and Catholicism of the Holy City, the poignancy enhanced by the proximity of Shelley's spot to the final resting place of John Keats.[8] The nook was then quiet and attractively rustic, rather than the rather dusty and well-trodden place that it became in later years. When one future poet laureate, Alfred Austen, was there in 1863 the tomb was already covered in lichen and grass, and he had to tidy it up.[9] Today the cemetery borders a road junction heaving with suburban traffic and with a bustling metro station close by.

We shall return later to Percy Shelley's drowning in the Bay of Spezia on one of his beloved yachts – water fascinated him both in nature and as a metaphor of the human condition[10] – as well as the rather gruesome aftermath of a necessarily improvised cremation. But if there was a totemic moment in the history of the Anglo-Mediterranean cultural encounter, this was it; even, it seemed in long retrospect, the quintessential embodiment of English Romanticism.[11] It is certainly hard to think of any comparable event touching the same chord in the canon of British culture, including its global outreach. The death of Byron himself in Greece two years later did not come to resonate in the same way, for reasons we shall discuss.[12] The effect came about not only because of who Shelley was – he was detested by many of his own countrymen as a revolutionary and an atheist far more than he was ever admired in his lifetime – but because of *where* the event occurred, and how it relates to a quasi-sanctification occupied by the Mediterranean in British life.

As the literary critic Marilyn Butler has explored,[13] Shelley's literary career and his death were framed by a process in which the Mediterranean lent itself as a laboratory for ideological, political and cultural struggles within Britain. The Mediterranean was inherently flexible and protean – it could be turned to any number of conflicting purposes by British protagonists. No other overseas region had a similar resonance in British mentalities, a reference point and defining idea of what is beautiful or desirable reflected in the pictures of olive-studded landscapes in houses and flats, preconceptions of the perfect holiday, or the ideal setting for all sorts of fulfilments painfully elusive at home. These symbols of a shimmering mirage of wants and desires have remained remarkably stable across centuries. In Britain the finer arts reflecting such vibrations are still to a large degree instinctively viewed through a Mediterranean prism. Where did this fixation – what the Anglophile French-Swiss writer Madame de Staël termed 'the sensation of the South'[14] – come from, and how did it evolve in modern British history?

This story begins in the early decades of the eighteenth century, when what Linda Colley in her influential book *Britons: Forging the Nation 1707–1837* terms the 'would-be' nation of Great Britain – constitutionally formed by the Act of Union in 1707 – was first fully immersed in the affairs of Continental Europe. Indeed, the fact that the Anglo-Mediterranean interaction was itself a facet of a wider European involvement will remain vital throughout this account. But it was the traction that the Mediterranean gained across British artistic, intellectual and even emotional life by the end of the eighteenth century that shaped the evolution to come.

This approaches an important missing link in the general understanding of British historiography. That there was, from the loss of the American colonies in the 1770s onwards, a 'swing to the East' in Britain's external orientation, meaning one towards India and an expanding Eastern empire, has become something of a truism, even if the exact timing is debated.[15] True or not, however, these decades were critical in other ways. Linda Colley writes that, 'In the half-century after the American war, there would emerge in Britain a far more consciously and officially constructed patriotism which stressed attachment to monarchy, the importance of empire, the value of military and naval achievement, and the desirability of strong, stable government by a virtuous, able and authentically British elite.'[16] The 'virtuous' here is critical because, compounded with elements of morality, it encapsulated the cultural bearings and claims to fitness to govern possessed by an aristocratic oligarchy reacting to the necessities of a new age. That cadre's old binding ideology based on shared but now rather fading historical reference points, combined with the banalities of Anglicanism, had begun to lose something of its firepower. Yet, as J. C. D. Clark has argued, the 'old society' this underpinned was sufficiently resilient to recast itself to survive.[17] The Grand Tour, that pattern of trips by young British gentlemen (and not many women) to southern Europe for their general education, was one aspect of a refurbishment of the credentials behind the existing order.[18]

This is relevant because one of the enduring themes as the eighteenth century proceeded was that, despite – indeed, in no small degree *because* of – the material and territorial successes of Great Britain against which the loss of America was to be just a temporary setback, the relatively new and fragile Union after 1707 lacked a secure identity of its own. What was more, increasing intimacy with other European countries in the era of Enlightenment meant that the governing class became sensitive to the greater cultural prestige of other Northern nations, and above all that of the great rival, France.[19] 'For the first time,' a historian of Britain's shifting cultural foundations in the eighteenth century has stated, 'many Englishmen thought it important that their arts should have a history and their taste should have a guide' (this was written in 1970, when what English *women* had thought in the past was still often passed over).[20]

In seeking to fill such a glaring gap in the nation's makeup, and to counter the perceptions of other Europeans that the otherwise generally successful British polity was crude and untutored in the finer arts, there arose an instinctive and increasingly urgent tendency to look towards the South. The process was foreshadowed when Charles Montagu, the 1st Duke of Manchester, was sent to Venice as ambassador extraordinary in 1707, 'keenly aware of both the strengths and the weaknesses of his own countrymen'.[21] When he returned to England the duke took with him two Venetian artists and designers, Giovanni Pelligrini and Mario Ricci, who stayed for some years providing rich Whig patrons with what they felt fitted contemporary life in the new Britain: an Italian sophistication suitably purged of Catholic pictorial rhetoric. The inward flow of such artisanship continued in the decades ahead. Ricci, for example, played a part in transforming theatre stage sets in London, with colourful backdrops and pulley-driven cut-outs denoting ships and other moving contrivances. Meanwhile, during the Hanoverian decades after 1714 Europe still overwhelmingly dominated the British world view; there was 'at most a merely incipient consciousness of empire'.[22] Nor did this fundamental relativity between Europe and 'beyond Europe' framing the British world view, in geopolitics and even more in culture, ever really change radically.

Just as important, and indeed more significant, than any swing to the East by Britain was a turn towards the Mediterranean that subsequently intensified during the wars against France from 1793 to 1815. It was in very large part, though not exclusively, from the southern regions of Europe that the British sought the cultural wherewithal to make their nation great in the manner required to dignify its status and that of the changing elite presiding over it. The degree to which this cultural strategy succeeded has important implications for how one assesses the underlying self-confidence and psychological character of the ensuing Victorian civilization in Britain, and indeed for the post-Victorian era as well.

Our subject spans the Mediterranean, and combines the ancient and the modern, since they are inseparable. For the British, Italy and Greece always blended at the edges in terms of their cultural meanings (there was something appropriate in Byron, rare among his countrymen in having more or less fluent Italian, having begun to learn that language while travelling in Greece). In this regard Sicily assumed a special role, since it was there that so many currents came together, and in particular it was where British travellers often had their first, and for most of them only, direct encounter with *Greekness*, not only through ruins but also through the social and mental traces of Hellenism. 'If you want to understand Greece, go to Sicily,' a writer of one of those innumerable Mediterranean travelogues stated as late as 1901. 'At Syracuse the poorer inhabitants . . . are unaltered since the days of Dionysius.'[23]

Nor, as the example of Spain will show, is it possible to leave the western Mediterranean out of the overall picture, since British cultural engagement spanned the entire region. Italy, Greece and Spain predominate; and although other places will crop up – such as Malta, where Samuel Taylor Coleridge spent an important interlude in his life, and which became so emblematic of heroic resistance to fascism in the Second World War – it is through this triptych that the Anglo-Mediterranean factor in British cultural flows is explored. Each country had its distinctive place in the British imaginative order, but it is the way they overlapped and fed collectively into successive artistic movements in Britain that is striking.

Despite this omnipresent phenomenon, there are few works that treat British engagement with the Mediterranean in an integrated manner. This is itself only a reflection of the region's broader historical traits, whereby centrifugal, or disintegrative, impulses usually outweighed any unifying elements. What pulled and pushed the Mediterranean into a common pattern for any length of time was usually war. It is telling that one of the few latter-day publications to treat British culture in its relation to the Mediterranean as an entity appeared in 1941, when British armies had been ejected from northern Continental Europe by Hitler and the Mediterranean constituted what Winston Churchill called 'Britain's first battlefield'.[24] That year, Fritz Saxl, a distinguished Austrian Jewish art historian who had been instrumental in bringing the Warburg Library, with its rich holdings in Mediterranean bibliography, to London, and fellow-refugee scholar Rudolf Wittkower arranged an exhibition entitled *British Art and the Mediterranean*. After opening in London, this exhibition, which spanned ancient Roman civilization in Britain all the way through to the war against the Axis powers, went on to tour the provinces. The links between the historical subject matter and the contemporary situation would not have been lost on a British population at that moment hungry for news from the Mediterranean theatre. In their introduction to the publication that had to wait until 1948 Saxl and Wittkower wrote, 'At a period when inter-European relations were disrupted by the [recent] war, it was stimulating to observe in the arts of this country the age-long impact of the Mediterranean tradition on the British mind.'[25]

The subterranean workings of that tradition did not diminish after 1945. Given an instinctive southerly bias in British sensibilities, it was logical that visions of the Mediterranean – in literature and art, travel and even food – offered the natural counterpoint to drab domestic austerity, and through them the tantalizing possibility of a return to happier days. Paradoxically, too, just as the United Kingdom's colonial stake in that region began to slip away – Cyprus became independent in 1960 and Malta in 1964[26] – the human density of Anglo-Mediterranean interaction actually increased. From the early 1960s, holidays in Mediterranean beach resorts became a feature of Britain's consumer society, though the dreamy idyll of what the eighteenth-century British artist in Rome Thomas Jones described as 'Magick Land', and the American novelist Nathaniel Hawthorne in the mid-nineteenth century termed a 'fairy precinct',[27] remained much the same as ever: in the popular 1989 film *Shirley Valentine* a middle-aged woman, dissatisfied with her pedestrian life in Liverpool, accompanies a friend on a two-week break in Greece, and unexpectedly discovers new fulfilment, both emotionally and sexually.

By the 1980s, indeed, British communities of sun-seeking retirees were emerging across a swathe of southern Europe. (One of the most popular serials on British television in that decade, *Duty Free*, evoked this world, including British class obsessions operating as vigorously as ever in a Mediterranean setting, in this case Marbella – a trait that went back to the Grand Tour.) This was paralleled after the financial crash of 2008 by a counter-flow of mostly younger Mediterranean workers seeking employment in the United Kingdom. All round, this is a timely juncture to look again at the relationship of the Mediterranean to the often uncertain growth of British culture over a long period; and all the more so when the British have slipped once more into acute uncertainty as to what their identity actually amounts to, and how it relates to Europe. As some historians have concluded about Spain (the peculiarities of which have striking British parallels), the United Kingdom 'possesses a unique history, but also a fully European one',[28] and this Europeanness carries an ineradicable impress of the South.

There have in fact been many different Mediterraneans. To begin with there was the noble simplicity of the ancient Greek heritage, with its sun-kissed transparency in sculptural forms that was such a building block of European Enlightenment. This came to be filtered through a Romantic – especially Italian – lens; the vision mutated into the Victorian dream of a warm and cultured South that has never really been dislodged. John Singer Sargent captured this essence in many of his Mediterranean watercolours – Tuscan, Corfiote, Majorcan, Andalusian – but quintessentially in *Breakfast in the Loggia*, painted at Villa Torre Galli at Scandicci on the outskirts of Florence in the autumn of 1910, when he was staying there with friends. Here are core elements in the everyday routine of a

Mediterranean idyll: the dappled shade of an interior courtyard, a statue of Venus as the epitome of beauty at one end, the vividness of the scene, a lively conversation between guests in their Victorian summer best, the intense engagement of which is triggered by the surroundings, as if 'coming home' to a truly leisured, humanistic culture. Successive versions of such an ideal have been harboured by generations of the British middle and upper classes, as they still are today, as any glance at more upmarket tourist brochures (featuring, say, opera in Verona's amphitheatre or cookery classes in Tuscan hilltop towns) will easily illustrate.

Nor indeed was it necessary to be actually in or around the Mediterranean to prove susceptible to its magic. The only requirement was certain antennae of the senses. Robert Browning, who will feature prominently later on, made this point in his poem 'A Toccata of Galuppi's' – that is, a snatch of music from the Venetian composer, Baldassare Galuppi – which appeared in Browning's collection *Men and Women* (1855). The first-person narrator, in classic Browning style, has in fact never been to Italy, but is transported to eighteenth-century Venice by the sheer power and melody of the music. Vivid renderings of this kind were always liable to caricature or condescension. Browning's grasp of Galuppi's music may have been fragile, whilst pictorial idealizations of the Mediterranean of the sort that Sargent produced once he tired of portraiture earned him some criticism by younger art radicals for their essential lightness of mood. Yet the imagery itself has never been devalued and is irony-proof. One need only look in the window of fine art print shops in any British or North American town today, rarely without some alluring Mediterranean imagery, to see that this holds true.

There was, however, from the start another kind of Mediterranean altogether. This was a sinister, sometimes violent, morality-free, even depraved Mediterranean, full of masques and deceptions and disillusionments. Most frightening was the very suddenness with which such forces might manifest themselves. Robert Browning in his narrative poem *The Ring and the Book* (1868), concerning vicious killings in Renaissance Florence, and E. M. Forster in *A Room with a View* (1908), in which young Lucy Honeychurch is confronted with a stiletto assassination that comes out of the blue in a tranquil Florentine piazza, entertained such possibilities.[29] Patricia Highsmith's chilling portrayal of Italy as dream-into-nightmare in her murder story *The Talented Mr. Ripley* (1955) indicates how this trope has never gone away. Apprehension that behind all the colour there was something else entirely was often rooted in Anglo-Protestant hostility to the assumed falsity of Roman religion, with ramifications often extending to allegations of sexual abuse (scandalous goings-on in convents being widely alleged). Such imaginings of a brutalized and pitiless Mediterranean were to be set most starkly against Spanish backdrops, in part because of the darkness and fanaticism of Iberian Catholicism lodged in British consciousness, where the word 'Armada' still echoed with a national and even personal vulnerability. The religious implications will keep coming back in this account in all sorts of shapes, as well as, overall, parallel and highly contrasting versions of the Mediterranean as a moral and aesthetic conception. That this marked a pathology about the Mediterranean in a British cultural setting – not merely, as an important retrospective study has stated,[30] a passion for it – is important for our discussion.

Such a pathology connects with another issue running through the subject: was the lure of the South felt by so many British artists and writers conducive to their creative impulses, or rather sometimes counter-productive in deflecting their energy and abilities, with all the opportunity costs this implied? William Wordsworth, with his love for the Cumbrian landscape, got fed up with the endless travel memoirs recapitulating the supposed superiority of Mediterranean sunsets, views and general topography. 'Nothing is more injurious to genuine feeling,' he grumbled in his *Guide to the Lakes* in 1822 – just, as it happens, as the unfortunate Percy Shelley was being carried off by that fierce Ligurian squall – 'than the practice of hastily and ungenerously deprecating the face of one country by comparing it to another.'

The key here was the *genuineness* or otherwise of the feeling, and with it the danger of falling into an entirely false idiom in gushing about the Mediterranean. Just a few years later the novelist Edward Bulwer Lytton, who was then about to write one of the biggest selling books ever about the Mediterranean in English literature,[31] put into the mouth of one of the actors in his story *Godolphin* (1833) the acid statement that, 'So far from a sojourn in Italy being friendly to the growth of ambition, it nips and almost destroys the germ.' This was in line with the thrust of the novel itself, which was to satirize the English governing class and its various predilections in the wake of the recent Reform Act. But that there *was* a creative cost, a sort of illusory contentment, in drawing upon the Mediterranean for British literary and visual practitioners, to be set off against an undoubted capacity to inspire, is a factor that needs to be put into the balance.

Instinctive awareness of such pitfalls was why some artists regarded the Mediterranean with a certain tentativeness, or kept clear altogether. The painter J. A. M. Whistler, though one of the few in the Victorian era to be influenced by a previous Spanish master in the form of Diego Velázquez, and who spent some time in Venice, has nonetheless been described by a biographer as 'not a man for the South'.[32] This was even truer of W. H. Morris, whose love of all things Nordic arose naturally from his distaste for Italy. 'I quarrel now with Morris about Art,' noted the painter Edward Burne-Jones sadly, with whom he had enjoyed close relations. 'He journeys to Iceland and I to Italy – which is a symbol.'[33] There was always a lure to the North that counteracted the one to the South, and the resulting bifurcation is of significance in the underlying dialectic of British cultural development.

Yet at the same time these two directional impulses within the British imagination ran in parallel and had a curious tendency to conflation. The *Poems of Ossian*, published by the Scottish writer James Macpherson between 1760 and 1763, the authenticity of which was fiercely contested for decades, were to be founding documents in not only British but also European Romanticism (Napoleon Bonaparte was a great admirer). They were widely regarded as a Celtic counterpart to the classical writers, especially Homer, underpinning a northern Gaelic tradition quite independent of Greece and Rome.[34] But in their epic quality, with stories of endless battles, fateful love affairs and unresolved yearnings for happiness, the Ossianic and Homeric styles crossed each other frequently. This gyration in Romantic modes between rival poles of cold North and warm South was to continue through the nineteenth century. Somewhat fittingly, when John Everett Millais set about painting his *North-West Passage* (1874) – an evocation of the heroic search for a route between Canada and the Arctic which had cost Sir John Franklin and his crew their lives just a few years before – he insisted on using as a life model for the painting's haggard, defeated old sailor Edward Trelawny, whose role in the burning of Shelley's corpse on the sunbaked Viareggio beach we have seen. Yet Trelawny's many adventures in a very long life had always been in hot southern climes and nowhere near *real* ice at all.[35] Just as one writer on the idea of North in British minds observes that it was a 'shifting idea . . . always going away from us',[36] so was the idea of South constantly recessive. The two phenomena were in fact part of an intimate whole, representing something distinctive about the British. Where the Germanic people had a homing instinct to disappear into their own forests, Wagner-style, the British more often than not looked to somewhere else entirely, just over the horizon, but not always in the same direction or zone of temperature.[37]

Perhaps this has some bearing on why for a good few Britons the Mediterranean, far from being a route towards self-discovery and the refinement of their art, led instead to personal dislocation and inner confusion. The Grand Tour is often supposed to have been, at least in popular memory, the most delightful experience imaginable. For more than a few it was a lonely time and they could not wait to go home. Nathaniel Hawthorne caught this susceptibility to depressive fragility in *The Marble Faun*, his story set in Rome during the early decades of the nineteenth century, when one of his expatriate characters remarks, 'Here it seems as if all the weary and dreary Past were piled upon the back of the Present. If I were to lose my spirits in this country – if I were to suffer a heavy misfortune here – methinks it would be impossible to stand against it.'[38]

But there was something even more complex in this flipside of Mediterranean reality hinted at by Byron with unerring acuteness in his reference to Italy's 'fatal gift of beauty', a beauty that could deceive, betray and even destroy – what the Victorian historian of the Renaissance A. J. Symonds labelled the agony of 'continued unsatisfied desire' amid the beguiling southern heat. In his case it was the demon of homosexual desire: 'All kinds of young men,' he once recalled, 'peasants on the Riviera, Corsican drivers, Florentine lads upon Lungarno in the evenings, *facchini* [porters] at Venice . . . used to pluck at the sleeve of my heart.'[39] But such yearning could have many sources and indicated deeper personal uncertainties the very exquisiteness of which the Mediterranean could evoke mercilessly. This yearning ravaged more than one character in Henry James's Italian fiction – and perhaps to some degree, James himself.

What dislocation might mean in such contexts ranged from everyday banality to ghastly horror. Bulwer Lytton's breakdown with his relatively new spouse travelling in Italy in 1833 led to one of the most envenomed personal ruptures leaving its traces in print during the nineteenth century. It was in Italy, too, in 1844 that Charles Dickens, who wrote a light memoir of his journey, got drawn into the psychological troubles of the wife of a Swiss doctor he met en route; his vision of himself as rescuer in this case was an illustration of the heightened, often destabilizing, consciousness that the Mediterranean could induce in British visitors.[40] Dickens's own marriage began to wobble as a consequence, though it took some while to unravel. The remark by William Hazlitt in the 1820s, meant as a warning to British artists and writers on their stays in the Mediterranean, that when we go abroad 'we are not the same but another',[41] encapsulates what could be a hazardous transformation affecting both life and art.[42]

Just how hazardous, perhaps, was shown by the tragedy of Richard Dadd, originally in his profession a painter of fairies. He set out with a companion in July 1842 and travelled through Europe to Syria and Palestine, returning through Italy. He felt under enormous pressure to complete the usual sketches executed under such circumstances, straining to see from the interior of a carriage or jolted by the roads, but nevertheless producing notebooks crammed with tiny heads, trees, boats, canals and fragments of architecture and sculpture.[43] He first showed signs of a cata-strophic breakdown while staying in Rome in August 1843, becoming highly erratic on religious matters and later confessing to a desire to attack the pope as an incarnation of the Devil. On returning to Britain, he knifed his father to death in what appeared a planned attack, and, despite escaping to France, was arrested and spent the rest of his life in an institution, where he continued to paint travel pictures and watercolours.

Dadd's case was obviously very unusual. But there were quite a few examples of writers and artists, seeking in the Mediterranean some boost for a sagging impulse, cracking under pressure in a way that might have been averted at home. Arthur Symons, one of those so-called decadents whose standing had been hit in the censorious public reaction following Oscar Wilde's trial and imprisonment for homosexual practices, went to Italy in 1908 to rejuvenate his poetry but while there suffered from mounting depression. In a harrowing personal account, Symons recalled the onset of his troubles in Venice, associated in his mind with the stifling warmth of a hotel room's closed windows, beds enclosed by mosquito nets, and besetting insomnia.[44] He ended up in an asylum in Bologna, and his biographer writes that although he recovered some equilibrium and returned to his family in London, 'his spiritual perspective returned to the Methodist vision of his childhood. He became tiresomely obsessed with sin, damnation and girls' underwear', his writing abandoned completely.[45] Just as North and South went round and round in the British cultural universe, so did enchantment and disenchantment, growth and decay, and vulnerable individuals could easily get crushed in the process.

The conditions surrounding ordinary human relationships in these settings were usually constraining for visitors. Meaningful contact with local people apart from innkeepers and other providers of everyday services was often extremely limited. In Spain this was especially the case, and to some degree too in Greece, where outsiders could easily get enmeshed in simple misunderstandings. An event in August 1874 illustrated this to almost comic effect: the British embassy chargé went for a walk up Mount Lykabettos, directly opposite the Parthenon, and got involved in a punch-up with a policeman whose job was to stop people trampling the shrubs and dropping cigar-ends, leading to an embarrassing diplomatic incident; the local Greek authorities were browbeaten into an abject apology, though the distribution of fault was not at all clear.[46] We shall see that misunderstandings were a frequent pitfall in modern Anglo-Greek encounters and not only because of linguistic barriers.

In Italy things were easier, but not always vastly so. As far as sex was concerned, the desperate attempts by the young James Boswell on his own Grand Tour to effect a liaison with a series of 'respectable' local women almost invariably ended in humiliating, and surprised, rebuffs. '[V]exed and angry' he described his feelings in his diary for 15 January 1765 after one more anticipated pleasure proved illusory.[47] The Mediterranean myth in the British imagination was always strongly tinged with sensuality: 'Beauties of deeper glance' was how John Keats put it in his sonnet 'Happy is England' (1817), referring to the imagined lure of southern womanhood eclipsing previous contentment with the 'simple loveliness' of Britannia's daughters. (The fact that this temptation worked for both genders was less transparent in literature at the time, though not unknown.) Keats wrote with little hard experience where adult love was concerned – that recognition, the sense of not yet having *lived*, was to be part of the tragedy on his

Roman deathbed. Certainly for British travellers any climax to expectant eroticism – unless, like Boswell in a number of Italian cities, one fell back on a purely commercial transaction – more often than not retained the air of ethereal, dreamlike fulfilment, though arguably all the more powerful as a consequence. Socially, there were the impressive *conversazioni* in the Roman palaces of leading noble families to which Boswell's aristocratic superiors amongst the tourists might get an invitation, or in early Victorian times the bourgeois receptions of the Duke of Tuscany's court in Florence, not to mention the Venetian masques with all their intriguing possibilities. Such occasions, however, were governed by minute etiquette and a chilling formality.[48] A. J. Symonds, despite his obsession about his sojourns with young men and his toil on Renaissance history, was said to be always uncomfortable with Italians themselves,[49] though his daughter later remarked, perhaps coyly, that his own death in Rome was 'a fitting end to his life'.[50] In terms of ordinary human dealings, a sense of being on the margins of Mediterranean society was the norm, even for somebody like Elizabeth Barrett Browning, for whom Italy in some larger mental realm was a metaphor of freedom and ease.[51]

Nor did the passage of time and new conditions in the twentieth century necessarily alter things. The 'strangeness' that kept a veil between the foreigner and local inhabitants when occupying the same physical space was the subject of an early sequence in D. H. Lawrence's *Twilight in Italy* (1915), recording his first visit to the country in 1912–13. One commentator describes how Lawrence conjures up a 'mismeeting', or a midway point between being a neighbour and an alien, an uneasy ambivalence underpinning subtle gambits of avoidance and studied indifference between wary parties.[52] For a slightly later generation intimations of such clumsy awkwardness became embarrassing, especially among a more popular readership wanting a happier tone to things, and the emphasis shifted to creating an impression of genuine involvement with surrounding society, as in Lawrence Durrell's genial evocations of expatriate life on Greek islands. The effect, however, was often unconvincing, if not quite bogus.[53]

Such limitations on pedestrian human intercourse connect with interpretations of the 'otherness' of local societies in the eyes of British and Western visitors generally that have become central to postmodern analysis, especially as described in Edward Said's highly influential work

Orientalism (1978). As Said's title indicates, the problems involved have usually been conceived of in Middle Eastern contexts. Nevertheless, an Italian writer on Anglo-Mediterranean cultural intercourse aptly remarks that this is curious insofar as the legacy of picturesque elements of the 'other' in British cultural practices derived overwhelmingly not from the Holy Land or, say, Syria, but from the more proximate lands of southern Europe, interaction with which was naturally much more dense.[54]

This bears on why the oriental and Islamic Mediterranean falls largely outside the framework of this book. The rationale for such a balance of treatment can best be illustrated by real-life examples. Lady Mary Wortley Montagu's *Turkish Embassy Letters*, originally composed over a brief period in 1717–18 during her husband's diplomatic appointment to the seat of the Ottoman Empire, have been an inspiration to female travel writers in modern times, and have assumed something of a cult status. But when personal troubles later assailed Lady Mary it was Italy, not somewhere more exotic, that she saw as offering an alternative road to a lost happiness, and where she was to spend many years before, as she wrote, 'dragging my ragged remnant of life to England' to die in 1762. (Lord Byron, an admirer, was to attempt to research her stay in Venice when he lived there himself in 1817.)[55] The doyen of the High Victorian art establishment, Frederic Leighton, travelled to Egypt and Syria, though not, as is often said, to 'the Middle East', insofar as such a designation had no currency at all at the time. But Leighton was much more significantly the product of his early upbringing in Rome and above all an obsession with classical Greek art. He might have installed a so-called 'Arab Hall' at the entrance to his west London house, the richly coloured Damascus tiles of which can still be admired by visitors, but the hall's design was actually modelled on the twelfth-century Siculo-Norman palace of La Zisa at Palermo; the exterior of the house itself is essentially Italianate.

This is emblematic of how even stylistically oriental influences percolating into Britain were more often than not mediated through the classic European South, and not anywhere truly 'Eastern' at all. During the era of Enlightenment, admittedly, a small bevy of European scholars – Edward Gibbon among them – considerably increased Western *knowledge* of Muslim accomplishments, amassing, interpreting and anthologizing Islamic texts.[56] But with rare exceptions this did not feed into the mainstream of either

British, or indeed European, cultural practices or popular consciousness. Behind this, too, lies something fundamental into which D. H. Lawrence, ten years after his original visit to Italy, provides a more modern insight. During 1921, when he was living in Taormina in Sicily with his German wife, Frieda, they decided on a fresh excursion as they pondered their post-war future. Lawrence rejected Naples and Rome as destinations, where so many thousands of other visitors had over centuries trawled the relics of an all too familiar classic past. He needed somewhere different to evolve the sorts of novel ideas in his mind, with their rejection of the purely rational and known. But just how different? He recalled this choice beginning with elsewhere in Sicily: 'Girgenti [Agrigento] and the sulphur spirit and the Greek guarding temples to make one madder? . . . Tunis? Africa? Not yet. Not yet. Not the Arabs, not yet.'[57]

In the end the decision for the Lawrences was between Spain and Sardinia, and they chose the latter (though in fact Sicily always remained at the heart of Lawrence's thought and feeling). But why this outcome and definitely *not* the North African or Arab lands? One writer on Lawrence comments that it was because Sardinia lay 'outside the circuit of civiliza-tion' – Lawrence's own phrase, and really meaning off the beaten track of most cultural forays – while still being indubitably European.[58] And this was the point. Lawrence appreciated that more fabled destinations were simply beyond his own understanding and sympathetic grasp as an English writer. Perhaps one day – for him, or more likely for a later generation – they would not be, but that was not the present reality. The recurring impulse among some British travellers who had ventured to the Arab world to dress up in local fancy costume – as the Grand Tourist Francis Dashwood, with his jewelled turban and gold-encrusted shirt, had done in the 1730s, as well as, slightly less richly, the later Victorian poet and trav-eller Wilfrid Blunt, not to mention quite a few thereafter – did not affect the substance of the matter.[59] It was the more 'familiar otherness' in the non-Islamic Mediterranean that impacted most powerfully on British minds, but still in ways that could produce an uneasiness of which Lawrence was all too keenly aware. These Mediterranean societies fell into a zone which was both sufficiently known to facilitate recognition and instinctive attraction, and yet also profoundly apart from England. As such, for a Northern sensibility this triggered an exquisite sensation of being so near and yet so far, of a desired consummation just beyond the realm of what was possible, itself the tantalizing essence of the Romantic disposition. This complicated ambiguity – an ambiguity impossible beyond the frame of a shared Graeco-Roman inheritance – is key.

To this logic there is one outstanding exception. The aspect of Islamic civilization filtered through British imaginings of Mediterranean experience that does come firmly within our parameters is the Moorish legacy in Andalusia, above all the Alhambra in Granada. As a motif this entered into Victorian culture, for example in ways that were striking in exuding admiration for its fine traceries and tranquil effects, attitudes far removed from the deprecations of the conventional orientalist paradigm. The fact that in 'discovering' the beauties of old Moorish Spain the contribution once made by Islamic rulers was often valued considerably above that of the succeeding Christian monarchy of the Reconquista fits poorly with Edward Said's academic suppositions.[60]

In truth, the vast majority of Britons we are dealing with here did not, anyway, go to the Mediterranean or take it up as a theme in their art out of any supposed engagement with local society, whatever its own character may have been; criticisms based on their failure to do so are misplaced. They were almost wholly preoccupied with discovering themselves, and their purposes were defined in terms of their own lives and contexts. They were not really equipped to do anything else. Even the exceptions were partial, so that whilst Byron's poetic style, especially his most satirical and searing work, *Don Juan*, was deeply affected by Italian chivalric romances, he still essentially exploited Mediterranean forms as a filter for critiquing the hypocritical and degraded British society at home that he so despised.[61] Damning that society, in fact, lay at the root of Byron's life whether writing or travelling. When it is said, therefore, as has been remarked of David Roberts's painting in Spain during the later 1820s and early 1830s, that the images he produced did not fairly represent the country 'on its own terms',[62] any truth is slippery. Roberts in Spain, or any number of British writers and painters in Italy, let alone more distantly, had no idea at all what such terms might actually mean. How did their visions and representations of this warm southern world, and the larger Mediterranean tradition behind it, come to affect the changing shape of British culture itself?

A brief comment on what might be meant by 'the British' is required. I shall be at pains to separate out the Scottish, Irish and Welsh as well as the English contributions along the way. For example, such a leading figure in the evolution of national taste in architecture and design as Robert Adam first discovered his British identity in the Mediterranean. Adam went to Rome as a Scot and came back a rather self-conscious Briton.[63] His reasons were not least commercial and professional, but more profoundly, expatriate society in the superheated cultural world of the papal capital provided a venue in which those from the British islands cleaved to each other with a new intimacy, obscuring all sorts of accumulated historical differences among themselves. 'Britishness' and its nuances often evolved with a Mediterranean imprint on it.

At times, 'British' necessarily slides into a wider Anglo-American definition. I have already mentioned several figures whose transatlantic experience was also filtered through the Mediterranean. In the conditions of nineteenth-century Anglo civilization it could not be otherwise. A biographer of America's first female foreign news correspondent, Margaret Fuller, comments that in departing the United States in August 1846 aboard a British Cunard steamer she was 'leaving behind not only America, but the constrictive aspects of her Americanness'.[64] Sadly, after serving in June 1849 as an emergency nurse in defence of the insurrectionary Roman Republic, and spending her last night in Florence with Robert and Elizabeth Barrett Browning, Fuller set off with her Italian husband and young son on the voyage home in May 1850, only to be drowned when the ship foundered off New York's Long Island. But there were to be many Americans like Fuller for whom experience in Italy helped to prise open whatever that constrictiveness consisted of. Indeed, by 1858 some two thousand Americans a year were visiting Florence alone. That destination had a special attraction for women artists and writers, something that Nathaniel Hawthorne, who thought they could quite easily get their inspiration back at home, put down to the relative freedom of life to be had ('the toxic effect of Rome on female [expatriate] sensibility', in John Pemble's words, was one of Hawthorne's pet themes).[65] Thus, in a complicated cultural irony, whilst countering any narrow American provincialism by time spent in the Mediterranean, travellers from the United States often found themselves cohabiting for long periods alongside their transatlantic cousins with their finicky old-country ways and sometimes opposed political instincts. 'Americans are, for the most part, merged into the English,' Catharine Sedgwick wrote to her compatriots in *Letters from Abroad*, perhaps as a gentle reminder of the frustrations awaiting itinerant New Englanders.[66]

In one of those generational loops running through this account, one young seven-year-old who heard the news of Margaret Fuller's death while on a ferry from Manhattan (in fact from the mouth of the creator of Rip van Winkle, Washington Irving) was Henry James, destined to become the epitome of an Anglo-Saxonism refined by life in Italy.[67] James himself once remarked that the British and the Americans were just 'different chapters of the same general subject',[68] and in the European South it was not surprising that separate elements in this blend were often hard for others to make out. This was only beginning to cease to be true by the very end of the nineteenth century, when a mutual irritation could be triggered in Mediterranean settings. Again, in E. M. Forster's *A Room with a View*, the Anglican clergyman, Mr Eager, travelling in a horse-drawn victoria on the hills above Florence, gestures towards a house lived in by 'Mr. Someone Something, an American of the best type – so rare!', by which barbed compliment he meant to privilege any American recognizably like himself. Yet thereafter the British and the Americans in the Mediterranean were often still to be shunted together, if only by wider events, and overlapping identities remained. When Ernest Hemingway used Spain, the Mediterranean country he loved most, as the backdrop for his portrayal of a 'lost generation' in the wake of the Great War of 1914–18, he saw no need to distinguish between the Anglo-Americans in his story.[69] By then the rising star of English literary modernism was Missouri-born T. S. Eliot, whose own grand conception of a unified English-speaking tradition was soaked in classical and Mediterranean reference points. Somebody who knew Eliot well once remarked by way of cultural metaphor that his clothes were British and his underclothes American.[70]

Of course, the shaping of British culture through Mediterranean forms and experiences took place against a much older backdrop. In the summer of 2017 a stunning fourth-century AD Roman mosaic was unearthed in Berkshire, initially by the dog of a local archaeological group, said to be the finest such find in fifty years.[71] It depicted the Greek hero Bellerophon riding the winged horse Pegasus, and showed that the villa owner had been well versed in both Greek and Roman mythology. Romano-British civilization did not disappear completely when the legionnaires departed somewhere around AD 410. The Venerable Bede, dedicated to his monastery at Jarrow in the Kingdom of Northumbria four centuries later, looked constantly to Rome and to Italy; one of the lavishly illustrated Latin Bibles he inscribed ended up in the Laurentian Library in Florence.[72] England's great medieval cathedrals were constructed overwhelmingly in the northern Gothic style, but King Henry III had brought Italian craftsmen to make pavements, choir stalls, canopies, pulpits and tombs, all with a flourish and colour that often carried their own distinctiveness. Such a mingling of Northernness and Southernness is inherent in our story. Henry VIII broke with the canonical authority of Rome, but as a self-styled great Renaissance prince both Italian and Greek scholarship was brought into the old universities through his patronage. A little later it was natural for Elizabeth I, anyway an able linguist, to converse in Castilian with Philip II's representatives at her court.

Thereafter the breadth of Anglo-Mediterranean exchange increased rapidly as the seventeenth century proceeded. The Prince of Wales Charles Stuart's interest in Flemish and Dutch paintings, for instance, was more than equalled by his fascination with Mediterranean riches. When he went to Madrid in 1623 he was thunderstruck by the beauty of the Baroque and Renaissance art in the royal galleries there, contrasting so painfully with the absence of imagery of almost any kind that was the dour legacy of the Reformation in England. Although he failed in his main goal to bring back the Spanish Infanta as his bride and future queen, he did acquire a baggage-load of densely coloured canvases, including Titian's portrait of Charles V, then the most important 'master' painting ever to be brought into the kingdom; and although it was sold outside the country after Charles's execution following the English Civil War, it was said to have left an indelible impression on English artists.[73] Sir Henry Wotton, the immensely well-travelled scholar and twice England's envoy to Venice, expressed in his *Panegyrick* to Charles I, written while the reign was proceeding on its fateful course, what he saw as the underlying trend: '*Italy* (the greatest Mother of Elegant Arts) or at least (next the *Grecians*) the Principal Nursery, seem by your magnificence to be translated into *England*.'[74] That such an interlocking process could be identified in the 1640s, and restored in 1660 along with Stuart authority and the abrupt reversal of Protector

Cromwell's disbandment of the royal collections, is telling about its growing significance in the history of the Anglo-Celtic islands. But it is the translation of the Mediterranean into *Britain* in modern experience, and its enrichment and undergirding of a national culture ill at ease with its own status and fineness despite mounting successes in other spheres, which lie at the heart of this book.

Chapter Two

THE ANTIQUE, THE NOBLE AND
THE STUPENDOUS
THE TURN TO THE MEDITERRANEAN, 1740–1800

All appears enchantment: it is with some difficulty we can believe we are still on earth.

Patrick Brydone, *A Tour through Sicily and Malta*, 1773

O n 16 March 1787 two Germans, one a scholar and writer and the other an artist, approached the country villa of Sir William Hamilton, the British diplomatic representative to the Kingdom of the Two Sicilies.[1] The residence was at Portici, twenty miles north of Naples, nestling in the margins of the ornate Bourbon palace of Caserta. The two men – Johann Wolfgang von Goethe and Johann Tischbein – had travelled from Rome along one of the most dilapidated roads in Italy, passing through a region of lonely shepherds and roaming herds of cattle, buffalo and wild horses. On the way Tischbein had painted perhaps the best known of all the images of his famous countryman, *Goethe in the Campagna*, with the Alban hills glowing in the background. But having arrived at last in sophisticated Naples, they were expectant about the visit to Sir William Hamilton's home. He was, in addition to being a prominent British diplomat, one of Europe's most notable connoisseurs and under his roof were several curiosities Goethe and Tischbein were keen to see.

One was his antiquities, including exquisite vases acquired from the excavations at Pompeii and Herculaneum (a number are now in the British Museum).[2] Most of Sir William's impressive collection of treasures was at his *palazzo* in Naples itself, but some were at the Caserta residence. There was another presence, however, about which Goethe and Tischbein were especially curious. The previous year a young female companion from England had joined the considerably older diplomatic widower in Naples; rumours inevitably abounded. This was Emma Hart (later Hamilton), and she had soon added a fresh twist to Sir William's obsession with classical civilization: a *tableau vivant* of theatrical display or 'Attitudes' embodying ancient Greek beauty in its most alluring form. Tischbein had hopes of painting Emma in the guise of King Agamemnon's daughter, Princess Iphigenia. Goethe, for whom Italy had offered a sexual awakening after years of celibacy in his native Weimar, just wanted to see what had already entranced others in the elegant circles of cosmopolitan Naples.

Describing what followed in his diary, Goethe noted Emma's lithe figure, and the simple white dress specially commissioned by Sir William as suitably 'antique', which, Goethe said, 'became her extremely'. He went on:

> Dressed in this, letting her hair fall loose, and making use of a length of shawl, she exhibits every possible variety of pose, expression and aspect so that in each the spectator imagines himself in a dream. Here one sees in perfection, in ravishing variety and movement, all that the greatest artists have loved to express. Standing, kneeling, sitting, reclining, grave or sad, playful, triumphant, reflective, alluring, menacing, anxious, all states of mind flowing regularly one after another. She suits the folding of her veil to each expression with wonderful taste . . . as an entertainment it is quite unique.[3]

Goethe recalled how Sir William, 'the old knight', had held a lamp by her throughout to heighten the effect and generally entered into the performance heart and soul, as if Emma was the embodiment of those antiquities he had collected over many years with lustful zest. Afterwards, back at their lodgings, Goethe, never without a trace of hardness, commented on the unfortunate fact that, from what they had heard at dinner following

Emma Hamilton as 'The Muse of Dance'
Engraving by Friedrich Rehberg (1794)

the entertainment, Emma's mind did not live up to her beauty. Tischbein, with characteristic sympathy, 'saw her with the eye of a painter, and was content with that'.

Emma's 'Attitudes' became famous in Europe when another German artist, Friedrich Rehberg, published drawings of the same scene just a few years later. The subsequent engravings sold very widely.[4] The celebrity this generated through Europe has never lost its sheen. Emma's performance has been described by one writer as the prototype of modern performance art and, as such, 'something to be perpetually reinvented in modern aesthetic experience'.[5] The great Victorian actress, Ellen Terry, for example, developed a rather similar routine, described on one occasion as 'doubly classic . . . she curls herself into innumerable graceful poses . . . her snake-like draperies fall into the exact folds of the garments of an ancient Greek statue or a Pompeian fresco'.[6] The shades here of Emma's Neapolitan displays are clear; traits were also detectible in Maud Allan's highly eroticized choreography of Salome's 'Dance of the Seven Veils' that led to a celebrated libel case in 1914.[7] Certainly Emma never gave up a classical

Greek consciousness of herself. After the death of her guardian and lover, Admiral Nelson, at the Battle of Trafalgar in 1805, she wore her hair *à la grecque* as a sign of mourning.[8]

The striking scene at the Hamilton villa in Caserta in 1787 included a whole complex of elements and polarities – cosmopolitanism, sexuality, gender, the European North meeting the Mediterranean South, an obsession with antiquity interlaced with a bursting sense of the present – that are relevant to this book. The British played a key role in the 'discovery' – itself necessarily a kind of pose – of the Mediterranean during the second half of the eighteenth century that shaped European culture between the onset of the Enlightenment and the impact of the French Revolution. Sir William Hamilton epitomized a synthesis of gentlemanly acquisitiveness, classical scholarship and sardonic humour about the human condition characterizing key aspects of the British involvement with the process.

Whatever may have been the case in strategy and economics regarding a 'turn to the East' after the war in America – and it has been remarked that even in 1800 the part of the East uppermost in British consciousness was, in fact, not India at all but the Levant[9] – the argument here is that there was a matching cultural orientation towards the broader Mediterranean. This did not pivot on the intrinsic significance of the Mediterranean countries themselves; rather it was that 'the warm South', ancient and modern, lent itself as a laboratory or theatre for articulating cultural change in Britain when increasing wealth and power were transforming society.

Much of this is bound up with an Age of Romanticism emerging in the last third or so of the eighteenth century, though in fact the term 'Romantic' to denote retrospectively a huge array of tendencies and heightened sensibilities did not become current until the 1860s. 'Romanticism' itself was a still later invention (the twentieth century, as an era of 'isms', imposed such collectivities on earlier periods). Indeed a falsity of language can bedevil this whole subject. 'Neoclassicism' is another label we cannot avoid using. As a description of shifting uses of the ancient and especially the Hellenic past, lumping together all sorts of different traits, it was first used in England in an article in *The Times* in 1926,[10] but that has not stopped cultural historians using it as if the tag meant something coherent even at the time. Realities, however, were much messier.

British engagement with the Mediterranean went back a lot further than this. Shakespeare's plays abounded with Italian locations. Although it seems unlikely that the playwright ever went there, plenty of travel guides existed concerning the country to obtain the necessary information to build up a plot.[11] The modernization of London's architecture in the 1620s was profoundly shaped by the visits made to the Venetian Republic and Rome by Inigo Jones, whose trail-blazing Banqueting House in Whitehall (in front of which Charles I was later to be executed) was inspired by the style of Andrea Palladio. The influence of the Palladian 'school' was to shape significantly the built fabric of the country. Examples included the elegant Augustan villas – one inhabited by Alexander Pope and supposedly based on Cicero's Tusculum residence outside Rome – along a stretch of the Thames at Richmond and Twickenham, which was to be England's answer to the mansions gracing the Veneto's River Brenta.[12]

But the most practical starting point is the evolution of the Grand Tour, a term first used in Robert Lassels's posthumously published *The Voyage of Italy* in 1670 (Lassels was an English Roman Catholic priest, and

A Palladian villa
Chiswick House (1781)

interactions with the Roman faith were to be a key thread in the phenomenon).[13] 'Grand Tour' as a description conflated a diverse range in which younger members of the British aristocracy set out on their journeys towards southern Europe, accompanied by tutors and guides. British travellers found little to detain them after Paris as they headed towards their ultimate goal of Italy. (Far fewer included the Iberian Peninsula in their itinerary, and Greece, though often dreamed about, remained beyond the realm of possibility except for rare individuals until the early nineteenth century, and really well beyond that.) Some Britons halted at larger provincial towns in France, such as Arles or Nîmes, to see Roman antiquities, but rarely for long.[14] Unforeseen public events sometimes complicated matters, so that Lady Mary Wortley Montagu got stuck in Avignon due to the War of Austrian Succession in the 1740s, but felt, as she said, philosophically detached from her surroundings.[15] Such a detachment represented an instinctive hesitation, an inwardness, felt by most British in French-speaking environments. Right up until the 1850s, when railways altered the logistics of travel, those heading for Italy usually moved on speedily by taking a boat from Marseilles to Genoa, or following a landward route across the Alps by various forms of horse-drawn transport or diligence, crossing the border with Savoy and down into the Italian states with all the rich sightseeing of art treasures and ancient, exquisitely nostalgic ruins to follow.

The driving aim of all this movement was to absorb some tincture of refinement, tokens of an expanded mental universe, as a provincial and often boorish landowning elite adapted to a new form of political and social leadership, a trend intensified after the Glorious Revolution of 1688. Samuel Johnson, the great writer and lexicographer of Britain's ensuing Augustan Age, put this in personal terms. 'A man who has not been to Italy,' he remarked, 'is always conscious of an inferiority from not having seen what it is expected a man should see.' Johnson's ambition to do so himself was never fulfilled, but the fact that, of his many aphorisms on English life and letters, this is arguably the most quoted, indicates that it struck a deep chord in his own culture. It was to remain true in the nineteenth century, when some measure of Italian experience, and ideally a usable knowledge of the language, was a token of the superior Victorian gentleman. As an architectural historian has commented, the frequent tendency to treat the Grand Tour, broadly defined, as a special, highly colourful aspect of eighteenth-century history underplays its long-term effects in British life.[16]

Already by the 1720s and 1730s the Grand Tour had become frequently discussed in Britain's growing print culture. It overlapped with a process in which England had, politically and strategically, been integrated after 1688 into Continental affairs under a new Dutch king, William III, who was constantly fighting his enemies. Many people were opposed to this, and the stereotypical figure of 'John Bull', lover of small beer and domestic peace, and fierce critic of foreign entanglements, arose at this time. Most controversial had been the country's participation in the War of the Spanish Succession after 1700, during the course of which Gibraltar and Menorca were seized from Spain, territories retained by Great Britain after the Treaty of Utrecht (1713). Here were the first glimmerings of her role as a Mediterranean power proper. That this coincided with the challenges of consolidating the new state created by the Anglo-Scottish Union is significant.

One person who moved to London from Italy during the struggle over Spanish succession was the German composer George Frideric Handel. His first opera in Italian written specifically for the London stage, and with an all-Italian cast of singers, was *Rinaldo*, which opened in 1711 at the Queen's Theatre in London's Haymarket.[17] Written in two weeks, and with the English libretto translated over a few days, the performance included real fire, water, live birds, painted backdrops and machinery-driven sets, an overall effect that electrified audiences. Singing by Italian castrati was a key element in the new style and almost immediately these productions were all the rage. Women went mad over a series of soulful castrati, wearing their miniature images, fainting in the theatre, sending them private messages and installing their busts at home. The castrati craze reached a peak with the singer Farinelli (real name Carlo Broschi), whom Handel after much persuasion lured to London in 1734; allegedly he could earn up to £5,000 for a season. Such Italian enthusiasms suggested a new realm of experience and formed a perfect target for another fresh genre, that of satire – and William Hogarth, artist and engraver, lampooned the phenomenon mercilessly.[18] The cultic ambience of London's Italian opera scene, Handel included, was captured sardonically in one of the scenes of

Hogarth's series *A Rake's Progress* (1732–4). Arguably this was why Handel soon moved on to a piece, *Alexander's Feast* (1736), based on an ode by John Dryden, marking a transition from a now endless Italian repertoire to distinctively English choral works, which must have been greeted by the relief of at least a few members of London's musical world.

Anything associated with the Grand Tour itself and outside influences in general received similarly barbed treatment from the English satirical school, although what it mostly objected to was not anything alien as such

George Frideric Handel's libretto *Giulio Cesare*
First performed at the King's Theatre, Haymarket, 20 February 1724

but the surrounding self-preening connoisseurship. Hogarth, the self-styled 'Britophil' who rarely travelled himself, disliked what he saw as idle sauntering abroad because he felt it stifled a revival of 'native' English art that could thrive best in a domestic setting.[19] The circle he created, centred on Old Slaughter's Coffee House in St Martin's Lane, propounded an edgy, almost anarchic rejection of superficial sophistication for which the Tour overseas provided a ready metaphor – although ironically, the first coffeehouse in London, with stimulating effects on intellectual and social life in the capital, had been established by a local Greek employee of the Levant Company.[20] As for the growing fashion for Palladian-type country houses, their high ceilings and open colonnades were said by some to be highly unsuitable for English conditions, leading to mockery of those who were 'proud to catch cold at a Venetian door'.[21]

Reflected in this was a pattern that would recur endlessly in British cultural interaction with the Mediterranean: a circularity in which rapture and enthralment with a southern European world offering experimental ways of seeing and feeling was offset by a relapse into seemingly less stirring but realistic English (and Scottish) frames of reference. That was the moral message of Samuel Richardson's novel *The History of Sir Charles Grandison* (1753), whose protagonist's sexual longing for a beautiful Italian girl during his youthful travels haunts his mature life back in England, until he is ultimately reconciled to a more pedestrian but workable marriage to an Englishwoman. It proved even more popular with the new novel-reading public than Richardson's preceding work, *Clarissa*. (Jane Austen was later influenced by the Grandison story, and its theme foreshadowed Madame de Staël's *Corinne*, which consolidated the Mediterranean myth in English literature.)[22] The theme of desire and ways to control it and make everyday life bearable was to undergo endless permutations in the Anglo-Mediterranean engagement.

Already by the 1760s, however, the Grand Tour had passed its heyday in the guise of an educational jaunt (one which, the Scottish economist Adam Smith said, had only thrived in the first place because the universities at home were so dire).[23] It progressively overlapped with a more diffuse phenomenon in which British practitioners of the visual arts, literature, antiquarianism and nascent archaeology spent protracted periods in the Mediterranean; though, since the average stay was about two years, networks of patronage still remained essential for many of these by no means always well-heeled travellers. Architectural students appear to have been the most impecunious, and if they can be said to have had a Grand Tour as such, it was often the least grand of all.[24]

Underlying personal motivations for all these sojourners – a search for better health in a warmer climate, making money go further where living was cheaper, escaping from disastrous marriages, alleviating all sorts of intimate griefs, or driving professional ambition – were to remain as varied as always. To these could be added an alienation from home, so that Horace Mann, the long-time British diplomatic representative in Florence and a port of call for generations of British visitors, was said to harbour 'a coldness and dislike of England'.[25] Yet what made such alienation complex was that it often ran alongside a sense of keen isolation from what was loved best. Lady Mary Wortley Montagu had, like Mann, escaped Britain, but living in the city of Brescia for ten years she read the novels of Henry Fielding through the long nights to inhale their quintessential spirit of Englishness, and when her son sent her a box of china, 'everything was precious to her, even the straw used in the packing' because it was redolent of home.[26]

This milieu of fluctuating emotions and needs surrounded many members of an organization prominent in our subject. This is the Society of Dilettanti, from the Italian *dilettare*, meaning to delight: a title suggestive of the foppish insouciance characterizing the society's origins but mixed up with a considerable record of cultural entrepreneurship (it still meets four times a year in London). The Society of Dilettanti was originally formed in 1734 out of a milieu of specialized grand touring, speculation and the forging of connections between like-minded cognoscenti – or virtuosi as they thought of themselves. One such manifestation was the Roman Club, formed in 1723 by a number of patrician artists and dealers who dressed up in togas at meetings. Two of its members, Arthur Pond and George Knapton, began a series of visits to Italy, not least to see the startling excavations that had just got under way at Herculaneum, and sent back plaster casts from the antique originals. Later, Pond published a series of engravings drawn from the work of local artists entitled *Italian Landscapes* and *Roman Antiquities*, appearing into the 1750s.[27]

The Dilettanti's characteristics went beyond a penchant for Roman cross-dressing and love of masquerade. Horace Walpole famously remarked in 1743 that if going to Italy was a requirement for membership, getting drunk was another.[28] To this could be added holding Whig political loyalties hostile to the Hanoverian dynasty, though the members' Whiggism was that of a landed magnate class quite aloof from the masses. One man Pond and Knapton befriended in Rome was Sir Francis Dashwood, also a founder and later arch-master of the Dilettanti, whose escapades in the papal capital became notorious. According to Walpole, whose prejudice could often get the better of his imagination, Dashwood allegedly once 'secreted himself in the Sistine chapel before the penitential scourging of holy week and emerged from the darkness at the most sacred part of the ceremony lashing out . . . with an English horsewhip'.[29] Back at home, Dashwood's Grand Tourist circles overlapped with a brotherhood he established at a former Cistercian abbey at Medmenham in Buckinghamshire, a sort of Hellfire Club for those with Mediterranean connections, complete with rituals, chamber music, pornographic wall murals and 'nuns' drawn from London brothels (making fun of Roman Catholicism was part of the mix).[30] The radical politician John Wilkes, whose travels in Italy had coincided with those of Boswell, was a prominent member. Acting as grand master of these rural proceedings, Dashwood was said to have once administered the sacrament to a baboon; when Knapton painted his picture for the Dilettanti in the guise of 'St. Francis of Wycombe', named after his country house stuffed with ancient artefacts, he did so in an attitude of devotion before the delicious figure of Venus de Medici.[31] All this was extreme, but tamer versions existed. In the 1730s and 1740s there was a Hellfire Club in Dublin on Montpelier Hill, with an elite – and naturally Protestant – camaraderie drawing on its members' Mediterranean experience.[32]

Yet in a profoundly eighteenth-century manner, lasciviousness went hand in hand with the deeply serious. Perhaps this may be seen as inherent in the instinct to probe more deeply the human psyche. Dashwood was, intellectually, a profoundly reflective man. On his European travels he had met and discussed philosophy with Montesquieu. He became a vice-president of the Foundling Hospital in London, and was one of those in 1757 who protested at the execution of Admiral Byng after the loss of Menorca to the French, temporary as it proved, saying that at most Byng had been guilty of misjudgement. (In Europe Voltaire excoriated the glaring injustice whose base motive, he wrote, was merely *pour encourager les autres* – the phrase was to stick.) Regarding the political crisis in the American colonies in the 1770s, Dashwood, as a leading independent in Parliament, called repeatedly for moderation and reconciliation. The point here is that his Dilettantism embodied sexual, aesthetic and intellectual impulses converging in a self-consciously Enlightenment fraternity where it was possible to think that a small group of people could incorporate all human understanding and experience in an interconnected, humanistic Deism. In this milieu the lines separating eroticism, fine art, travel, scholarship, humanity and the changing 'Taste' of the times all came together.[33]

One ambitious, but far more cautious, young Scot who turned up in Rome a bit later than Dashwood in early 1755 was to have a lasting effect on all sorts of tastes across the British islands. This was Robert Adam, whose family architectural firm had imbued in him a now somewhat old-fashioned Palladian-style classicism, not to mention still older Scottish

The Dilettanti Society
Engraving of painting by Sir Joshua Reynolds (1778)

baronial forms. On arrival he had reckoned it would be sufficient just 'to pick up a new set of thoughts' on his profession before going home to exploit a claim to novel credentials. But he soon concluded that matters were more complicated. For one thing, mixing for the first time with English peers, he decided that London was his ulterior goal. In that metropole, however, he said, with an eye on future patrons and customers, 'you have rivals – and those not unformidable . . . Unless one can appear equal, if not superior, to these antagonists, so as to acquire the preference from the connoisseurs, all attempts to succeed . . . will not continue for any length of time, so that after a little blaze you are sent home [to Scotland] with little honour and less profit.'[34]

This anxiety about failure – an oppressive sense to be felt by many British artists in Rome – explains the brittle feverishness with which the essentially bourgeois Adam set about equipping himself for the professional battle he saw looming back at home. He arranged a kind of intensive crammer's course in design from an artist on the fringes of the distinguished local French Academy, Charles-Louis Clérisseau, whom Adam regarded as a kind of elevated servant, the Frenchman padding along on foot after Adam's coach through the streets of Rome. (The relations of English artists with their French counterparts were generally uneasy in a manner not replicated with other expatriates – one remarking that the French in Rome were 'as distinct from the rest of Mankind as the Chinese'.)[35] But Adam would probably have treated Giovanni Piranesi, the only contemporary Italian artist with whom he had close dealings, the same as he did Clérisseau, except that Piranesi, in the spirit of his own oversized, elemental drawings of old Rome, could not be dominated quite so easily.[36]

Adam immersed himself hungrily in classical culture, embracing architectural plans, painting, sculpture and above all the decorative arts. After two years in Rome, a biographer writes, Adam 'succeeded in transforming himself from a rather green Scottish architect into a cosmopolitan figure, ready . . . to put into effect "the Antique, the Noble and the Stupendous" '.[37] On getting finally to London, Adam wrote home to Scotland signing himself 'my dearest Mother's British Boy'. A new pan-British (as well as Anglo-Irish)[38] awareness was forged in the hothouse world of the expatriate community in Rome, when the alien surroundings accentuated what was shared between them rather than the accustomed differences. One historian ascribes a significant role to renewed emphasis on a common Roman inheritance in the 'nationalistic definition of what it meant to be British in the modern world', a definition capable of bridging the chasm between Whigs, Tories and Jacobites when 1688 was still not so very long before.[39]

The real prize Adam brought back from Rome was his collection of drawings, copies of ancient motifs and figures. These – unlike the larger paintings and antique objects he acquired – were transported in his own personal luggage. They were too valuable to risk losing because they constituted his portfolio which he would display to potential customers and patrons in London. Their outstanding characteristic was sheer eclecticism and scope for creative adaptation to Northern circumstances in which an *allusion* to Southern 'Antiquity' was as important as anything strictly antiquarian. One historian of Georgian architecture concludes that Adam 'invented an exciting stylistic synthesis that embraced Roman, Hellenistic, Etruscan, Greek, Italian *Cinquecento* and Second Palladian Revival in one fecund Neo-Classical soup'.[40] The quintessential Adam style – overseen by the Italian craftsmen he brought back with him – quite quickly attracted criticism for an excessive fancy and lightness, a too smooth blend of the picturesque and the classical. Nonetheless, it was never entirely to be eclipsed, surviving as a caricature of its own century, as James Lees-Milne once remarked, where terraced houses in London, Edinburgh and Dublin might contain 'a single "Adam" fanlight or a portico, with inside an "Adam" stairway, an "Adam" grate or just an "Adam" frieze'.[41]

There was one thing Adam did not do during his stay in the Mediterranean about which he was a little sensitive: he did not go to Greece. There was already a growing feeling that Italy, and above all Rome itself, was being exhausted as a mine of cultural inspiration. Even worse was the unsettling possibility that ancient Roman art was not quite what it was cracked up to be – in fact only derivative, a mere copy, of the greater glory that had been ancient Hellas.[42] In April 1748 two Grand Tourists, James Stuart and Nicholas Revett, and the Scottish painter and art dealer Gavin Hamilton (who was to be a key figure in the artistic life of Rome during the later decades of the eighteenth century) had gone to Naples, and while there had formed the idea of an expedition to Greece itself, though Hamilton travelled with them no further. Naples – the original Neapolis – was, after all, a Greek city in origin, part of that overflow of ancient Hellenic cultural and economic expansion, *Magna Graecia*, which the Dilettanti who helped finance the adventure were increasingly keen to promote in their researches.[43] British travellers had certainly made it to Athens before. The botanist Sir George Wheler had spent a month there in 1675–6 and recorded his time in great detail.[44] But this new venture in that direction was conceived with a very precise purpose: to explore Athens, 'the Mother of Elegance and Politeness', as offering the perfect model for modern society to follow before its remaining testimonies were wholly obliterated by the destructiveness of Turkish Ottoman rule to which the Greek lands were still subject.[45] In practice, this meant recording in pencil and accurately measuring the physical dimensions of what classical remains might be found there.

During February 1751 Stuart and Revett left Venice for Greece, though Hamilton did not go with them.[46] The two men arrived in Athens several months later. Getting the necessary official permission, or firman, to set about their tasks was not their only challenge. After all, this was not like Rome. The classical heritage in Athens was then by no means so visible to the naked eye at street level as subsequent excavations and clearances made it seem. Stuart and Revett also had very little idea of what actually to look *for*. For instance, they had no idea how important the Parthenon – at that time still occupied by a Turkish garrison – was as an edifice. They were neither historians of ancient art, insofar as such people then existed, nor indeed even practising architects; Stuart was originally a painter of fans. What they really wanted to discover and record were purely decorative styles, the sort of thing that might have an impact back home on that gentlemanly preoccupation of the age, 'Taste', and through it on the shape and texture of the ideal life in society of the day.

Stuart and Revett remained in Athens, involved in various quarrels with Greeks and Turks, before escaping in September 1753 from an outbreak of local disorder to Salonica (today's Thessaloniki). They travelled through the Aegean before arriving in London in October 1754, where they set about preparing their drawings for publication. The first volume – featuring what later would be seen as mostly minor works of art – appeared as *The Antiquities of Athens* in 1762, and its successor volume not until 1790. The delays led to a personal break between the two men. This sumptuous serial publication, however, promoted through the Dilettanti network, had a wide albeit necessarily elite readership. But that did not mean Stuart and Revett's recipes for emulation in Britain were instantly adopted. Robert Adam was a particularly fierce critic. When he saw the ceilings designed by Stuart for Spencer House in London he growled, 'They may be Greek but by God they are not handsome', whilst Stuart himself always remained more deeply affected by the eight years he had previously spent in Rome than by the more chaotic period in Athens.[47] Nevertheless, *The Antiquities of Athens* was in the end to prove the principal design source for the Greek Revival climaxing in Britain in the early nineteenth century.[48]

The 'Grecian Taste', as tentatively advocated at this stage by Stuart and Revett, was anyway a mere supplement to a much larger turn in the culture of European Enlightenment. The key figure here was the German scholar Johann Joachim Winckelmann, librarian to Cardinal Albani in Rome after November 1759. The cardinal had close English connections, above all through the court of the Old Stuart Pretender based in the city, and Winckelmann was to mix frequently in these circles. Even before arriving in Rome he had become obsessed with a conception of Greek art as possessing a simple grandeur never subsequently equalled. It now became an overwhelming obsession, though to what extent Winckelmann's adoration of Greek statues of male nudes bore any relation to his homosexuality remains vague.[49] The truth was that whilst Winckelmann knew something about Greek literature, he knew very little about Greek art, and that little was derived from what was available in Rome (there was then virtually nothing in Germany). But as a latter-day scholar once commented, 'Had he known the Greeks better, they might have lost half their power over him.'[50] Certainly his close friend, Goethe, though hardly untouched by Hellenism, remained essentially Roman in his preferences, and always a wry critic of what he saw as shallow 'Grecising'.[51]

Yet for Winckelmann the point was anyway not about Greek realities, but a desperate search for some fresh secular divinity to worship, a framework within which to order man's cultural evolution in contemporary minds. His *Geschichte der Kunst des Alterthums* (*The History of Art in Antiquity*) published in 1764 – four years before he finally left Rome, only to be murdered in Trieste on his rather uncertain travels – presented a picture of civilization's early climax in the wonder of Periclean Athens of the fifth century BC, before inexorably declining through the accumulating barbarity of imperial Rome and the complete darkness of the Middle Ages. Winckelmann's legacy was prominent in a book called *The Tyranny of Greece over Germany* by the British cultural critic E. M. Butler, writing in the 1930s and seeking to explain the connection between Nazi ideology and its frequent use of ancient Greek symbols.[52] The argument was highly controversial and no doubt exaggerated, but insofar as there was any 'tyranny' of what later became neoclassicism in Britain it was a paler reflection of an essentially German phenomenon. Nevertheless, here was a deeper and more intensively cosmopolitanized European culture in which Britain was caught up.

It has often been thought curious that Winckelmann never travelled to Greece himself. At least Robert Adam got as far as Spalatro (today's Split) in Dalmatia to make drawings of Emperor Diocletian's palace,[53] though after considering making Athens the goal of a more extended stay in the Mediterranean, he decided to go home instead.[54] What is interesting in both these cases, however, is that they help to identify a general tendency: a powerful attraction to the *idea* of seeing Greece, but one more often than not accompanied first by hesitation and then a flinching from actually doing so. This hesitation was to continue even when travel became easier and safer.

There were very practical reasons for this. In Ottoman Greece all sorts of authorizations were needed to access almost anything, including ruins. Admittedly, permissions were needed to copy artworks in Italian galleries, but usually one could get round these strictures through contacts and 'introductions'. Greece was much more difficult. The infrastructure of aristocratic hospitality that made Grand Touring viable elsewhere did not exist. In the Ottoman Balkans no readily comprehensible directions were available as to how to get from one place to another, entailing a dependence on guides who might or might not prove reliable or well intentioned. This was why when antiquarians from Britain did start to penetrate the Greek lands they matched their scholarly interests with recording topographical directions. As if this was not enough, travelling in Greek provinces held considerable physical dangers. John Bouverie, who visited

Athens and died shortly afterwards from an infection on the coast of Asia
Minor in September 1750, was just one example.

Yet there was something deeper too. At the heart of Winckelmann's
obsession with Greek art was a conception of idealized beauty. A preoccupation with beauty – how best to represent it, and how its sensory
impact on the human mind actually operated – was to mark British as well
as Continental European artistic debates for decades ahead. A sense of
Grecian perfection, however, was an internalized and above all imaginary
affair. To see actual and all too often mutilated examples in their original,
inevitably crude, settings – rather than through a few carefully selected,
and often 'restored', Roman copies of Greek masterpieces elegantly
installed in the Vatican Museum or the Palazzo Borghese – might even
cause aesthetic confusion. There was in this psychology a strong legacy of
the Baroque age that still exerted a powerful hold. Certainly the reluctance
on the part of many cultivated northern Europeans to push beyond the
cultural and emotional frontiers of Rome was based on invisible as well as
purely logistical barriers.

The reason for underlining this, however, is that it makes the engagement of British writers, artists and collectors in southern Italy and Sicily
which *did* take shape from the 1770s onwards all the more striking.
Cultural exploration in the realm of old *Magna Graecia* was a fortuitous
alternative – almost a placebo – to Greece itself. Naples was its epicentre.
The city made an impression completely different from Rome on the
Britons who went there. Rome was dour, repressed, papal, with no public
theatres or opera except at Carnival time, full of ruins and, indeed, ruin.
Women were hardly to be seen at most events.[55] Naples, by contrast, was a
shock to the system. It was a great metropolis, its size comparable in the
late eighteenth century to any other city in Europe, possessing gas lighting
decades before London. Its pulsating street life – with sellers of melons,
cooked apples, corn, truffles and fried pastries – found its most vivid visual
record of the day in the portrayals of the Anglo-Neapolitan artist Peter
Fabris, who catered to a Grand Tourist market.[56] Neapolitan Catholicism –
unlike the profoundly hierarchical clericalism of Rome – was exotic,
popular, relic-rich, full of symbols and miracles; the most famous of the
latter was the annual liquefaction of the blood of St Januarius that foreign
visitors flocked to see. A pronounced sexual consciousness, as felt at least

by susceptible outsiders, was part of the thrill;[57] as was the 'blaze of splendour' that was its opera house, the Teatro di San Carlo.[58] After a cadet branch of the Spanish Bourbons assumed the Neapolitan throne in 1734, bringing many treasures with them from Parma, there was a flurry of prestigious new construction, notably the theatre, the most lavish in Europe, but also palaces at Capodimonte and in the country at Caserta (though the latter was not finished until the rule of Napoleon's representative, Joachim Murat, in the next century). Naples had its own ancient heritage, mostly underground, in the city itself, but it was the here and now, the inescapable sense of the present, that visitors repeatedly described.

There was another aspect of Neapolitan life widely commented on: the extreme poverty of its ordinary people. In Rome human need was concealed behind fading grandeur; in Naples it hit you in the eye. 'Such dreadful sights,' the actor David Garrick said when there in 1764, after a famine had recently claimed many thousands of lives.[59] Slightly later, when 'the beautiful, gay and fascinating Lady Craven', as James Boswell described a woman dogged by scandal, first arrived in the city where she was to die many years later, it was the indigence haunting almost everybody, from the nobility to ordinary people, that forcibly struck her.[60] One writer has evoked the impression the city's life made on Goethe with its 'unreflecting naturalness . . . the singing, the quarrelling, the chaffing . . . this was life, direct, simple, intense'.[61] That general effect was why the further south from Rome any cultural engagement extended, the less overwhelmingly preoccupied with the past, and the more human, ethnographic and even sociological the focus often became. One might more properly say that it was the way that the past and the present intersected that was critical, so that the *then* and the *now* could hardly be separated. This represented a considerable step towards an incipiently modern intellectual perspective affecting a whole range of disciplines.

The gradual uncovering from the 1730s onwards of the remains of Herculaneum and Pompeii close to Naples bore on this sense of the closeness, the tactile quality, and by extension the continuing relevance of the ancient. Buried under volcanic ash in the great eruption of Mount Vesuvius in AD 79, the human and material life of these towns was captured at the point of extinction. This exquisitely painful sense of being both dead and yet somehow framed in life was never to go away (and was to be the subject of one of the biggest publishing sensations in Britain in the nineteenth century).[62] But there was also something special about the treasures these excavations yielded. They included in their original completeness colourful walls and murals depicting plain domestic affairs, and mosaic floors and vases with perfect cameo designs, illustrating the taste of an ancient society and making it vivid in a way that oversized statuary could never really do. Not only did the revelations of Herculaneum and Pompeii give the classical tradition in European culture a boost when otherwise it might have flagged, they offered a stock of motifs and flourishes that were to appear on furniture, tripod tables, walls, perfumeries, cutlery, teacups – the whole fabric of a society taking shape in the later decades of the eighteenth century. Indeed, viewed in narrowly material terms, this was simply just one expression of the consuming classes' craze for *having things* – visions of Turkish luxury introducing the *sofa* as a new feature in the drawing room was another[63] – which unleashed economic forces driving first a commercial, and then an industrial, revolution in Britain.

Sir William Hamilton, as British diplomat and confidant of the Bourbon court, was perfectly placed to make the most of the laboratory of new ideas and concepts that Naples became from the 1760s onwards.[64] His main residence, the Palazzo Sessa, hosted a kind of permanent salon for cultivated enjoyments, including music. His first wife, Catherine, who died in 1782, was said to be one of the best violinists in Italy, her performance in May 1770 complimented on by Leopold Mozart when he and his brilliant young son attended a reception.[65] Hamilton took a great interest in excavations of the buried towns – he was sometimes present when burial sites were opened – and acquired particularly beautiful artefacts. It was considered a privilege, even by a personage like Emperor Joseph II of Austria, to be invited to see what Sir William called his 'lumber room' of art.[66] There were rumours that some of these valuables had strayed from the royal museum at Portici to the Hamilton palazzo; a French diplomat once caustically observed that it was not quite clear whether Sir William supported the arts or the arts supported Sir William.[67]

Hamilton's collection of paintings was notable in its great range, including works by Canaletto, Rembrandt, Raphael, Veronese, Rubens, Poussin and Titian, amongst others. It was the vases, however, that were perhaps most unique and which distinguished *Antiquités étrusques, grecques et romaines* (1767–76), Hamilton's joint publishing project with the Frenchman 'Baron' d'Hancarville, whose mix of the risqué, fake nobility and genuine scholarship embodied something of the age. This collaboration has been described as 'one of the most influential art publications of the eighteenth century',[68] a product of the international republic of letters at the heart of the Enlightenment.[69] Not long after the first volume appeared, Josiah Wedgwood – to whom Hamilton had personally sent a copy – opened his pottery works at 'Etruria' in Staffordshire and started producing basalt vases in the style of Hamilton's much-loved possessions.

If vases formed one main pole of Hamilton's many interests, the other was volcanoes. During Hamilton's time in Naples Vesuvius erupted in 1767, 1779 and 1794. Fascinated by the phenomenon, he made careful observations which were published by the Royal Society in London and formed the basis for much scientific discussion. His major work on the subject was *Campi Phlegraei* (*Flaming Fields*), with the subtitle *Observations on the Volcanos of the Two Sicilies*. Appearing in 1776, this was accompanied by gouache images of eruptions, lightning and other natural events, subsequently widely reproduced in prints. Here was the Neapolitan countryside in its most powerful and 'picturesque' form (though, as the English writer and art critic Sacheverell Sitwell once pointed out, the Neapolitans themselves never iconified Vesuvius as the Japanese did their own Mount Fuji).[70] A climb up the blackened slopes of that open peak, or alternatively those of Mount Etna, remained ever afterwards a staple of British tourism long into the Victorian era, and still is today. Thanks not least to Hamilton, such volcano worship became symptomatic of an emergent Romantic consciousness in which sudden eruptions fused awe and horror, a metaphor for the sublimity of man's intense emotional states.[71] The sexual connotations of this were not far from the surface. A good deal of the imagery in what we regard today as classic Romantic literature, especially poetry, in the early nineteenth century has some of its roots in Hamilton's *Campi Phlegraei*.[72]

There was an entirely logical connection running from this near-obsession with natural external forces to man's (and woman's) internal psychology. In February 1783 a big earthquake hit southern Calabria. Up to 40,000 people died. Hamilton visited the devastated localities. In writing of the characteristic 'attitudes' in which the deceased were found by the rescuers, he wrote that:

> the male dead were generally found under the ruins in an attitude of struggling against the danger; but that the female attitude was usually with hands clasped over their heads, as giving them up to despair, unless they had children near them; in which case arms are in some attitude which indicated their anxious care to protect; a strong instance of the maternal tenderness of the sex.[73]

This perhaps reflected a certain gender stereotyping, but also a new desire to penetrate the deeper recesses of the human psyche – and there was a sense in which this could not yet be easily executed in the social and mental evolution of any northern European country. Although by the latter part of the eighteenth century in the richest European nations there was an intense consciousness of heightened sophistication and materiality, of which the preoccupation with the right 'taste' was one aspect, this novel sophistication also gave rise to a countervailing instinct amongst the intelligentsia to look beneath the human exterior with its growing flummery, and examine the fundamental and inherently *unstable* roots of thoughts and motivations. To do this with any clarity, though, it was necessary to carry out an analysis in a relatively primitive, sensual but still accessible society. Southern Europe – and above all southern Italy – lent itself to such purposes. Here was a drive towards nascent anthropology.

The most striking example of this development was to prove controversial back in Britain. In May 1785 Hamilton travelled to the province of Abruzzo to investigate rumours of a surviving ancient cult of Priapus. This Dionysian worship consisted of votive offerings to combat sterility accompanied by much phallic symbolism. Hamilton wrote it all up and sent his composition to a friend and member of the Dilettanti, Richard Payne Knight. Knight subsequently published an extended version privately as *An Account of the Remains of the Worship of Priapus*, keeping the frankness of Hamilton's description along with the phallic illustrations. What made the book more explosive still, however, was the more general thesis that sexual symbolism lay at the basis of all religions. Knight even suggested an analogy between Priapus and Christ, with the cross as a later transfiguring of the phallus.[74] The scarcely veiled implication was that Catholic clergy over time had consciously incorporated pagan rites into Christian practices as a way of enticing the credulous masses.[75] Only eighty copies of the *Account* were published, but not surprisingly it was widely passed round informed circles. Titillation was very much part of the Dilettanti sensibility.

Knight's book has been seen as proto-Freudian, and indeed it foreshadowed James George Frazer's in many ways more coy *Golden Bough* by more than a century.[76] Probably it is best considered in the context of Enlightenment debates on the nature of Christian belief. Here it had contradictory implications. On the one hand it had the potential to stir anti-Catholicism in Britain, which was still very close to the surface. On the other, however, the cultural and ethical relativism inherent in Hamilton's and Knight's musings suggested a tendency to lump Catholicism in with other branches of faith, as no worse and no better than others; there was propensity in this for draining off deeply embedded prejudices. Shifting attitudes to Catholicism were always to be a feature of Anglo-Mediterranean experience. But so was a raffish experimentalism that had marked the

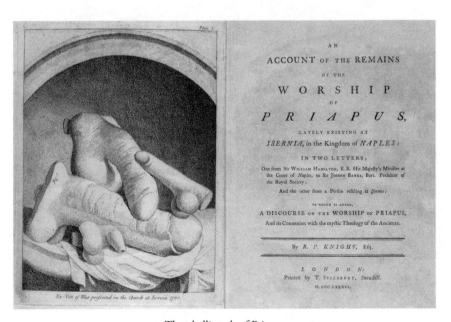

The phallic cult of Priapus
Frontispiece to Richard Payne Knight's book (1786)

Dilettanti mind, and which before long, as political moods changed, was to expose it to blistering attack by conservative commentators.

The web of curiosities epitomized by the freethinking account of Priapus characterized an impulse to venture still further southwards from Naples. The stout Doric temples at Paestum, inland from today's Salerno, provided the next marker. The old Spanish authorities had come close to removing them to the vicinity of Naples but had fortunately desisted; from the 1750s the site attracted growing interest from foreign visitors, even if aesthetic appreciations were mixed.[77] Robert Adam's brother James did get that far south in 1762 but in his opinion what he saw did not merit the considerable exertion of penetrating the Calabrian interior. He called the remains 'inelegant and unenriched',[78] and it was true that their archaic, primitive quality – with massive rough columns thickening towards the base – grated with those whose eyes looked for harmonious Roman

Interior view of a Doric temple at Paestum
James Bruce (1762–3)

smoothness. But responses to ancient forms were becoming more eclectic, and Thomas Major's extensive description with engravings, *The Ruins of Paestum* (1768), granted them an intriguing place in the British imagination. Their very remoteness, and the way that such enormous structures loomed unexpectedly out of the luxuriant Calabrian countryside, started to gel with shifting appreciations. It still remained, however, more than just an aesthetic frontier. Very few foreign women were to visit until into the next century.[79]

More than Paestum, however, Sicily was to become the quintessence of an extreme South in the British imagination and, as an island in a key strategic situation, it was also shortly to acquire significance for British naval purposes. When Patrick Brydone, a Scotsman who had previously travelled widely in Iberia, visited the island in 1770 it was still almost unknown to British visitors. His two volumes *A Tour through Sicily and Malta* (1773) proved very popular; Samuel Johnson's only quibble was that the books did not have enough biblical references, but by then he was an old-fashioned Augustan.[80] It went through nine editions and was soon translated into French and German. Brydone's work inaugurated a particular kind of travel writing, or poetic geography, whose influence was later to be detectible in the vastly more famous fictional work of Lord George Byron. There were soon to be many imitators of the travel genre,[81] anticipating that pile of future Victorian reminiscences, so many of them about the Mediterranean. Yet Sicily retained a certain magic because of its hybridity, a melting pot of influences and cultures spanning Europe and extra-Europe,[82] though it was not until later that its Arab and medieval Norman legacies were to be seen alongside its being – as Goethe put it when there on the most southerly of all his journeys – 'essential Hellas'.[83] For one thing, it saved all the bother of going to that searingly hot, dusty and essentially Ottoman destination of Athens.

Although British explorers of Sicily were impressed by the ancient Hellenic remains of Girgenti (today's Agrigento) and Syracuse, and often dwelt on the jarring juxtaposition of faded glory and contemporary decay, what struck them most was the island's evocation of classical pastoral poetry: effects of light and shade, rippling streams, balmy air, shaded groves. This was a romanticized landscape that shortly acquired its most dramatic and Gothic literary exponent in Ann Radcliffe, the most pioneering English novelist of her generation, hailed at her death in 1823, after years of silence on her part, as 'the great enchantress'.[84] Three of her six novels had Italian backgrounds, though Radcliffe herself never went to Italy, but the most popular of all was *A Sicilian Romance* (1790). 'Through all the sublimest Italian scenery she had ever heard of,' as one writer put it, 'Mrs. Radcliffe caused her villains to chase her heroines.'[85] In that pursuit female virginity was besieged by rampant misogynistic males, whilst on a larger historical plane the transition between feudalism and the present was characterized by gaping fissures that all too easily gobbled up lives and happiness, epitomized by caves, ravines and sheer drops. In Jane Austen's *Northanger Abbey*, the fevered Catherine Morland was said to have read too much Radcliffe.[86] The mixture of beauty, love, enchantment, sadness and horror, unfolding against the backdrop of southern heat, itself by turns relaxing and terrifying, looked forward to the more refined, intellectualized and after 1815 increasingly Mediterraneanized introspection ('Romanticism') of the Shelley generation.

The descriptions of wild nature in Radcliffe's stories were suffused with the lush and melancholic landscapes of the seventeenth-century Italian artist Salvator Rosa. In Britain the practice of landscape depictions was generally regarded as a lower form of art, or what William Blake, who was to avoid it other than as mere background to pastoral engravings, later disdained as a 'vegetable universe' (that is, having little imaginative power).[87] But by the time Radcliffe was writing, British landscape painters were, against all impediments, gradually assuming a distinct 'school', an advance facilitated by the prestige of Roman and Neapolitan backdrops. Two Welshmen played key roles in this development. The most important was Richard Wilson, who first came to Rome in 1751. A biographer states that 'by the mid-1750s Wilson was already doing what future landscape artists were to do habitually: making a highly finished landscape painting devoted to the accurate and emotive depiction of the natural world . . . within a composition consisting of sky, light, trees and water'.[88] This was the basic method of later portrayals in the Romantic spirit, which in capturing local atmospheric conditions anticipated J. M. W. Turner (who greatly admired Wilson) and indeed later still the French Impressionists. It was Rome that opened up for Wilson the possibilities of Welsh landscape, and after his return to Britain in 1757 his *Snowdon from*

Llyn Nantlle and *Holt Bridge on the River Dee* translated the special effects he had developed in Rome and Naples into rather different Welsh climatic conditions. Previously north Wales had been regarded as a remote and forbidding part of the British Isles. It was Wilson's 'sublime' Italianate versions of it that first brought the area within the vista of domestic tourism.[89]

Wilson's fellow Welsh student, Thomas Jones, was in Italy between 1776 and 1783, the last three years of which he spent in Naples, painstakingly discovering the technique of accurately rendering ilex and olive trees on canvas and experimenting with blue pigments from 'the inkiest darks of deep water to the clear blue of soaring skies'.[90] Unlike the affluent Wilson, Jones was often financially hard up and he felt that in Naples he moved 'in a Cloud of Obscurity', relieved only by a young Danish widow he had met in Rome and later married. This was just one of many cases where expatriate life was often anything but idyllic; few led the charmed existence of Sir William Hamilton.[91] There were hazards, always with an extra touch of alarm in a foreign setting. Jones got mugged several times in the streets at night. Vulnerability to infections was a serious danger. When the wife of an English painter, William Pars, died from a disease in Rome in June 1778, Jones later described – melodramatically but evoking a tightly knit, slightly off-kilter community – the night-time funeral in the Protestant Cemetery beyond the walls of the city:

> At the funeral all the English Artists who were then in *Rome* walk'd in procession with torches to the number of 18 or 20 . . . The Scene was grand and striking – The Moon just hid behind the tomb of *Caio Sesto* [Caius Sestius], cast her silvery tints on all the Objects around, save where that large dark Piramid threw its broad shadow over the Place in which the solemn ceremony was performed by the dusky Light of Torches.[92]

After returning to Wales in 1783, Jones found little fame but enjoyed a comfortable rural existence, turning out Italian scenes for a ready market amongst local gentry keen to brighten up their farmhouse parlours. Landscape, more than any other branch of painting, assumed in these decades a distinctive shape through the practice of British artists in Italy like Wilson and Jones, as well as others like the English watercolour artist Francis Towne. They took their insights and aesthetic instincts home with them, where they took deep root (the modern English painter, Eric Ravilious, for example, was to be influenced by Towne's work).[93] By the time that J. M. W. Turner started trudging English waterways with his paintbox in the 1790s, concerned not only with river scenes but also with marine views and distant mountains, the rendering of landscape – so often revealing Mediterranean influences – was starting to challenge the old preoccupation with 'history' as the dominating medium of painting in Britain.

The complex relationship between the emergence of a home-grown British 'School of Art' and Mediterranean experience, however, went beyond the hitherto little-regarded branch of landscape painting. After the Anglo-Scottish Union of 1707, Britain had become not only wealthier but more influential internationally. The victorious outcome of the Seven Years' War in 1763 sealed its place as a military and imperial power. Yet there was a residual sense that Britain still lacked a fine culture to buttress this new rough strength. No less a figure than Samuel Johnson could still conceive of 'art' as a skill, as in the art of boiling sugar, rather than anything more sophisticated (but then Johnson was never very visual).[94] Foreigners sometimes rubbed in such a national stereotype, if only as a way of sneering at England's material prosperity. 'It is well known,' one German art critic unkindly put it, 'that in matters of art the Little Island is of no account . . . Whatever treasures she may possess she covers with the ashes of a cold egotism.'[95]

But if a nation is to have a high art, it must rate artists above mere coach-painters. Often this was not the case in Britain (in fact artists there sometimes *were* originally coach-painters).[96] After all, many would-be artists even much later – Samuel Butler and Roger Fry were examples – faced a hard struggle within their bourgeois families when trying to take up their preferred career. But part of the appeal of the Grand Tour in the eighteenth century was that it provided artists with the possibility of making a contribution to their country's struggle to elevate its position in the finer arts while also enhancing what was hardly yet a respected profession in the domestic social hierarchy. One measure of artists' lowly status was that in Britain they had no means of representing their collective interests. When they managed while abroad to gain membership of such bodies as the Accademia del Disegno in Florence or the Accademia di San Luca in Rome, therefore, it was an object lesson in how to develop collegiality and boost personal standing. Not only artists saw the advantage in doing so, though sceptical observers at home remained hard to impress. For instance, the Scottish architect Robert Mylne, newly returned from Rome in 1759 having won the Concorso Clementino of the Accademia di San Luca, was declared the winner of the competition to design London's new Blackfriars Bridge; he was duly satirized by one critic in an engraving (entitled *Arrived from Italy*) showing him returning to Edinburgh laden with Italian academic honours, implying that a foreign and therefore decidedly dubious prestige was the key to advancement in the new dispensation.[97]

It was out of debates about the need for similar institutions in Britain, including lobbying by the Dilettanti, that the Royal Academy in London emerged in December 1768. Its first president was Sir Joshua Reynolds, subsequently recognized as the founder of an authentic British 'School of Art'. His own experience abroad had been relatively brief. In Rome after Easter 1750 he had soaked himself in the work of the old masters, though he was sceptical about the endless hours that some foreign artists spent copying them on their travels. His somewhat wry perception of the latter activity was exemplified by his parody of Raphael's *The School of Athens*, depicting an almost grotesque assortment of 'milords', tutors, painters and picture dealers, distinguished by exaggerated facial expressions, bandy legs and dogs milling around, all set in Gothic gloom. Athens or indeed Rome this was most certainly not. The message was clear. The British could copy and seek to emulate whomever they liked, even the idealized Greeks of ancient times, but British they were and stolidly British they could only ever be.

Reynolds returned to London in 1752, taking with him a young Roman factotum, Giuseppe Marchi, who stayed with him until Reynolds's death in 1792. Reynolds never went to Italy again, but in his later role at the Royal Academy the Italianate ideal provided the benchmark that he set for the development of art in Britain. Aspiring British artists should, Reynolds said, go to Holland to learn the mechanical necessities 'as they would go to a grammar school to learn languages. They must go to Italy to learn the higher branches of cultural knowledge.'[98] What they did with this knowledge, how they applied it to national circumstances, was another matter. Reynolds's discourses at the Academy, a staple of British art theorizing for decades thereafter, embedded assumptions of Italian superiority (though the superiority Reynolds recognized was that of *dead* Italian artists, certainly not contemporary ones such as the then most famous practitioner, Pompeo Batoni, renowned for his portraits of Grand Tourist gentlemen shown in mock-casual proximity to an antique fragment just for effect, about whom Reynolds was scathing).[99] By comparison, Spanish art – apart from that of Bartolomé Esteban Murillo, whose soft textures and lightness of touch were considered distinct from the harsh realism of most of his country's other notable painters – was very little known, and treated as a decidedly inferior, even deviant, subcategory of Italian.[100] Admittedly, the old Whig prime minister Robert Walpole once had two canvases by Diego Velázquez displayed at his Norfolk country home at Houghton Hall, and from its inception Britain's first public art gallery at Dulwich possessed several paintings by Murillo, but generally Spanish art was only bought by the occasional British collector in the eighteenth century as a slightly eccentric addition to the mainstream.[101] This was to change only very slowly and partially, whereas Reynolds's Italianate prescriptions for an emergent art establishment in Great Britain broadly held even through to the early 1900s.

This did not stop tension within the Royal Academy arising from the start between those who could claim the imprimatur of Italian experience and connections and those who could not. There remained a nativist impulse that jibbed at perceived alien presences flowing in to sit alongside old master principles. Two individuals, connected through their life histories, are interesting here because they raised art-related issues of Mediterranean-derived foreignness and its link to gender. The first is Angelica Kauffmann, Swiss-born but as a painter 'made in Italy'. From 1759 she mixed closely with British Grand Tourists and artists in Florence, Rome and Naples. It was in the latter in 1763–4 that she painted the actor David Garrick and made the contacts that assisted her move to London two years later. But for outsiders London was an easy place to make enemies. Her friendship with Reynolds – 'his Angelica', the sneer went – led to allegations of a love affair. For this, other than that they painted each other's portraits, there is little evidence, any more than there is for the claim by the pockmarked French revolutionary Jean-Paul Marat to have slept with her in London.[102] A deeply attractive woman, she lived her life under a cloud of sexuality.[103]

A good deal of this was jealousy at her success. She was a founding member of the Royal Academy and although her ambitious 'history' paintings garnered mixed reviews, she became very fashionable as a portraitist and above all for her work in interior decorative art. Gracefulness – with 'delicate female figures in light, finely draped fabrics'[104] – was the essence of her style, which is why it worked so well in association with 'Adam' settings. In England and in Dublin many villa walls, ceilings, porcelains and furniture had designs composed either directly by her or by others copying her work.[105] But one biographer remarks that Kauffmann 'always dreamed of Rome',[106] and after marrying Antonio Zucchi, chief designer in Robert Adam's decorative workshop, they both returned to Italy in 1781. Some admirers in London penned poems in regret at Kauffmann's departure.[107] She spent the rest of her life in Rome, a pillar of the old cosmopolitan art community, where she played a key role in cementing the dominance of neoclassicism in a city where the old Baroque had always obstinately persisted.[108] After the occupation by French troops in 1798 she was said to have suffered from her British connections; certainly she had continued to supply British clients with her work, and to send paintings back to the Royal Academy for display in the annual exhibition. When she died in 1807 a letter was read at the Academy describing her funeral, arranged by the sculptor Antonio Canova and attended by all the foreign academies in Rome. Goethe – someone else rather obsessed with her during his time in Rome – was not alone in finding her work charming and tasteful, but lacking in the finest ability to draw.[109] But in matters of style, and as the first really successful female painter in the country,[110] Kauffmann made an impact on British cultural life.

A second female career that is relevant here – and one that parallels Angelica Kauffmann's in several respects – is that of Maria Cosway. She was the daughter of an English couple, the Hadfields, who ran an inn in Florence frequented by many foreign visitors, including the historian Edward Gibbon. Made much of by British artists passing through, the young Maria abandoned her musical interests and took up the paintbrush, laboriously copying in the Uffizi Gallery and later moving to Rome to exploit the opportunities there. It was her mother's ambition that she become 'another

Angelica' that took them to London in 1779 (though Maria never lost her Anglo-Italian accent). Married shortly thereafter in St George's, Hanover Square to the miniaturist Richard Cosway, with Angelica Kauffmann present, Maria was a highly successful painter in the 1780s as well as a celebrated salon hostess at Schomberg House in Pall Mall.

Always strongly religious, Maria Cosway's themes were mythological, literary and biblical. But her religiosity did not prevent frequent insinuations of sexual liaisons, including involvement with the libidinous Prince of Wales; one person who really did fall in love with her on a visit to Paris was the American ambassador and future President of the United States Thomas Jefferson.[111] As an artist, Cosway's portrait of Georgiana, Duchess of Devonshire was found by a critic in the *Morning Chronicle* to be worthy of Reynolds himself,[112] but other Royal Academicians denigrated her work, most notably the Swiss-born Henry Fuseli, who allegedly got upset even at the mention of somebody closely associated with the phenomenon of the female artist.[113] But then Fuseli never lost the traces of a brilliant but misogynized eroticism, an aspect of what an admirer terms his 'passionate apprehension of life' acquired during his own years in Rome.[114] Maria eventually found London too unsettling – her themes began to feature grieving, prostrate women – and in 1790 she left for the Continent, returning eventually to Italy. Although she revisited London at intervals while her husband was living to see to his care, she spent many years presiding over and funding a convent school for girls in Lombardy, where she died in 1838. But her earlier work had significantly affected the style of late eighteenth-century England, a considerable achievement for an Anglo-Italian innkeeper's daughter.[115]

One key to the unsettlement of both Angelica Kauffmann and Maria Cosway in London was their Catholicism (an uneasiness only underlined by the anti-papist Gordon Riots in 1780). During her time in Rome Cosway had mixed in circles close to the Young Stuart Pretender, and in 1790 his widow, Princess Louise of Stolberg-Gedern,[116] became godmother to Cosway's son. By then, however, the palmy days of the exiled Stuart network in Rome had passed. For many years, since Protestant Britain did not have an embassy in the Papal States, making use of Stuart connections had been necessary for any Scot or Englishman who wanted access to galleries or salons. Until the debacle of the Jacobite Rebellion of 1745 this remained sensitive, since the Stuart court in Rome was held to be a threat to the Hanoverian regime itself.[117] Such suspicions, however, ebbed in the following decades. Boswell found the Jacobites in Rome in the 1760s mild and accommodating.[118] Abbé Grant, the most prominent Scottish Catholic in Rome over many years, devoted so much of his time to promoting the interests of British Grand Tourists regardless of religious denomination that he was known as *l'Introduttore*.[119] Grant was especially intimate with Pope Clement XIV and was one influence making the latter friendly to British visitors in particular, reflected in such changes as the scrapping of the rule that Protestants genuflect before papal eminences. The second youngest son of George III, Prince Augustus, lived in Rome between 1791 and 1796, a significant marker in relations between the reigning British dynasty and the Papacy. In 1800, with the Union of the Kingdoms of Great Britain and Ireland, the Court of St James and the Holy See exchanged informal envoys for the first time since 1534.

The wider significance here was that as British Mediterranean experience deepened, appreciations of the Roman faith and Catholic societies became more complex and nuanced. Such a tendency ran parallel with gradual changes in Britain itself, where after 1778 it was legal to hold Catholic services in public chapels, though they were usually only to be found in quite remote rural districts.[120] When Tobias Smollett was living in Leghorn – he died and was buried there in 1771 – the mere sight of a Catholic procession could still raise his blood pressure.[121] Yet only a couple of years later, when observing simple Sicilians at their devotions, their awe and sense of the divine struck Patrick Brydone as wholly sincere and unforced.[122] Indeed, although the so-called Age of Enlightenment has sometimes been interpreted as ushering in a process of dechristianization throughout Europe, this has to be highly qualified; if anything, aggressive secularism caused a pietistic reaction in parts of southern Europe especially.[123]

Yet relics and relic worship seem to have had a diminishing capacity to arouse Protestant disgust. British non-Catholics, when encountering the old rituals abroad, could feel what was for them a rather novel if also uneasy tug towards, rather than away from, the religious sensuality and physical appeal of Catholic ceremonial.[124] This was particularly so amidst the majesty of the Papal Basilica of St Peter in the Vatican, so that even the atheistic Shelleys when attending a service there in 1819 experienced a queasy fascination with the event.[125] In this there was a suggestion of a modern sensibility that came later: the Catholic rite, especially with its rich Italian trappings, could embody a salving power *qua* rite, wholly independent of the need to believe in any specific doctrine or alleged facts in the Bible. John Pemble writes on the resulting paradox: 'In the age of modernity it was not necessary to be Catholic or even Christian in order to feel this powerful force of attraction. The allure of Rome was now greater among many Protestants and agnostics than it had been among devout Catholics in the pre-Reformation days of papal hedonism and clerical abuse.'[126]

Yet, because religious difference was the most instinctive tingling apprehension that British Protestants felt almost as soon as they crossed the English Channel, such shifts sometimes remained glacial and irregular, and were prone to reversal once the evangelical spirit of the early Victorian era took hold. A distinction also has to be made between Italian and Spanish Catholicism. Whatever may have been the case with the former, the latter lost nothing of its reputation for extreme piety, devotion and allegedly idolatrous imagery,[127] all grist to the mill of English Protestant horror. This was but one, if especially powerful, facet of the persisting 'Black Legend' of Spain (though the term itself was only coined in 1914), characterized by the Inquisition, the burnings of the old *auto-da-fé* and a militant dislike of foreigners.[128] 'Don't let your imagination loose upon Spain – it is a hideous parched-up country,' William Beckford, the author of the bestselling oriental tale *Vathek*, once advised Lady Craven, putting in a good word instead on behalf of Portugal.[129] Beckford was one of the relatively few Grand Tourists who nonetheless included Spain on their itinerary in the eighteenth century, leaving luscious descriptions of the strangely illusory experience of wandering through royal palaces in Madrid and Aranjuez: 'cages of gilded wire, and in every case a curious exotic bird in full song'.[130] Beckford's wealth could get him access to most places, but the great majority of British visitors to Spain found very limited access to anything, and did not much enjoy themselves. The cloistered life of the grand Spanish nobility epitomized a general social impenetrability lasting well into the nineteenth century (one reason why it was an unpopular posting for British diplomats).[131] The persistence of an ingrained Hispanophobia was reflected in Matthew Lewis's sensational novel of murder, rape, incest and generally unbridled passions in a Madrid convent, *The Monk* (1796).

There was one city on the classic Grand Tour route – usually fitted in on the return leg – where religion did not enter significantly into British responses: Venice. The Veneto was the least papal part of Italy, its religious institutions often alleged by foreigners to have a suspect discipline, such that Edith Wharton in her much later historical novel *The Valley of Decision* could tartly observe that 'it was a common thing for the noble libertine returned from Italy to boast of his intrigue with a Venetian nun'.[132] Certainly an ingrained secularism fitted with a different resonance whereby Venice offered to English minds a model of constitutional government and mercantile expansion. After the Glorious Revolution of 1688 this Veneto-tropism (or the drawing of analogies between the destinies of England and the Serene Republic) became commonplace. The parallel merged into broader spheres. Palladian architecture became, as we saw, the particular hallmark of a Whig, anti-Hanoverian gentry. Thomas Otway's 1682 polit-ical drama *Venice Preserv'd*, featuring prostitution, treachery, conspiracy and death on the gallows, became the most popular stage play in the highly theatrical age of Georgian London, partly because it was easy for audiences to read English references into the plot.[133] It was still drawing in the crowds at the end of the century, when the theme of regime change gave it a fresh relevance.

For British visitors Venice could not sustain an agenda of cultural or intellectual engagement on a par with Rome or Naples. It lacked an intel-ligentsia along the lines of these cities (or indeed of Milan). There were no galleries with classical statues, no famous *Apollo Belvedere* or *Laocoön* sculp-tures to linger before with carefully arranged expressions of adoration. Nor were there any ruins as such, though that was a relief to many people, who had seen quite enough farther south. Venetian painting commanded some attention. Reynolds spent several months there in the summer of 1752 on his way home, admiring the works of great Venetian colourists such as Titian, Tintoretto and Veronese. Still, it was in the nineteenth century that the classic achievements of Venetian painters were to dominate so much of British art criticism. In the eighteenth century it was Venice as a *social* phenomenon, including masquerades and the Carnival in February, that offered the most intriguing dimension.

Social in this context included having one's portrait painted, ideally by the pastellist Rosalba Carriera. To have a likeness done by her, or to purchase one of her signature productions of womanhood with winsome, genteel eroticism and typical rococo qualities – the '"gracefulness" of the image, the "lightness" of touch and the brilliant gem-like quality of the colour'[134] – became a highly competitive matter amongst young expatriate gentlemen, especially the British. The latter were so pressing that Carriera said she was '*attaqué par des Angles*', and even worked by a kind of mail order to keep them at bay.[135] The Rosalba Carriera style, more risqué than the sort of formal Augustan portraits done at home, presented exactly the type of assured image of itself that a new British aristocracy hankered after. There were also rumours that Carriera, always in need of money to keep her own large family going, could act as 'go-between' in making a reality of that heightened sexual consciousness with which Venice, like Naples, was conventionally associated by Grand Tourists.[136] Certainly go-betweens were needed because Venetian society was renowned for being inaccessible to outsiders.[137] As for the Venetian Carnival, it was practically a metaphor for a wild, almost abandoned, existence, but the reality was very different, its little rituals conducted in a grave, oblique spirit.[138] In truth, Venice was

An Italian carnival
Etching by Paul Sandby (*c.* 1781)

often found by outsiders to be an alien, unknowable city,[139] inscrutable behind its noble polish and Carnival masks.

The Venetian imagery that more than any other lodged in the British cultural canon, however, arose from the canalscapes of Giovanni Antonio Canal, better known as Canaletto. Their popularity in Britain was a reflection of the ordered vitality and sheer materialism which was the principal self-idealization of the Georgian age in Britain. Canaletto's leading patron was the foremost English collector in Venice, Joseph Smith, who had arrived in the city in 1700 and first started commissioning works by the great Venetian 'view-painter' from the 1720s. In 1744 Smith became British consul, adding to his local prestige. In the Palazzo Balbi on the Grand Canal, which he had renovated in elegant Palladian style, Smith kept rooms bulging with Canaletto's drawings and paintings in gleaming frames to reflect the sparkle of lamplight at night; from them visiting Grand Tourists could select the sort of thing they wanted for themselves, and put in an order accordingly. But Smith did not only collect the views of Canaletto. Amongst his favourite possessions was *Winter*, one of Rosalba Carriera's most alluring depictions of young Venetian noblewomen, fur-wrapped, red-lipped and full of fuchsia skin tones. This collection, combined with the display of Smith's equally precious books – he set up a press of his own to produce richly illustrated works – caused the Venetian playwright and librettist Carlo Goldoni, who wrote a play about Smith, to call the Palazzo Balbi 'the most perfect union of all the sciences and arts'.[140] It was, in essence, a Venetian counterpart to Sir William Hamilton's treasure house of arts and antiquities in Naples, and finally enriched British culture itself, since so much of its contents also ended up in the United Kingdom.[141]

It was through Smith's encouragement and patronage that Canaletto came to spend extended periods in London between 1746 and 1756 (the War of the Austrian Succession in the 1740s had disrupted the Grand Tour, and made it difficult to transport paintings and other acquisitions in Italian cities to Britain). Canaletto's productions while there spawned a vision of London as a kind of Venice-upon-Thames, with the new Westminster Bridge as its Rialto, leading conveniently to Vauxhall Gardens, a distinctively bawdy, less enigmatic variety of English masquerade. It has been argued that Canaletto's London as *Venice redivivus* was stranded between Englishness and Italianness, reality and fantasy,[142] just as Joseph

Smith was held responsible by some for debasing Canaletto's style, fore-shadowing the commodification of Venice that later became so widely deplored.[143] When he went back to Venice, Canaletto's originality certainly seemed to desert his work.[144] But over and above any such criticism is the telling observation by one art historian that Smith and Canaletto were a well-matched pair: an Italianate Englishman and a Venetian shaped by English taste.[145] As such, their interaction, however idiosyncratic and inde-finable, mirrors perfectly the subject of this book.

In some of these traditional roles, however, Venice progressively lost its old symbolic uses for Britain as the eighteenth century drew on. After the dazzling gains that Britain made at the Peace of Paris following the Seven Years' War, the parallel that attracted British minds was increasingly with the ancient territorial empire of Rome, not the narrowly mercantile imperium of Venice. The not-so-Serene Republic's slide into oligarchic corruption and political feebleness against the background of the French Revolutionary Wars that broke out in 1792 was exactly what the English and Scots wanted to avoid for themselves. Nothing epitomized this more than the ignominy of Venice's fall into the hands of Napoleon Bonaparte's troops, fresh from their victories in Lombardy, on 14 May 1797. Bonaparte displayed towards Venice an animosity beyond any other military occupation in his entire career, partly as an assertion of his accumulating personal power, but also because its Grand Tour associations clashed with everything he stood for. The twenty Venetian master paintings, five hundred precious manuscripts and the four bronze Roman horsemen ripped from the roof of St Mark's were a harbinger of much treasure-looting to come elsewhere.[146] Old master paintings and other artistic riches previously funnelled through an interna-tional market often dominated by British agents were now to be carted off to Paris by the French Army. Yet at least they were then safe from the 'improvements' to which British purchasers had often resorted as a way of inflating the artworks' commercial value.[147]

The occupation of Venice, in fact, was what made the British public first aware of just who Napoleon Bonaparte was. He had been largely unknown before the northern Italian campaign of 1796–7 in which he led the French armies; the strategic implications of the whole war from now on included a slant towards the Mediterranean. Afterwards, one writer states, Venice became just 'another sort of ruin to visit' for British travellers, the liquidation of its political independence 'a necessary precondition of the wistful Veneto-philia of Byron, Ruskin and other nineteenth-century observers'.[148] The ending of Venetian statehood opened the way to that later concentration on the city's stricken beauty so resonant amongst British Victorians and their cosmopolitan American cousins.[149]

Napoleon's seizure of Venice intensified the process of the latter's loss of cultural prestige in relation to other Italian cities which had already begun; the most distinguished Venetian artist of the day, Antonio Canova, left for Rome at this time.[150] But it also heralded the collapse of the social and political foundations of the faltering Grand Tour. In June 1797 Napoleon declared a Cisalpine Republic – the first of so many confected entities with classical name tags – and on 10 February 1798 French troops entered Rome. British artists started to flee the occupied papal city. One who decided to stay was Gavin Hamilton, who along with Thomas Jenkins was one of the two dominant British art dealers in Rome at the height of the Grand Tour. Hamilton died, however, only four months after the imposition of French control, his death put down to grief at the changing world around him;[151] and indeed when Thomas Jenkins fled shortly after, he suffered a fatal heart attack within hours of arrival on the English coast, again attributed by some to the sheer stress of the times.[152] Soon very few Britons were left in Rome. A similar exodus had occurred in Naples. During December 1798 Sir William Hamilton, Emma (whom he had married some years before) and the Bourbon royal family escaped on one of Admiral Nelson's warships to Palermo;[153] in a terrible storm the son of Queen Maria Caroline died in Emma's arms. Naples became, for a short while, the Parthenopean Republic, another Napoleonic entity conjured up in purely titular terms out of ancient literature. A bewildering disorder was seeping into virtually every sphere, in which discontinuities in private and public life all too easily converged. It was in Palermo that any attempt by Emma and Nelson to conceal their affair was abandoned.

The subsequent – albeit temporary – return to Naples of the Bourbon royals under British naval protection, and the fierce counter-revolution in which Emma in particular acted as a conduit for absolutist revenge against French-leaning rebels (being responsible for rejecting their pleas for clemency before execution), is too well known to need repeating here. It is said that Emma's pitiless behaviour reflected that of the Neapolitan queen to whom she was so attached, and who was the sister of the guillotined Marie Antoinette. But her behaviour also mirrored that of her husband, only intensified by virtue of her own headstrong character. Sir William's hatred for the Neapolitan revolutionaries was intense. This was not just because they had become the enemies of his native country. More profoundly it was because to him – as to Goethe, now back in Germany – the Revolution was alien to the cultured and aristocratically enlightened world around which his life had revolved. Even amidst all the tensions of the Bourbon collapse Sir William's thoughts were bound up with the fate of his collection,[154] and especially with the new set of precious vases he had acquired since he had given his first benefaction to the British Museum twenty years before. The vases themselves embodied a universe of cultured and pure sensibility. Before escaping to Palermo, he had carefully packed and shipped them off to Britain on HMS *Colossus* (British warships, too, were acquiring more classical names than ever). The ship's foundering off the Scilly Isles was one of the greatest setbacks in Sir William's life – bigger than Emma's desertion to Nelson, to which he accommodated himself really quite easily.[155] He was now an old man, and physical – rather than aesthetic – passion had never been a dominant characteristic.

Fortunately, some of the vases submerged with the *Colossus* proved retrievable and were soon safely in the British Museum, where Sir William went to see them after arriving back in London together with Nelson and Emma in November 1800.[156] As he peered through the glass cases, what a world of Neapolitan experience with all its desiring and collecting and appreciating in the spirit of the age must have passed across his tired mind! In his refinement, free thinking and mission to spread a more cultured taste across a wider face of society, Sir William, who died in April 1803, was the quintessence of the British Enlightenment with all its quirks of acquisitiveness and political conservatism.[157] It was appropriate that this cosmopolitan and essentially humanist mindset had been defined under Mediterranean conditions.

The Britain to which Sir William had returned, however, was also deeply affected by the current turmoil. As the war with Revolutionary France unfolded, a powerful political dialectic got under way. On the one hand there was a radical attack on the aristocracy. Yet on the other there was an intensely conservative reaction. Anything that smacked of experimentalism, of being outside the accepted frame of things secular or religious, became subject to violent abuse. An angry John Bull peered out from a thousand prints. One group that found itself under attack was the Dilettanti.[158] Sir William Hamilton was one of those made fun of in the *Anti-Jacobin* journal. The satirist James Gillray was soon to produce a famous cartoon, *Dido, in Despair!*, portraying a blowsy Emma and poking fun at her antique-loving husband's complaisance in her affair with Nelson.[159] The old controversy over Priapus with its phallic allusiveness got dredged up, one writer foaming at the mouth against the 'obscene revellings of Greek scholars and their private studies', with 'all the ordure and filth, all the antique pictures and . . . generative organs in their most odious and degrading protrusion'.[160] Here was an intensified nativism triggered by acute uncertainty, a rejection of anything foreign and a reassertion of introverted Britishness.

But there was also the glimmering of something that had important implications for the future. Radicalism and loyalism were bitterly opposed in the Britain of the 1790s. But neither was static. There were already the outlines of an updated conservatism that did not simply rely on a restatement of Edmund Burke's belief in continuity with feudalism, but which held out a vision of a more flexible commercial society and elite. That elite was still to be bound together by the privileges of birth and wealth, though the balance between those two things was shifting rapidly. But underpinning such a strategy and seeking to give it moral legitimacy was a heightened awareness of shared 'civilization', a refinement of taste writ large.[161]

One indication of this, it has been argued, lay in the displays of the old master paintings that had flooded into London in recent times as distressed nobility, both in France and Italy, sold off their assets. Successive portions of the collection of the Duke of Orléans – who as the self-styled Philippe Égalité was guillotined in Paris in November 1793 – came to London and were seen by thousands in private exhibitions for the entrance fee of one shilling. The main lot, including masterpieces from the Italian Renaissance, was bought by a consortium of aristocrats and put on display at the Lyceum in the Strand in 1798. The special ticket price of two shillings and sixpence did not deter viewers drawn from a considerably wider social sphere than in the past; and these viewers were sometimes conscious of a step change in the nature of their responses to what they saw. 'A mist passed away from my sight; the scales fell off', as the future critic and radical William Hazlitt, used to hiking the countryside to see minor works in isolated mansions, recalled of the paintings by Titian, Raphael and Domenichino on display there. '[A] new sense came upon me, a new Heaven and a new Earth.'[162] This was art indeed.

Such a new artistic and civilizational sensitivity, an awareness of culture as a sacralized activity worthy of being worshipped in its own right,[163] in what yet remained a rough, tough and instinctively insular society, came from many directions but not least from the medley of taste makers, Grand Tourists, authors of new travelogues and novels, painters, picture dealers and sometimes fabricators (motives always being mixed) emerging from Britain's accelerating exposure, direct and indirect, to the Mediterranean. Meanwhile a bitter war was being fought with intensifying restrictions on the ability to travel freely through the Continent, restrictions that were especially hard to evade in its northern parts. More than ever at the close of the eighteenth century, when the British wished to deepen their understanding of civilization's roots and its contemporary meanings, they turned above all to the south of Europe, ancient and modern. The Mediterranean was to remain a testing ground for how the British responded to modern changes and assessed their place in a world now transformed by Napoleon's seemingly unstoppable conquests.

Chapter Three

THE DISTORTED MIRROR

THE SOUTH IN BRITISH CULTURE DURING THE AGE OF BYRON,
1800–30

He is deeply discontented . . . in the distorted mirror of his own
thoughts.

Shelley on Byron in Venice, 1817

*T*he fusing of culture and war – or what has been called 'the culture
of power'[1] – was one of the many striking aspects of Napoleon
Bonaparte's genius with its latent imperial ethic. To Venetian treasures stripped in 1797 was soon added the booty from Rome, including
from the despoiled Vatican collections. The sculptural glories of Graeco-
Roman civilization, the *Laocoön and His Sons* and the *Apollo Belvedere*,
once so entrancing to Johann Winckelmann, were taken to Paris and
paraded through the streets before being installed in the Musée du Louvre
as a sign of popular sovereignty. Before long followed artefacts from
Napoleon's invasion of Egypt after July 1798 – he had taken with him a
swarm of artists, archaeologists and other savants.[2] What was renamed the
Musée Napoléon formed the prototype of a universal museum testifying to
man's highest endeavours, and also marking a new stage in the world-
historical process of transferring the moral and artistic leadership of the
world from Periclean Greece[3] to Rome and now to Revolutionary France.
Here, too, was a new religion of art to replace the Christian ecclesiocracy
Napoleon was bent on destroying.

This released an electric current as powerful in Britain as in France. As a chronicler of national taste once remarked, since 1660 the British had looked to the French for guidance on such matters.[4] (Significantly, during the Napoleonic conflict there was no visceral contempt of France of the sort that was to be levelled against Germany in Britain during the world wars of the twentieth century.) With peace made by the Treaty of Amiens in March 1802, many rushed across the Channel to see masterpieces which previously would have involved all the time and expense of going to Italy. This was a godsend for penurious young British artists. The Musée du Louvre put any private exhibition in London in the shade, even the Orléans collection in the Strand that had so mesmerized the young William Hazlitt. He now spent four months in Paris, laboriously copying his favourites, with Titian's *Man with a Glove* standing out above all else. For Hazlitt, destined to be the greatest critic of his generation in Britain, the experience was a formative one.[5] He was one Englishman (though his family was of Ulster origin) always to remain faithful to French Revolutionary ideals, and never more so than after 1815 when the emperor was bathed in the glory of defeat.

'We live in giant and exaggerated times, which make all under Gog and Magog seem pigmean,' Lord George Byron declared, and an exaggeration of personal visions, aspirations and desires was a thread running through many of the individuals concerned here.[6] In that sense Napoleon was the true portent of the age on both sides of the Channel.[7] This volatility carried a tendency to political invective, physical restlessness and sexual angst; one writer stresses the hedonism of the circles in which Byron moved once *Childe Harold* established his fame.[8] Mediterranean experience provided a template for such brittle psychologies, just as it had for the Enlightenment generation of Sir William Hamilton. But as always, ideologically and in other ways the resulting patterns pointed in multiple directions.

The restrictions on Continental travel for British citizens (though not for Americans) as Napoleon's grip extended across Continental Europe threatened to limit the outlets for such pressures. There were different ways of responding. One was to turn inwards into Britain itself. There was a sense of discovering one's own island for the first time, embodied not least in the riverways that so attracted the youthful J. M. W. Turner. 'We have been strangely neglectful in celebrating our own SEVERN, THAMES or MALVERN,' one critic commented, 'and have therefore fallen into trite repetitions of classical images.'[9] William Wordsworth's highlighting of the poetic possibilities of 'low and rustic life' in his *Lyrical Ballads*, shaped by Lake District existence, carried with it an explicit condemnation of those who looked beyond native shores for inspiration. The sardonic dismissal by Byron, amongst others, of the narrowness of the school of poetry of 'the Lakers' arose from this difference. Wordsworth's praises of Cumbria constituted an instinctive turning away from the soft murmurings of Italian-inspired verse characteristic of certain branches of eighteenth-century English literature.[10] Instead they pointed Northwards to a harder-edged, more primitive imaginary life, which the English and the Celts shared with other northern peoples in Scandinavia. We shall return to this recurring counterbalancing to the lure of the warm South in the pages that follow.

A contrary way round Continental closures to British travelling, however, was by an enhanced bias *towards* the Mediterranean, circuitously approached through northern routes such as the German states or even Russia, or by sea via Gibraltar. Although it always remained true that going to Greece called for a mental as much as a physical leap over and beyond any visit to Italy, more Britons did so from the late 1790s onwards. John Tweddell was a classical scholar and barrister whose early enthusiasm for the French Revolution led him into a close association with such prominent radicals as John Horne Tooke. Allegedly it was disappointed love for the famously beautiful Isabel Gunning that led him into extensive European travels, for which Greece became the focus. Arriving in Athens during December 1798, with the help of a French artist Tweddell set about copying 'every temple, and every archway . . . every stone and every inscription . . . with the utmost fidelity' (it was an index of their own uncertainty about themselves that British artists often sought the help of other, in their eyes more artistically accomplished, Europeans when abroad).[11] At the same time Tweddell recorded in detail the '*ceremonies*, and *usages*, and *dresses* of the people'. This matching of the past with the present marked a shift that was to become more and more important. Tweddell died of fever in Athens in July 1799, and was to be lauded at home as a genius cut off in his prime. Indeed Byron a few years later marked his grave with a block of marble from the Parthenon.

In the immediate wake of Tweddell came Edward Clarke. After an extended Grand Tour in Europe through much of the 1790s, Clarke had been in Alexandria following the Battle of the Nile helping to secure for Britain sarcophagi, maps and manuscripts that had originally been seized by Napoleon's *savants*. Arriving in Athens in October 1800, Clarke toured adjacent provinces. His main 'discoveries' were at Eleusis, including a large ancient female figure he levered out of place with an improvised machine and transported to the seashore, where it was put on a British ship and subsequently donated to the Fitzwilliam Museum in Cambridge. The increasing density of British shipping across the Mediterranean as commerce found a vent outside Napoleon's stifling 'Continental System' was an essential backdrop to acquisitions of this sort. The career of Edward Dodwell provided a marker for such an expanding ambition. Initially an architect by profession, Dodwell was another for whom a conventional Grand Tour morphed into a more extended phenomenon. He set out from Venice with his friend William Gell in late April 1801 with the aim of making a special exploration of Greece. Leaving Gell in Corfu, Dodwell visited Ithaca and Patras, passing through the Greek archipelago to Constantinople. More important was his second visit in 1805–6, accompanied by the Italian Simone Pomardi, exploring western Greece, on to the Attic mountains and down into the Peloponnese. Dodwell and Pomardi made over 1,000 drawings of antiquities and landscapes, some later published in *A Classical and Topographical Tour through Greece* (1819); a genre of ancient Corinthian vase painting was later named after the Englishman ('the Dodwell Painter'). In September 1806 Dodwell got back to Rome, and spent the rest of his life there and in Naples, marrying a much younger aristocratic woman and devout Catholic whose remarkable beauty was legendary. To the Countess of Blessington, confidante of Lord Byron, Teresa Dodwell was 'one of the most faultless models of loveliness ever beheld'.[12] She survived her husband sufficiently long to be responsible for organizing the escape of the besieged pope from Gaeta amidst the revolutions of 1848.[13]

In the British penetration into the eastern Mediterranean after 1800 diplomacy and various forms of exploration interacted. Once Napoleon took control of Corfu from a Russo-Turkish occupation of that island as a springboard for further French expansion, the British tentatively began to experiment with a counter-stake of their own in western Greece. This meant establishing a relationship with Ali Pasha, the warlord with a local empire based in Yannina in north-western Greece. From this flowed the sinuous part played by the British government in the fate of the Orthodox Christian community of the Souliotes in Epirus, who resisted their Ottoman ruler; the climax came in December 1803 when, at Ali Pasha's bloody hands, a group of their womenfolk threw themselves off a cliff to escape an even worse fate. This was subsequently plaintively captured in paintings of the women's Dance of Zalongo, incorporated into the recurring imagery of liberal Romantic sentiment in Europe.[14]

It was in this period that Dodwell's companion William Gell – who in 1801 had already been one of the first to claim to fix the site of Troy by inspection on the ground, and who later published *The Topography of Troy* (1804) – was sent by the British government on a mission to the western Greek lands, travelling widely in the Morea. In future years Gell would become a prominent figure in British circles around the Mediterranean. William Martin Leake, who as a colonel with the British Military Mission to the Ottoman Empire had travelled widely in the eastern Mediterranean, was dispatched by London to central Greece in 1804, becoming one of the few Britons thus far to visit the monastic haven of Mount Athos and, drifting further eastwards, the island of Cyprus.[15] Leake published about these travels extensively, and later became a founder member of both the Travellers' Club (1819) and the Athenaeum (1824); the emergence of London's 'clubland' was to have a strong Mediterranean imprint. Gell and Leake, with their wide classical learning, constituted the high point of a literary topographical tradition in Britain, the aim of which was, as Gell expressed it, that 'a student reading the account of any [ancient] battle may be certain that here stood such a height & there ran such a brook'.[16] By the time of Gell's death at Naples in 1836, such laborious literary exactitude was to seem old-fashioned, and Gell himself the relic of an exhausted generation in Anglo-Mediterranean affairs. But it provided a link between an older world of Enlightenment learning and a more professional, academic milieu that was to become dominant in the nineteenth century – but which had its own, really more dangerous, pitfalls of mind-numbing pettifoggery.

In the tradition set by Stuart and Revett's *Antiquities of Athens*, architecture remained as central as ever to a vision of Greece in Britain. Robert Smirke studied at the Royal Academy Schools, and, after visiting Sicily on a Grand Tour commencing in 1802, he spent 1803–4 in Athens dedicated to a close examination of classical remains. According to Joseph Farington, a diarist of British cultural life, no young architect was better prepared than Smirke when he got back to London in 1805. His mainly Greek Revival designs over the next years won many customers, helped by his Royal Academy and Tory Party backers. His first big success was the rebuilding of the Theatre Royal in Covent Garden. This broke bounds in its pure Doric style, which years before in its manifestation at Paestum had evoked widespread distaste, but was now felt to have 'Grandeur of effect'. The theatre opened on 18 September 1809. In 1823 Smirke went on to design, in the spirit of a 'Greek Temple of the Arts', what is today the core and main façade of the British Museum, though it was not to be completed for thirty years. Raised to a knighthood, he never departed from the view that Grecian models offered the best testimony to the fabric of Britain's national stature, and although by the 1840s the repetitiveness with which

Temple of Concordia, Girgenti (Agrigento), Sicily
Robert Smirke (1802–4)

this was executed had begun to pall, the imprint left on the country's public culture and self-image proved lasting.[17]

'Grecian' architectural taste was also the stimulus for the British apotheosis of what in retrospect we call neoclassicism: the relocation to Britain of Athenian marbles or ancient fragments by the Scottish aristocrat Lord Elgin, as an exemplar of the nation's cultural evolution. In 1799 Elgin had been appointed minister plenipotentiary to the Ottoman Empire. His mission was to win the Sublime Porte over to Britain's side in the escalating regional rivalry with France. Admiral Nelson had just destroyed the French fleet at the Battle of the Nile, but Napoleon's invasion force remained ensconced in Egypt. Having built a new 'Grecian' country house, Broomhall, on the shore of the Firth of Forth, Elgin's plan was to match his diplomatic activities at Constantinople with a plan to 'improve the arts in Great Britain' by forging a special national connection with the classical legacy of Athens. This involved making yet more drawings of ancient buildings, but also obtaining small-scale plaster casts of architectural and sculptural features which at that time artistic and professional education in Britain lacked in sufficient quantity to design from. What Elgin did not initially envisage, however, was dismantling chunks of ancient Athens and shipping them home.

Lord Elgin, en route to his diplomatic posting, went to Palermo and recruited for his purposes Giovanni Battista Lusieri, a painter and former protégé of Sir William Hamilton in Naples, who had also gone to Sicily with the Bourbon court. The team of designers Lusieri assembled, mostly from Rome, arrived in Athens in September 1800. The situation there was not easy. Louis Fauvel, the French consul and archaeologist, was very popular locally and not easily pushed aside. Elgin had to seek a firman from Constantinople to allow the drawing of various ruins to commence. Meanwhile bribery greased the way. Consequently, the work commenced spasmodically. It reflected the extremity of the times that, quite soon, an alternative plan presented itself to Elgin's mind and that of his local agents, headed by his chaplain Philip Hunt: to lower the most desirable fragments to the ground and take them away wholesale. On 31 July 1801 a ship's carpenter and seventy-five crew, using a windlass and cordage, detached the best of the surviving metopes (the decorated bands running across the top of an ancient frieze) from the Parthenon and transported them by gun carriage to the port of Piraeus.[18] There they awaited a British warship for transportation. How far such removals might actually be taken hung in the balance, not least depending on Elgin's leverage in the Turkish capital.

Having excised material from the main temple on the Acropolis, the temptation was to similarly remove the beautiful adjacent structure of the Erechtheion. But once manhandled to the shore – a major exercise in itself – a big ship would be needed to take it away and no man-of-war was available. Instead only some particularly attractive parts were hacked off. Philip Hunt also had his eyes on other ancient sites. He went to Mycenae and initially thought that the Lion Gate was a manageable proposition, but the site was too far from the sea. Over ten months after the first detachments from the Athenian Acropolis, seven metopes, twenty slabs of frieze and almost all the figures from the temple pediments were processed in this way. From Piraeus they were shipped either through Smyrna or Alexandria, and then reconsigned at Malta, a British possession after September 1800. The main cargo eventually arrived in Britain in January 1804, though supplementary batches followed at intervals.

The debate about the moral niceties of Elgin's removals of classic Athenian patrimony was to reverberate endlessly. It has in modern times become a touchstone of alleged cultural imperialism. The historical context of Elgin's activities was one in which the use of financial muscle to whisk away all sorts of art treasures morphed under conditions of a spreading war into outright purloining where growing naval power often gave the British an edge. The argument of Elgin and his helpers was that the marbles were best relocated in an ordered fashion because the ancient fabric of Athens was already being destroyed by both Ottoman depredations and the piecemeal greed of successive waves of European tourists. Anyway, it was said, if the British did not get hold of them, the French would.

Nevertheless, the repetition of these rationales elicited a distinct queasiness from the start. It was one thing to arrange the acquisition of paintings from an Italian gallery, or to seize stone hieroglyphics in Egypt,[19] but quite another to remove large portions of ancient Greek temples. The act of their lowering and the contingent damage made an impression on many who saw it, and their recollections over time were to strike home. Robert Smirke witnessed the removal of a Parthenon frieze. As the heavy stones, dislodged by crowbars, smashed against the ground, he recorded that 'it seemed like a convulsive groan of the injured spirit of the Temple'.[20]

Etching of horses' heads from one of Lord Elgin's Marbles

Edward Dodwell similarly recalled his 'inexpressible mortification' at observing the destruction, and the 'shattered desolation' in which the remaining Parthenon was left.[21] Elgin's team in Athens, indeed, was unpopular not only with Fauvel's faction, but also with most of the Latins (or western Europeans) there, and other English people.[22] When Byron was to arrive there later on, he found the bitterness well entrenched. But even before then his own strong feelings on the matter fed into his first literary work to have a major impact, *English Bards and Scotch Reviewers*, in which he uttered a *cri de coeur* on behalf of these 'maimed antiques', fulminating against those like Elgin, in his new country house in Scotland, who 'make their grand saloons a general mart / For all the mutilated blocks of art'.

Byron's most intense sympathies were always with those without defence, perhaps because, behind all the fierce irony, there was something in him that was likewise utterly defenceless. Ancient Greek stones came into that category. But in London high society, such sensitivities were not common. The practical question was what was actually to be done with these materials, usefully subsumed under the catch-all title of 'marbles'. At first they were laid out in a rented house in Piccadilly, and then in a temporary museum. Elgin, his diplomatic career in Constantinople ended in effective failure, set about trying to sell the treasures to the British government. But this raised the key question: just how valuable and innovative, in artistic and aesthetic terms, were they? They were lumps of seemingly rather primitive, masculine art, compared to the soft, creamy and feminized texture of Graeco-Roman sculptures now residing in the Musée Napoléon, which had become so embedded in the eighteenth-century European, including British, imagination as the acme of excellence and beauty.

An artistic propaganda war surfaced as different aesthetic schools took shape. Getting tickets to view the marbles became a preoccupation for London's fashionistas. Elgin was good at hyping what he had to sell. In June 1808 the All-England prize-fighting champion, Bob Gregson from Lancashire, agreed to stand almost naked in the museum striking various attitudes to reveal his own anatomy as a comparison with some of the statuary around him (a curious male version of Emma Hamilton's more famous 'Attitudes' in Naples some twenty years before).[23] The noted actress, Mrs Siddons, in what might be regarded as the first public expression of the theatrical 'luvvie', burst into tears as she gazed on the display. J. M. W. Turner came and, very usefully for Elgin, said afterwards how invaluable the collection was for the nation. The most influential supporter was the sculptor and key Academy figure John Flaxman, who pronounced that collectively it was far superior to all the treasures of Italy.

Significant parts of those treasures were, of course, now in Paris, so an attraction of the Elgin Marbles was precisely that they were 'our' marbles and as such a counterweight to Napoleon's cultural acquisitions. They provided what Britain so conspicuously lacked: a tangible and national claim to greatness in the visual arts. It was only much later that the emphasis shifted to the universal role that Elgin's fragments played in the world cultural setting of the British Museum (the argument becoming one in which the insights and feelings generated by these distinguished offcuts in Bloomsbury would have been impossible had they remained in their Athenian provenance).[24] But for the moment there were those still unconvinced as to their value viewed through whatever prism, though the motives underlying this critique were suspect. For decades, British nobles on the Grand Tour had been acquiring their own marbles according to very different principles of taste – an 'Italian' taste – from these Athenian importations. If the latter were to be accorded primacy, the cash value of previous ensembles was bound to depreciate. Sir William Hamilton's old friend, Richard Payne Knight – who, as the author of the noted *An Analytic Inquiry into the Principles of Taste* (1805), a volume translated into German by Goethe, was somebody whose opinion carried weight – sought to undermine the status of the Parthenon (or ex-Parthenon) slabs. He told Elgin, 'Your marbles are over-rated', in fact not classically Greek at all, merely Roman designs from the time of Emperor Hadrian's rule in Athens.[25] So an argument unwound, though it was not to come to a climax for several years more. Meanwhile, the passage of time had one great advantage: the original idea of temporarily sending the marbles to Italy for 'restoration' and improvement was finally abandoned, and they stayed unimproved – that is, not further hacked about – in London. For posterity, this was a stroke of good fortune, but more importantly a pre-echo of a modernist, and even more postmodernist, insight: that truth and beauty could lie in incomplete but authentic entities, in shards and fragments made even more meaningful by certain absences, rather than in some over-crafted unity.[26]

These travels and marble-grabbings were the background to the craze in Britain for all things Greek that broke out in the early years of the nineteenth century. We saw that in Athens John Tweddell had sketched the clothing of present-day inhabitants. Ancient Greek costume was now filtered back through English female fashion into designs with high waists, plunging bosom-lines and semi-transparent material, worn only with a tight-fitting petticoat and a *chiton* or drape over the shoulder.[27] As the cultural historian Alexandra Harris has noted, this was 'all very well for a few hours in fine weather or a heated ballroom, but impractical if you wanted to be comfortable or get anything done. This was the hey-day of "catching a chill".'[28]

Such mimicking of diaphanously draped classical statuary, known as the 'English' or sometimes the 'naked' style, had potential for controversy in a period when the overtly sexual was capable of being interpreted as part of a French Jacobin plot to undermine sturdy British society.[29] When the actress Mrs Jordan appeared on stage wearing a garment of flimsy classicism, she got derisively whistled.[30] That 'Greekness' could carry risqué connotations was essential to the storm soon to be created by Byron's love poetry – an outburst that did not therefore come out of the blue. The passion for Greek forms extended well beyond female dress, poetry and public and private architecture, embracing tea-caddies shaped like urns, classical-style furniture and a host of everyday articles.[31]

These applications were possible because it was only around 1800 that there existed the vast mass of evidence from which pure classical styles in so many forms might be reconstructed.[32] But if fastidious purism was important in certain circles – 'The hand of Phidias was on that,' Flaxman would enthuse as he showed Academy students around Elgin's marbles[33] – elsewhere ancient Greek principles were improvised and blended into something rather different. A key figure was Thomas Hope, whose London mansion in Duchess Street became a repository for contemporary taste and design (he had bought some of Sir William Hamilton's much-loved vases). Hope is remembered as the arch-protagonist of neoclassicism, but in fact his aims as a cultural entrepreneur were wider and more complex.[34] His voracious thirst for acquisition and display mixed up Greek with Egyptian, Indian, Turkish and what had evolved into a mongrel species of 'English Picturesque' imagery. In fact quite a few Grand Tourists had returned home with collections of antiquities including Egyptian artefacts that had ended up in Italy, or just marble Roman copies of Egyptian originals (suggestively, when the Italian artist, Giovanni Piranesi, had decorated the English Coffee House in Rome in 1767, he had done so in a neo-Egyptian style).[35] Thomas Hope was not alone in the growing belief 'that Greek art was merely a more elegant restatement of the aims and practices of Egyptian artists';[36] and where Greekness was to be found, Turkishness was never far away.

The eclecticism embodied in Hope's Duchess Street home was transferred after 1806 to his country villa at Deepdene in Surrey, where Disraeli was to begin writing his novel *Coningsby* in September 1843. Hope was in one of his many roles a novelist himself. His *Anastasius* (1819), full of dramatic incident and lashings of sex, ranged over the Ottoman Empire. Byron, to whom in Ravenna the publisher John Murray sent a copy in the spring of 1820, said he wept on reading it because he had not written it himself (and indeed many of Anastasius's tribulations around the fringes of the eastern Mediterranean had parallels in Byron's Don Juan).[37] But above all Hope was a self-conceived paragon of taste committed to synthesizing a highly refined system of cultures. This was cultural globalization even before material globalization got fully into its stride. In this system anything Greek might be *primus*, but it was also very much *inter pares*. What made Greece, ancient and modern, so resonant in British cultural life in the long term was precisely this ability to be recycled, matched with other elements and constantly reinterpreted.

But Ottoman-ruled Greece was not the only place brought into sharper focus by the intensifying southerly bias in British life, especially when war with France was resumed in May 1803 after the Amiens interlude. Samuel Taylor Coleridge referred to his stay in Malta after May 1804 as 'the most memorable and instructive period of my life'. This followed an intense time when his imagination had been drifting steadily Northwards. Like many of his generation, Coleridge had got to know large parts of rural Britain by tramping through it, in his case hiking with William Wordsworth and his sister, mainly in the Lake District. He then spent several years in Germany, nurturing his intellectual cosmopolitanism. Coleridge was already the author of *The Rime of the Ancient Mariner*, moving from a phantasmagoric world of mist and snow into an icy and endless oceanic waste, imagery he largely concocted from scraps of knowledge about Captain Cook's colder explorations.[38] The poet embodied a North–South dichotomy, above all emotionally, that was to be a trait of so many British writers and artists.

Coleridge departed from Portsmouth southwards on HMS *Speedwell* on 9 April 1804 for reasons of health and because there were positions suddenly available for job-hungry Britons in the new Maltese possession in the central Mediterranean.[39] But it also came at a point when his life was in a state of disruption: his marriage was shipwrecked, his great friendship with the Wordsworths was unstable and he was tormented by love for another member of their Cumbrian circle, Sara Hutchinson. But as the *Speedwell* sped towards warmer waters some of these tensions eased, and he became alert to fresh experiences, though the reference points remained home-centred. The mountains he glimpsed in North Africa passing through the Straits of Gibraltar reminded him of Grasmere, and when he arrived at La Vallette (today's Valletta) its Baroque architecture seemed like that of

Bath.[40] But Coleridge was soon entranced by the exquisite colours of the wildlife on the island, his notebooks recording brilliant green lizards with their gold spots and 'darting and angular movements'.[41] Lulled by heat, novelty and a growing opium habit – though also irritated by the sheer noise of Maltese life, even the squealing pigs passing through the capital's streets – Coleridge was compelled to look into himself.[42] This was the primal effect that the Mediterranean often had on susceptible, Northern British minds.

The deep introspection triggered by the Mediterranean took for Coleridge two basic forms: the personal and the political. William Wordsworth had identified his friend's 'promptitude to love' as a defining characteristic, something not uncommon amongst a generation raised on the uncontrollable and unfulfilled passions portrayed in Goethe's *Werther*, and played upon by the sheer turbulence of the times. Coleridge became obsessed in Malta with a sense of lovelessness and sexual frustration that only became more intense from this point in his life. The pivot was an incident when he made a visit to Sicily, where a British presence was also becoming entrenched.[43] In Syracuse he attended an opera performance set in the ancient Greek theatre. For British travellers to the Mediterranean, opera had long since become a cliché for inducing heightened emotional states (something that was to be true of both Shelley and Byron, whose first actions when visiting any Italian city included going to the opera house). On this occasion, after the performance Coleridge went to the changing room of the singer, Anna-Cecilia Bertozzi, and was, by his own account, only saved from being seduced by a vision of Sara Hutchinson's innocent purity. A modern biographer states, 'it was the directness of Cecilia's feelings, her sunny Italian spontaneity, that seemed to frighten him. It was too simple, too sexual'.[44]

What actually happened in that cramped space in Syracuse is, of course, not the point at all. It was what Coleridge made of it. After returning to Malta, he spent many hours as the guest of the chief British administrator, Captain Alexander Ball, sitting in the delicious garden of San Antonio palace, with its orange blossoms and beguiling fragrance. There he wrote 'The Blossoming of the Solitary Date-Tree', a lament that the more exquisite any individual's capacity for joy may be, the more devastating was the experience of being crushed by its elusiveness. 'Why was I made for Love and Love denied to me?' the unfinished poem asks as it trails into nothingness. Here was Coleridge's sense of the richness and fecundity of the Mediterranean entwined with a sense of personal exile and uselessness.[45] Such paradoxical effects made by the crucible of the Mediterranean on British feelings and self-examination were to play out endlessly. They certainly left a permanent mark on Coleridge's uneasy and visionary life.

Coleridge was also notable, however, as a poet engaged with practical politics. Even before going to Malta his early enthusiasm for the French Revolution had been tempered by suspicion of Napoleon's power-lust. Once there he became acutely conscious of Britain's isolation against France, and why the Mediterranean mattered increasingly to Britain's future. Appointed by Alexander Ball as public secretary in Malta, he came to enjoy the regularity of responsibility and the comradeship of the naval officers.[46] His patriotism entered into his religious philosophizing, central to his own development, as (surrounded by an alien Catholicism) he concocted new ways of reformulating Anglican doctrines. Leaving Malta at last in September 1805, he was in Naples when he heard the news of Nelson's recent death during the defeat of the Franco-Spanish fleet at the Battle of Trafalgar that October. Coleridge later recalled the people who greeted him as an Englishman in the street, full of tears for the fallen hero who had once saved Naples from the Jacobins.[47] He moved to Rome and when Napoleon ordered all Britons to leave the city, hovered for a while in Pisa, a city shortly to be so critical in the lives of Shelley and Byron. Coleridge finally left for England aboard a British warship on 23 June 1806. By this time his anti-French feelings were acute.

These were the sentiments that fed into the journal that, with the still platonic help of Sara Hutchinson, he wrote and collated once back in Grasmere, the last edition appearing in March 1810. It was entitled *The Friend*, the essential theme being a critique of the origins of French Revolutionary thought going back to Voltaire. But a prominent supplementary topic was Coleridge's adulation of the civil commissioner of Malta, Alexander Ball, who had died in Valletta in 1809, as the epitome of a wise and effective governor.[48] Thomas de Quincey, famous for his own opiate ramblings, ascribed this to Coleridge's habit of filtering his views through dominant figures.[49] Yet such hero worship on Coleridge's part in this case arose from his concern to pursue theoretical issues of politics and religion in a framework defined by his personal experience in Malta. Crucially, the Mediterranean as a means of refracting British political culture held all sorts of possibilities. It could be used for conservative or radical purposes. Coleridge was to be denigrated as a political apostate by Shelley and Byron, whose own experiences passed through a Mediterranean gauze had very different ideological textures. But in the longer term, Coleridge's principled conservatism, shaped in part by an incipient colonial ideal in Malta, influenced an early and mid-Victorian generation for whom Byronic recklessness became something to avoid.

Coleridge's vision of the Mediterranean as a theatre in which the British might play out a new future for themselves coincided with the considerable impact of a book then framing the same involvement in rather different terms of human sensibilities, life-shaping choices and relations between the sexes. This was Madame de Staël's *Corinne, or Italy* (1807), the title arising from the fact that the eponymous heroine of the novel *was* Italy personified. The author was the daughter of one of Louis XVI's most reforming ministers – Anglomania was part of her family tradition – and she had struggled as a liberal thinker to remain loyal to a revolution in her native France that had gone off in such troubling directions.[50] In doing so she sought to define the wider problem of European civilization in terms of physical, moral and emotional geographies. One of de Staël's starting points was the climatic theory of the Enlightenment thinker Montesquieu, who had argued in his *Lettres persanes* (*Persian Letters*, 1721), and more systematically in *De l'esprit des lois* (*The Spirit of the Laws*, 1748), that environmental conditions predicated a basic dialectic between an icy, stiff North and the hot-tempered South. Already in her *De la littérature considérée dans ses rapports avec les institutions sociales* (1800), de Staël had gone further and developed a broad cultural spectrum between North and South, the Romantic and the classical, reason and passion.

At that juncture she had still retained some hope that Napoleon, at the head of a consulate, might tug the Revolution back to a line conducive to human progress. By 1807, banished from Paris at the dictate of the emperor who was himself close to obsession with the personal feud between the two of them, she had given up such possibilities. Great Britain, Bonaparte's natural enemy, instead loomed for a while as the sole prospect of blocking a downward spiral in European civilization. But was that country, so long admired in its purely constitutional and material capacities, mentally equipped to develop the new human paradigm that de Staël dreamed of, one combining the soberness and moderation of the North with the sheer *enthusiasm* for life embodied in the South, a commitment to duty but also open to the compulsions of love and beauty, just as de Staël was in her own life? Without both kinds of sensibility mankind could never move forward in a sustained manner. This was the challenge that the author explored in *Corinne*.

The story of the novel, captivating to a new readership but especially amongst women, may be simply told. Oswald, from a Scottish baronial family, is an archetypal melancholy Northern wanderer who travels to Italy to escape some 'cruel attending circumstances' that so often prompted prolonged visits to the warm South (he represented, J. Christopher Herold comments in his biography of de Staël, essentially 'all the men Germaine ever loved').[51] Oswald attends a poetic festival in Rome during which the winner of the competition – with the crowd shouting 'Long Live Corinne! Long live genius! Long live beauty! – at first appals him with her sensuous and fiery virtuosity but then exudes a profound fascination, her loveliness likened to that of a Greek statue. They fall in love, but in doing so Corinne has finally to divulge her great secret: she had been brought up in England before fleeing its cold constraints, and was in fact the half-sister of the girl, Lucile, whom Oswald had been intended by his father to marry at home. A test of sincerity, love and loyalty looms as the couple visit Naples and are caught up in its pulsating excitement (as de Staël had been during her own stay in that city in 1805). Oswald and Corinne visit a British warship at anchor in the Bay of Naples. De Staël explains that 'The subordination, the seriousness, the regularity, the silence that could be observed on that vessel were the image of a severe and free social order [in] contrast with the city of Naples, so lively, so passionate, so tumultuous.'[52]

Naples in its raw spirit and emotion here stood for the very antithesis of the England represented in such a vessel, although the dualism also embodied that of the genders.[53] But could sturdy English qualities and preferences, buried deep in Oswald himself, ever truly merge with the spontaneity, the ability to improvise at every level, the instinct to *live* that made Corinne what she was, something so much at odds with Anglo-Saxon preconceptions? Despite the unexpected revelation of Corinne's previous history

Corinne declaims her poetry
Illustration from the novel by Madame de Staël

Oswald gives her a ring as a token of his love, but when he goes back to Britain he is sucked into the old pedestrian calculations and family wishes. He renews his commitment to Lucile, and when Corinne covertly follows him and sees this, she finds a means to return the ring and leaves. She picks up her own brilliantly lived life in Rome, but falls ill and dies lamenting her betrayal, though not before Oswald revisits the city and ponders the awful possibility that the choice he made had been one for safety, with all the mediocrity and the narrowing of soul this entailed. Beyond a consciousness of a road not taken, however, de Staël leaves Oswald's ultimate conclusions about his own conduct ambiguously suspended.

That very ambiguity, however, was one that de Staël implicitly attached to the British themselves. Did they know what they really wanted for themselves, or even how to live? The ideal – the 'sensation', as de Staël put it – of the South as a *possibility* that might be made real in one's own country and one's own life, vaguely formulated as we have already seen

1 John Ruskin, *St Mark's, Venice. Sketch after Rain* (1846). Ruskin's passion for medieval architecture grew during the visit to the city when this sketch was made, shortly to climax in his book *The Stones of Venice*. The Basilica of St Mark's afterwards remained central to his moral and aesthetic critique of modernity.

2 David Allan, *Sir William Hamilton and the First Lady Hamilton in their Villa in Naples* (1770). The couple are portrayed surrounded by favourite possessions – a classical bust of Zeus, a violin, a canvas by Correggio. Hearing her play, Leopold Mozart reckoned that Catherine was one of the best violinists in Italy.

3 Katharine Read, *British Gentlemen in Rome* (*c.* 1750). Dundee-born Read lived in Rome between 1751 and 1753 and had a clientele among the Italian aristocracy and Grand Tourists. She later became a fashionable portraitist in London.

4 Thomas Patch, *British Gentlemen at Sir Horace Mann's Home in Florence* (*c*. 1763–5). Mann was Britain's representative in Tuscany from 1740 until his death in 1786. His receptions at the Palazzo Manetti were described as 'remarkably brilliant', with fashionable Florentine ladies in attendance, although here the artist – a noted caricaturist – captured an exclusively male society.

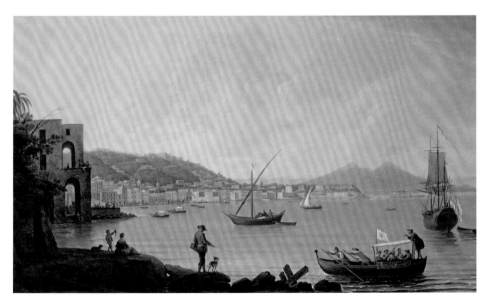

5 Pietro Fabris, *The Bay of Naples from Posillipo* (1770). The Anglo-Neapolitan painter presents a view of the city, bathed in evening warmth and crystalline light, from what became a classic viewpoint.

6 Joseph Wright, *Vesuvius in Eruption* (*c*. 1776–80). Wright described this scene as 'the grandest effect of Nature ... I suppose can be', and although he painted many versions, this was the most lurid. Vesuvian imagery became an iconic motif of British Romanticism.

7 Thomas Jones, *The Garden of the Villa Borghese* (*c*. 1776). The garden was a focus for the British community, the site of fêtes and receptions often lit by torchlight in the evenings.

8 Francis Towne, *St Peter's at Sunset, from above the Arco Oscuro* (1781). After seeing this an admirer at home wrote to Towne of 'his Delight at finding myself in Old Rome … by your Pencil'. Towne's work influenced modern British colourists, including Eric Ravilious.

9 David Roberts, *Old Buildings on the Darro, Granada* (1834). The river surrounded the city's exotic medieval architecture that Roberts loved. When first exhibited, a critic called this picture 'an exquisite thing'.

10 John Phillip, *The Antonia* (1863). The blackness of the image combined with the limpid beauty and penetrating gaze of the female subject embodies characteristics of much British art concerning Spain.

11 Robert Smirke, *Kalamata, Greece* (1802–4). Smirke visited Kalamata on a Grand Tour that was part of a growing British intrusion into western Greece after the renewal of war with France. He became a leading figure in Greek Revival architecture in Britain.

12 Edward Lear, *Town and Harbour of Gaio, Paxo* (1863). After entering the little port Lear wrote that it 'looked sparkly and bright and quiet in its moonlit silver and black shade'. Some consider this to be the finest of Lear's Ionian lithographs.

13 Hiram Powers, *The Greek Slave* (1844). Evoking a girl abducted into Ottoman slavery, this work was a much-discussed feature at the Great Exhibition in Britain. It was already controversial in Powers's native United States. 'It is not her person but her spirit that stands exposed,' the Florence-based artist claimed in defending the figure's nudity. The image was prominent in pro-abolition publicity before the civil war in America.

14 Archibald Archer, depiction of the Elgin Marbles in the British Museum shortly after their arrival (1819). This triumphant portrayal of the arrival of the Parthenon sculptures elided previous criticisms in some quarters as to the Marbles' value. Afterwards the picture was hung above the fireplace of the Museum's boardroom as a mark of the new consensus.

15 Edward Burne-Jones, *Cupid and Psyche* (*c.* 1870). The narrative of Cupid's obsession with Psyche preoccupied Burne-Jones, interwoven as it was with his affair with Maria Zambaco, the Anglo-Greek heiress and Pre-Raphaelite model. Of his various portrayals, this recumbent Psyche is said to be the most reminiscent of Maria's striking beauty. The affair foundered, but illustrates how Victorian artists often sought to express inner struggles through Greek mythology.

over decades, was now made concrete in *Corinne*, allied to a newly resonant claim of 'the realm of culture as a province for women'.[54] This *idea* of
the Mediterranean as a theatre within which some British women might
be able to expand their selfhood, even their fantasies – shadowed as a latent
instinct in the craze for castrati in the era of Queen Anne – was to take far
more substantial intellectual forms in the rest of the nineteenth century.
De Staël herself was to move on, and her theories, still revolving around
antitheses of North and South, were to be most sharply defined in her
greatest book *De l'Allemagne* (1810), since by then it was the Germans, not
the British, who appeared the most formidable in their opposition to the
author's enemy on the imperial throne in Paris. She died still in exile in
1817, yet another whose dream of one day going to Greece remained
unfulfilled.[55] But the Corinne myth subsequently entered deeply into
British and European sensibility, refracted through many literary imita-
tions. Although Byron was left uneasy by the image of female power over
men's happiness that de Staël revelled in underlining,[56] he was himself to
exploit the emotional currents in a far richer poetic vein. As for Napoleon,
when he tried to read the novel in exile on St Helena, he expostulated of
de Staël, 'I can see her, I can hear her . . . I want to run away.'[57]

The war itself meanwhile had not stood still and, in line with a south-
ward bent in strategy as well as cultural awareness, Spain came to define
central aspects of Britain's struggle against Napoleon. Here is a paradox
extending into the twentieth century: if Italy had a greater cultural resonance for Britain, the impact of Spanish events sometimes cut deeper
politically. It was as if that country were capable of hitting an old Tudor
nerve in the British psyche. After a popular rebellion against the French
occupation of Spain broke out in May 1808, an expeditionary army sailed
from Cork under Sir Arthur Wellesley, soon to be the Duke of Wellington –
a Dubliner by birth and further testimony to a deep Irish vein running in
British Mediterranean experience. The Convention of Cintra (August
1808) temporarily stopped the Iberian fighting, but caused a storm in
Britain; one of its fiercest opponents was Wordsworth, moving, like
Coleridge, steadily towards a strident patriotism. After the renewal of the
campaign, and the dispatch of a fresh expedition, the ensuing Peninsular
War forged a consensus between Tories and the Whig opposition in Britain.
'England is herself again,' the poet Robert Southey enthused.[58] The

Quarterly Review, the great mouthpiece of nineteenth-century British Toryism, was also set up at this point, originally to agitate about Spain. The historian of British Romanticism, Marilyn Butler, has remarked on how sensitivity to the Mediterranean and its peoples in British cultural life intensified alongside these Spanish developments in the war.[59]

Such sensitivity, however, did not necessarily mean sympathy. British troops who fought in Spain seemed to show little interest in the towns in which they were billeted and the life that went on there.[60] The one painter who witnessed parts of the campaign, Denis Dighton, mainly recorded military uniforms (though we shall return to British images of the war produced after 1815). The French remained in control of most of the country, and it was they who were principally responsible for purloining the riches of Spanish art as opportunity offered. Marshal Soult, Napoleon's commander, had claims to connoisseurship, and his additions of old Spanish masters to French holdings ensured that for the rest of the century that country remained ahead of Britain in appreciation of Hispanic painting.[61] Relations between the British and the Spanish population meanwhile were tentative. 'Between his men, the officers included,' a biographer of Wellington has written, 'and the inhabitants of the Peninsula was a gulf of prejudice, suspicion and incomprehension.'[62] Something of this can be glimpsed in what one writer calls the 'surprisingly haunted' portrait of the duke made by Francisco Goya (1812–14), who spent these years in Madrid keeping a careful distance from the various foreign occupiers.[63] Intimate in size and texture, this painting is perhaps the most revealing ever made of Britain's most famous soldier. It is telling that it was the work of a wary Madrileño.

In cultural and political relations, nevertheless, purely personal intimacy is not the point. It was against the backdrop of the Peninsular War that a constitutional saga unfolded ultimately affecting both Britain and Spain. Lord John Russell, later one of the greatest figures in mid-Victorian politics, spent two years in Spain during the early phases of the war observing political life. He was present at the reconvening of the Cortes on the Isla de Léon off Cadiz in March 1812, under the protective cover of the Royal Navy. There he learned 'a gigantic lesson in constitutional history'.[64] This sprang from the failure of the Cortes to bridge the divisions amongst Spaniards opposed to the French. The reason for this failure,

Russell felt, was the lack of a centrist and moderate class. Translated into British terms, which is what really interested Russell, this meant the need for a form of Whig politics moderating the extremes of Radicals and Tories. Later on Russell took little interest in Spain. But his Iberian experience shaped his role as an architect of what finally became the British Liberal Party, and indeed 'liberal' as an English political usage was in the 1820s taken directly from the *liberales* then active in Spain.[65]

Given the wartime British public's emotional stake in Spain, it was not surprising that Lord Byron set the first two cantos of his poem *Childe Harold's Pilgrimage*, published in 1812, in that country. These cantos were not principally about politics – though English chauvinism on display in Iberia got its comeuppance in them – but rather about what always mattered most to Byron: love and its illusions. In his rhapsody of Spanish womanhood Byron's languorous and tactile verse ran:

> The seal Love's dimpling finger hath impress'd
> Denotes how soft that chin which bears his touch . . .
> Who round the North for paler dames would seek?
> How poor their forms appear! how languid, wan, and weak![66]

Here was the polarity between a frigid North and sexualized South that hit an almost desperate chord with many thousands of British women, some already alerted by the message of Madame de Staël's *Corinne* that there were societies – not in some half-mythical Eastern realm, but just over the horizon, bathed in Latin sunshine – where life might be freer, more natural, truer to real instincts. The importunate and often fantasizing letters dispatched to the poet through the office of his publisher, John Murray, 'disclose', Fiona MacCarthy writes, 'a whole small world of early nineteenth-century female isolation'.[67] The publication of *Childe Harold* introduced an author who not only before long became the first European celebrity in a modern sense, but also embodied Anglo-Mediterranean interaction in its most complex and meaningful form. Nobody else ever really came close. Quite how Byron's sensuous but also curiously Calvinistic nature – Lady Byron said Calvinism 'was the rock on which all who had to do with him were broken'[68] – interweaved with his experiences in southern Europe touch basic concerns in this book.

Divided inner drives, indecisiveness and acute frustration with both himself and his country provide the keys to Byron's conduct, and it is from these that life in the Mediterranean came to offer some muddled resolution or escape. Where many Britons had decided views on the French Revolution, either as paradise gained or hell to be avoided, Byron was equivocal. He was contemptuous of the British political elite, but hated arguably even more the radical demagogues on the other side. He was flexible in his own sexual as well as political tastes.[69] All his love affairs, it has been observed, were really 'sentimental attachments',[70] and this applied regardless of gender. In literature he was set on being modern himself, but preferred old-fashioned Augustans – always reading Pope or Swift – to what he regarded as shoddy contemporary writing.[71] His first major poem, *English Bards and Scotch Reviewers*, was a tirade not only against the current literary world but against British culture as a whole, since none of his own instinctive preferences seemed to fit.[72] The spirit of his departure on his own Grand Tour on 2 July 1809 reflected this inner rejection. 'Hark! The farewell gun is fired,' he versified to a friend the night before he left, and in his innermost heart he was always afterwards bidding farewell to England.

Byron's travels in 1809–11 went beyond what he dismissed as 'the Common Turnpike of coxcombs and virtuosos'. His route included Lisbon, Seville, Cadiz, Malta, Albania, western Greece (including Missolonghi, where he was eventually to die much later), Athens, Smyrna, Constantinople (where occurred what he saw as one of his greatest achievements, swimming with his club foot across the Hellespont), and then back through Athens and the Morea. Byron's interests on this itinerary were scarcely political. When at Patras he met Frederick North (the son of George III's old prime minister) who on an earlier visit to the Greek lands had adopted the Orthodox faith, he was left unmoved by North's philhellenism.[73] Byron finally embarked for home on HMS *Hydra*, ironically along with the last large consignment of the Elgin Marbles. He arrived back at Portsmouth, along with these ancient slabs, on 14 July 1811.

This uncommon turnpike might be taken as the last authentic tour in the grand eighteenth-century manner,[74] since after all the public acclaim of *Childe Harold*, of which it was a kind of account, such travels could only henceforth be mimetic. Comparisons were inevitably made between the conflicted, lovelorn sufferings of Byron's Harold and Goethe's Werther, since these figures more than any others personified the essence of Romantic *angst*. But whereas Goethe's novel had been situated in a sleepy provincial town in eighteenth-century Germany, Byron's epic poem 'unravels the panorama of history and brings far-distant countries into view'.[75] Certainly henceforth the Mediterranean had a tangibility and meaning for much less travelled British readers that had not been at all possible before.

If only because of the later climax of Byron's life, it is his time spent in Greece, and especially Athens, that resonates in his biography. He took a particular dislike to the antiquity-loving virtuoso (or Dilettanti) types he found amongst the English residents of the city,[76] and although this was special to Byron's cast of mind – to him antiquities were something to carve your name on, as he did at the temple of Sounion[77] – it also represented a subtle shift of mood. Despite, or perhaps because of, the preoccupation of English cognoscenti with the Greek past, here was the start of a counter-impulse that such an obsession could be stifling of any truly modern tendency to thought or feeling.[78] *Childe Harold* was to mark the end of deference,[79] and one of those deferences was to classical deadness: the fictional Harold, like Byron himself, and like the new mass readership he reached, wanted instead to *live*. One of the achievements of Byron in this regard, John Pemble writes, was not to invalidate the appeal of the antique as such, but lay in 'reversing the chemistry of melancholia', and imposing on the marble legacy of ancient times 'the burden of his own suffering. For Byron, those heaps of broken stone were tragic less as witnesses to history . . . than as reflections and projections of his own inward ache of dereliction and bereavement.'[80] This, in its relationship to inner worlds of desire and disillusionment, was to give to past Mediterranean ruins the capacity for endless resonance in modern, and also postmodern, sensibilities.

To subsequent Victorians, the most memorable, and estimable, thing Byron did in Athens was to fall in love with a twelve-year-old girl (what a later age might think of as paedophilia was then seen somewhat differently).[81] She was Teresa Macri, daughter of the British vice-consul and his Greek wife, her youthful bloom later rendered in Byron's adoration of the 'Maid of Athens'. Although there was a sordid undertone to Byron's worship of Teresa,[82] it was the aching pathos – 'Maid of Athens, 'ere we part, / Give, oh, give me back my heart' – that helped trigger many of those fan letters sent via John Murray the publisher. For Byron, innocence and sordidness always went together, and his later frenzied – to Shelley, degraded[83] – sexual life in Venice was a kind of graffiti being inscribed on his own desire and need of love, just as he had scraped letters on the Sounion temple. But as always with Byron, what was special to him had a larger echo. Here was that double life of horror and loveliness – 'The fatal gift of beauty', as he put it in *Childe Harold* – which for many British writers assumed its most poignant form in Mediterranean settings.

Elevated to an unparalleled fame by *Childe Harold* in 1812, Byron went on to develop the essential Byronic figure in such poems as *The Giaour*, *The Bride of Abydos* and *The Siege of Corinth*. That figure was usually an aristocratic and 'culturally alienated anti-hero, bearing within a dark secret'.[84] There was much self-conception in these portrayals, and their edge came from his detestation of Britain's growing militarization – especially as he was not part of it. Byron found vulgar the celebration put on in Vauxhall Gardens, that now shabby eighteenth-century London pleasure ground, after the bloody Battle of Vitoria in Spain (June 1813). He hated Wellington and even more the triumphalism of 1815, suffering always from a sense of his being *belated*, of being left behind by great events elsewhere, not least by those who were beneficiaries of the reflected glory.[85] Whether the 'dark secret' of alleged incest with his half-sister Augusta was true or not, Byron felt that on leaving England after the formal separation from his wife on 21 April 1816 he had been hounded out of the country. (Somebody who made an unavailing attempt to prevent the final implosion of the marriage had been Madame de Staël.) Throughout this disintegration Byron dreamed of escaping to Greece: for him that country and a vision of youth were now fixed as synonymous.[86] But in bidding farewell to England, again, and for the last time, his actual destination was Italy. The latter remained the real world in a way that Greece could not.

Byron's route lay through Switzerland, where that summer he met and forged a fateful friendship with Percy and Mary Shelley. A generation of Enlightenment writers and artists had fallen in love with the majesty of the Alps, and after 1815 the region enjoyed a boom in British tourism.[87] Byron was captivated himself, the stupendous light of the Jungfrau, he wrote, 'shining like truth'; a glacier near Grindelwald was 'a frozen hurricane'.[88] Such an apotheosis of Nature, redolent of what has been called 'a Romantic engagement with ice',[89] was conjured up in the poem *Manfred*, with its picture of a superhero conventionalized in European Romanticism after 1830 (Ford Madox Brown was to paint the scene Byron portrayed in verse, and Robert Schumann set the work to music). Here was a crystalline and unambiguous beauty – Shelley's term for the Swiss mountains was 'God's ballet'[90] – that pointed straight to the heavens, and connects Byron to the Alpine obsessions of John Ruskin.

This is relevant because, whatever romanticism belonged to Italy, it was not like this, as Byron's subsequent life there epitomized. Italy's beauty was more mysterious, unpredictable, indeed even impure; hence its fatality. It is Byron's stay in Venice after May 1817 that has above all fixed his image in retrospect (just as Byron fixed the image of Venice itself for the coming Victorians). He rented the sea-smelling but magnificent Palazzo Mocenigo, its basement inhabited by animals that the poet always picked up along the way, like the dog Muntz from Freiburg or the squirrel kept in a cage which he purchased in Chamonix. There is, perhaps, some obscure truth in the observation that his growing debauchery there 'went far deeper . . . [than] mere time-wasting and superficial self-indulgence; one might almost suggest . . . that it had a moral basis'.[91] Such behaviour challenged the Calvinism that he tried, but never succeeded, in ridding himself of; a challenge defined by Byron's adoption of an Italian view of life as essentially a performance, with all its movement, vivacity and delight in the grotesque, as well as the imagined sexual nonchalance of the city of gondolas and masks.[92] Summed up in his poem *Beppo*, at heart this was not about any real Italy; rather it was for Byron about England, about what England had done to him, and a desperate desire to experience some differently constructed reality. This was only, in very intense form, what experience in the Mediterranean meant for many Britons in the years ahead.

Here, too, for all their differences, is the drive that united Byron and Shelley, described as 'a battle in defence of the classical and Mediterranean south' against the reactionary, dour, enclosed Gothicism of the North embodied in post-Waterloo Britain.[93] Byron's most enduring masterpiece, *Don Juan*, which Marilyn Butler calls 'an assured epic of the south', revelled in 'a cult of sexuality, its beauty and naturalness' precisely because for

Byron these qualities went to the heart of the matter.[94] Byron 'defined the chief value of living as the feeling of being alive', another critic writes, and love and sensuousness lay at the centre of *Don Juan* because they constituted such feelings at their most exquisite.[95] But at the polar opposite lay hate, and it was inherent in Byron's own life that Don Juan's experience of unfolding 'Love–Tempest–Travel–War' set in revolutionary times climaxed in its final cantos, perhaps the most devastating critique of the British ruling caste ever written.

This southern blast aimed at British repression in the years following the Peterloo Massacre roughly coincided with another great public tumult in Britain with an Italian dimension – though as always in the British context, one with shifting moral implications.[96] This was the trial for adultery of Queen Caroline, wife of George IV, who had separated from her after his succession in January 1820. Successful prosecution hinged on getting suitably salacious evidence of the queen's behaviour during her extensive Mediterranean travels as Princess of Wales,[97] but especially with her alleged Milanese lover, Count Pergami. A commission was sent to Italy to collect what incriminating titbits it could. One of the prosecution's chief pegs was what had allegedly happened in an adjoining room when Caroline retired during a ball held by the King of Naples in 1815, taking Pergami with her. The trial after August 1820 sparked a period of intense popular agitation, and the legal procedure in Parliament was 'one of the most spectacular and dramatic events of the century' in Britain.[98] After Caroline's acquittal and early death the agitation subsided, but the outpouring helped to frame public opinion in a new way. After 1822 the old English order was back in the saddle but things could not be quite as they had been before. Here were the roots of profound shifts in British political culture that were to crystallize at the outset of the following decade.

After May 1819 Byron left Venice and began his prolonged relationship with Countess Teresa Guiccioli and her family near Ravenna. This marked for him a turn away from flaunted depravity and towards Italian politics proper. The Gambas were discreet conspirators, as so many aristocratic Carbonari were,[99] and in a way this is what made them congenial to Byron: they had education, pedigree and civilization – so different from common English radicals – but were still at odds with the status quo, in this case an

Austrian one.[100] One event more than any other captures the essence of Byron through its spontaneity. He happened to be on the spot in Milan when the Austrian military commander, whom he knew, was shot dead. He sat by the bloodied body in the confusion of the event: it was 'the underlying strangeness, what it said about the human condition',[101] and its inherent savagery regardless of political affiliation that gripped his thoughts. Gazing at that corpse in Milan, hating the Austrian despotism the commander had represented just as he despised its British counterpart, but somehow attached to it and grieving for its pain, strikes to the heart of Byron's complexity.

A similar ambivalence prevailed, too, when Byron joined the Shelleys and other expatriates at Pisa to form what Shelley conceived of as a colony of like minds and shared experience, but one organically embedded in local society. Therein lay the rub, for though Percy Shelley claimed that 'our roots were never struck so deeply as at Pisa' after October 1821,[102] and whilst it has been argued that this represented a transplantation of a Romantic Anglo-Italianism,[103] the story suggests something more ordinary. These cosmopolitan Pisans slid into a pattern of existence where the women, including Mary Shelley and Teresa Guiccioli, kept closely to a villa engaged in conversation and embroidery while the men engaged in a very English life, playing snooker and shooting and riding their horses around town, where on one occasion a fierce contretemps arose with the local authority.[104] A sense of strained exile grew, accentuated by Shelley's awareness that Byron possessed the fame that he had so clearly missed out on himself; their 'ironical companionship' became a burden to him.[105] Beneath the intellectual banter, here was a banality into which Anglo-Mediterranean lives often collapsed. Shelley once expressed the belief that Italy – by which he meant an obsession with it – 'ends in nothing and produces nothing',[106] and it was true in a way of his own fate when, as we saw at the start of this book, he drowned off Viareggio on 8 July 1822. His very recklessness in going to sea in an unsuitable vessel is telling.

The roots of the Pisan circle were sufficiently shallow that Shelley's death unearthed them quite quickly. Mary Shelley, once she had ensured that her husband's ashes were to be moved close to the grave of one of their children in the Protestant Cemetery in Rome, soon returned to England.[107] Her attitude to Italy afterwards always remained equivocal.[108] Byron, digesting his own delayed grief and perhaps guilt at the death of his daughter, Allegra, in an Italian convent, then started his profoundly hesitant move towards a decision to go to Greece in support of the rebellion against Ottoman rule that had erupted in February 1821. Byron had previously supported 'freedom' for Greece, but had only envisaged wider autonomy under the Turkish sultan.[109] Although in England a philhellenic movement got under way, it never quite caught on with a wider public and, like the agitation on behalf of Queen Caroline, finally sputtered to a halt. Shelley in his Pisan prime had resoundingly declared 'We are all Greeks' in his last published poem, *Hellas*, but this was in the vein of that Intellectual Beauty which was his only tangible belief; the declaration had to do with universal mind and spirit, not actual events. When a real-life Greek politician, Prince Mavrocordatos, turned up in Pisa, Shelley had been rather equivocal towards him, especially once Mary Shelley – all too aware of her husband's continuing infidelities – appeared to develop a friendship with the cultivated prince.[110] When Lady Blessington, whom Byron visited in Genoa in 1823 and spoke to frankly about his own life, later published their conversations, she stated, 'On one thing those who knew him were in no doubt. He was not doing it for the Greeks.'[111]

Why, then, did Byron leave for Greece in mid-July 1823? Finally discarding 'the conceits and fripperies of his Italian existence', and after hesitating again for a long period in the British-ruled Ionian Islands, he eventually arrived in the western Greek port of Missolonghi on 4 January 1824 with an entourage including his Newfoundland hound, Lyon. In truth, Italy was played out for him. He was always drawn to the realm of the intenser feelings,[112] and after much reflection he decided where those feelings now were for him. 'I mean to stick to the Greeks to the last rag of canvas or shirt,' Byron wrote,[113] his determination all the sharper because he knew that he had failed to stick to so many affective ties before. As one narrator of his long path to Missolonghi writes, Byron's personal 'war' was above all a war against mortality,[114] and, aware that his own body was shattered and failing, Byron decided that his last stand should be in Greece, where youth had once been so glorious. This is why the judgement that he 'did not do it for the Greeks' is ultimately flawed, because for once Byron's fate had become fused with something other than himself in a way it had never been in Italy or indeed in England.

As it turned out, Byron did not actually fight in Greece. For all his poetic bellicosity, it would have been against his nature. He contracted fever, and died surrounded mostly by German volunteers on the evening of 19 April 1824. His body was taken back to England and after remaining in London for respect to be shown, a cortège of forty-seven carriages accompanied the hearse out of the capital – an echo of the great *equipage* with which he had once gone about the Mediterranean. Coleridge, prompted by the occasion into one of his gushing rhetorical reflections, watched it go past on Highgate Hill to final interment at the family seat of Newstead in Nottinghamshire.[115] It was one of those nineteenth-century deaths where many people recalled the moment they heard of it; the young Edward Bulwer Lytton later wrote about 'the singular, the stunning sensation, which the intelligence produced . . . so much of us died with him . . . it was as if a part of the mechanism of the very world stood still'.[116] Not everybody was sympathetic. Goethe, still living in Weimar and now rather Anglophobic, remarked that Byron's death had 'occurred at exactly the right time. His Greek enterprise had something impure about it, and could never have ended well.'[117]

This acerbity was extreme, but embedded in it was the kernel of why Byron's death at Missolonghi did not, as Shelley's death in Italy did after a prolonged interval, come to assume a totemic cultural status in British life (and in telling contrast with some European countries, such as France, where the flame of Byron's fame burned intensely). Whereas for High Victorians Shelley's intellectuality and ethereal character proved reclaimable despite his moral notoriety when alive, there was always something too subversive of England itself, too *clashing* about Byron, and perhaps as well something simply too equivocal about modern Greece with which he came, finally, to be so associated. Matthew Arnold (for whom the *dirtiness* of Byron was incompatible with his dream of 'sweetness and light' as a guide for Britain's future) conveyed something of this feeling in 1850 in his poem 'Stanzas from the Grande Chartreuse':

What helps it now, that Byron bore,
With haughty scorn which mocked the smart,
Through Europe to the Aetolian shore
The pageant of his bleeding heart?[118]

This did not stop Byron becoming for many, if not for the more priggish Arnoldians, one of the public gods of Victorian England.[119] But it did mean that in a curious way the death was separated out from the life, whilst the poems admired and selected for study were the early romantic ones, not the dangerous verses of *Beppo* or *Don Juan*.[120]

There had, however, been another death in the Mediterranean shortly before those of Shelley and Byron that in rather different ways also proved defining for English literary consciousness: that of John Keats. The two slightly older writers had for some years been disdainful of the struggling Keats. Byron disliked Keats's soft-focused classicism and scoffed at his half-educated culture (probably because Keats's Greek references all came from translations).[121] Byron's reference on one occasion to 'Johnny Keats' piss a-bed poetry' was an instance of his letter-writing mode at its most savage.[122] Even more a butt of ridicule was Keats's patent lack of hardened life experience of the sort enjoyed by Byron and Shelley.[123] *The Eve of St. Agnes* (1819) was hardly the work of a dedicated seducer. Keats himself confessed to a friend, 'I have not a right feeling towards women',[124] by which he meant a difficulty relating to the other sex. Awkwardness, even distrust, in these relationships plagued him to the end.

Confronting the same illness that had killed his brother, Keats left under doctor's orders for Italy on 18 September 1820 accompanied by a friend, Joseph Severn.[125] It was now that the jibes to which the richly scented youthfulness of his published work had made him subject cut to the quick of his troubled mind. The voyage towards what he termed in one of his symbol-laden odes 'the warm South' – a beguiling existential zone in which by force of imagination one might escape the psychological limitations of the human condition[126] – was a dreadful one of sleeplessness and sombre thoughts. However, early in the journey he did manage to write out in Severn's copy of a Shakespeare play, in his own shaky hand, the famous lines 'Bright Star! Would I were steadfast as thou art', expressing ardent love for his neighbour in Hampstead, Fanny Brawne. Keats and Severn arrived in Naples, where, after the frustrations of quarantine, Keats tried to distract himself by reading Richardson's *Clarissa*; like Byron, he admired the Augustans. A move to Rome approached on 15 November, though the forlorn landscape of the boggy Via Appia did nothing to alleviate Keats's now desperate spirits. Taking up lodgings in the Piazza di

Spagna, he felt he was now living a 'posthumous existence',[127] and according to Severn, suffered from an unbearable physical frustration and fear of losing Fanny Brawne to others.[128]

In the circumstances, what this meant was a crushing awareness that although in his poems he had self-consciously balanced polarities of celibacy and passion, love and death,[129] the bitter reality for Keats was that he would never himself know the full range of human feeling. He contemplated suicide, but died naturally at 11 p.m. on 23 February 1821.[130] The funeral in the Protestant Cemetery three days later was small, with only nine people present. Severn intended to give his friend a grave arranged like a Greek altar, lyre included, but the suddenness of events meant it was unfinished. During the long years he subsequently spent in Rome, Severn attempted to make up for the omission of a more elaborate memorial, as well as recording for posterity as good a death for Keats as the uncomfortable facts allowed.[131] The corner of the graveyard by the wall, once Shelley's ashes too had been transferred to the same nook, became a kind of consecrated ground for the English poetic tradition, and Severn looked after it assiduously – if, some felt, with questionable taste.[132]

And this was the point because, ironically, it was the fact that Keats's experience, expressed in his sensuous and rich language, was so chaste and expectant, but also as it turned out *foreshortened* in sad Mediterranean circumstances, that made his poetry perfectly congruent with the exquisiteness of mid-Victorian feelings and aesthetics. After the middle of the century Keats was to be elevated to the highest plinth in the British cultural pantheon, so that Matthew Arnold put him on a par with Shakespeare.[133] The final revelation in the 1870s of Fanny Brawne's identity as Keats's muse assisted the transformation. In a curious manoeuvre of memorialization, Shelley's posthumous repute was disengaged from Byron – whom he had known so well, if ambiguously – and connected more closely to that of Keats, smoothed by the fact that a copy of Keats's poems had been found stuffed in Shelley's back pocket when his partially clothed body had washed ashore in Viareggio.[134] As a result, the building in Rome where Keats had died – which was immediately, to Severn's disgust, fumigated by the local authorities – is today the Keats-Shelley Memorial House, and attracts many thousands of Anglo-American literary pilgrims every year. Very few of them would think of going to lagoon-washed Missolonghi in western Greece to see the location of Byron's scarcely easier death, from where any physical fragment from 1824 has long since disappeared.[135]

In his final days on the Piazza di Spagna, Keats had not been visited by any of the British artists drifting back into the city since the coming of peace. As after 1802 with the Treaty of Amiens, so the Treaty of Paris in 1814 had unleashed an immediate flood of British travellers escaping from what the *Westminster Review* called their island prison.[136] Napoleon's escape from Elba had then sent some scurrying ingloriously back across the Channel. Only Waterloo made Europe definitively secure for them, and the flow was recommenced on a bigger scale. In 1816, therefore, Byron and Shelley had been among some thousands eager for an experience so long out of reach. The concourse in that year also included one already rather retiring ten-year-old, Elizabeth Barrett, along with her family, who would years later cross the same stretch of water in the most famous British elopement in modern times.

The phenomenon of rediscovering Europe had psychological repercussions, not least because, as one contemporary observed, frantic travel abroad, much of it to the Mediterranean, provided a sort of substitute for the expired excitements of war.[137] The French historian of Italy, Jean-Charles-Léonard Simonde de Sismondi, lamented 'the swarm of English . . . on the rise', a feeling shared by his compatriot and fellow Italy-worshipper, the writer Stendhal.[138] Stendhal had special reasons as an old Bonapartist for believing that the British were now loathed on the Continent for shackling Europe with a restored absolutism. Certainly English manners, often lambasted as arrogant, now became a matter for constantly carping criticism. The post-Waterloo British were relatively rich and seemingly victorious. Such people are rarely popular, and their pound notes became a frequent symbol of satire, tinged perhaps with envy – the most bitter satirical combination of all. The fact that the British themselves were barely conscious of the undertones made the critique all the more telling.

Although in retrospect Rome in the 1820s was to appear as a golden age for the British artist abroad, the reality was more pedestrian. The community was quite small and not particularly illustrious. Its members complained constantly about the superior status of their French counterparts still entrenched in the splendid Villa Medici,[139] and whilst German painters, like the nascent Nazarene community, did not have a palazzo at their disposal either, they had a collective identity and intellectual prestige that the British lacked.[140] To boost their presence the latter set up the British Institute in Rome and sought some form of public subsidy through the Royal Academy. The last thing the Academy wanted, however, was to encourage a rival body into existence, and 'the Roman party' was viewed with disdain in London. The most revealing sign was the unflattering positioning of their pictures when sent home for the annual Academy exhibition. Charles Lock Eastlake was the de facto leader of Anglo-Roman arts in these years, spending ten years in the city, but he was in effect the local agent for Sir Thomas Lawrence, president of the Academy in London. As such, he was not likely to go out on a limb for the new Institute. It was no accident that the final demise of the latter coincided with the return of Eastlake – destined to be one of the figureheads of Victorian public culture – to Britain.[141]

One of the problems of the British 'Romans' was that the foundations of cultural taste back at home were changing, but in ways that were opaque. Classical literature as an inspiration for painters continued, but there was a feeling that it was getting stale.[142] Even the best painters kept plugging away at it, but the strain showed. The recent war had in this sense changed things invisibly but fundamentally. It had made the present – the real world – so much more engrossing and vital. Measured by such events, who cared a straw about Cicero or Plato? It was not the Italy of hazy classicism that many were now interested in, but the Italy of today, the one that Napoleon had strode across with such transformative strides – Italy 'as it is', as yet another travelogue of that country put it even when the fighting at Waterloo had not quite ended.[143]

But capturing Italy 'as it is' visually, or indeed in print, was not an easy task. The eighteenth-century Grand Tourists had found the countryside deeply depressing, depopulated and poverty-stricken. They had no desire to take home any images of it; their preferences were almost entirely urban. William Hazlitt was one critic now calling for fresh subjects to be adopted, and one of the suggestions was to get further out into the country districts.[144] But the Anglo-Roman artists of the 1820s lived in an easy manner that meant this did not come naturally to them. They did not hike across rural Italy in old boots or make long journeys by horse as Edward Lear was to do twenty years later, or indeed as at least one or two solitaries, such as Oliver Goldsmith, had done decades earlier.[145]

Driven by the necessity to respond to a new marketplace, and the fading of aristocratic patronage, one method was to take up some subject or genre with a contemporary feel likely to gel with shifting taste. Eastlake, for example, became famous for his renderings of Italian *banditti*, a subject of much fearful gossip after the notorious murder of a honeymooning English couple when visiting the temples of Paestum in 1825. For Eastlake, *banditti* as a theme had the advantage of providing that frisson of excitement that a British public sated on Byron wanted, whilst keeping clear of anything too sensational.[146] For one thing, both Eastlake and Severn enjoyed social lives in Rome on the margins of the aristocratic whirl presided over in the city by the Countess of Westmorland, just as a similarly Anglo-expatriate, if somewhat more polished, milieu was emerging in Florence under the oversight of the British diplomatic resident, Lord Burghersh, himself a dilettante composer in his spare time.[147] This did not lend itself to a spirit of experimentalism. The reputation of Eastlake – who also specialized in 'fancy' portraits of young British women dressed in Italian costume – as 'The Archbishop' of taste in the world of the visual arts was already taking shape. After getting back to London and becoming a Royal Academician, he stuck rigidly to highly prescribed Italian and Greek themes, where there was little danger of making a false move.[148]

It was logical that, as Waterloo opened the floodgates to cultural tourism from 1815, a counter-reaction was triggered. Not since Hogarth in the 1720s was there such an explicit attack on those who thought that practising the arts, or discovering the acme of beauty, meant going abroad, above all to the Mediterranean. William Wordsworth's rejection of Italian landscape as affording a universal definition of the sublime was made more explicit than ever in his *Guide to the Lakes* (1822), a publication that often accompanied later Victorian generations on their Cumbrian vacations. English skies and their cloud formations offered a distinctive definition of sublimity all their own, he wrote, adding that any inhabitant observing them properly 'will often congratulate himself on belonging to a country of mists and clouds and storms, and make him think of the . . . cerulean vacancy of Italy as an unimaginative and even sad spectacle'.[149]

The most devastating contemporary critique of Mediterranean-worship, however, was by William Hazlitt in an essay entitled 'English Students at Rome' following his own trip there in 1825 (though the fact that he travelled with his wife while the marriage was disintegrating, as all his desperate lunges after love and happiness did sooner or later, was not helpful to his even-mindedness). He found the museums, especially the Vatican, simply too big and disorganized. They lacked the coherence and unity that the Louvre had possessed in the great era of the Musée Napoléon, now partially stripped – not least under British insistence – of many treasures which had been sent back to their original institutions (the Prince Regent personally covered the expenses for repatriating some of the looted artefacts to the papal collections).[150] As for the Anglo-Roman artists themselves, Hazlitt derided their proneness to social diversions, lack of professional seriousness and 'presumptuous self-importance'.[151]

Hazlitt's spleen was extreme. But there was a campaign of muttering against those like Eastlake who could be seen as 'mouldering away' under the Italian sun.[152] This prefigured an analysis that modern critics have taken seriously, to the effect that those British painters who flocked to Italy in the post-Napoleonic era did so 'against the grain of their own genius'.[153] Samuel Palmer provides an example. Deeply influenced by William Blake, he was an artist who in the 1820s, living on the southern English coast, evoked in his watercolours a distinctively native vision of 'the divine vitality of nature, and man's spiritual place amidst landscapes of sacramental golden corn'.[154] But subsequent travel to Italy, and attempts to transpose his visionary Sussex moonscapes and dusky colours to very different atmospherics, really led nowhere. His renderings declined into a kind of gaudy picturesque.[155]

For Britons desperate to find some personal mode of expression for themselves, the Mediterranean did not always hold much appeal. It had none, for example, for John Constable. *The Hay Wain*, displayed at the Paris salon in 1824, was an implicit rejection of 'the Heroic, the Historic or the Grand' and an affirmation of the primacy of native art with, in Constable's mind, its authentic modesty.[156]

These artistic dilemmas came to play a prominent part in the career of somebody with whom Constable famously had a brittle professional relationship: J. M. W. Turner. Turner's great Victorian champion, John Ruskin, was later to contend that his hero's time in Italy, and especially in Rome, had harmed Turner's development by dragging him into the 'false and fantastic world' of Michelangelo and Bernini.[157] Sir Thomas Lawrence persuaded Turner to go to Italy in 1819, arguing that his talents 'want a scene like this'.[158] What Turner had wished for at the time was royal patronage, and some Italian subject matter seemed likely to assist (an unavailing hope as it proved). He went to Italy but at first he was disorientated, as the slightly bizarre, Piranesi-like rendition of *Rome, from the Vatican* suggested. It did not go down well at the Academy.[159] Turner took up antiquity as a theme, but the fact was that antiquity bored him,[160] and it showed a bit in the paintings. The classical river scenes looked like the Thames by Isleworth, which is what he really knew and cared about; whilst his *Venice, Looking East from the Giudecca, Sunrise*, painted in 1819, is hardly distinguishable in general effect from his renderings of the east Kent coast.

On his various trips to Italy thereafter, though not again to Rome after 1828, Turner never seriously got to know any Italians. This was not unusual for expatriate artists, and it must be said that Turner's enigmatic cockneyism posed special challenges for compatriots, let alone foreigners. But what he did do was to read Byron's *Childe Harold* and look closely at the southern light. Turner never met Byron, though they were once in Rome at the same time, but they had one thing in common: their real affinities were essentially eighteenth century. Neither strove to look ahead, because the pathos of the immediate past and present was enough to preoccupy them. It has been said that Turner's images of Italy were a visual filter for Byron's poetry, satiated by 'the beauty of fallen greatness . . . torn between enchantment and melancholy, rapture and heartbreak'.[161] Turner's Venice was 'a distant vision created by atmosphere and light',[162] and it was suggestive that it was instinctively seen *at a distance*: stunning, evoking as Hazlitt remarked 'the first chaos of the world', but not suffused by the immediacy of human sadness of, say, his *Fighting Temeraire*, said by some to have been observed by Turner from Cherry Garden Pier (or thereabouts) in Rotherhithe. In the end the dour but familiar North always drew Turner back.[163] He caught the intensity of the Mediterranean sun, but the effects it set off – as in his *Regulus* (1828) – still remained recognizably English.[164] Turner, like Wordsworth and ironically also like Constable in this respect, was fundamentally a cultural nationalist in feeling that British art had to be grounded firmly in its indigenous setting.

One thing that Turner did which nonetheless helped embed Italian scenes in contemporary British culture was to illustrate Samuel Rogers's poem *Italy*. The stilted Augustanism of this work wilted under later critical tastes, but at the time more than any other evocation of the Mediterranean it struck a popular chord. Rogers had visited Italy in 1815, and the first full edition of the extended poem published in 1828 was based on the journal of that original trip. The publication flopped, but the lavish edition of 1830 with handsome new steel engravings of Turner's images hit the jackpot, and many reissues followed. The combination of travelogue, historical survey, scholarship (even including footnotes), luxuriousness and pictures unusually placed alongside the verses themselves made for something novel. Notably, those fragments of the original journal recording the sheer physical distress of immediate post-war Italy found no jarring place in the later poem. But the visual authenticity, a sustained exploitation of the picturesque – the blue transparent mist along the surface under the black mountains at Naples, or a girl leaning from a balcony in Rome – was turned up a notch.[165]

Byron, who knew Rogers in Italy in 1822, had lampooned the 'finicky elegance' of a man who was also a very rich banker.[166] But by the end of the decade finicky – that is, ostentatiously learned – elegance was coming into vogue. Italian art and landscape offered the perfect foil. Of more long-term significance than Samuel Rogers was Anna Jameson, daughter of a Dublin miniaturist, who in 1826 published *Diary of an Ennuyée*, purporting to be the musings of a young woman struck by both a lost romance and declining health, but experiencing the visual glories of Italian cities. The style prefigured Jameson's later more erudite art criticism with its preference for the ideally beautiful and dislike of any hint of horror.[167] A certain kind of early feminist, Jameson embodied the origins of what became the archetypal Victorian lady with a taste for pleasurably improving reading.[168] Still more important for our subject, however, is that by the end of the 1820s, rebounding from the excesses of Regency England, a new cult of respectability was forming, and with it the implicit notion of culture as a religious sanction.[169] The Dilettanti of Sir William Hamilton's day had admired Italian old masters, with their air of worldly nonchalance, but they did not worship them as people now began to do. There was in this a developed form of social snobbery,[170] but the snobbery was itself only part of an incipient bourgeois order for which the fusing of culture and civilization, with its Mediterranean roots, was a fundamental preconception.

Significantly, the underlying stability of Victorian Britain was closely connected with this phenomenon.

Greece's place in this setting was to remain more unstable than that of Italy. The 'craze' of the early 1800s had flagged. Admittedly, in 1816 a special parliamentary procedure led to the British government purchasing the Elgin Marbles for the nation. Its protagonists hailed the final triumph of pure classicism as a future template for the arts in Britain. Yet the essentially Graeco-Roman character of what was still called 'Grecian taste' in Britain was never really displaced, if only because it was too ingrained. Purism was anyway never the point; the mixing and matching of styles, as championed by Thomas Hope, continued. Although Charles Barry, destined to be Victorian Britain's most distinguished architect, went to Greece with Charles Lock Eastlake in 1818, on his return he tended towards an Italian palazzo style as being more functional for everyday purposes than any imitation of ancient Greek temples.[171] The new building for the Travellers' Club (1829) on Pall Mall, for example, consequently invoked the spirit of the medieval Florentine Republic. As for literature, by the end of the 1820s the myths of Greece began to lose some of their inspirational power, liable to be discounted as merely pretty and fanciful, though the process was gradual and by no means permanent.[172]

The fragile character of Hellenic enthusiasms in Britain outside anything strictly classical and architectural was reflected in the life of Frederick North, the acquaintance of Byron in Greece during 1810.[173] North had succeeded to the peerage as Lord Guilford in 1817, but in 1820 he went off to be director of education in the new British protectorate in the Ionian Islands. There he was responsible for setting up what has been described as the first Greek university in modern times,[174] the Ionian Academy, the official regalia of which was designed by Guilford himself from ancient statues. Given to eccentricity, Guilford was described as going about 'dressed like Plato with a gold band around his mad pate and flowing drapery of a purple hue'.[175] He donated his extensive collections of books and manuscripts to the new Academy's library. Back in England, however, his enthusiasm for anything Hellenic was ridiculed, and although the bestowal of his valuable books was meant to be in perpetuity, when he died in 1827 his heir used a technicality to insist on the return of the collection to London, where it was sold off at auction. Afterwards a generation of

Greek scholars regarded Guilford as having played a key role in the development of modern Greek language and culture, whereas in his home country he was mostly recalled as someone whose constant travelling and curious interests had sent him gradually round the bend.

The ambiguous outcome of Guilford's dedication to Hellenic ideals coincided with a general disillusionment in Britain with the course of the revolution in Greece itself. Some years before, the Tory *Quarterly Review* had noted a greater level of engagement with contemporary Greeks rather than only with their ancient forebears. Instead of being written off as 'degraded and oppressed' by their Ottoman masters, increasingly they had come to be seen as 'in a fair way of rising to something like a level with the inanimate relics that surround them'. This too was perhaps double-edged, but the *Quarterly* went on that, 'as we are assured that the Greeks improve, and are likely to still further improve, we shall become anxious for means of watching their progress, and calculating the chances of success'.[176] Unfortunately, apart from those in Britain who shared the unflagging sympathies of Byron and Guilford, the opinion of most of those who took any interest was that the ensuing revolution – including the horrific mass killing of civilians and prisoners – showed the Greeks as being little if any better than the Ottomans. In such conditions the best to hope for was simply to see the hostilities come to an end as soon as possible. As prime minister, the Duke of Wellington described the sinking of the Ottoman fleet at the Battle of Navarino on 20 October 1827 not as an event to hail, but as 'an untoward event', which was to say *undesirable*;[177] and although, under British surveillance, Greece afterwards crept towards becoming an independent state, it was clear that it would be – and in the opinion of Lord Palmerston as foreign secretary, *should* be – small, indebted and definitely subordinate. We shall see that these doubts about the success of modern Greeks in making a state of their own were not to go away in the decades ahead.

As for Spain, the gloss of the Peninsular War against Napoleon wore off quite rapidly after Waterloo, though Wellington saw to it that for many years afterwards those officers with Peninsula experience creamed off the best promotions in the British Army. The final stages of the Iberia campaign had ended on a note of something close to estrangement between the British and their erstwhile allies the Spanish patriots, reflected in the war poetry generated by the experience.[178] Britain's frail influence in Spanish affairs generally fell away, and despite Byron's own continuing enthusiasm, any sympathy in Britain for the revolution that erupted in Spain in 1820 was scant. Three years later the British looked on, helpless, when the new Bourbon regime in France invaded Spain to restore 'normality', and with it prime French oversight of Spain's future. This was, strikingly, the first assertion of French power abroad after the destruction of Napoleon.

The renewed dip in the rollercoaster of Britain's political engagement with Spain had one rather tawdry postscript. During 1830–1 a number of radically inclined Cambridge friends joined a small band hoping to excite a fresh outbreak against the local Bourbons, and, led by General Torrijos, a London exile from the 1820 outbreak, invaded Spain from Gibraltar. One of this group, Robert Chevenix Trench, a later Archbishop of Dublin, escaped before things went wrong, his young cousin, Robert Boyd, having been captured immediately upon setting foot on Spanish soil and executed alongside Torrijos on Malaga beach in December 1831. When the matter came before Parliament, Foreign Secretary Palmerston remained unmoved, saying only that the executions had been carried out under legitimate Spanish law.[179] Keeping toxic Spanish politics at arm's length was a British trait in the nineteenth and indeed twentieth centuries.

Against this background there was one significant shift of perspective in viewing Spanish history and culture: a new prizing of the medieval Islamic heritage and, in particular, Granada's Alhambra. An ex-Dublin bricklayer, James Cavanah Murphy, played a key role (testimony to how artistic interests and social mobility were interacting more than ever). Murphy had secured some funds from the Royal Irish Academy to continue his real interest in architecture. While engaged on minor diplomatic duties in Cadiz, he focused on the Islamic period. Subsequently in London he drew up his notes on the subject, and although he died in 1814, his large work *The Arabian Antiquities of Spain* was published in parts between 1812 and 1816, with accompanying plates.[180] As a consequence it was an Irishman who thus came to be seen, even by some Spanish scholars, as having originated the Moorish Romantic idea in Hispanic culture that was to be so important in various fields.[181] By 1827, when the American traveller and writer Washington Irving and the Scottish painter David Wilkie (who was trying to shake off a recent nervous breakdown) arrived in Spain more or

Hall of the Abencerrajes of the Alhambra
James Cavanagh Murphy, *Arabian Antiquities of Spain* (1812–16)

less simultaneously, Murphy's work had reframed interest in the Peninsula along oriental lines, though this orientalism, whatever may have become true later, was one that looked back with wistful admiration at the Muslim legacy in Europe.

Irving and Wilkie, who became friends and travelled together, began to explore the folklorist possibilities of Spain as a subject. Another of Wilkie's tasks was to acquire paintings for the Tory politician and art connoisseur Sir Robert Peel, as he had previously done in Italy. But it was also necessary to come up with some Spanish formula that would generate cash by finding an assured market at home, and so Wilkie began a series of paintings of the resistance to the French during the last war, all conceived on a large scale that contrasted with the relatively small scenes of impoverished Scottish life for which he had previously been known. The most famous of these paintings was *The Defence of Saragossa* (1828), featuring the patriotic maid that Byron had heroized in Canto I of *Childe Harold* (at least one of Byron's maids not highlighted for other reasons). Notably in Wilkie's paintings Catholic clergy played prominent roles, writing dispatches in the background, or bravely holding out their crucifixes towards the oncoming enemy. 'The question of Catholic and Protestant I have considered a theme for art,' he said, and that this came from the son of a Scottish Presbyterian minister was suggestive of a crucial flux in religious, and therefore also political, feelings (significantly Wilkie later painted a portrait of Daniel O'Connell, the leader of Catholic Irish nationalism).[182] It was equally telling that these paintings, showing Spanish Catholicism positively, were bought by King George IV himself following Wilkie's return to London in July 1828, having spent, he later reckoned, the most fruitful period of his life in Spain.[183] This was just six months before the final parliamentary triumph of Catholic emancipation, including the all-important royal assent. In Rome, in celebration of that auspicious occasion, the English College was illuminated and *Emancipazione Catholica* spelt out in transparencies across the façade of the palatial building.[184]

There was one Englishman of rather special character, however, who not long afterwards touched Spain on a protracted Mediterranean journey also to recover his broken spirits, the consequences of which in British history were to be full of implications. This was a young writer called Benjamin Disraeli, whose recent novel had not been a brilliant success. That patterns of travel and self-display were adjusting to a post-aristocratic age was indicated by the fact that, whereas Byron had travelled to Italy on land with a cavalcade of carriages and dependants, Disraeli now passed through the Straits of Gibraltar in July 1830 as a lone seaborne passenger, boasting, with his jet-black curls, coloured waistcoats and gold chains, that he was the first to do so 'with two canes, a morning cane and an evening cane' – that is, outrageously vivid and over-embellished, but essentially bourgeois rather than aristocratic.[185] Convinced that his family was of Spanish Sephardic descent, and briefly exploring Andalusia ashore, powerful emotions took hold of him. He wrote home, 'Oh! Wonderful Spain! Think of this romantic land covered with Moorish ruins and full of Murillo! . . . I thought that my enthusiasm was dead within me and nothing could be new. I have hit upon the only country which could have upset everything.'[186] As Disraeli's most distinguished modern biographer notes, this ecstatic reaction to the rich, Eastern tradition of Spain deepened his instinctive fascination with the whole idea of Mediterranean civilization. 'Every further stage in his journey,' Robert Blake adds, 'consolidated this strange love affair.'[187]

It was also a love affair with Byron's memory. Disraeli's father, Isaac, himself a noted literary commentator, had known Byron well, and Disraeli always felt in adulthood that his nature was entwined with the late poet, whose spirit was to pervade his later novels with their constant interweaving of rival essences of North and South.[188] In Malta Disraeli hired Byron's old boatman, Tita Falcieri, and they continued the journey together. In Greece they visited the Romantic destination of Yannina, with its shades of Ali Pasha, but missed out Missolonghi, since Disraeli never had much truck with Hellenism.[189] Having spent some time in Jerusalem – where Disraeli revelled in the proximity of what he felt to be 'the race' from which he came, but without expending time actually meeting any of its members – Disraeli and Tita headed for England, gathering news as they did of a revolution in Paris, and potential commotion in Britain from a looming attempt to reform the parliamentary franchise. On arrival, Disraeli retained the services of Tita, who for many years ahead was to be part of the Disraeli family and political entourage.

Writing of Disraeli's preoccupation throughout his life with 'being Byronic', Fiona MacCarthy argues that it was an impulse 'entangled with Disraeli's own sexual mysteriousness'.[190] It also encompassed the role that a powerful Mediterranean consciousness played in his political mystery; for few modern British leaders at historic junctures had more opaque motivations and methods of operating than Disraeli. Although there is little to be gained from straining excessively to see a connection between Disraeli's travels in 1830–1 and the great political struggles regarding what became known as 'the Eastern Question' – 'East' in this case meaning Turkey – in which he was later to play one of the two main British roles, Robert Blake nonetheless concludes that such a link exists, however imprecisely.[191] It is striking that the two political giants of Victorian Britain, Benjamin Disraeli and William Gladstone, were both men whose interests and natures were deeply affected by the Mediterranean, though their approaches differed entirely through temperament and spiritual bent as well as party affiliation. The powerful interaction between the United Kingdom and Europe's southern margins, both culturally and politically, was clearly, then, not going away. It was, indeed, to help make British Victorians what they were, and to affect how they expressed and defined their inner as well as public lives.

Chapter Four

BLUE SOLITUDES

THE MEDITERRANEAN AND THE SHAPING OF VICTORIAN BRITAIN, 1830–60

No rampart excludes
Your eye from the life to be lived
In the blue solitudes.

> Robert Browning, 'The Englishman in Italy', 1845

What has inspired me with all sorts of strange reflections . . . is the thought that I am on the Mediterranean – for how much is implied in that one circumstance!

> John Henry Newman, 1833

John Steegman, a historian of Victorian culture, wrote as follows about the faltering of the 'Rule of Taste' that, in some rough and ready way, shaped aesthetic preconceptions in Britain in the late eighteenth and early nineteenth centuries:

The Rule was showing signs of breaking down before the death of George IV in 1830, and during the reign of William IV it may be said to have collapsed. The passing of the Reform Bill in 1832 could be cited as the point at which the collapse began, for it is one of those convenient labels with which historians like to mark off an epoch.[1]

This cultural flux was one in which Mediterranean connections continued to reverberate powerfully. During the early and middle years of Queen Victoria's reign – she ascended the throne in 1837 – the poetry of Elizabeth Barrett Browning was to rhapsodize the struggle for Italian national freedom as a metaphor for individual liberation. The most acclaimed object at the Great Exhibition of 1851, a defining event of the mid-Victorian climax, was undoubtedly Joseph Paxton's Crystal Palace building itself;[2] but arguably the most discussed artefact inside was *The Greek Slave*, a sculpture by Hiram Powers, an American artist based in Rome, which mixed exquisite sentiment, classicism and alluring sensuality.[3] The classic statement of British liberalism in the nineteenth century, John Stuart Mill's *On Liberty*, was, the author claimed, first conceived as a theme when mounting the steps of the Capitol in Rome in January 1855 (though there was, perhaps, a conscious desire here to echo Edward Gibbon, who in his autobiography stated that the idea of his own great work on the decline and fall of the Roman Empire came to him in a flash of inspiration on the same spot on 15 October 1764).[4] Such instances could be almost endlessly listed.

None of this meant that the Mediterranean exerted a uniformly positive pull. The mere mention of Rome could for many Britons still trigger negative vibrations – 'odious; built on shams' was the response of the novelist George Eliot on a visit.[5] When *Punch* discussed the foreign influences that the Great Exhibition at Crystal Palace might bring into the country, scrofula from Naples, mumps from Greece, rickets from Spain and scarlet fever from Italy's Papal States were highlighted.[6] But when British people wanted to articulate their deepest uncertainties and aspirations, it was to Mediterranean analogies past and present that they continued to turn. Growing materiality reinforced this orientation. In *Little Dorrit* (1855–7) the house of the Meagles family in Twickenham was described by Charles Dickens as a 'lumber room' of art and impedimenta drawn from that region – tessellated pavement from Pompeii, Roman cameos, Spezian straw hats, Spanish fans, images of Egyptian gods and pharaohs. Victorian generations grew up surrounded by such object matter with all their associations.

Any discussion of Victorian cultural life is hindered by a stereotype: that it was an age of intimidating confidence and national, increasingly imperial, certainties. The truth was very different. Leading Victorians were wracked by fears of individual and collective decay and outright break-down, often fomented by disturbing Mediterranean experience, real or imagined. This had religious, mental and sexual connotations that we shall come to. But from the outset of this period there was also fear of political dissolution. We saw that by the time the flamboyant young Benjamin Disraeli returned from his southern European and Levantine travels Britain was already entering a severe domestic crisis. In July 1830 the Bourbon regime in France collapsed at the barricades. The Orléanist regime of King Louis-Philippe succeeded to power in Paris. Contamination by disorder from France always cast a shadow over British affairs.

Regime change in France coincided with a backlash against the reac-tionary, hyper-aristocratic style of Regency England. The massively popular 'silver fork' novels of the day epitomized an ugly social reality characterized by foppery and an arrogant flaunting of wealth. The activist George Grote who, to appease earlier disappointments about a new political dawn, had retreated into writing about ancient Greece as a template for Britain's condition, remarked that by mid-1831 agitated public feeling was at a height resembling that in France before 1789.[7] In England protest took the form of rick-burning and cattle-maiming – the 'Captain Swing' riots. A Whig ministry elected in September 1831 was jolted into framing legis-lation on the old 'rotten' franchises to quieten matters down. The perilous question of the Great Reform Act crisis of 1831–2 had arrived.

For our purposes, it is axiomatic that this crisis was as much cultural as political in nature. In targeting aristocratic hegemony, radical reformers struck at the existing structure of British life. The middling classes were mostly as determined to see the end of that hegemony as any impoverished farm labourer or urban radical. Yet aristocratic values, bound up with assumptions and hierarchies secreted within the word 'civilization', was another matter. Indeed, the nub of Whig policy was to disentangle rational and moderate reform from the dictates of what Prime Minister Lord Grey, writing to King William IV, typified as the 'irrational mob'.[8] A descent into chaos loomed when the House of Lords threw out legislation on a reformed electoral system in May 1832. At this stage the critical role was played by the Duke of Wellington's successor as Tory leader, Robert Peel. It was his refusal to head a government of outright reaction that allowed a fresh Whig cabinet to push a reformed parliamentary franchise through

Parliament a few weeks later. No other single event was to be so crucial in the genesis of the long Victorian equipoise in the nineteenth century, though it did not feel like that at the time.

Peel's centrality to the reform outcome of 1832 is suggestive, however, because it had implications for the role of culture and the state in shaping a new national stability. The historian Antonia Fraser has drawn a connection with the National Gallery whose relocation to a new building in Trafalgar Square, itself the result of reconfiguring the adjacent street neighbourhood in the 1820s, was decided in Parliament simultaneously alongside the enlarged franchise. The National Gallery had been set up in 1823 to meet the criticism that Britain still had no public institution for the fine arts to compare with the Louvre in France, operating by open admission rather than a socially exclusive system of tickets. Its foundation came about when the British government paid £57,000 to endow the Gallery with paintings – mainly by Italian artists such as Titian and Raphael, but also more unusually the Spanish master Velázquez – bequeathed by Sir John Julius Angerstein, a Russian émigré who had played a vital role in the infant Lloyd's insurance market. Initially situated in Angerstein's old house in Pall Mall, parliamentary legislation was required to facilitate the Gallery's move to larger premises of Greek Revival design by William Wilkins. Part of the rationale was that the revamped Trafalgar Square was where the rich families of the West End overlapped with the popular classes further east, or, as Peel said, borrowing an expression from Samuel Johnson in arguing this case, where 'the great tide of human existence flowed' through the city.[9] In the same way a new conception of state-sponsored arts might form a bridge across the social divides of which current political instability had given such disturbing proof.

Robert Peel's support for the expanded National Gallery combined a reluctant acceptance of political change with a telling indication of how it might be contained.[10] He was a man whose own collection of paintings, acquired as a side effect of so much European turmoil during his lifetime, was said to be the thing in his life that he most prized; he had been advised in his purchases at one point by David Wilkie fresh from his Spanish travels. 'In the present times of political excitement,' Peel told the House of Commons at the end of July 1832, 'the exacerbation of angry and unsocial feelings might be much softened by the effects which the fine arts had

ever produced upon the minds of men.'[11] In this he echoed a recent assertion by the connoisseur Allan Cunningham in his *Lives of the Most Eminent
British Painters* that the mob only ceased to be a mob when they acquired
taste.[12] The concept of taste as a tangible whole – so quintessentially eighteenth century in origin – was already dissolving. But even such a sharp
critic of exclusivity as William Thackeray, whose *Vanity Fair* (1847–8)
portrayed that system with searing accuracy, still felt that the social goods
of fine arts and civilization were so essential to continued public order that
on those grounds alone the British aristocracy, who embodied their values,
needed to be retained.[13] On such grounds aristocratic influences, instead
of disappearing altogether, continued to flow freely and became enmeshed
in the shibboleths of the emerging Victorian middle class.[14] Those influences, in their cultural form, always had a deep Mediterranean imprint.

One ambitious newly elected member of parliament during the crisis of
1831–2 was the controversial young writer Edward Bulwer Lytton. He was
a passionate advocate of radical change – albeit change to be guided by a
new cultural elite of which he saw himself as the embodiment – but had
been shocked by how close the country had just come to implosion. In
thrashing about for a theme to evoke, as dramatically as possible, the
continuing dangers of social decay and wholesale dissolution, Bulwer
Lytton dipped into Roman history. With this idea crystallizing in his
mind, he set off in the autumn of 1833 with his wife Rosina, an heiress
originally from County Tipperary, on a leisurely honeymoon to Italy
delayed by rifts in the marriage that had appeared almost as soon as the
couple emerged through the doors of St James's, Piccadilly. Italy unfortunately did nothing for the relationship. Neither felt settled, and Rosina
wrote to a friend, 'Poets ought to be strangled for all the lies they have told
about this country.'[15] In Naples, witnessed by a house servant who was
drawn into the legal divorce tussle that went on for years, Edward allegedly
beat his wife 'black and blue'.[16] One writer ascribes significance to Rosina's
implacable quest for revenge – principally by impugning Bulwer Lytton's
name in any way that came to mind, including allegations of sodomy with
Benjamin Disraeli[17] – in the 'unresolved nineteenth-century war between
the sexes' in Britain.[18] Mediterranean experiences were to consistently
impact on the shifting identities of at least some elite portions of Victorian
womanhood.

Something else occurred during the Lyttons' wretched stay in Naples: Edward set about drafting a fictional tale set amid the destruction of the bustling town of Pompeii, engulfed in the eruption of Mount Vesuvius in AD 79. His researches on the subject were superficial, but he had the benefit of being conducted around Naples by the aged Sir William Gell, whose publication *Pompeiana* had summarized much of the information produced by the long-standing excavations. The ancient domesticity, with its rich human dimension, that had been revealed allowed Bulwer Lytton to evoke for readers an effective if bogus intimacy with the fate of the town.[19] By the time he left Naples the manuscript was virtually complete, and it was published as *The Last Days of Pompeii* in London in July 1834 with a dedication to Gell. It ended up becoming the biggest publishing sensation of the century in Britain. No other work of fiction went through so many impressions, including sixteen in France during its first thirty years. An Italian film version (*Gli ultimi giorni di Pompei*) in 1908, loosely based on Bulwer Lytton's text, inaugurated the genre of the historical epic on the big screen that was to be such a feature of twentieth-century entertainment. The sheer immediacy of Bulwer Lytton's imagery, because it was florid and overdrawn to an extent that a later generation found hard to take, was also why the critic G. K. Chesterton wrote of Lytton that 'You could not have the Victorian Age without him'.[20]

Bulwer Lytton's novel portrayed a Roman town caught in a vortex of luxury, hedonism and corruption whose heedless rush towards physical as well as moral extinction was symbolized by the boiling lava careering down the Vesuvian slopes. The central figure of the melodrama was not actually Roman or Pompeian, but the Egyptian priest Arbaces, combining 'the three great Victorian sins of religious hypocrisy, sexual degeneracy and foreignness'.[21] More immediately it was a parody of Regency excess, burgeoning consumerism and the shaky foundations of William IV's England. Arguably its principal effect – one that was to be constantly recycled in Victorian culture – evoked the trembling eroticism of life-in-death, epitomized by the last desperate clawing movements of the human form encased in molten material. After *The Last Days in Pompeii*, art forms of any kind in Britain, if they were to be successful, had to be *visual* in a more direct way – what one writer terms the Victorian 'visualization of experience'.[22] In this sense the apparent archaism of Bulwer Lytton's writing –

despised by Thackeray for its self-conscious finery[23] – was in fact quite modern. Strikingly, Disraeli was once said to have remarked that Bulwer Lytton was 'among the two or three persons whose minds had exercised a distinct effect upon his own',[24] an effect not least of a Mediterranean-tinged exoticism. His vision of Pompeii's fate captured an anxiety of national *dégringolade* and a deep uneasiness within the British political order that was always ready to reignite.

Intense religiosity was sometimes part of this volatility, though it was to take many forms. Scepticism stemming from strictly rational and historical scholarship about the Bible appearing in Germany was already unsettling minds in Britain, although this phenomenon was to become more prominent later. But much more immediate was the way in which debates about reform raised questions concerning the privileges of the established churches in England and Ireland. In such a milieu one Englishman's Mediterranean voyage laid claim to being the most important single visit of its kind during the nineteenth century, because it bore directly on shifts central to Victorian public culture. This was that of the thirty-one-year-old John Henry Newman, who was to play a key role in Catholic revival in Britain and end up a Roman cardinal. A Fellow of Oriel College and ordained as an Anglican priest, Newman by the end of the 1820s was already steeped in his reading of the primitive Church in the early centuries after Christ. For Newman, fear of revolution was wrapped up with 'how to prevent the [Anglican] Church from being liberalized' alongside the Westminster Parliament.[25] As the crisis of parliamentary reform peaked he was already undergoing what he described as 'inward change' – one towards a new reformation, or even counter-reformation, of the Anglican order – when he was invited to go on a Mediterranean tour by his college friend James Froude.

They set out onboard ship from Falmouth on 8 December 1832. On reaching Mediterranean waters Newman's spirits were already elevated, as he mused on the centrality of that sea in world history where Romans had fought Carthaginians, Phoenicians had plied their trade and St Paul had been shipwrecked. These sentiments became decidedly feverish off the coast of Corfu, where Newman felt 'full of joy to overflowing – for I am in the Greek Sea, the scene of old Homer's song'.[26] On the island he was impressed by the fervency of local Orthodox clergy with their strict regime of fasting. These powerful whirling feelings on Newman's part were undoubtedly sincere. One later account of Newman's theological trajectory, however, accounts for them in part as arising from his suppressed desire for his travelling companion – Newman having taken a vow of celibacy due to his preoccupation with a projected scheme for Anglican monasticism.[27]

The pair of friends next headed for Sicily, 'drawn', Newman said, 'as by a lodestone'. Visiting ruined hilltop temples in classical landscapes impressed on him the genius of early Greek worship, and perhaps archaic Greek ways more widely. From Sicily they crossed the Strait of Messina and travelled to Naples, though Newman found the 'animal gratification' of the city offensive. This revulsion against Neapolitan life amongst British visitors was to become more general as evangelical moralism infiltrated the Victorian mentality.[28] It was in Naples, too, that the friends heard of the Irish Church Reform Bill back in England, which Newman confessed made him 'hate . . . the Whigs . . . more bitterly than ever'.[29] Mediterranean travel did not always provide the medicine for a troubled mind that the poet Samuel Rogers had recently claimed.[30]

Inevitably, Rome was the climax for what had become a kind of itin-erant meditation on Newman's future life. But precisely because he took the state of the Catholic Church in Rome itself as being a measure of where his own benighted English Church was heading,[31] Newman's senti-ments cut in conflicting directions. He believed that Rome as a city was 'still under a curse', and the Church there cruel in its demands on followers. But at the same time he felt drawn towards its rituals and worship, and began to make a distinction between Rome as a *place*, which he abhorred almost as much as Naples, and as a *Church*, to which he felt himself impelled. In early April 1833 Newman and Froude had an interview with Nicholas Wiseman, the rector of the English College, an institution which had reopened in Rome in 1819 after years of dereliction, and which had thrived in recent years, its clerical students often to be seen walking arm in arm in their regular collective afternoon promenades through the city.[32] This meeting was a notable occasion because Wiseman, Spanish-born but with Irish antecedents, was to have an impact on religious life in Britain running in parallel with that of Newman himself, though the relationship between two such different men – Wiseman approachable and enjoying the conviviality of a good dinner table, Newman ascetic and sometimes conflictual – was to be far from close. Certainly their conversation in Rome did not clarify the doctrinal and practical dilemmas that disturbed Newman's thoughts.

It was in this highly ambiguous but excited state that, when Froude left for England, Newman decided to return to Sicily. He did so because, as he wrote, whereas Italy as a country left him cold, 'Greece has ever made my heart beat, and Sicily is Greece in a way'.[33] The beating of the heart was due to the paganism of ancient Greek rites, and from them the comforting deduction in the face of contemporary secular challenges that man was an instinctively religious being, even before Old Testament Christianity had appeared. In Catania Newman endured a nearly fatal fever that he interpreted as an intervention by the Devil to prevent him returning home to undertake an as yet undefined mission.[34] The days and nights of sweat and agonized tossing and turning he later recalled as the determining factor in his later development; it divided his life in two, and he wrote about it for years afterwards.[35] This Sicilian climax had not decided Newman between the pulls of Anglicanism and Romanism, but it gave him a sense that time was short. Once back in England, he was to set out on a long journey during which, as the leading light of the Oxford Movement (arguably the most controversial phenomenon in Victorian public life), he was to try and make Anglo-Catholicism a tolerable *via media*, before giving up and finally being received into the Catholic rite by an Italian Passionist missionary in Birmingham in September 1845. The repercussions in early Victorian England of this most famous conversion to Catholicism were to be very powerful.

These episodes embody ways in which Mediterranean experiences cut across emotional and intellectual currents in Britain on the cusp of Victorianism. In the context of southern European travel this was a distinct era between the liquidation of the old Grand Tour and the later spread of railways across the region in the 1860s, bringing mass tourism in their wake. In social terms it was a shift from a still dominant aristocratic ethos to one that was overwhelmingly bourgeois. In these decades Italy remained an echo chamber for a huge variety of British sensibilities. But both the timing and the tone of this engagement fluctuated. After the convulsions in Britain in 1831–2, what the propertied classes wanted was a respite from the shadow of any upheaval, near or far. Italian secret societies, revolutionary oaths and desire to exploit some wider conflagration in Europe in the cause of their own national freedom and unification – aspirations which had once appealed to the aristocratic radicalism of Byron and Shelley – now cut Italy off to some degree from middle-class British sympathies. John Ruskin, the art critic whose ties with Italy, and above all with Austrian-occupied Venice, eventually framed one of the quintessential expressions of refined Victorian feeling, remarked, 'For a long time I regarded the Austrians as the only protection of Italy from utter dissolution.'[36] The Venetians themselves, he also once stated, were 'a horde of banditti'.[37] Not all Ruskin's compatriots shared this bias by any means, but for most Britons the movement for Italian liberty – far from being 'the cause of a generation', as has sometimes been claimed[38] – was something to keep at a very discreet distance, if they did not necessarily welcome its complete suffocation.

Botched local uprisings and authoritarian crackdowns in Italian states continued to bring a stream of distressed exiles to Britain during the 1830s and 1840s, adding to those of the immediate post-1815 generation. They came to constitute a distinct, if marginal, feature of London intellectual life in a way that their Spanish counterparts never did (though a greater awareness in Britain of the art of Francisco Goya has been attributed to the prints that the Spanish brought with them).[39] Spanish exiles rarely attracted much patronage. On one occasion Thomas Carlyle observed such a group in their usual haunt of Euston Square, looking pinched and threadbare.[40]

In contrast the Italians were mostly middle class and better equipped to make their way in London society, including the circles around Lord and Lady Holland ('the Holland House set'), that epitome of Whig elitism. The philosophic radicalism that went with this particular turf came naturally to exiles like Ugo Foscolo and Giuseppe Pecchio.[41] Still, occasional good dinners and an invitation to contribute an article to liberally inclined journals like the *Westminster Review* did not keep body and soul together. Language teaching often helped supplement incomes when it was still true that some knowledge of Italian was a token of the genteel educated Englishman.[42] A whole generation of Victorian political leadership – Gladstone (who translated portions of Dante), Palmerston, Grey, Russell, Derby and many others – possessed a reasonable proficiency in at least reading in the language.[43] As for women, Italian, far more than, say, the dead classical languages, was often a part of the curriculum in girls' schools, supplemented by private tutors, 'a relic', one historian remarks, 'of the eighteenth-century conception of Italian as a "light and frivolous language", best suited to sonneteers and tender lovers'.[44] If sometimes it was remarked that Italian instructors had a habit of falling in love with their English pupils, this only fitted a lasting stereotype.[45]

The galling dependence of an exiled existence, however, could prove too much, and it was easy to fall by the wayside. Foscolo died in poverty in Turnham Green.[46] Keeping up a respectable family life was a hard struggle even for somebody with a university position like Dante Gabriel Rossetti, and quite likely it was having to listen to the endless homesick complaints of Italian residents spending their evenings in the Rossetti parlour close to Tottenham Court Road that persuaded the young Gabriel, later a founder of the Pre-Raphaelite movement, never to go to Italy himself.[47] But for an exile like Antonio Panizzi, who had perseverance, ability and a thick skin, it was possible to go far. With the help of the radical Whig leader, Lord Brougham, Panizzi initially got a position as assistant librarian at the British Museum in 1828, and gradually worked his way up, though taking British nationality did not stop his Italian roots being used to try and block his promotion in 1836 – opposition aired in *The Times* – and his appointment as principal librarian in 1856.[48] Those who opposed his frenetic pursuit of bringing the library up to date could always seek to undermine him, for instance calling him a 'vagabond Italian'.[49]

Navigating a path through the Victorian professional labyrinth required intense caution for such an outsider. Panizzi avoided any expression of sympathy for Italian revolution abroad, and he kept a distant relationship with his fellow exile and extreme nationalist Giuseppe Mazzini. But these qualities of calculated moderation, summed up by one contemporary observer as the quintessence of liberal Italianate Englishness in the nineteenth century,[50] won such respect that Panizzi's bust was finally erected by colleagues in a niche above the entrance to the Reading Room, where it remained until the British Library was moved from Great Russell Street to Euston in 1997. John Morley, who knew Gladstone intimately, wrote in his seminal biography that Gladstone's enthusiasm for Italian liberty was owed not least to Panizzi's influence on him on a matter that crucially defined the origins of the modern British Liberal Party.[51]

Giuseppe Mazzini is particularly relevant here because he provided a significant touchstone in the shaping of mid-Victorian political culture.

That it was possible for an Italian to do so at all is notable. It would not have been so at a later period. Having been embroiled in a series of failed insurrections in the name of 'Young Italy' (*La Giovine Italia*), whose unluckier participants ended up in front of firing squads, Mazzini came to live in London in 1837. The authorities kept him under surveillance, and the revelation that the Foreign Office had been opening his letters and allegedly passing information that led to more executions in Calabria proved highly sensitive. For some in Britain, the republican fervour of Mazzinian rhetoric was alienating. Although the Italian was a regular visitor to the household of Thomas Carlyle in Chelsea, the latter dismissed Mazzini's evocative calls on behalf of his oppressed homeland as 'rosewater imbecilities' and pressed him to focus more on literary than political subjects.[52] On one occasion, when both were invited for tea at the lodgings of the visiting American journalist and writer Margaret Fuller, Carlyle subjected Mazzini to a particularly rough assault on his libertarian ideals (Carlyle himself only supporting any liberal cause when it was safely wrapped in the past). Suggestively, Jane Carlyle, also present, noted afterwards that what were but opinions to her truculent husband were to Mazzini, caught up in a struggle where friends and accomplices had gone to the scaffold, matters of life and death.[53] Fuller's own decision to go to Italy, with ultimately tragic consequences for herself and her later family,[54] was much influenced by Mazzini's encouragement.

In one important respect, living in London affected Mazzini's perspective. It gave him a social awareness that previously had not been evident. A Genoese bourgeois through and through, in Italy he had hardly had any dealings with working-class compatriots. Ironically, it was only when Mazzini came to London, where he developed a taste for English tweed suits, that he also discovered the human face of an Italian proletariat in cameo. The Italian community in London in the early nineteenth century, congregated around Holborn, had consisted mainly of craftsmen making looking glasses, picture frames and precision instruments. At their social apex were the designers and fresco artists with whom the Adam brothers and some other Grand Tourists had returned as part of their paraphernalia.

Grinding social conditions in Italy during and after the Napoleonic wars, however, brought many poor Italians, often from the south of the country, to London, where they scraped a living by playing street music on harps, fiddles, hurdy-gurdies and barrel organs, with white mice or even a monkey to add to the entertainment.[55] Clerkenwell became the centre of this Victorian 'Little Italy'.[56] The social evils connected with a white slave trade in young organ players attracted notoriety and triggered a famous court case in 1845. Mazzini set up a school for poor Italian boys and girls in Hatton Garden, supported by a donation from Lord Byron's widow, though it only lasted for a few years.[57] Given the conditions, crime became associated with districts where the gaggle of men and boys on street corners sometimes gave a Neapolitan feel. It was not accidental that the den of young thieves in Dickens's *Oliver Twist* was located in Field Street, on the borders of Clerkenwell, whose long-standing reputation for disorderliness assumed an extra layer.

Such an assumed link between an Italian presence and criminality had a wider aspect. What had become the classic preconception of Italy in the British Romantic imagination was soft-focused, feminized and passive, so much so that it had been subject to parody.[58] But by the 1840s the literary market was saturated with these fuzzy effects. Readership was growing and changing rapidly. Its more varied social makeup meant a desire for greater edginess and realism as well as impatience with the flowery and the insipid. Thackeray captured this mood when he wrote, 'How long are we to go on with Venice, Verona, Lago di so-and-so, Ponta di what-d'you call 'em?'[59] Similarly the craze for Italian opera in Regency times now sagged. Its exclusivity – a tight cabal of promoters and overpaid imported singers – was out of sync with the times, whilst wall-to-wall Rossini had become tedious.[60] Although the Theatre Royal in Covent Garden reopened in 1847 as the Royal *Italian* Opera, a newly restless musical audience started to demand some variation from productions overstuffed with lyrical frills and unconvincing plots (oddly enough, this was in some ways simply a repeat of a cycle already gone through in the 1730s).[61] This meant a turn to French and German opera, though the process was to take some time before maturing in the age of Wagner.[62]

This did not mean, as has been said by one writer, that interest in Italian themes 'died of exhaustion'.[63] But it did mean that in selecting an Italian theme it had to serve some specific purpose, and preferably possess a different mood-music. The young poet Robert Browning indicated fresh directions, though it was not to win him much praise for some time. G. K. Chesterton in his brief but characteristically astute biography, writing in 1903 when the issues raised had assumed new meanings, pinned down something about Browning that is worth quoting because of its wider sense:

> There are thousands of educated Europeans who love Italy, who live in it, who visit it annually, who come across a continent to see it, who hunt out its darkest picture and its most mouldering carving; but they are all united in this, that they regard Italy as a dead place. It is a branch of their universal museum, a department of dry bones . . . they keep Italy as they might keep an aviary or a hothouse, into which they might walk whenever they wanted a whiff of beauty. Browning did not feel at all in this manner; he was intrinsically incapable of offering such an insult to the soul of a nation. If he could not have loved Italy as a nation, he would not have consented to love it as an old curiosity shop . . . he is interested in the life in things.[64]

But in being interested in life, Browning had an acute sense of its blemishes and failures as much as any beauty or fulfilment it might have. His first trip to Italy was in June 1838 and, looking back much later, it was in Asolo that Browning felt he discovered his own lasting preoccupations.[65] Prime amongst these was the nature and decay of sexual love.[66] In *Sordello* (1840) the first glimmerings were reflected obliquely in the bare-legged beggar girls from Venice and Padua who hang around the narrator as he recites a winding narrative of medieval Italy, the very obscurity of which embodied Browning's dawning realization that truth and meaning have no fixed centre but fluctuate according to circumstances, relationships and opportunities.[67] Young girls, too, were central to 'The Englishman in Italy', one of whom, Fortú, sits on the Englishman's knee as he reflects on the seductive naturalism in Italian life symbolized by its rich harvest – ripe pomegranates, pulpy red love-apples, purple slices of gourd, glossy and luscious fruit-balls – as preparations are made for the Feast of the Virgin on the following day. His thoughts, physical in every sense, might, he concludes, be considered trifling, but for one thing:

> Fortú, in my England at home,
> Men meet gravely today

And debate, if abolishing Corn-laws
Be righteous and wise.

Typically with Browning, seemingly casual and banal throwaway lines enshrine the heart of the matter: in Italy a world of fecundity proceeds according to eternal rhythms, whereas his England was increasingly dead-locked over how to respond to political and social dilemmas. On one side an organic, holistic naturalism undimmed by complex choices; on the other, a killing preoccupation with public policy amidst the contradictions of a rapidly industrializing nation.

Such a contrasting duality of Britain and Italy entered into the inspiration of the poem that many were to consider as Robert Browning at his finest. This was *Pippa Passes*, appearing in his first, if still modestly, successful collection *Bells and Pomegranates* (1841). The poem traced the experience of Pippa, a poor young silk winder from Asolo, who walks on her only day off during the year through the neighbourhood, singing as she goes. Those she meets on the way often contrast with her innocent naivety. Browning's first biographer said that the story actually originated with a girl he had seen idling in a wood in Dulwich on London's southern reaches, and the image had flashed on Browning's mind of a young female walking through life, with traps at every turn.[68] One literary historian remarks: 'The precision of these images helps explain why Browning could never have set "Pippa Passes" in Dulwich. He may perhaps have watched shop girls there chatting but never with the fascination that they had for him in Asolo where they represented not only the new and the exotic, but the forbidden . . . For him Italy held the excitement of evil.'[69]

The reason perhaps goes deeper still. Charles Dickens was about to describe poverty and want inside English society with a directness that was novel and sometimes grated with his critics but which was accepted by the public as having moral legitimacy. But to explore sexuality and evil, as Robert Browning was setting out to do – as he put it in the poem 'Bishop Blougram's Apology', 'Our interest's in the dangerous edge of things' – it was necessary to look rather more distantly for a context since otherwise any hope of a sympathetic and receptive public at home might all too easily evaporate. Browning himself said, 'Italy is stuff for the use of the North, no more', by which he meant writers from northern Europe like himself, whatever their purposes may be; but the 'stuff' in his case, far from being merely sexually touristic, as has been argued, broke moral and intellectual ground.[70] The Italian setting allowed him to get away with it, just about.

Robert Browning's subsequent marriage to fellow poet Elizabeth Barrett and their clandestine flight, the most celebrated real-life love story in nineteenth-century Britain, was in line with his own mental cast. 'He was . . . true to his vision,' it has been said about Robert Browning's enigmatic persona, 'the poet erecting beauty in his mistress by his love of her.'[71] The love began in London's Wimpole Street – against the background of the 'verriest slavery' of Mr Barrett senior's patriarchal domination[72] – but was largely played out in Florence, where after a sudden departure in the early summer of 1847 (accompanied part of the way by the art critic Anna Jameson) the couple settled down in a villa apartment, Casa Guidi, directly opposite the Palazzo Pitti. With its gilt armchairs and marble consoles it was so different from the gloomy décor of Wimpole Street. It was from the balcony there, amid mounting unrest at Habsburg oppression, that in early 1849 Elizabeth watched a lively political demonstration. In *Casa Guidi Windows* (1851) she crafted the most lyrical description of popular protest in nineteenth-century English literature, but it was also a lyricism of motherhood – she had given birth to her own 'Florentine boy', Pen, on 9 March 1849[73] – and an implied comparison with the triumphant, but to her merely pedestrian, commercialism of the Great Exhibition currently dominating public interest back in Britain.

This was the start of a literary fame that in Elizabeth's lifetime eclipsed that of her husband.[74] Ironically, later on her aesthetic style and (some said) ill-judged political emotion was to find critics: Henry James was one who felt that her commitment to Italy had been a liability for her art.[75] Robert Browning was always more guarded about swirling contemporary events,[76] and once the tide turned against the springtime of revolt in Florence, as elsewhere in Italy and Europe, Elizabeth confessed to a 'certain political latitudinarianism . . . creeping over me',[77] by which she meant toleration of Austrian military occupation. But in *Casa Guidi Windows* Elizabeth had already hinted broadly that the surface of politics was not anyway the main thing. The fictive observer in the poem has herself grown weary of looking at the scene in the piazza below and eventually retreats behind closed shutters with the rumination, 'souls have inner lights'. For Elizabeth those lights were not essentially political, which was probably why the publication attracted little interest in the Italian reviews.[78] Her own *social* beliefs were anyway instinctively conservative. When visited at Casa Guidi by Margaret Fuller, although the two women took to each other, Elizabeth afterwards noted that the American was 'one of those out and out Reds, and scorners of grades of society'.[79]

Siding with Italian hopes was for Elizabeth Barrett Browning really a metaphor for healing wounds of a very intimate nature,[80] wounds that had been inflicted in another place entirely. This was an exploration carried further in *Aurora Leigh* (1856), with its more direct implications for the concerns of Victorian women.[81] The Brownings, indeed, wrote about different things. She could not easily grasp the evil that fascinated him, and he could not truly empathize with the strident public engagements that had, so unexpectedly, liberated her inner being and made her opium habit redundant.[82] They came to live essentially separate, though still mutually devoted, lives at Casa Guidi, occasionally at odds as to how to dress the infant Pen, Robert preferring sober trousers and short hair, and Elizabeth, whose considerable royalties kept the household afloat financially, insisting on velvet pantaloons and large curls.[83] In a way, the psychological predispositions this reflected were the same that framed contrasting approaches

Elizabeth Barrett Browning

to Italian political nationalism. But for both of them Italy was a necessary instrumentality – their shared 'dangerous edge of things' – that the accident of life had thrown in their path.

Although the Brownings were drawn into the expatriate community around them in Florence, they were far from being its heart. That was the Villino Trollope, after 1843 the home of the novelist and travel writer Mrs Fanny Trollope and her extended family.[84] Fanny Trollope's books rivalled in mass popularity even those of Charles Dickens. Anthony Trollope, one of her younger sons, who spent some time at the Florence villa, later drew a good deal on characters and themes in his mother's fiction, so that the classic Trollopian world of the cathedral close, middle-class mores and strong-minded women that has so shaped a certain vision of Victorian England was in fact first conjured up in a Tuscan milieu.[85]

This was just one instance of Anglo-Florentine residues in later Victorian culture. The rich allegories of the painter George Frederic Watts, who was to be a major influence on later symbolist art in Britain, also took shape in Florence. First arriving at the old Medici-built Villa Careggi of Lord and Lady Holland for a few days in 1843, Watts ended up staying there until 1847.[86] Lady Holland saw it as her task to encourage the young man's art in approved directions. In such ways aristocratic patronage survived into a bourgeois age. Watts recast himself, as a self-portrait made at Villa Careggi epitomizes, into a self-consciously Renaissance man just when the very term 'Renaissance' – the capital letter was important – as a way of describing an era in medieval Italian history was taken up for the wider purposes of charting the emergence of Western civilization (as a term it had scarcely any currency before this period).[87] The label was to be endlessly recycled in British cultural debates, though again, like 'Romanticism', it was an essentially nineteenth-century construction of vague meaning, though one that proved in the end too useful as a tool of analysis to give up even when later scholars queried its veracity.[88]

The Anglo-Florentine milieu was to leave a special legend behind – what Henry James summed up as an 'excess of serenity'.[89] It was the result of a particular conjuncture. There had long been a British presence in the city. In 1781 Mrs Thrale, visiting with her Italian husband after a marriage that so crushed the last romantic hopes of Samuel Johnson, had found an English inn cheerfully serving up a 'Dish of Beans and Bacon, and Currant

Tart' (James's serenity was to come later).[90] Florence was usually seen as lacking the allure of Rome and Naples, in fact as being rather dull. Bulwer Lytton thought it 'inferior to Cheltenham'.[91] But as Italian politics grew unstable after 1830, being dull and cheap was an advantage. The increasingly Protestant evangelical temper of early and mid-Victorianism was also a factor. The 'animal gratification' of Naples that had so offended John Henry Newman was nothing new, but now it caught in the craw of a hardening moral consciousness that the English increasingly took with them overseas (the broad-minded Irish much less so). There was to be no echo in Victorian poetry of Shelley's 1820 'Ode to Naples'. As for Rome, the British presence there had never had a truly separate identity of its own, being – as George Eliot was to describe it in *Middlemarch* – part of a north European, mainly German, cultural enterprise.[92]

By the time Edward Lear passed through Florence at the end of the 1830s it could seem that 'The whole place is like an English watering place'.[93] This Englishness was being modified but not undermined by a growing American contingent only very partially distinguishable from their English cousins.[94] Nathaniel Hawthorne – famous as the author of the bestselling *The Scarlet Letter* (1850), who spent some years in Italy – was more acerbic than most in finding Florence acceptable in a way that Rome and Naples could never quite be.[95] In the latter cities those devotional rites Hawthorne described as 'course and sensual, with only an impudent assumption of penitence and religious sentiment', were more intrusive, and grated against a Puritan inheritance.[96] Yet it was also true that there was something *free* in the atmospherics of Italian society that could strike a chord with some visiting Americans. Recalling his time in Florence a quarter of a century before Hawthorne, James Fenimore Cooper, author of *The Last of the Mohicans* (1826), often regarded as the first great American novel, said, 'Italy haunts my dreams and clings to my ribs like another wife', adding that it was 'the only region that I truly love'.[97]

The phrase 'Anglo-Florentine' was a misnomer in one way, since the expatriate interface with local society had strict limits. When a historian writes of Hawthorne that in Florence 'he was hermetically sealed in a foreign substance',[98] the same could equally be said of the English. Elizabeth Barrett Browning, for all her emotional engagement, felt outside Italian society,[99] but this was typical, and reflected the guardedness not only of

Anglo-Americans but also of local upper-class Florentines whose social status might, in theory, have made them proper soulmates for the Anglo-Saxons (to use Hawthorne's term in this context). The fact that the latter tended to flock out of the city when political trouble loomed (as they mostly did from Rome during the 1848–9 uprising, for example) and to come back only when things were calmer, did not help bridge a psychological gulf.[100]

There was also a physical difference to reinforce an arch social formality. The Anglo-Americans came 'down' into Florence from their villas perched on the hills of Bellosguardo (where Florence Nightingale, named after the city, was born in Villa Colombaia) and lofty Fiesole.[101] Facility in the Italian language did not necessarily make things better. The poet Walter Landor, a rare case of someone fluent in the Tuscan dialect, argued with his Italian neighbours more violently – even physically – than he did with almost anyone else, driven by a hyper-sensitivity about his own status as poet-gentleman.[102] Some expatriate authors did try to convey to readers at home the more ordinary life around them sympathetically. The novel *Marietta* (1862) by Thomas Adolphus Trollope, Fanny's eldest son, was praised in *The Times* for offering a true and vivid picture of 'the domestic life of the Italian',[103] whilst George Frederic Watts, in his *Peasants of the Roman Campagna* (1845), empathized with conditions in a region which was sunk into a state of disease-ridden miasma – what the Irish novelist and travel writer Lady Morgan had called in her description of Italy in 1821 a place of 'dreary frontiers'.[104] For all its rich classical associations, this was an area hitherto usually dashed through by British visitors eager to avoid contagion. Watts's painting had caught a stark reality, stripped of romance.

As social questions were increasingly coming to the surface in both Britain and Italy, Watts proceeded to illustrate, at least implicitly, how poverty in the two countries could be compared through the same lens. On returning to London he set to work on images of suffering and want there, most starkly in his *Found Drowned* (1848–50), which portrayed the prostrate body of a young woman who had committed suicide by throwing herself in the Thames by Waterloo Bridge,[105] and *The Irish Famine* (1850), depicting cadaverous parents and their desperately malnourished baby.[106] Embedded in these various works was a question that was to reverberate in future: was the hardship evident in Italy's relatively static social system, however grinding, less destructive of human lives and happiness than what you could see through your own eyes in dynamically industrializing Great Britain? Watts seemed to think so, and he was not to be alone.[107]

The ambivalence lodged within Anglo-Italian interaction was soon powerfully illustrated by the most intense controversy in Britain in the early 1850s. John Henry Newman's conversion to Catholicism in 1845 stoked fears of an escalating revival of 'Roman religion' on the British mainland, its flock enlarged by poor Catholics fleeing the famine across the Irish Sea. Nicholas Wiseman, who left the English College in Rome to become vicar apostolic of the Catholic Church in the diocese of London in 1848, was at the heart of this controversy. Whereas the local Catholic leadership in England had always clung to a minimum of ceremonial out of prudence, Wiseman and the cadre of highly enthusiastic converts around him relished full pageantry after he took up his post in Britain. He genuinely believed what many Protestants feared, that the country was on the verge of returning to full Roman obedience. When Pope Pius IX restored the panoply of Catholic episcopal hierarchy in Britain in September 1850, with Wiseman elevated to be cardinal and first arch-bishop of Westminster, the latter issued a pastoral letter ('Pastoral from Out of the Flaminian Gate') open to interpretation in its wording as hailing the restoration of juridical Roman authority in Britain, leaving Queen Victoria to wonder in private 'Am I Queen of England or not?'[108]

Wiseman's Flaminian rhetoric was castigated as 'Papal Aggression' by a Whig government whose leaders, ironically, had previously supported Catholic emancipation, but who now saw a way to milk popularity. The intensity of the ensuing outburst of Protestant emotion in both England and Scotland threatened to trigger something like the anti-papist Gordon Riots in the 1780s.[109] There were even calls for the inspection of Catholic convents in Britain on the grounds that young women were being tricked into conversion and sexually abused by foreign priests. This was merely to 'flip' for current use the lurid claims often made in old Grand Tour days about convents in Italy.

Whig ministers shortly gave up their 'anti-popery' line for fear of losing control of the situation, and before long animosities ebbed. There were some who thought that what had happened had been cathartic in draining off the remnants of large-scale anti-Catholic prejudice in Britain, and in fact there was never again to be such a phenomenon on the mainland. Nevertheless, anti-Catholicism in England was to linger into the 1860s and beyond, and although the primary distorting effect of this was always in relation to Ireland, it entered too into interactions with Italy. More broadly, the 'Papal Aggression' episode had shown in its intensity how acutely insecure the British still were about their own identity and institutions.

Here was a crucial paradox about mid-Victorian Britain. The Great Exhibition in 1851 displayed the new material and industrial strength of the country. But far from reflecting cultural confidence in nationhood, an essential fragility remained. This was also expressed in a dual social fracture. Disraeli had stated this in his 1845 novel, *Sybil*, evoking two nations, rich and poor, lodged within the new industrialism, 'between whom there is no interest or sympathy . . . who are as ignorant of each other . . . as if they were dwellers in different zones, or inhabitants of different planets'. But the gulf also readily became one between different regions, captured in Elizabeth Gaskell's *North and South* (1855), where tellingly the central rift was transposed into the still wider terms of world civilizations. Here the English South became conflated with an idealized ancient Greek world of relative stillness, pastoral pursuits and abiding preoccupation with beauty, and the North with more thrusting and vital, if pedestrian, qualities. Mr Thornton, the rough-hewn northern manufacturer from the fictional town of Milton, says to Margaret Hale, whose southern English beauty he secretly idolizes, 'I don't mean to despise them [the Greeks], any more than I would ape them. But I belong to the Teutonic blood; it is little mingled in this part of England . . . we retain much of their language; we retain more of their spirit; we do not look upon life as a time for enjoyment but as a time for action and exertion.' Margaret Hale's response – 'You are regular worshippers of Thor' – neatly combined admiration with gentle sarcasm about this northern English breast-beating. The Milton industrialist's credo was a million miles from the earlier South-seeking idyll of Sir William Hamilton, fresh from Naples at the outset of the century, with his Greek vases and desire to infuse British life at home with the essences of their delicate beauty. Did this very different Victorian Britain of the Great Exhibition belong to the South or the North within the world's grand civilizational order? It was not entirely clear, because the British, with all their differences, did not know what they actually *were* as a collectivity, despite their sudden accretion of wealth founded on the hardier ideals represented by steam and iron rails. As John Steegman has observed on this theme, 'In [mechanical] knowledge the men of 1850 in England were masters of the world, and they had no doubts about it. In feeling, in aesthetic sensibility, they did not seem to be masters of anyone, let alone themselves.'[110]

Perhaps most profoundly, Steegman adds, mid-Victorian Britons did not know where, for them, 'home' really was.[111] They had looked everywhere, be it to Italy as an aesthetic ideal, to Germany as the home of that sturdy Saxon race fast becoming a Victorian fixation,[112] to the Gothic realm, to Olden Time nostalgia, including in its most ancient forms. But still they had not found it, and that uncertainty was as much a part of the Victorian reality as any consciousness of material and imperial success.

Indeed, during these decades a series of polarities constructed around North and South, darkness and light, Gothicism and classicism, 'bright Mediterranean clarity and the smoke and damp of industrial production', came to revolve within British cultural consciousness.[113] Some of these competing impulses were at work in the battle of the styles surrounding the architectural and decorative schemes for the new Westminster Parliament, the burning of the old medieval palace on 16 October 1834 being for many Londoners the most dramatic event of the age. What was to replace it? Artists and designers with very opposed preferences jostled for commissions. In the end the replacement palace was to be dourly Gothic and Northern, what the twentieth-century cultural historian and anti-Goth Kenneth Clark, writing with the brazenness of youth, was to lambast as 'a great necropolis of style' (though even Clark ended by having a grudging admiration for its inspirer, Augustus Pugin).[114] The corridors inside, by contrast, were to be full of frescos painted by British artists in a pure Italian spirit with bright pigmentation.[115] This experiment was to go badly wrong, since the imported egg tempera before long cracked under English climatic conditions, and the whole scheme had to be abandoned. What worked, technically and artistically, in Italy did not necessarily do so in Britain, or indeed vice versa. This was not, however, to be the last time that an attempt was made to revive the use of Italian tempera in British art, since it was just one token of a deep-rooted instinct.[116]

But a North–South dialectic inside British mentalities was not just about strict geographically defined categories. For one thing, as Alexander Pope had written in *An Essay on Man* as early as 1734, whether the 'North' began at the Tweed, the Orkneys, Greenland 'or the Lord knows where' signified little; it depended on your angle of vision. It was in the wake of the Napoleonic Wars that the first Royal Navy expeditions to the Arctic fanned out from Chatham and Portsmouth to ascertain just how far north one might actually go. Meanwhile the romances of Walter Scott gave a new if darkened glamour to a more familiar 'old north', whilst from the early years of Queen Victoria's reign there was a mounting interest amongst provincial antiquarians and nascent archaeologists, as well as sections of the reading public, in the Viking age and its legacies in much of Britain – neglected cairns, fragmented crosses, primitive jewellery.[117] This of course had special resonances in Scotland, Wales, Ireland and assorted border-lands. But more generally it established a fault line 'between Viking-age and Graeco-Roman cultures, between northern and southern European values' within Britain itself and the way its present-day inhabitants saw their origins and fundamental attachments.[118]

The North–South dichotomy in the British mentality, however, took a particular shape in these decades, pivoting on Germany. The magnetic attraction of German *Kultur* in Britain was hardly new. But after 1830 the flow of British writers, artists and intellectuals of one sort or another to the German states grew considerably, and the role of Prince Albert of Saxe-Coburg and Gotha in British public life after 1840 as Victoria's Consort intensified it.[119] Thackeray, for example, was steeped in German literature, drawn to its fable-rich romanticism.[120] But the most assertive intellectual presence in British public debate with a Germanic bent was Thomas Carlyle. His written style, first formulated in *Sartor Resartus* (1836), was self-consciously German, and in his special lectures in London between 1836 and 1840 one of his basic messages was that the greatest achievements of British culture were Teutonic in nature.[121] Carlyle's Teutonism included bringing Goethe back into British literary and philosophical focus (though an English Goethe Society was not set up until 1886). When Carlyle later excoriated what he saw as the absurdities of mid-Victorian art and thought, their hollowness and falsity, one of the things he implicitly despised was their tendency to reflect the textures of a soft

Mediterranean South.[122] To him, Dante represented an 'obsolete theme'.[123] Carlyle never travelled south of the Alps, and although at one time he had taught himself Italian, this did not greatly affect his approach or, as we saw earlier, at a human level his wryness towards what he saw as the 'overwrought' figure of Mazzini.

Carlyle is interesting because he represented a powerful contradiction to our main theme. There were many more, however, who simply straddled the North–South frontier in British consciousness. Edward Bulwer Lytton early on in his career looked to Germany as offering sources of self-discovery absent in Britain, 'a practice', his biographer notes, 'he would continue . . . for the whole of his life'.[124] But he was nonetheless still irresistibly drawn to Pompeii and its ancient Vesuvian disaster for his greatest literary invention. But especially telling here is the critic Anna Jameson. Her 1826 novel *Diary of an Ennuyée* had popularized Italian art for a new mass readership, though her larger reputation rests on her *Sacred and Legendary Art* (1848) which distilled years of inspecting European galleries into lessons which profoundly influenced popular Victorian reactions to high culture, especially amongst women. In her later years she spent increasing time in Germany. Her greatest friend there was Ottilie von Goethe, the daughter of the great German scholar, and together they retraced some of his Italian journeys. Yet as a chronicler of Jameson's life observes, there was a subtle but crucial difference in the role that Italy and Germany played for her and in the British imagination generally. This is summed up as follows:

> There is a radical difference between the attitude of Anna, the traveller in Italy, and Anna, the traveller in Germany, a difference which seems to reflect the prevailing attitude of the English. In Italy she was enchanted, but superior, a commentator on its art treasures, but never an intimate of its people; in Germany she finds a society which is intellectually and socially superior to her own, a society of which she stands in awe, and before which she is humble.[125]

In culture, as in politics and diplomacy, Italy and the Mediterranean generally were to play this role in the orientation of modern Britain: an inflection brought about by British insularity and its difficulty in engaging effectively with Continental, and above all German, counterparts. Instead

Britain got repeatedly sucked back into a southern drift that suited its tastes and capacities, but also reflected a certain lack of self-confidence. Years earlier the Dilettanti and Grand Tourists of the day had by their travels, collecting and varied entrepreneurship set about counteracting such cultural vulnerability, but in the age of the Great Exhibition, despite all its engines, designs and endless products, it still did not seem to be abating.

This mindset, unstable and liable to implosion, was the key to the troubled world of the painter-critic John Ruskin. It was why he was a quintessential Victorian, and why his pronouncements on art and much else were amongst 'the most valuable expressions of that society'.[126] The most lasting of those pronouncements was the three-volume *The Stones of Venice* (1851–3). The first two volumes were essentially a guidebook on how to 'read' the city architecturally, but also in moral and historical terms.[127] The larger goal, however, was to inaugurate Ruskin's attack on the Renaissance as the harbinger of that worldliness and cold rationality which he despised and found embodied above all in his own native land, now riding, as he saw it, for a great fall.

The Stones of Venice famously began, 'Since first the dominion of men was asserted over the ocean, three thrones . . . have been set upon its sands: the thrones of Tyre, Venice and England. Of the First of these great powers only the memory remains: of the Second, the ruin; the Third, which inherits their greatness, if we forget their example, may be led through prouder eminence to less pitied destruction.' The 'ocean' was the Mediterranean – the Atlantic was still far from dominating British maritime awareness. Indeed, the idea that the fate of Venice held dire warnings of a pitiless demise for Britain went back to the eighteenth century. It assumed fresh urgency, however, in the 1850s when the British Empire was seemingly growing ever larger, but when – as the panics surrounding the war against Russia in the Crimea indicated – hostile forces were felt to be hovering all the more threateningly. It was as if the more powerful in material and territorial senses the British became, the more their inner nerves frayed. Ruskin was to display such sensitivity at both political and cultural levels.

Ruskin himself came from a wealthy commercial background, his father being an importer of sherry into Britain from Jerez in Andalusia, though the son never showed any inclination to visit Spain. Alpine Switzerland – the mountains he loved, 'sacred and unassailable', as the surest evidence of God's creation – and Italy were the twin poles of his interest revolving through science, geology, art, architecture and sociology. This bifurcation between Swiss Alps and Italian cities was John Ruskin's imaginative polarization between North and South, as it was for others.[128] With his devoted parents he enjoyed in his youth many educational trips to the region by horse-drawn carriage, but it was during his first trip alone in 1845 – when he had already published the first volume of his *Modern Painters*, eulogizing J. M. W. Turner and crystallizing a body of art criticism that was to dominate later nineteenth-century British appreciations – that his real concerns began to emerge.[129] He stayed a week in Lucca – further south, especially Rome and Naples, horrified him – and confirmed his growing fascination with early ('primitive') art and architecture, viewed through a prism that contrasted old and new Italy, medieval order and a modernity the ghastliness of which he found summed up in the present-day inhabitants who were 'bad enough for anything'.[130] The dire vision pivoted on the church of San Frediano, its once lovely frescos brutalized, it was alleged, by previous French occupiers – a nation always despised by Ruskin, especially for their art. Any hint of loveliness was wrecked, 'all going to decay', he lamented, 'nothing rising but ugliness and meanness'.[131] His first thought was to trace what remained of the frescos before they fell entirely to pieces. It was this kind of laborious copying of anything Italian of the 'right' pre-High Renaissance age that epitomized his later mission to rescue timeless treasures from the depredations of the current times he detested.

These preoccupations were grafted in intensified form onto Venice during the successive winters that Ruskin and his wife Effie, whom he married in April 1848, spent in the city over the next few years. The Ruskins both felt comfortable with the reimposition of Austrian control after the doomed revolutionary republic of 1849 collapsed. John saw the local revolutionaries as having been even less respectful of the medieval fabric than the foreign occupiers, whilst Effie was happy mixing socially with Habsburg officers. Her friendship with one of the latter indicated that perhaps all was not well in the marriage.[132] John Ruskin was little impressed by the Venetian nobility and intelligentsia. As he explained in

The Palazzo Contarini-Fasan, Venice
Drawing by John Ruskin (May 1841)

the preface to his celebrated book, he had first gone to the city expecting that at least the dates of the principal buildings – buildings that Edward Gibbon rated 'the worst architecture I ever saw', but which for Ruskin became the quintessence of ethical worth – were already well established.[133] To his consternation, he discovered that not even the grand façade of the Palazzo Ducale could be dated with precision to the right century. Ruskin explained that as a result he had personally to go over the various palaces along the great canal 'stone by stone', measuring the exact proportions and measurements in every direction, and assessing chronologies, a task that was, Ruskin stated, 'a subject of great surprise to my Italian friends'.[134] There was in this, perhaps, something of the same minute and unbending exertions that George Eliot in *Middlemarch* was to embody in Mr Casaubon's grail-like pursuit of a Key to All Mythologies.

Ruskin's mythological key had by the end of the 1850s come down to one principle: the worship of beauty. This underpinned his ultimate disillusionment with the sombre Gothic he had once venerated.[135] Beauty, indeed, constituted for him a religion in itself, gradually replacing a personal faith that had once threatened to veer towards Romanism, had reverted to a staunch patriotic Protestantism during the 'Papal Aggression' episode in Britain, and then displayed the first signs of wavering altogether as new geological knowledge, to which he was so sensitive, had a chilling effect on assumptions of a God-created universe.[136]

The trouble was, however, that as Ruskin looked about his world he saw beauty suddenly under attack from many sides. There were railways and mass tourism, assisted by John Murray's increasingly ubiquitous guidebooks. There were people, including an increasing number of Britons, who desecrated the lonely majesty of Swiss mountains by actually climbing them rather than looking at them with awe. (Ruskin's preferences in this respect were at odds with the Alpine Club, founded in 1857, in which Virginia Woolf's father, Leslie Stephen, was to be a leading light.)[137] There was the digging of the archaeologists, making the natural beauty of ruins into some kind of building site.[138] There was the definition of sensuousness primarily as romantic and sexual desire, rather than being consecrated at the level of art in its purest sense.[139] This was why Ruskin's doubts about the Pre-Raphaelite painters who sought to break with the existing establishment in the visual arts, and whom he had initially encouraged, morphed into suspicion. The original trio of the 'PRB' – Dante Gabriel Rossetti, William Holman Hunt and John Everett Millais – had been inspired by Jacob van Eyck's *Arnolfini Portrait*, the first Netherlandish acquisition by the National Gallery in 1843, arousing sensational public interest by its contrast with the Gallery's hitherto almost exclusive focus on paintings with a southern European provenance. The dark canvases Rossetti and his circle produced in imitation of van Eyck were deeply at odds with Ruskin's growing predilection for light and transparency. Nor after a while was there any mistaking in Pre-Raphaelite images models and girlfriends ('stunners') conveniently repackaged in mythological roles. This clashed directly with Ruskin's view that the primary role of art was to provide the moral grounding that theological truth could no longer do with certainty.

Perhaps inevitably, Ruskin's personal life could not be cordoned off from these assaults. Much has been written about the break-up of his marriage to Effie in 1854, the formal annulment being on grounds of non-consummation. The story circulated by Effie, and generally believed, was that when Ruskin discovered on the wedding night that her lower body was not exactly like the alabaster smooth and hairless idealization of the ancient Greek female statues he knew so well, he proved incapable of the physical act.[140] (Effie later married Millais, the most 'respectable' of the Pre-Raphaelites.) Insofar as this cut across an underlying obsession with perceived imperfection as a shadow haunting Ruskin's mind, it touched on many other cultural sensitivities.

Of all Ruskin's growing aversions, later to cause years of mental strain, a loathing for English industrialism, epitomized by the northern cities, became increasingly prominent.[141] And although he had often taken swipes at present-day Italy, as his critique of contemporary Britain deepened Italy appeared in a generally better light, because at least it retained a continuing link between past and present as well as a sense of beauty amongst ordinary people. In Britain such connections had, in his view, snapped altogether. In his 1859 lecture at the Bradford Mechanics' Institute Ruskin compared that city to Pisa, whose central Camposanto he had also striven hard to protect from blighting 'improvements'. In making an unflattering contrast Ruskin was careful to tell his workaday hearers, 'I do not look for any possible renovation of the Republic of Pisa at Bradford in the nineteenth century . . . We don't want either the life or the decoration of the thirteenth century back again . . . but rather to raise the historical consciousness of the working people by invoking a time and place where there was an aesthetic dimension to even the most humble lives.'[142] Here again there was arguably a grave misunderstanding: that modern Italian poverty, either morally or materially, was not so degrading in its effects as equivalent distress in Manchester, Bradford or the rabbit-warrens of London, because it was relieved by a national aesthetic principle cutting across classes. Had Ruskin spent more time in Rome or Naples, where absolute poverty hit you right in the eye, any such thought might have been counteracted. But still, as Britain's nineteenth-century industrial civilization approached maturity, it remained credible for Italy to provide, for one of the most defining and sensitive Victorian minds, a way of measuring its own character and failings.

One aspect of Ruskin's evolving sensibility was that his interest in the strictly classical legacies of the ancient Mediterranean dwindled, a reflex of his alternative idealization of pre-Renaissance medievalism.[143] He was not alone in this depreciation. The young Rossetti, despite or, contrarily, because of his Italian roots, felt 'no charm in the antique', part of Pre-Raphaelite rebelliousness.[144] 'The heroes of antiquity,' it was asserted in the *Library of Fine Arts*, 'are now quite out of date.'[145] George Eliot also had reservations about what she regarded as 'mouldy ancients'.[146] Thackeray and Dickens did not greatly like each other, but they shared a dislike of the Greek and Latin languages. Thackeray's alienation from the classics as a whole sprang from a severe beating he was once given for his errors in Greek grammar by a brutish teacher at a small private school in Southampton.[147] Years later when he visited Athens he stood in front of the royal palace – today's Syntagma Square – and 'cursed the country which has made thousands of little boys miserable'. His supporting observation – that there was no point going to Athens to peer at the ruins when you could quite easily go and see Greek Revival buildings in Liverpool that were in much better condition – simply drove the knife in a bit deeper.[148]

Dickens also saw a connection between dead languages and hateful educational brutalities, even sadism, especially in the minor public schools of the day.[149] But his antipathy went wider. Dickens wanted to invent a distinctively English authorial voice that chimed with the industrial and urban world of Victorian Britain. The very 'literariness' of language in the classical tradition, the artificial balancing of phrase upon phrase, was precisely what he wanted to ditch, which is why classical references in his novels are relatively few. That absence, the historian Edith Hall remarks, was part of Dickens's own class consciousness.[150] The imitation of classicism in all its little linguistic tics, still then prevailing amongst many British writers, and the habit, characteristic of Walter Landor for instance, of stuffing into a poem as many classical quotations as possible as a sign of erudition, started to pall with many Victorian readers.[151]

This fits with the general interpretation that the principal role of the classic Mediterranean in nineteenth-century Britain was inherently conservative. It helped shore up the existing social order, a function Robert

Peel had conceived for the fine arts generally. 'It was access to culture and power,' one writer concerned with the sphere of gender writes, 'to which the classical languages, and especially Greek, with its exotic alphabet, held the magic key.'[152] The possession of a semblance of competence in these dead languages was a sure indicator that individuals had a secure place in the existing order. The industrialist Mr Thornton in Elizabeth Gaskell's *North and South* finds the time to learn Ancient Greek in the evenings because acquaintance with those 'mysterious sentences' promised to add a tincture of refinement to his social standing that is otherwise lacking.[153] Acquiring elements of classical knowledge also had a special application for many upper-middle-class women looking for points of entry into a public world hedged about by male privilege. Some – George Eliot was one, however mouldy the texts may sometimes have seemed to her – took private lessons to acquire the classical rudiments that their brothers were given, punishingly or not, in the schoolroom.[154] This may have been second best, but the acquisition and use of what in *Aurora Leigh* Elizabeth Barrett Browning had called 'lady's Greek / Without the accents' helped expand at the margins the roles and horizons of bourgeois English women. Whether this gently subverted the status quo between the sexes or merely altered its modus operandi is debatable.

Ancient Greek language, literature and history generally had a greater 'pull' over the Victorian imagination than its Roman equivalent. At least in part the reason for this was that concrete knowledge about any aspect of Greece still often remained somewhat hazy.[155] It could therefore be turned to almost any purpose without too many facts getting in the way. 'Writing about [ancient] Greece,' Frank Turner states, 'was in part a way for the Victorians to write about themselves.'[156] An example was George Grote's twelve-volume *History of Greece*, appearing between 1846 and 1856, described as 'one of the chief monuments of mid-Victorian intellectual life'.[157] The thrust of Grote's work was to take issue with earlier histories, mostly of a conservative bent stressing the turmoil and defects of ancient Athenian democracy,[158] portraying instead an admirable experiment in popular constitutionalism, while identifying pitfalls that may have proved fatal to the Athenians but which could be avoided by their British succes-sors with some tinkering (such as a secret ballot). Grote may be criticized for interpreting ancient Greek history in terms of English affairs, and for using nineteenth-century terminology to describe fifth-century BC Athens,[159] but this is to miss the whole point, which was to engage with contemporary Britain itself. The result was that, after Grote, 'Englishmen looked at [ancient] Athens and saw a reflection of their own best selves' – selves, that is, that had not succumbed as had so much of Europe to revolution and disorder in 1848. When J. S. Mill, who had encouraged Grote in his gargantuan task, invited him to come along on a visit to present-day Greece, he refused.[160] Grote's idea of Greece was one that did not need any physical manifestation or reality.

There is one classical Greek preoccupation in mid-Victorian Britain that needs emphasis: Homer. As Richard Jenkyns remarks: 'It is striking how many public men engaged in Homeric Studies. Lord John Russell passed the time at Geneva in translating a book of the *Odyssey*. Lord Derby translated the entire *Iliad* into blank verse . . . Homer's deepest admirer was the most eminent of all Victorian statesmen. Gladstone wrote in 1886 that he was reading the *Iliad* for the twenty-fifth . . . time, and every time more glorious than before.'[161] The reason why Homer came so alive for this generation was because the questions that came to surround its study – how to treat the text, even the authenticity of authorship – echoed so clearly the troubling debates that sceptical scholarship had already posed regarding the Bible. Even the chronological rhythm of the disputes over the New Testament and Homer flowed together.[162]

It is telling that the one Victorian statesman who never bothered with Homer at all was Disraeli. This was not only because he thought Hellenism was a 'got-up' enthusiasm; it was also because by his background he had no personal investment in the Christian religion, nominal Anglican though he was. For him there could be no read-across from a possibly mythical Greek poet to matters of belief in an age where theological doubt was starting to dislocate many people's beliefs. For Gladstone, whose three-volume *Studies on Homer and the Homeric Age* appeared in early 1858, it was wholly different. His obsession with Homer came from a determination to locate the roots of revealed religion as far back as one could possibly go, even before Christianity proper (as his friend John Henry Newman had pondered years before). As Richard Jenkyns concludes, Gladstone was in the end 'remarkably successful in what sounds like the almost impossible task of demonstrating Homer's moral excellence according to conventional

Victorian standards'.[163] But then, probing current-day truths and false-hoods, and in Gladstone's case asserting a religious truth that matched those fiscal verities in his self-balancing budgets as chancellor of the Exchequer, were what it was all about. Nor was that to change even when ideas about ancient Greece became, with time and archaeology, much more complex than Gladstone ever contemplated.

Oddly enough, Gladstone's *Homer and the Homeric Age* was one reason why Bulwer Lytton, who at the time was colonial secretary in Lord Derby's Conservative government, chose him in the late summer of 1858 to carry out the task of lord high commissioner extraordinary to the Ionian Islands. The glitzy job title and Gladstone's Homeric expertise were meant to dazzle the local Greek population. The episode is interesting as being Gladstone's only experience of British administration of an overseas territory. A British protectorate since 1817, Corfu and the other Ionian Islands ('the illus-trious seven') had seen their affairs get progressively worse. The chief administrator during the 1830s had summed up the problem by saying that the islands under British supervision constituted 'a sort of middle state between a colony and a perfectly independent country, without . . . the advantages of either'.[164] In other words, the Ionian situation was exactly the kind of halfway house – the worst of all possible worlds – in which rulers and ruled ceased to have any real comprehension of each other. By the end of the 1850s this misunderstanding had become endemic. The local Greeks overwhelmingly wanted to be ceded to the adjacent Kingdom of Greece. The British had the idea that the islands should become formally part of the British Empire, a bit like self-governing Australia or Canada. This was what Gladstone sought to effect, albeit in a circuitous way, by first 'undeceiving' the impossible aspirations of the majority of the population to become truly Greek.

The deadlock that followed showed that if ancient Greeks could easily be put at the beck and call of the contemporary British imagination, modern Greeks were less pliable. This was not for want of trying on Gladstone's part. As he reflected in his diary, 'it may seem strange but so it is that my time and thoughts are as closely occupied . . . in the affairs of these little islands as they have been in almost any period of parliamentary business'.[165] This was a remarkable confession. But the fascination deep-ened as Gladstone toured an area with all the classical associations that meant so much to him; this constituted the most enthralling overseas experience of what proved a very long life. It came to a climax on the island of Ithaca, Homer's alleged birthplace. 'The [naval] salute in this beautiful harbour,' he wrote on leaving, 'was one of the grandest things from its regular circles of thundering echoes, that I ever heard.'[166]

Unfortunately, disillusionment followed when it became all too clear that the path towards British colonial citizenship, which was all Gladstone had to offer, was simply of no interest to the local Greek population. Worse, far from anybody being 'undeceived', each side thought the other had tried to bamboozle them. For the Greeks, Gladstone's prime interest was seen to have been concerned with little more than polishing Britain's good name. Gladstone effectively admitted as much when writing back to London.[167] The British politician, with all his pre-existing Greek sympathies, left for home on 19 February 1859, fed up 'with the Greeks in general and the Ionians in particular'. An English official in the islands afterwards offered a more sarcastic summary: 'One great genius [Bulwer Lytton] had sent out another great genius [Gladstone] and had failed unmistakably.'[168] When Lawrence Durrell visited Corfu decades later, he still found echoes of this debacle circulating in the local folklore.[169] It was, in Gladstone's career, for all its interest, little more than a footnote, but nevertheless it presented a kind of parable for modern Anglo-Greek misunderstanding.

There was one English resident of Corfu in the later 1850s, however, who left a much-loved legacy: Edward Lear. Probably no other British artist can be said to have conjured up so atmospherically the Mediterranean landscape. Lear had spent ten years in Rome, and was rare in the thoroughness of his exploration of southern Italy, recorded in his *Journals of a Landscape Painter in Calabria* (1852). Few foreigners ventured into the remote recesses of the Mezzogiorno as Lear did on both foot and horseback, enduring a great deal of hardship which affected his health. In April 1848, however, he decided to leave Italy before political conditions worsened. He considered going back to England but could not stand the prospect of being 'demoralized by years of mud and fog and gnats'.[170] He went instead to Corfu, drawn by his infatuation with a friend, Franklin Lushington, who had been appointed a judge in Corfu Town. Lear spent most of the next fifteen years there. A biographer tells us that the island

Campagna of Rome from the Villa Mattei
Lithograph by Edward Lear (1841)

'entered deeply and subtly into him . . . and made him what he was, as his years . . . in Italy did not . . . His contentment in the scenery and light of Corfu is visible in the way he luxuriates in the olive groves . . . and in the way that what had been exotic becomes familiar and domestic.'[171]

This was Lear's achievement for a mass British public: to fix an image of the Mediterranean, more realistic than the older picturesque tradition, and conveying a certain fragrance and experience of actually *being* there, even for those who were never likely to see an olive grove in reality. Lear was never to resolve his own intense restlessness, just as he was never to resolve his ambivalent sexuality. Nor did garrison life in British-ruled Corfu – in his nonsense language he referred to it in a letter to his sister as 'a disorganised fiddlefaddle Poodly-pumpkin place' – provide Lear with the artistic camaraderie of expatriate Rome. But, with his endearing insecurities, and anyway always preferring the solitary life, Lear felt happy and safe there, and it showed in the tranquil imagery he left behind.[172]

Relationships between Britain and the independent Kingdom of Greece itself, however, remained highly tentative, not helped by the Ionian deadlock. It was as if Byron's legacy had become inverted into a wary dislike, even repugnance, for the state that had emerged after his death. That state was in any case made in the image of Bavaria, not of England. Not only was the first King of Greece, Otto, a Bavarian, but the rebuilding of central Athens was designed by Bavarian architects who came with him from Munich. It is their work that gave the heart of the city its modern, neoclassicized flavour, and the British – in contrast to the simultaneous reconfiguring of Corfu Town[173] – had little to do with it. Those Britons who had fought in the independence struggle and stayed in Athens tended to have fragile relations with the new authorities. The Glaswegian-born George Finlay set about writing a multi-volume *History of Greece* taking up chronologically about where George Grote left off, even covering the revolution after 1821, in which Finlay himself had been a player. Finlay always believed in the essential qualities of the Greek people, but was a scathing critic of the country's governance – a double-edged view with a long future ahead of it.[174] The radical free trade politician Richard Cobden, visiting Athens in April 1837, reflected a general British feeling about Greece and its modern pretensions when he wrote sardonically in a private letter of 'the *papier maché* Court and Capital of a doughty empire comprising seven hundred thousand paupers'.[175]

Tensions between Britain and a Bavarianized Greece approached a climax at the end of the 1840s, however, in a way that was to significantly impact on British public culture at home. The British minister in Athens was Sir Thomas Wyse, a County Cork man, and the first Roman Catholic to hold a senior post in British diplomatic representation overseas in modern times. Wyse was an acidic personality with some foundation in a rocky personal life. He had married a Bonaparte – Letizia, the daughter of Napoleon's younger brother, said to be the most physically attractive of her family's generation. The marriage foundered venomously, the resulting feud even rivalling the bile between the Lyttons.[176] Wyse's temperament was no smoother when it came to conducting relations with the Greek government, and those relations dived over British claims for compensation from the Greeks by a Gibraltar-born businessman called Don Pacifico. In a swaggering style characteristic of the prime minister of the time, Lord Palmerston, the Royal Navy appeared in mid-January 1850 in the Bay of Salamis to back up the demand for prompt payment by the Greeks to Don Pacifico – or else.

Under threat of bombardment the Greeks did pay up, but when British Liberals and Radicals attacked Palmerston in Parliament for bullying a weak and vulnerable country on wholly specious grounds, the prime minister turned the occasion into an opportunity for stringently asserting the rights of British nationals abroad. At the climax in the chamber on 8 July 1850, Palmerston, quoting directly from the legal doctrines of Cicero, stated it to be a fundamental principle of British foreign policy that just as 'the Roman in days of old held himself free from indignity when he could say "*Civis Romanus sum*", so also a British subject, in whatever land he may be, should feel confident that the watchful eye and strong arm of England will protect him against injustice and wrong.'[177] The fact that Don Pacifico was almost certainly a crook did not prevent this patriotic enunciation from emerging as the definitive statement of British power overseas in the mid-Victorian age, and even in the 1920s it could be said to resound in British diplomatic practice.[178] Indeed, it lodged permanently in English-speaking political culture as a whole. In an episode of the popular American television political saga *West Wing*, the fictional President Bartlet, faced with a situation of US citizens at risk abroad, unleashes a rhetorical tirade precisely echoing Palmerston's classical outburst in the British Parliament in 1850, including its Ciceronian strapline.[179] Tellingly, the scriptwriters could be confident that an early twenty-first-century American television audience would recognize, however subliminally, an ancient Roman principle filtered through a British Victorian experience relating to nineteenth-century Greece.

If contemporary Greece – the one that was most tangible – always remained maddeningly out of kilter with British conceptions and expectations, Spain remained similarly elusive. That country continued to slip in and out of British consciousness depending on the intensity of its bitter internal divisions. The savage if dispersed civil conflict that erupted there in 1833 – the First Carlist War – attracted a volunteer British Legion about 10,000 strong. Since so many monasteries and convents were caught up in the devastation, one side effect was a sudden outflow of religious art, a good deal ending up in Britain.[180] British opinion was for a while captivated by the drama. The celebrated actress Fanny Kemble trembled daily for news; her brother was a volunteer, and fate on capture was not infrequently execution on the spot by Carlist *guerrilleros* (over 400 Britons died in Spain at this time). The Legion's record, though, was patchy. The British minister in Madrid, George Villiers, said its behaviour almost drove him mad with frustration,[181] and although those British critics who alleged that the Legion blundered across the Spanish plains with 800 baggage mules and 500 prostitutes, avoiding any military engagements whatsoever, were mostly Tories driven by ideological prejudice,[182] by the time the fratricidal fighting petered out in 1838 nobody had covered themselves in any glory. The country had again briefly been a vivid British preoccupation but the events were mostly seen as a repetition of the confused bloodbath that had accompanied the Peninsular War before 1815. What was actually going on remained wholly obscure even to British observers on the ground. Richard Cobden, visiting a bit later, pronounced views on the country just as dismissive as those he held on Greece, stating that any attempt to regenerate Spain was purely quixotic.[183]

The most renowned British traveller to Spain of this era, George Borrow, shared that opinion in spades. The British and Foreign Bible Society sent Borrow there in 1835 to distribute Christian scriptures but instead he spent several years drifting rather aimlessly across the country in a dreamy, rambling adventurousness conjured up in his three-volume *The Bible in Spain* (1843). This was a great popular success in Britain when it appeared, its condescension towards local habits and failings appealing to the more evangelical section of the mid-Victorian reading public.[184] In fact Borrow seems to have had relatively few sustained exchanges with Spaniards other than with the tavern keepers where he stayed.[185] However, in one revealing instance of accelerating intellectual currents across Europe, he did come across a village *alcalde* (mayor) who tried to engage him in a discussion about the social theories of Jeremy Bentham (or the 'great Baintham', as the mayor referred to the social theorist, while pointing proudly to Bentham's collected works on his bookshelves). As a strong Tory, Borrow had no interest at all in pursuing a further discussion about British utilitarian liberalism, stomping off and leaving the *alcalde* rather puzzled.[186] Still, such gaps of instinctive sympathy were not exclusively British. Théophile Gautier, the outstanding figure of French Romanticism in this period and a noted Hispanophile, once said, tongue half in cheek, 'I know Spain very well. I once spent half an hour in Cadiz.'[187]

Spain as a subject for British representation was inherently unstable given its tentative character, but it developed certain traits. As seen earlier, in the 1820s British artists first 'discovered' the country as offering a market for images a bit different from well-worn Italy. On the other hand, these practitioners were above all in the business of making money, and the market at home remained chiefly for what the Italian stereotype still embodied: warmth, luxuriance, richness, fertility. Painters like David Roberts and John Frederick Lewis made a speciality of visiting and representing Andalusia, with its searing heat, orange trees and perfumed sensibility. What Richard Ford, author of the much-used *Handbook for Travellers in Spain* (1839), termed 'bewitching' Andalusia was epitomized in its tantalizing dances,[188] and this involved distinctly sexual overtones. Whereas in Italy a certain coy reserve was usually thought appropriate, in 'passionate' southern Spain something more direct, including a good deal of décolleté, was permissible. Lewis's *Sketches and Drawings of the Alhambra* (1835), featuring Spanish women in romantic poses by shimmering pools and framed in medieval arches, and girls gaily strumming guitars as a symbol of easy pleasure, struck all the conventional notes (the sound of castanets at this time became embedded in Northern understanding as an infallibly sensual signal in any story or musical score set in the country). A theme frequently repeated in Spanish contexts was that of female devoutness and erotic vibration. The Scottish painter John Phillip, who more than any other British artist of the day was dedicated to Spanish topics – so much so that he was known as 'Spanish Phillip' – has been said to have been 'well aware of how exciting the connection between religious observance and the male gaze can be'.[189]

Appreciations of Spanish art in Britain therefore remained skewed and limited. One who did take an interest, Sir Edmund Walker Head, later governor-general of Canada, complained that the British remained almost totally ignorant of Spain's rich legacy, and by way of compensation published his own succinct account. A more scholarly breakthrough came in 1848 with the publication of William Stirling's volumes *Annals of the Artists of Spain*, placing the country's art for the first time in a broad social and historical context.[190] Suggestively, he also brought his discussion to bear on the larger theme of an assumed intellectual and moral superiority of northern Protestantism over Spanish Catholicism. He wrote with a gentle but pointed inference: 'But to the simple Catholic of Spain the music of his choir and the pictures of his ancient shrines stood in the place of the theological dogmas which whetted and vexed the appetite of the Protestant peasant of the north. He discoursed about them with as much delight, and perhaps with as much moral advantage; and he clung to them with as much affectionate resonance.'[191]

Stirling was a strong Scottish Tory – British cultural engagement in Spain continued to come from the conservative end of the spectrum, in contrast with twentieth-century patterns – and his seat of Keir House in Stirling housed the finest collection of Spanish paintings in Britain, including Goya and El Greco. When the deposed King Louis-Phillipe's large holdings of Spanish pictures that had constituted the *Galerie Espagnole* in Paris were sold at a London auction in 1853, Stirling had been able to make key acquisitions and carry them triumphantly back northwards. Queen Victoria particularly appreciated the Spanish paintings of Edinburgh-based John Phillip, buying several of them, including his large-scale *The Letter-Writer of Seville*. Interestingly, John Phillip's biography also connects with a psychological thread in our subject. In 1846 he had married Maria Dadd, only a couple of years after her brother, the painter Richard Dadd, had been committed to Bedlam for killing their father. Afterwards she developed the mental instability that plagued the family, and the time Phillip devoted to seeing and representing Spanish scenes with their vividness and warmth seems to have offset in some indefinable way the sadness surrounding his life back at home and Maria's eventual long-term hospitalization. As so frequently, the south remained an escape from mental and emotional anguish at home.

Meanwhile, whatever might be the case in the realm of private taste, British public art galleries, with their finger on the pulse of what wider society could absorb, still recoiled from most things Spanish. One of the lingering characteristics of early and mid-Victorian 'taste' was an instinctive reaction against portrayals of physical agony, an element, for example, never to be found in any painting by Turner;[192] but in the art of Spain – somewhere Turner never visited – agony seemed to be everywhere you looked. The National Gallery in London under its director Sir Charles Eastlake certainly did not go in for anything graphically painful. There was something not far short of a fixation on making graceful – meaning High Renaissance – acquisitions in Italy. Eastlake spent at least six weeks of every year there searching out possibilities, and any reference to the Gallery's holdings over these years indicates the dominance of that country (he visited Spain only once, in 1859).[193] When the Gallery bought a painting by seventeenth-century Spaniard Francisco de Zurbarán (*Saint Francis in Meditation*), its action was criticized in *The Times*, one collector calling the purchase 'small, black, repulsive'.[194] This was another way of saying it was both Spanish and Catholic. But 'black' – the darkness of characteristic Spanish tints – was the giveaway. The colour, a historian of Anglo-Spanish cultural interaction remarks, was

> associated in British minds with an extreme form of naturalism. The refusal of Spanish artists to idealize, coupled with the menace of darkness in Victorian minds, led critics such as Ruskin to claim the moral inferiority of the Spanish school, especially as compared with the lighter-toned, pre-Catholic Reformation paintings by Italian artists. Even Mrs Jameson warned her readers of the possible ill effects of viewing Spanish art, confiding that 'many Spanish pictures . . . oppress the spirits'.[195]

It is suggestive, given that interest in painting Spanish scenes or in Spanish art itself appears to have been more Scottish than English (testified to by figures like David Roberts, David Wilkie, John Phillip and William Stirling), that the blackness so conventionally associated with Spain was also a trait within Scottish art.[196] Such a quintessentially Scottish image as Henry Raeburn's *The Reverend Robert Walker Skating on Duddingston Loch* (*c.* 1795), with the black garb of the reverend dominating the frame against the whiteness of the ice, is a case in point. In fact, Wilkie had once himself noted a parallel between Raeburn and Velázquez. Arguably the Scottish Kirk and Spanish Catholicism overlapped in possessing a deeper sense of the darkness of life than was usually found in the more facile mentality of English Anglicanism. There was to come a time, indeed, when a 'refusal to idealize', far from being seen as a fault, was to be considered a mark of serious engagement with the human condition.

Yet in a very gradual way Spain was emerging in British awareness as a 'real' country, not merely a largely imagined construct with certain inbuilt prejudices, even if this was a bumpy process. Owen Jones, for example, was the first to study the Alhambra in a truly scholarly, rather than romantic-picturesque, spirit. Notwithstanding the Elgin Marbles, he described the aesthetic system embodied in the great Moorish palace as the most perfect that had ever existed in the history of art,[197] and that admiration found expression in Jones's interior design for the Great Exhibition. Subsequently

The Alhambra Court in the Crystal Palace, Sydenham, designed by Owen Jones (1854)

his *The Grammar of Ornament* (1856), a design bible for the generation ahead, led to the proliferation of a neo-Alhambra style applied to textiles, ceramics, fabrics and wallpapers, as well as glass and decorative woodwork, not only in Britain but also in Continental Europe and the United States.

The advent of photography also had an effect. A Welshman, Charles Clifford, has been described as 'the master photographer of nineteenth-century Spain'.[198] For more than a decade after 1850 Clifford recorded the country's monuments, sending plates back to the Photographic Society in London. His *Photographic Scramble through Spain* (1861) provided new angles and approaches even to medieval buildings previously the subject only of rather mannered painting.[199] It also provided a sense of a contemporary urban Spain hitherto largely ignored, including Madrid, that bête noire of most British visitors because it fell so far outside their comfort zone. Clifford captured, for example, Madrid's great central space, the Puerta del Sol, as it took shape in its present-day form.[200] He died in the city in 1863 and was buried in the British cemetery. Still, the old Anglo sentiment against Madrid lived on.

But if the British still viewed Spain only at an oblique angle, right at the end of the 1850s Italy suddenly returned to the centre of their vision. Indeed, when Gladstone and his wife travelled through Tuscany in late February 1859 after their problematical stay in Corfu, they saw the beginning of what were to be dramatic times.[201] The birth of an independent and unified Italy under the Savoy monarchy (the 'Risorgimento') was one of the most momentous events of the day; indeed, to the historian G. M. Trevelyan, writing in the early 1900s, it seemed 'the main historical fact of the nineteenth century'.[202] Yet at the time it appeared to come out of the blue. British opinion had for some time continued to regard Italian aspirations with suspicion. Gladstone a few years earlier in 1851, following a visit to a prison in Naples, had written a pamphlet lambasting the appalling condition of political prisoners and calling the Bourbon regime 'the negation of God erected into a system of government'. The phrase had catapulted him into a politician of genuinely European reputation,[203] and indicated that English Tories as well as Whigs and Radicals could lose patience with the status quo in the Italian peninsula.[204] Still, such interventions could peter out very quickly, and in the case of Naples in particular, and Italy in general, they largely disappeared for a while from British debates. Sympathy towards Italian aspirations, always hesitant, could even regress, as in the wake of the expulsion of an Irish Protestant proselytizer from Florence, seen by the authorities in the Grand Duchy as a political agitator; this was interpreted in Britain as Catholic aggression.[205]

This was despite immense efforts by some Italian sympathizers in Britain. A remarkable example was Jessie White, for whom Italian hopes became synonymous with faith in humanity at large, an idea reinforced by a period spent in Paris mixing with intellectuals of the new sociological school such as Victor Cousin.[206] After a subsequent meeting with Mazzini in London she went off on a lecture tour around northern English cities for the Friends of Italy. Her eloquence, head of flaming auburn hair and penchant for cigars were bound to attract attention, and this campaign was striking as the first in which a female *speaker*, not just a supportive assistant, played a prominent part. When visiting Italy afterwards Jessie White's Mazzinian enthusiasms extended to marrying one of his associates, Alberto

Mario, with whom she was briefly imprisoned in Genoa by the authorities. Her radicalism was by now too much even for the Brownings, with whom she had previously stayed in Florence. But Jessie White Mario, as she now was, and Elizabeth Barrett Browning shared one opinion: that Italian freedom was more likely to come with the help of the French emperor, Napoleon III, than that of any time-serving English government.

This was borne out by events. It was the combination of French and Piedmontese diplomacy (the latter overseen by Camillo Benso, Count of Cavour), including war against Austria after April 1859, that set in motion the train of events leading to a new unified Italian state. The culmination of a highly muddled process was the entry of King Victor Emmanuel into Naples in November 1860 (though his kingdom was not yet to include Rome or Venice). Throughout the greatest regional crisis in the Mediterranean since 1815, the British manoeuvred for position to ensure that France did not end up as the dominant factor in the Peninsula, and especially so that British naval power remained unchallenged in its old Neapolitan and Sicilian haunts. Yet British actions and, just as important, refusals to act – allowing Garibaldi's Redshirts to sail unhindered from Genoa to Sicily, and then to cross the Strait of Messina to Calabria – were absolute preconditions for bringing the drama to its eventual southern climax, over which the warships of the British Mediterranean Fleet presided as they lay at anchor in the Bay of Naples. Afterwards an Anglo-Italian myth was created that the Risorgimento had unfolded *all'inglese*,[207] that is, in a way typified by liberal moderation and English pragmatism. Indeed, at the end of it the new Italy looked to Great Britain as its special patron, something that was to endure for some time.

The emotional forces unleashed by these events had a great impact on many Britons as well as on Italians precisely because they conveyed a sense that forces of change were breaking loose across a wide front. The tension could be too much. It was said by those close to her that Cavour's sudden death brought on the last phase of decline in Elizabeth Barrett Browning's brittle health;[208] but then the latter's well-being had always been played upon by a welter of factors. The Neapolitan apotheosis led to hysteria. We have seen that for complex reasons the Italian cause had frequently assumed a special resonance amongst the upper social tiers of British women. Some English ladies staying in the city cornered Garibaldi in his Neapolitan

The British Volunteer Legion arrive in Naples, 15 October 1860

hotel and cut off wisps of his hair, the Romantic hero demurely succumbing. Given the previous ambivalence in British attitudes more generally, it was hardly surprising that not everybody shared the enthusiasm. Amid the public confusion the leading concern of Charles Eastlake at the National Gallery and of John Ruskin was that the frescos in Italian cities and towns, which mattered to them far more than mere politics, might be damaged beyond repair, and an emergency copying fund was set up as insurance.[209]

The nuances in British minds surrounding the Italian drama were expressed in the responses of George Eliot, now married to the journalist George Lewes, who himself had a long record of pro-Italian sympathies. Eliot had just published *The Mill on the Floss*, and, escaping the furore when her male pseudonym was exposed as a ruse, she and her husband set out on her first trip to Italy in the early summer of 1860. This was at the height of the Risorgimento. Eliot, however, showed little direct engagement with events. Indeed, their very turbulence only induced further reserve, since, as Rosemary Ashton comments, 'in social matters, as in religious, the bent of her mind was to conserve rather than destroy'.[210] Appearing more interested in Giotto and Brunelleschi than in Garibaldi,[211] Eliot concentrated on that characteristic Victorian tourist occupation of ranking the treasures that she saw in relation to her own sensibility. In her journal she wrote, 'Among the ancient sculptures I think I must place on a level the Apollo [Belvedere], the

Dying Gladiator, and the Lateran Antinous; they affected me equally in different ways. After that I delighted in the Venus of the Capitoline'.[212]

But although Italian *politics* in all its confusions left Eliot lukewarm compared to the enjoyment of defining an aesthetic hierarchy of this sort, the profound displacement of the Risorgimento affected her in deeper ways. In Turin she felt herself being drawn, almost unconsciously, into 'the centre of a widening life', and on her return Eliot wrote that her visit 'had been one of those journeys that seem to divide one's life in two by the new ideas they suggest and the new veins of interest they open up'.[213]

The 'new veins' in Eliot's life marked a passage from anguished religious doubt to a liberating humanism, and the transition was to be worked out in her novel set in Renaissance Florence, *Romola* (1863), the erudite – some said excessive – research for which was carried out amidst the making of the new Italy. Although the local tradition that she actually wrote part of *Romola* in the Villino Trollope is not true, it seems quite likely that the essential plot was originally conceived when visiting the Trollope household on that first visit to Italy.[214] The idea of a historical romance surrounding the life of the radical cleric Savonarola certainly came to Eliot in the city at this time, and the point about the story was that, obscured amongst all the sordid political intrigue of fifteenth-century Florence, fundamental changes of a universal significance were taking shape – just as they were wherever you looked in 1860. One literary commentator has said of *Romola*'s later depiction of the Medici-ruled city-state that, 'philosophically confused, morally uncertain, and culturally uprooted . . . [it was] a prototype of the upheaval of nineteenth-century England'.[215] It was reflective of the blockages inside British society in the 1850s that in such works they found a vent in Italian historical experience rather than directly within.

Those blockages principally applied to domestic political reform, since the balances put into place in Britain after 1832 could also not last much longer. But just as importantly, as the critic Edmund Gosse recalled, a mood of literary and psychological rebellion was emerging. 'There was an idea about,' he recalled of the watershed of 1860, 'that in matters of taste the [current] age in England had for some time been static, if not stagnant. It was time to wake people up.'[216] This might mean waking up to the possibility of many things: to the need for an enlarged suffrage in political life, to fresh mental horizons cut free from religious agonizing, to the need for

The Grand Canal, Venice, around 1860

architectural options beyond the narrow battle raging between the Gothic and the classic, or to whatever deeply personal liberations were implied in the sado-masochistic verses of Algernon Swinburne's poem 'Dolores' that young male undergraduates in the 1860s chanted at their staid tutors in Oxford quadrangles.[217] The Mediterranean, directly and, even more, indirectly, both as something real and as an invention of the mind, had constantly impacted on Victorian society as it sought to make sense of its own circumstances. And that would remain the case as the British generation formed in the crucible of the first decades of the young queen's reign was succeeded by those of the High and late Victorian eras.

Chapter Five

AN ENCHANTED GARDEN

THE MEDITERRANEAN AND THE AESTHETICS OF HIGH VICTORIANISM, 1860–90

[W]e are sure that the endeavour to reach, through culture, the sweetness and light . . . which we call Hellenising, is the master-impulse of the life of the nation.

Matthew Arnold, *Culture and Anarchy*, 1869

Lovely, lovely, but oh how sad!

Henry James on Florence, 1867

*T*he 1860s marked a chasm in the wider cultural life of Europe. Nowhere was this truer than in France. Jean-Auguste-Dominique Ingres, hitherto an adherent of the old classical forms, declared that the Greek gods of European culture had died. His *Turkish Baths* (1862), one critic observes, marked by its cool, contemporary and highly erotic precision the death of *le pur classique*.[1] Simultaneously Charles Baudelaire uttered a startling call for artists to paint life as it was *now*. Out of such feelings issued the triumph of French realism and naturalism consummated through the novels of Gustave Flaubert (*Madame Bovary* had already appeared in 1859) and the stories of Guy de Maupassant, as well as, a bit later, Impressionism in art. Britain may have announced its material leadership at the Great Exhibition, but a decade later Paris was on its way to becoming, in cultural terms, the universal capital of the late nineteenth-century world. Not even defeat at the hands of unified Germany in 1870–1, and a Prussian victory celebration in the French capital before a quick withdrawal, were to halt this phenomenon; arguably both military and social debacle added an extra *edge*.

This is relevant because it establishes an essential context for British dilemmas in the field of culture during the High Victorian age. We have seen that the sense of a stagnating status quo and the need for fresh directions circulated in the United Kingdom. Architecture provides an example. In the same year as Ingres's Turkish portrait, James Fergusson's *History of the Modern Styles of Architecture* emphasized the sham in both the Gothic and Grecian schools that had so dominated debates about the built fabric of Britain. Fergusson was especially derisive in regard, for example, to the Acropolis replica of St Pancras Church in London's Camden Town dating from the neoclassical heyday of the 1820s, and he looked forward to a truly modern style reflecting mid-nineteenth century culture as it now existed. In the same spirit Robert Kerr in *The Gentleman's House* (1864) asserted the simple but surprisingly radical principle that 'an English gentleman is better suited to an English house than an Italian or Grecian one'.

But what was an English house? No such concept yet existed, other than an olden-time mock medieval idea that was little more up-to-date than the styles Fergusson found so lacking. John Steegman summarizes the ensuing confession of defeat once it transpired that there were, in fact, no stylistic notions to fill the gap that existed:

> Convinced at last of their inability to impress the character of their culture on their own age, the men of the 1860s resigned themselves to eclecticism, and to accepting a variety of styles on a scale unheard of since the Jacobean epoch. Among the most widely accepted varieties ... were the Elizabethan, the Rural Italian, the Palatial Italian, the French-Italian, the English Renaissance, the medieval or Gothic, the Cottage and the Scottish Baronial.[2]

Here Steegman may have had his tongue in his cheek, but such an almost desperate boxing of the compass in historical and geographical inspirations had parallels in almost all fields of creative endeavour in Britain. The most celebrated social critique was Matthew Arnold's *Culture and Anarchy*

(1869) with its central statement that the Hellenic – or *Hellenizing* – idea was the only available vision of 'sweetness and light' with the potential to save British civilization from falling yet further into the abyss of philistinism. To a post-Victorian generation this insistence on looking backwards, a clinging to timeworn ideals, was often to smack of a lack of imagination. Yet this took insufficient account of the limits working within the Victorian cultural imagination. The Britons of that period remade their world above all in material terms, but also – however reluctantly – eventually in political ones too. Many also confronted the frightening disintegration of their religious faith in the wake of Charles Darwin's *On the Origin of Species*. It is hardly surprising that in other matters, and above all in the cultural sphere, they sought ways of sticking to what was familiar about the past, or revising it in ways that did not entail the radical experiments or the *disruption* that they so deplored across the Channel. The point to underline is that the Mediterranean, so embedded in the existing imaginative landscape, continued to be central to themes pervading British aesthetic and stylistic preferences, though increasingly absorbed among a widening array of other influences as a globalized world system took shape in however messy and eclectic a way.

If one sought to pin down a precise moment at which mid-Victorian culture gave way, the death of Elizabeth Barrett Browning in her Florentine home of Casa Guidi on 29 June 1861 would be an appropriate suggestion. In her prime she had been the elegiac voice of her generation. The cause of death was an abscess on the lung, compounded by chronic weakness, her passing eased by large doses of morphine. Her final moments were spent in a drug-induced euphoria, her hands alternately touching her lips and quivering upwards to her husband. The Brownings' closest friend in Florence, Isa Blagden, on hearing of the passing, rushed to the *casa* and took the young Pen off to her Bellosguardo villa. A few days later Elizabeth's funeral took place, with many of the shops in the city closed. She was buried in the Protestant Cemetery – what Henry James considered the most beautiful place in Italy.[3] The tomb was designed by a young English artist in Rome, Frederic Leighton, a figure before long to be critical to the shape of the late Victorian artistic world. After the burial, Robert Browning left Florence almost immediately and never returned in a long life, though he was often to travel to other places in Italy. He sought a new refuge first

in Brittany, and later more permanently in London. But his was a personality split at so many levels that in some senses he always remained at Casa
Guidi. He wrote later to Isa Blagden, who remained his closest confidante
till her own death in 1873, saying how imaginatively he remained rooted
in the old life there: 'Oh me! To find myself some late sunshiny Sunday
afternoon, with my face turned to Florence – "ten minutes to the gate, ten
minutes home!" I think I should fairly end it all on the spot!'[4]

End it all on the spot – or, rather, freeze for ever in time a fleeting
moment re-imagined as utter, unrepeatable contentment. Such an exquisite sentiment of deathly sublimation was a quintessential element in this
subject (to be seen again in the life of John Singer Sargent years later).[5] The
'golden ring' of Anglo-Florentine society meanwhile did not die along
with Elizabeth Barrett Browning, as one writer suggests.[6] Its shades could
be felt, for example, hovering over Little Holland House, that social centre
of late Victorian arts in London, where the presence of the painter G. F.
Watts, amongst others, embodied old times in Tuscany.[7] But, with that
human tendency to disparage the 'near past', it was to become common to
condescend to the Anglo-Florentine connection for alleged superficiality.[8]
There were to be shades of this in E. M. Forster's formative fiction early in
the next century. Thereafter the Anglo-American presence in the city was
to be a self-consciously social rather than artistic elite, of the sort satirized
in Aldous Huxley's *Those Barren Leaves* (1925).[9] But the aura of the
Brownings and the Trollopes and their circles in a cultivated if self-
contained Florentine world never entirely went away, part of what Henry
James – for whom the immediate afterglow of that world cast such a spell
on his own life – called the 'irrecoverable presences' of a beautiful if always
ungraspable Italy.

Meanwhile the Italian Question, including its ramifications in British
affairs, had not itself ended with the formal inauguration of the Kingdom
of Italy on 17 March 1861, if only because the Papal and Venetian territories had been excluded from it. When Garibaldi marched with what
remained of his Redshirted enthusiasts against Rome once more in 1862,
he had been abruptly stopped by Italian government troops at the battle
(really a skirmish) of Aspromonte on a Calabrian mountainside. Wounded
in the foot in an exchange lasting only minutes, the hero was tended by
Jessie White Mario, still active in the ambulance corps.[10] The British prime

minister's wife Lady Palmerston even sent a special bed for his recupera-
tion. Despite such gestures, Aspromonte marked the limits of tolerance
amongst leading European powers for aggressive Garibaldinian gestures
with their dangers for international peace. But the continuing residues of
the Risorgimento in English political culture were illustrated by Garibaldi's
visit to England in 1864. It was one of the great popular events of the age.

Garibaldi arrived in Southampton on 1 April 1864, first made a detour
to visit the poet laureate, Alfred Lord Tennyson, on the Isle of Wight, as if
to give a special literary touch to the enterprise, before heading for London.
Large crowds met him virtually everywhere in what has been called 'the
greatest of all anti-papal demonstrations'. Garibaldi, after all, was a secular
nationalist par excellence.[11] The visit certainly played on continuing anti-
Catholic currents. But the sensitivities ran more widely. The underlying
question of suffrage reform remained stalled at Westminster after various
unavailing legislative attempts through the 1850s, and its opponents, or
those in Britain who feared a headlong rush towards it, were concerned
that any mobilization of large numbers on the streets might breathe
urgency into the question or even renew the Chartist disturbances of the
late 1840s. This was why the Metropolitan Police set strict guidelines, such
as forbidding flags and banners, for those radical figures in political life, as
well as London-based Italians, who were the organizers of Garibaldi's time
in the country.

The climax of the whole affair came at the Crystal Palace on 16 April
where Garibaldi was to be invested with the Freedom of London, ceremonial sword included. The event was billed as a 'people's festival' and special
trains were laid on by the Great Western, the London North-Western, the
South-Eastern, and the London and Brighton train companies so that
ordinary people could attend from the outer suburbs and beyond. On the
day the crowd totalled 25,000. It passed off peacefully, but alarm bells
began to ring in the Palmerston ministry, especially at the prospect of the
next stage of the visit, the itinerary of which was to include northern
industrial cities. In the end the authorities discreetly but very firmly hustled
the great Italian out of the country before the full programme was
completed. No one was more relieved than Queen Victoria, since amongst
the frissons set off had been a fresh wave of republicanism already fuelled
by the monarch's reclusive widowhood.[12] In British political history this

General Garibaldi received by a massive crowd of supporters in
Trafalgar Square, 16 April 1864

was not without repercussions. In July 1866 a reform meeting in Hyde
Park led to riots – this time the crowd was over 200,000 – and triggered a
set of consequences leading to the Second Reform Act of 1867 and with it
the introduction of a degree of genuine democracy into Britain. Garibaldi's
visit, through its evocation of mass feeling, had just provided an additional
shove along the way. It is impossible to think of a visit to British shores by
any foreign political figure since that has generated the same degree of
public clamour as Garibaldi's in 1864.[13]

Yet, paradoxically, at the same moment a sequence began in which
contemporary Italy gradually ceased to be internalized into British public
culture quite as it had been before. Superficially, the unfolding triumph of
Risorgimento forces, freshly demonstrated by the final eviction of Habsburg
authority from Venice in 1866, indicated that the liberal idyll of Anglo-
Italianism was in full spate. Lord John Russell, the most Italianate of British
liberal politicians, travelled to join the celebrations of King Victor
Emmanuel's entry into that city, a pageant of barges and gondolas adorned
in silk hangings proceeding down the Grand Canal, the gondoliers wearing
fifteenth-century costumes.[14] The excitement subsequently fed into the
poetry of Algernon Swinburne, but in a way that indicated an innate
fragility. Swinburne's first major publication, *Poems and Ballads*, had
shocked in its treatment of lesbianism, sado-masochism and anti-theism, a

call to revolt against mid-Victorian piety that established him as 'an international icon for progressive thinkers'.[15] But Italy remained part of the iconography. The young poet's 'A Song for Italy' worshipped before the altar of Italian freedom, whilst his ensuing *Songs before Sunrise* merged his quest for self-transcendence with adoration of Mazzinian republicanism.[16]

On the whole, latter-day critics have felt – not unlike some commentators on Elizabeth Barrett Browning – that the turn to a strident Mediterranean liberationism did Swinburne's creative genius no favours. The poet's character laid him open, then and later, to cutting psychological, indeed psychosexual, analysis. As one biographer remarks, 'it was always necessary for him to have some ideal before which he could prostrate himself, and *Italia* and Liberty were probably as good as any'.[17] In this interpretation *Songs before Sunrise* becomes an exercise in auto-intoxication, some of the verses, it was alleged, having been written on a bench in Regent's Park before Swinburne made one of his regular visits to a brothel in St John's Wood where flagellation was a speciality.[18]

Close to breakdown through drink and the shattering of his friendship with Dante Gabriel Rossetti, Swinburne shortly found salvation in a quiet suburban existence in Putney. Part of what Ezra Pound later dismissed as a 'facile compromise with life' was the evaporation through the 1870s of any residual interest in Italy and what it had previously represented for him. On one occasion, when a visitor to afternoon tea went into panegyrics on the beauty of Palermo, Swinburne quickly shot back, 'I doubt if you have seen anything there to match our Putney sunsets.'[19] By the 1880s his politics became those of a pedestrian Victorian conservative, including his attitude to anything foreign.[20]

The truth was that post-Risorgimento Italy was bound to prove at odds with what others expected of it. Furthermore, what aspired to be a new, secular, commercial and liberal-utilitarian Italy was not one recognizable in the old romantic ideal harboured even by sober enthusiasts like Lord John Russell. For one thing, the new state acted in unexpected ways. It introduced laws that made the export of artistic treasures more difficult. Sir Charles Eastlake at the National Gallery in London found that his efforts to purchase old master paintings sometimes now came unstuck. In fact he died in Pisa on Christmas Eve 1865 during his final such acquisitive venture and was buried in the Florence cemetery.[21] But whereas resting in an Italian grave like Keats and Shelley had hitherto struck in British minds a note of exquisite if sad romance, there was something now that detracted from such glamour. Lady Eastlake decided that something more in keeping with her husband's status was required, and his remains were brought back to London and reinterred in Kensal Green Cemetery, though only after a large cortège of the great and good had accompanied the hearse from Trafalgar Square. By then grumblings had already begun about the Italy that was emerging from the recent turmoil. Amongst the most acidic critics were sometimes Italian exiles occupying a prominent place in British life. Parma-born Antonio Gallenga, one of the most experienced foreign correspondents of *The Times* newspaper in the nineteenth century, writing when the Risorgimento had fully run its course, bitterly concluded that what had emerged was '. . . an *Italietta*, petty and bourgeois', combining all that was worst in the old Italian states.[22]

Other long-standing paradoxes were played out against this shifting background. Although British Protestants had often reacted strongly when coming face to face with the rituals of Italian Catholicism, this was nevertheless the Italy they were conditioned to, and the very strangeness of the encounter was for them part of the enthralment. Stories after 1861 of the abandonment of churches, despoiling of monasteries, and clergy and nuns being thrown out onto the streets at the hands of an anticlerical regime,[23] were oddly unsettling to Protestant consciences at a time when the real enemy was increasingly non-belief itself. Gladstone intervened personally at one point to ensure that the monastery of Monte Cassino was spared harassment, arguing that the rich library and its early charters needed to be kept together for cultural rather than just religious reasons. He even made a special visit to Italy to make this case to the authorities, taking his wife (to whom he had first unsuccessfully proposed on a moonlit visit to the Coliseum thirty years before[24]) and his daughter with him; allegedly he lectured them both daily on fragments of Dante at eight a.m. sharp.[25] In the event, Monte Cassino was one of the few large religious houses to escape disbandment.

As British prime minister after 1868, Gladstone consistently sought to ensure that if the Papal States were to become part of the new Italy, they should do so only through negotiation, and in a manner ensuring that the spiritual powers of the Papacy – claims recently enhanced in Pope Pius IX's encyclical *Syllabus of Errors* – should not be too rudely compromised.[26] In all of this, though he had never actually converted, were the traces of a theological Romanism that was part of Gladstone's highly complex make-up.[27] In the end the climax of Italian unification, and the final occupation of the old papal territory by Italian troops in November 1870, proved messier, but throughout the crisis, at Gladstone's behest, a vessel of the British Mediterranean Fleet was kept at the disposal of the pope should he need to make a quick escape to Britain's nearby and overwhelmingly Catholic colony of Malta.[28] Such a final humiliation the Catholic faithful were spared. Still, no British minister went to proffer any blessing for the climax of the Risorgimento in Rome as Russell had done in Venice four years before. Such ambivalence by outsiders was one marker that the future might not be brilliant. 'Idealists of the Risorgimento,' John Pemble states of the long-term process that followed, 'had argued that Rome, disencumbered of the papal incubus, would enhance united Italy. The sequel proved their opponents right. United Italy, encumbered with the incubus of nationalism, diminished Rome.'[29] Certainly that was how an insatiable late Victorian traveller in the European South, Augustus Hare, felt about it. In 1905 he was to express the view that United Italy had done more to destroy the artistic beauty of Rome than the invasions of the Goths and Visigoths centuries before. 'They,' he wrote of Italy's bourgeois democratic rulers, 'have done for the [entire] City what the sixteenth century did to the Forum.'[30]

Such a disenchantment with contemporary Italy, ranging from disillusioned radicalism through to the I-told-you-so amongst crusty English conservatives, interacted with a heightened sensitivity to social issues from the 1860s. Jessie White Mario, days of flaming nationalism now in the past, grew old writing from Italy for the liberal *Nation* newspaper in Britain, describing the evils in her adopted country of illegal abortions, boy labourers in Sicilian sulphur mines and paupers' graves. Perhaps the most striking example of such critiques were those of a Victorian writer unique in the contrast between the vast popularity of her two-shilling yellow novels and the utter oblivion into which she has since sunk in English literary history: Marie Louise de la Ramée, born in Bury St Edmunds, who wrote as Ouida.

After the vast financial success of her controversial romantic works in England, the most lasting being *Under Two Flags*,[31] Ouida moved to Tuscany in 1871 to escape public hounding. Somebody who knew both her and Italy well commented subsequently that in novels like *Pascarel* (1874) and *Ariadne* (1877), nobody interpreted more delicately for English readers a pervasive sense of beauty.[32] But in stories like *The Village Commune* (1882), Ouida turned her attention to the grinding injustices of the post-Risorgimento countryside and did not hesitate to draw awkward parallels with Ireland, where a violent land agitation was in progress from the 1870s.[33] These two contrasting themes in Ouida's preoccupations were not perhaps so contradictory. Her overarching concern was the pain of people's lives in romantic and material senses, and fate gave her a special Tuscan viewpoint, which was why she was one English writer who was actually read by Italians.[34] This won her little credit with the Anglo-Florentines who, in their increasingly rigid little community, heartily disliked her, though her own argumentativeness did not help.[35] Reduced to poverty and living in an apartment in Viareggio with many stray but pampered dogs, Ouida died in 1909. There is a memorial to her on the outskirts of Bury St Edmunds, appropriate to her oblique experience and character.

Yet if the Italy of the present day ceased to carry quite the same meanings in British cultural awareness, that is not at all to say that the Italy of the past, or themes that could be framed in essentially historical ways, lost their resonance. Italy was not, so far as British perceptions were concerned, cast into outer darkness like some orientalized 'other', though that has been contended in the vein of postmodernist analysis.[36] But it *was* freshly aestheticized so as to suit High Victorian sensibilities. John Ruskin's role remained critical. It is usually said that after 1860 his essential focus shifted from aesthetic to socio-economic issues, and that as part of the transition 'he looked at Italy . . . through a different lens'.[37] In fact aesthetics – and specifically the aesthetics of beauty – always remained at his core. It was just that around him Ruskin now saw material change blighting all that was best in being alive. His mission was to salvage what was possible. In England there was not much to be done, other than to alert the ordinary population to the slide into philistinism through his series of publications known as *Fors Clavigera*, purporting to be letters sent to working men in north-eastern England, and the organization of the St George's Guild, the latter inspired by the degradation of traditions he first identified in Swiss Alpine villages.[38] But in Italy at least certain practical goals in terms of preserving precious legacies of beauty could be set. Both Lucca and Verona became particularly important in this respect to Ruskin because these places appeared not to embrace corrupting change with the aplomb, say, of Milan, a city he now regarded as one only to pass *through*,[39] Rome, also fast losing its customary, if mixed, charms, and the always erring metropolis of Naples. Henry James's view of the latter as 'wild and weird and sinister' was one Ruskin certainly shared.[40]

Most deserving of protection of all, however, was undoubtedly Venice, and from the mid-1870s Ruskin was at the heart of what became a British mission to 'save' the city of lagoons and palaces from the ravages of restoration.[41] The city became, in Pemble's words, 'the quintessence of stricken beauty', and being *stricken* was an exquisite element in that Venetian obsession inscribed on the High Victorian emotional atlas. Far from being something to be 'improved', this quality of bereftness was deemed essential to Venice's embodiment of beauty and the sadness of the human condition. 'It is impossible for anyone to know the horror and contempt with which I regard modern restoration,' Ruskin stated,[42] and nowhere aroused his feelings more acutely on this score than Venice. One innovation he despised was the 'mosquito fleet' – a tellingly pejorative term for the new *vaporetti*, or steamers, that plied between the Lido and Piazza S. Maria after 1880, while the approach of the railway across the Veneto was even more galling.[43]

A conduit for protesting against innovations detrimental to Venice's role in Victorian consciousness was the Arundel Society, founded to promote awareness of old masterworks, its main activity being to issue chromolithographs of Italian frescos. Ruskin was a leading light in that organization, but so was the archaeologist and diplomat Austen Henry Layard, famous as the excavator of Nineveh, who retired to Venice in 1885 and was, with the energetic Lady Layard, until his death in 1894 prominent in the Anglo-American community. They spent their final years in seigneurial style in the sixteenth-century Palazzo Ca' Cappello, the hallway lined by fragments from his great Assyrian discoveries, and the stairways and saloons dignified by a large collection of pictures later bequeathed to the National Gallery.

The grandeur of the Layards' Venetian residence perhaps explains why younger expatriates in the city regarded an invitation to what they termed 'the refrigerator' as intimidating.[44] But a sense of being 'refrigerated', of being subjected to an insufferable aesthetic patronage, was becoming an even more distinct feeling among a younger generation of Italian intelligentsia. In the assessment of one English resident in Venice, the anti-restoration campaign in England had few resonances amongst most Venetians, who indeed strongly opposed it.[45] Buried in this was a process in which the 'special friendship' between Britain and Italy, which had underpinned the received version of the Risorgimento itself, gradually started to erode.[46] When a young British diplomat with a distinguished career in Mediterranean diplomacy ahead of him, Rennell Rodd, first took up a post in Rome in 1887, a contact at the Italian Foreign Office was to tell him that interaction with the British embassy was now at low ebb. The British, it was complained, 'regarded her [Italy] as a negligible quantity'.[47] Disillusion went both ways, and as ever politics, diplomacy and culture were not disconnected.

One of Ruskin's supporters in his campaign against the planned restoration of the façade of St Mark's Cathedral in Venice in 1880 was the painter Edward Burne-Jones. Burne-Jones's career encapsulated the continuing centrality of Italy in British painting, but also some of the instability surrounding it. In young manhood deeply religious and drawn towards Catholicism, he considered taking holy orders but turned to art instead. His first visit to Italy came in 1859, in the company of Ruskin, who encouraged him to examine the works of Botticelli, Ghirlandaio, Mantegna and Signorelli, full of religious motifs now important not so much as representations of faith but as testimony to the sacredness of art itself. They spent time in Milan and Venice, but Florence was always to be Burne-Jones's favourite. 'It was the model,' his biographer Fiona MacCarthy writes, 'for his enchanted garden of eternal beauty.' She adds, 'Burne-Jones returned [from Italy] with his mind full of friezes, the Annunciations, crucifixions, processions, angel choirs and great storytelling cycles, the Italianate concepts that . . . shape[d] his own artistic thinking.'[48]

Thereafter Burne-Jones liked to regard himself as almost Italian, sometimes signing letters 'Angelo' after Fra Angelico, the early Renaissance painter. It was the very strangeness of the works of the so-called 'primitive' Italians of that era which especially attracted the circles of Victorian Pre-Raphaelitism in which Burne-Jones moved, albeit with some independence on his part.[49] He made a second visit to Italy, again with Ruskin, in

1862, and because Ruskin's tastes and assessments could change with dizzying rapidity, this time Burne-Jones was directed towards the Venetian 'colourists' such as Titian, Tintoretto and Veronese.[50] Burne-Jones became concerned – perhaps all the more so since he lacked proper training in drawing – that this endless copying of Italian greats was stifling his own development.[51] Nor was it clear that such Italian models could provide a means of coming to terms, artistically, with his troubling personal experience. Ostensibly happily married, in the next few years he lost his religious faith and suffered from sexual anxiety, intensified by his affair with Maria Zambaco, daughter of a rich Anglo-Greek merchant in London, sculptor and archetypal Pre-Raphaelite pin-up with her red hair, pale skin and striking physicality. It is telling that in this phase of his life Burne-Jones turned rather to classical mythology as having the flexibility and meaning for his purposes, portraying Maria as a temptress in such works as *Cupid and Psyche* and *Phyllis and Demaphoön*, the latter notable as the first picture on public view in Britain to make explicit the male genitalia (the canvas, however, had to be removed from the walls of the British Watercolour Society). During 1870 Burne-Jones's entanglement with Maria came to a head. He refused to accompany her to Greece on a visit, and the affair foundered, though not before she had proposed a mutual suicide pact in Venice.[52] As Robert Browning once said, Venice was, among other things, a place of interesting suicides, at least in the British imagination.[53]

In what remained of his career, and against the background of a re-solidified family and growing professional recognition, Burne-Jones kept coming back to his Italian roots, with all the comfort that might hopefully be drawn from them. One of his main achievements was his mosaic, *The Heavenly Jerusalem*, for the American Church in Rome, the first Protestant place of worship built within the walls of the Vatican City, and unveiled on Christmas Day in 1885. But in keeping with the shifting connotations that attached themselves to the country, visits to Italy often now induced a sense of heartache. 'Italy breaks my heart,' Burne-Jones wrote to a friend '. . . to be in it, and have all the pining and longing . . . [and] to see long desolate streets and thoughtful, sorrowing faces everywhere . . . that makes tears come.'[54] Burne-Jones was an extreme but by no means rare case where Italy as it was now seen, or as it worked on the senses, precipitated a poignant awareness, not of the possibilities and

Edward Burne-Jones in his studio, 1890

excitements for which it once served as a metaphor, but of what had finally proved elusive and impossible in life. The old magic was there, but on it was now inscribed a sense of loss that was a hallmark of the aesthetic world of the High Victorians. That 'autumn consciousness' noted by one cultural historian as a distinctive trait of the Victorian zenith was not unrelated.[55]

Here, then, was a strong backward pull towards an old, eternal Italy embodying nostalgic sadness. The conservatism generated often, as in Burne-Jones's case, went with a strong distaste for the experimentation represented by the Impressionist salon in Paris, especially marked by the end of the 1870s.[56] Yet things were not always clear cut. Italy could be made to serve the purposes of those in British art and literature who also felt an urge to kick against the pricks of society. An example was J. A. M. Whistler, American-born but with close Scottish family links, whose career was overwhelmingly spent in Britain. Having trained in Paris, Whistler – now based in London – exhibited at the rebellious Salon des Refusés in 1863. Subsequently he found himself at the margins in his adopted city, with election to the Royal Academy passing him by. When Ruskin famously attacked him in *Fors Clavigera* in 1877 for 'Cockney impudence' and 'flinging a pot of paint in the public's face', a thinly veiled reference to his Impressionist tendencies, it led to a libel case (Burne-Jones testified on Ruskin's behalf). In late 1879 Whistler went to Venice for a year, and pointedly set out to paint, not the familiar stereotypes, but lesser-known commercial waterways and obscure viewpoints. This offered 'a visual answer to Ruskin's criticisms of Whistler's art'.[57] The outcome included such paintings as *Nocturne in Blue and Silver: The Lagoon, Venice* and *The Garden*, with all those moods and allusiveness that were Whistler's hallmark, vividly recreating 'a decaying city of rusty grilles, leprous walls, sagging, water-lapped steps – the Venice that was already in 1880 sinking into the mud'.[58] In one of his sketches, *The Beggars*, that hitherto largely ignored subject, *poverty* in Venice, was aired. Once exhibited at the Fine Arts Society in London that December, however, such images were criticized for a painful absence of feeling 'for the past glories of Venice' (strongly contrasting with the established conventions of Canaletto, whose rendering of Venetian water never *flowed* in the corrosive manner caught by Whistler). Starkly different interpretations of what was 'painterly' about Venice thus contributed to laying bare the fissures, aesthetic and emotional, now running through British art, for which Whistler was to be a principal touchstone not only through Italian but, as we shall see, also Spanish reference points.

In this vein the engagement of Samuel Butler with a rather different part of Italy during these years is relevant because it helped frame what finally became the most coruscating analysis ever made of Victorian values and ethos, especially of the patriarchal family. The youthful Butler, after his father had opposed his pursuing a career in art on the grounds that it would throw him into dangerous company, had gone off to become a farmer in the new and very remote colony of New Zealand, an experience recorded to much acclaim in *Erewhon* (1872). Already by the time of that publication he had, on return, begun his close acquaintance with the regions of Piedmont and Lombardy. Butler's main preoccupations were evoked in his *Alps and Sanctuaries* (1881). Elinor Shaffer writes of his descriptions of the religious shrines that fascinated him:

Amusing and readable, they also had a serious purpose: the rehabilita-
tion of the sites and artists of the counter-Reformation, the objects of
popular Catholic pilgrimage, but ignored by aristocrats on the grand
tour, by the new middle-class tourists, and by the connoisseurs and art
historical specialists. He takes up the cudgels for a form of art distasteful
to the sectarian narrowness and class prejudices of his own family and
the mass of his countrymen.[59]

In describing – and photographing – the intimacy of the family life of
Italian peasants and environments, Butler developed an internalized critique
of his painful English experience of society and familial home, and used
simple Catholicism as a means of exposing the hypocrisy he perceived in
English Protestant morality.[60] He painted the porch of Rossura Church as
his favourite place because of its very plainness. 'The impression,' he wrote
to a friend, 'that the porch could not be otherwise, that feeling of inevita-
bleness, was just one of its charms.'[61] This was even further from the grandeur of the stones of Venice than Whistler's nocturnes. As we shall see in the
next chapter, after publishing an evocation of the chapel art to be found in
the village of Varallo, *Ex Voto* (1888), Butler's interests were to take a more
strictly classical and literary direction, leading him to become immersed in
the life of Sicily. But the fundamental thrust – to find some means to shatter
the Victorian orthodoxies he despised – was to be the same.

That classicism remained, if in increasingly complicated and contested
ways, at the heart of Britain's tentative cultural growth through the later
nineteenth century is important. This would not have been entirely
predictable around 1860. We saw earlier that the mouldy Mediterranean
ancients had become the butt for a good deal of criticism ranging from
Charles Dickens to George Eliot. There were many educational experts
who felt that the primacy of classical subjects in the country's leading
schools was producing the wrong sort of elite, insufficiently attuned to
modern learning (here were the seeds of a strand in the interpretation of
British economic weakness that was to be prominent in the later twentieth
century).[62] A very distant Mediterranean past was at odds, too, with an
eagerness to reach out towards fresh realities – the world as it was
now – tangible in Britain by the end of the 1850s, a tendency even more
advanced, as we saw, in France. Such sentiments marked the circles of the

Pre-Raphaelite Brotherhood, for whom contemporary English painting on classical subjects seemed pompous and dated.[63]

Yet already by the end of the 1860s ancient Greece was making a comeback as an inspiration for British painters. The Royal Academy exhibition in 1869, the first to be staged in the new galleries at Burlington House on Piccadilly, provided a marker, with a number of younger artists contributing canvases of this type. In retrospect this was the start of what has been called by some art historians a school of 'Olympian Painting', though as so often that term is simply a latter-day rationalization of an essentially amorphous group. It was also just one aspect of the magnetism of Greek classicism as a whole for the High Victorian generation, offering, one historian notes, a very objective, and therefore comforting, contrast 'with the subjective, turbid, tangled art of their post-romantic era . . . [and] a yardstick against which the modern world and its art could be measured and found wanting'.[64]

This is not to say that the classical-Mediterranean impulse in Britain was inherently backward-looking in its cultural implications. It was just part of how the British sought to navigate change on their own very hesitant terms. A key aspect of this process was the return of the nude to British art, one reflection of the new radical secularism. The Royal Academy had been virtually nude-free for the first half of the nineteenth century, and especially so during the early and mid-Victorian peak of evangelicalism.[65] Artists who breached the rule did so at a cost. One who did was William Etty, for whom the disfiguring effects of smallpox, desperate shyness and a lonely personal life seem to have found some release in painting female nudes, a skill enhanced when he spent time at life classes in a Venetian studio.[66] He was attacked in *The Times* for painting 'mere dirty flesh'.[67] The same critic identified a lamentable failure – moral and aesthetic – to blend nakedness with purity. Etty's apparent fault lay in the very literalness of his rendering of the female body. This was not an easy problem to get over, and from the 1830s through to the 1850s, in contrast to practices in the Paris salon, not many British artists made the attempt.

In fact what was known as 'the Grecian' and nakedness went together in British art conventions throughout the nineteenth century (even in the 1890s at the 'progressive' Slade School of Art it was to be a rule that nudes must be viewed 'in the classical manner').[68] It was logical that after 1860, when, as part of that rebelliousness for which Swinburne's erotic poems and transcendent Italian nationalism had also been identifiers, there was a renewed interest in portrayal of the revealed body, it duly took a classicized, mythological and Mediterranean form. Frederic Leighton's full-length vertical nude, *Venus Disrobing* (1866), marked the start of the renaissance of the genre, but crucially it did so in the spirit of Greek art refracted through current tastes: a hand discreetly concealing the private parts, and redolent with the spirit of the ancient Greek master Praxitiles' Aphrodite of Knossos, in Ruskin's approving description 'one of the purest and most elevated incarnations of woman conceivable'.[69] This was an essentially aesthetic, un-literal view of feminine beauty, one frozen into ambivalence between warm flesh and deathly cold marble.[70] In one art historical assessment, the 'ambivalent, classicized bodies at the centre of Leighton's work threaten to disperse and break up into the parts from which they are assembled'.[71] At the time it was observed in the *Pall Mall Gazette* of Leighton's goddess that 'she is not a Venus, but a carefully studied and refined-looking Englishwoman about to step into the water, profoundly conscious that she is disrobing for the occasion'.[72]

If there were contradictory impulses at work in this, it was because the British Victorians were terrified of sex, at least in its public representations, and yet obsessed by it. Working this bind out was sure to be difficult, and 'Grecianizing' the process helped. For one thing, as has been observed, whereas nudes in French art – such as those conveyed with precise realism in Ingres's *Turkish Baths* – usually struck a note of having taken their clothes *off*, ancient Greek ones looked as if they had never thought of having any clothes *on*, which was far less suggestive of anything improper.[73] Wrapped up in this was the problem of male *looking*, so that the veiled distancing that went with suitably antique images was appropriate to an alternating attraction and repulsion, or what Simon Goldhill terms a half-looking, embedded in Victorian psychology when sexuality came to the fore.[74] The method offered a route into a more anxious, ambiguous and overtly sensualized world, without undue mental and moral displacement.[75] Richard Jenkyns again sums up this theme in relation to High Victorian culture over these years: 'Here was the paradox of Greek art: by the 1890s it had come to seem artificial and a little absurd; yet it could still serve to liberate the inhibitions . . . Greek art allowed one to contemplate

the naked body with a good conscience and at the same time to congratulate oneself on possessing good taste . . . The admirer of Ingres . . . had not
this consolation.'[76]

More should be said about Frederic Leighton because his influence on
later Victorian art was so significant. From an affluent professional family
spending (like John Ruskin's) much time in Europe, he lived in both
Frankfurt and Rome, where he received his first drawing lessons.[77] As an
art student in Rome he was closely involved with the German Nazarene
circle then in its dying phase; though, as one writer states, the attraction of
the Nazarenes for a certain group of British artists was because they were
religious in their inspiration, not because they were German.[78] Living in
London after 1860, Leighton set his sights on the Royal Academy, but here
the very 'progressiveness' of his European credentials constituted a potential handicap, and he was initially seen as an outsider.[79] This was where a
concentration on ancient Greek models came in useful because it allowed
him to straddle the boundaries of shifting tastes but also of the surrounding
cultural politics. As Leighton explained, he was drawn towards 'a class of
subjects . . . in which supreme scope is left to pure artistic qualities . . .
These conditions classic subjects afford.'[80] They were also entirely respectable and rooted in a distinct British tradition, though in fact traces of
Leighton's Germanism never entirely went away.

This strategy, allied with his undoubted talent as a visual artist,
succeeded. By 1878 he became president of the Royal Academy and was
knighted. In 1880 his self-portrait, commissioned for the Uffizi Gallery in
Florence, showed him in his studio wearing academic robes and standing
before a cast of the Elgin Marbles, now transmuted into an emblem of
Britain's special tie with Hellenic art. A contemporary remarked that
Leighton, with his Apollonian looks and highly refined manners, was 'like
a Greek deposited in London',[81] and this was the point about so-called
Olympian painting in Britain – in Scotland just as much as in England[82] –
as well as the Aesthetic school with which it overlapped: the blend of
modern Britain and ancient Greece underpinned a style quite apart from
that Continental experimentation so widely found repellent.

One viewer observed of Leighton's *Winding the Skein* (1878) showing
two young girls on a sunlit homely terrace manipulating the thread of a
textile against a far mountain background, that these 'Greek maidens are

naturally employed as we often see English girls in other surroundings', and such an idealization of a familiar occupation was indeed one of Leighton's hallmarks.[83] It was also characteristic of a wider genre evoking bourgeois Victorian lookalikes living contented ancient lives under a blazing Mediterranean sun in villas resembling vaguely the residences then spreading throughout the suburbs of English cities.[84] The mix of dream and recognizable reality, the time travelling, was all part of the charm, as in the classical pictorial reveries of Friesian-born Lawrence Alma-Tadema, though in his case the subject was Rome, not Greece.

Alma-Tadema's fascination with the ancient past stemmed from his visit to Pompeii in 1863 on his honeymoon; he moved to London in 1870 after being widowed. At first his paintings were of intimate domestic settings but moved on to capture the monumentalism of Roman public life, as in his *An Audience at Agrippa's* (1875). Such imagery conveniently gelled with a fresh sense of scale in Victorian London during its own imperial heyday. As an outsider himself, Alma-Tadema was all the more equipped to identify Victorian traits and evoke them through a Roman filter, just as his *Autumn* (1874) conveyed a seasonal thoughtfulness and pathos very much of its time. In a process that has been closely reconstructed, it was the ambiguity between the *then* and the *now*, fact and fiction, portrayed in warm Mediterranean settings, that helps explain his huge contemporary appeal.[85] It was also why, after his death, and even when, as with much Victorian art, his strictly artistic reputation was in sharp decline, Alma-Tadema's images still became an inspiration for filmmakers looting the classical tradition for whatever might engage mass consciousness. Cecil B. DeMille, when making *The Ten Commandments* in the 1950s, showed Alma-Tadema prints to his studio staff,[86] and the same traces can be seen in more contemporary films such as Ridley Scott's *Gladiator* (2000). 'Tadema might be a purveyor of hammy Victoriana. His pictures might even look downright ridiculous,' the art critic Rachel Campbell-Johnson states rather sharply, but goes on, 'Their sequels are still playing out in the British modern imagination.'[87] Alma-Tadema's paintings, alongside those of Frederic Leighton, with whom he had a close if not intimate friendship, may be regarded intellectually as heading towards a dead end, or as expanding the possibilities of British artistic life under the constraints – including moral – of their day, all depending on the angle of retrospection.[88]

There was one other High Victorian tendency indicating an underlying change. This was a growing eclecticism, so that even where Greek themes remained prominent in the visual arts, they were mixed and matched with other, sometimes totally contrasting, elements. Greek *and something else* became a common formula.[89] In the 1860s a fashion began for almost anything Japanese, with associated colours of blue and white; Liberty's, the department store in London's Regent Street, was established in 1875 to sell Japanese and other Eastern fabrics.[90] Painters like J. A. M. Whistler and Albert Moore subsequently took up the blending of Greek *and* Japanese motifs as a fresh aesthetic touch. Ellen Terry, who as a very young actress was briefly married to the much older painter G. F. Watts, alternated for a period between wearing Greek costume and a kimono, both supposedly marks at that time of highly cultivated living.[91] In the very different sphere of architecture, alongside the great variety of Italian styles mentioned earlier, the possibilities of 'something Greek' were expanded by a fresh interest in the Byzantine heritage. A key figure here was George Street, whose interests in medieval Greece were just one ingredient (Spanish Gothic was another) of what a biographer called 'the bold and character-istic – but ultimately exhausting – vocabulary of High Victorian architec-ture', a synthesis of which Street was the leading theorist and exponent.[92] The culmination of this movement in Britain was to be the construction of the neo-Byzantine Westminster Cathedral, not finally opened until 1903.

Such a hugely diverse eclectic impulse across a whole range of arts prac-tised in Britain reflected a process of globalization at a multitude of levels. An older Mediterranean primacy in a British cultural repertoire was there-fore subject to adjustment in a now more crowded, richer setting. But it also testified to a deep desire to go on searching for new combinations of art and design, and to graft them into the artefact of British culture, as a way of laying claim at last to the status of a truly elevated nation which some others, like the visiting French critic Charles Taine, continued to sneer at; in Taine's case at a country, he said, still churning out endless reproductions of antique busts in a vain attempt to fill a cultural empti-ness.[93] French contempt for English aesthetic shortcomings, British despising of French material and political failings, both testimony to what François Crouzet, a great historian of cross-Channel psychology, called the *'paradoxe' franco-britannique*: here were two countries in tense symbiosis, permanently bound by their dislikes and yet their intimate connection.[94] Britain's Southern bias, culturally and politically, was also one way it sought to deflect that tension so close to home.

As the Victorians passed their zenith, then, they remained gripped by old uncertainties and criticisms. Henry James, always with his finger close to the cultural pulse, and despite his love of England as an adopted homeland, caught this in his comment on the 'unaesthetic temper of the people' compared to their Continental neighbours;[95] and however exhaustively the practitioners of precious arts sought to press some button – or discover some magic formula, Mediterranean, oriental or whatever – to dispel the curse of British pedestrianism, they never entirely succeeded. To some, like Whistler, this was anyway a search for an elusive grail. There never was, Whistler remarked, an artistic people and there was no point in trying to make the British into something they were not.[96] Yet there remained an uneasy contrast between a nation that was now so great in its political and diplomatic power abroad, above all in its empire, and one which continued to harbour a very fragile understanding of what being British or English actually *meant* at home. A bit like Frederic Leighton's own enigmatic personality, as Henry James conjured it up waspishly in a fictionalized character in one of his novels, this imponderable was something all too apt on examination to disappear into thin air.[97]

The relationship of the Mediterranean to such cultural sensitivities had a fresh complication as the late Victorian era climaxed: it ceased to be altogether clear who the ancient Greeks – so critical to a certain vision of Southern living – had actually *been* or, more importantly, what they represented in modern terms. If they were to continue to offer an inspiring, liberally inclined, Hellenizing model along lines related to Matthew Arnold's dream of 'sweetness and light', then the assumption remained that of an idealized Greece of Periclean times, that is, made up of sunny, happy, natural, reflective and perhaps above all *beautiful* people. This was the vision of the classic past – or 'the wonder and beauty of the old Greek life' as Oscar Wilde called it[98] – infusing the essential *pose* of Aestheticism itself. The latter tendency could incorporate all kinds of possibilities, including an advocacy of greater sexual freedom, which in its relation to Hellenism had a special homoerotic meaning.

A key figure here was A. J. Symonds, whose *A Problem of Greek Ethics* (1883) was in practice the first history of homosexuality in English.[99]

16 John Singer Sargent, *Breakfast in the Loggia* (1910). With sprays of dazzling sunshine, dappled shade and classical-Renaissance echoes, Sargent's painting provided a visual definition of the Warm South, at once calming and stimulating for visitors.

17 Winifred Knights, *Italian Landscape* (1922). The smooth surface, contemplative mood and restricted palette conjure up the artist's early Renaissance feeling. Knights's years at the British School at Rome after 1920 shaped one of Britain's greatest twentieth-century painters.

18 Walter Sickert, *The Palazzo Eleanora Duse, Venice* (*c.* 1901). Named after the great Italian actress who lived in the palazzo, Sickert's depiction – uneven, almost tremulous structures fronted by vile green water – conjures up a decaying and vulnerable Venice in stark contrast to the bright majesty of Canaletto.

19 Arthur Melville, *A Barber's Shop, Spain* (*c.* 1890–5). The Scottish painter was a frequent visitor to Spain and this image, with its running pigments, offered a freshly modernist response to the country. He died there in 1904.

20 Roger Fry, *Le Petit Port, St Tropez* (1922). Fry's visit to the town from the autumn of 1921 confirmed his attachment to the French Mediterranean and its effect on his art.

21 Charles Rennie Mackintosh, *Port Vendres* (1926–7). Disillusioned at home, Mackintosh spent five years in Port Vendres near the Franco-Spanish border recording the interaction of hills, buildings and water fitting his philosophy of design. His wife spread some of his ashes from the town's mole in 1929.

22 Famagusta poster (1940). The Art Deco outlines feature the former Lusignan cathedral of St Nicholas. After Cyprus became a colony in 1925 British visitors there increased, mainly to see the classical and crusader heritage and stay at sanatoria resorts in the Troodos mountains.

23 Lady Mary Evelyn Chenevix Trench, *Kyrenia Harbour* (*c.* 1935). At this time, the later resident Lawrence Durrell recalled in his *Bitter Lemons*, Kyrenia, with its ravishing harbour, was still a Levantine port in the old Graeco-Turkish style.

24 Meredith Frampton, *Still Life*
(1932). In this meditation on
the tension between permanence
(the Roman marble head) and
rupture (a cracked pot, truncated
tree stumps), Frampton drew on
classicized forms and contemporary
Italian influences in art.

25 John Armstrong, *Pro Patria*
(1938). Influenced by turmoil
in Spain and a 1937 visit to
Rome with its pervasive fascist
propaganda, Armstrong's painting
used sun-bleached Mediterranean
imagery to convey a civilization
on edge.

26 John Craxton, *Galatas* (1947). Craxton first visited Crete in 1947, recalling that 'Greece at that time was magical beyond belief'. A sense of release from the restrictions of post-war England was reflected in the visual world he created of sailors, dancers, cats, goats and recurring Byzantine motifs.

27 Elizabeth David, *A Book of Mediterranean Food* (1950). The author recalled the origins of her first culinary classic as 'a personal antidote to the bleak conditions and acute food shortages' of late 1940s England. The cover and illustrations were by John Minton.

28 John Minton, *The Road to Valencia* (1949). Minton painted this after his first visit to Spain. 'I have felt very lonely sometimes,' he said on returning from a subsequent trip there, 'but the extraordinary beauty of this country is some compensation.'

29 Susan Hawker, *Pine Tree, Italy* (1979). The artist comments on the power of watercolour to transform the real world, 'always visually chaotic and full of confusing details, into a unified poetic idea'. This is what the Mediterranean has signified in the British imagination: a unified poetic idea amidst bewildering difference.

30 The Italian Chapel, Orkney. Built by Italian prisoners of war after 1942 from salvaged materials on a bare island, the chapel encapsulates the capacity of Mediterranean riches to blend with northern bleakness.

31 Damien Hirst, *Hydra and Kali Discovered by Four Divers*. Photographed by Christoph Gerigk. The shaggy dog story of Damien Hirst's 2017 Venetian exhibition *Treasures from the Wreck of the Unbelievable* embodies the endless ability of Graeco-Roman mythology to replicate itself in global culture whilst posing an age-old question: can the truly beautiful ever be found?

Symonds's tangled biography intersects with various themes to which this book keeps returning. Far from being a Decadent like Oscar Wilde, he disliked aesthetical priggishness as he saw it and resembled Byron in harbouring a strongly Calvinist streak.[100] His conception of Greek Love was deeply contradictory, on the one hand encompassing his fascinated gaze fixed on Corsican drivers, Florentine lads and Venetian porters,[101] and yet also having a recurring spiritual dimension anxious to leave behind the longings of the flesh. 'Italy,' he once wrote, 'devours the body and soul of me',[102] and it was to escape being devoured whole that Symonds turned to Switzerland on the opposite pole of his emotional map, living much of the time in the remote Alpine village of Davos after 1877. He oscillated between the transparency and purity of the Swiss mountains and the corrupt allure – in his own mind – of the Italian lowlands.[103] But the pull of the latter was irresistible, and perhaps it was this, as well as Symonds's preoccupation with notions of sinfulness, that led his daughter to say that her father's death in Rome in April 1893 had been somehow appropriate.[104] Symonds's ideal of Greek Love and enduring Hellenism, John Pemble concludes, 'constituted a rare and perhaps lost epiphany . . . his own transgressions confirmed its elusiveness'.[105]

One matter concerning the continuing applicability of ancient Greek models to contemporary life was dress reform for women: the encouragement of a fashion both healthier and more functional than the prevailing large domed skirts and corsets with all their constrictions of movement. Oscar Wilde took this issue up as editor of the *Women's World* magazine. Most discussion hinged on the clean-cut, flexible drapery of ancient Greek costume, though the advantages of looser Japanese clothing were also considered anew in this debate.[106] Somebody whom Wilde pressed towards a Greek style in her wardrobe was his friend, the society beauty and mistress of the Prince of Wales, Lillie Langtry. He encouraged her to adopt classical interests in a number of areas, including learning Latin and watching Greek plays in English, the latter becoming something of a fad at the universities. On a number of occasions Wilde accompanied Langtry to lectures on Greek archaeology at King's College, London, causing a stir amongst the students. Langtry – whose beauty, Wilde said, was 'a thing of genius' – had her own ideas on how to turn all this to her special ends. Writing to Wilde ahead of a social event to which they were both invited, she said she was looking forward eagerly to her next class in Latin, and went on that for the looming fancy ball she had chosen 'a soft black Greek dress with a fringe of silver crescents and stars, and diamond ones in my hair and on my neck, and called it Queen of the Night. I made it myself.'[107] This was Greek *and* bling, the sort of display that got derided as 'South Kensington Hellenism'. Dress reform and Wilde himself were satirized in the ensuing Gilbert and Sullivan operetta, *Patience* (1881).[108] But however much fun was duly made, there was still in all this a desire to become freer, lighter, more elevated in spirit and sometimes lovelier, even if the attempt could sometimes be a bit over the top.

Yet there was another vision of Greece in ancient times that contradicted such continuing visions of aery loveliness: one that was archaic in spirit, ugly and which spoke for very different forces at work in the here and now. George Eliot, always prone to love–hate where the ancients were concerned, hinted at this when Richard Jebb, Professor of Greek at Glasgow University, asked her how Sophocles had influenced her fiction.[109] Her reply was, 'In the delineation of primitive emotions.' In 1872 the German philologist, Friedrich Nietzsche, whose view of human nature had been affected by his experiences as a medical orderly in the Franco-Prussian War, published *The Birth of Tragedy*; the 1886 edition bore the telling subtitle *Hellenism and Pessimism*. Nietzsche explored not what was inherently progressive and forward-looking in classical Greek theatre, but what was tragic, mean and regressive.[110] Annual renderings of the old Greek tragedies became a staple at many British universities, and however ravishing Lillie Langtry may have looked, for example at King's College on the occasions she attended, such occasions testified also to an evocation of mankind's capacity for revenge and pitiless savagery. This was one way that the late Victorian mind took on a darker hue than the previous generation would have been comfortable with.

The growth of a new scientific archaeology widened the channels down which some of these tendencies flowed. Older idealizations of the distant Greek past never pretended to deep knowledge. Broad outlines were enough, and this meant that questions out of sync with comfortable orthodoxies could easily be brushed aside. But a process got under way parallel to what in Germany has been described as the 'conquest of the ancient world by scholarship'.[111] This remorseless academicism started to expose gaping holes in previous understandings. How come, for instance, the noble-minded, beauty-worshipping Greek ancients had been slave-owning and women-degrading? As for archaeology proper, the outstanding characteristic of the societies revealed by new techniques of excavation as the century advanced did not mostly concern all the wonderful treasures they had produced, but just how close to the edge they had lived in basic food supplies and a host of other privations.

The old purist hankering after ancient ruins and artefacts unencumbered with awkward questions was certainly still there, encapsulated in one of Oscar Wilde's neat summations, 'where archaeology begins, art ceases'.[112] Furthermore, the transition was gradual. Charles Newton's excavations in, and removals from, the Levant in the 1850s were redolent of a previous age of dramatic discoveries, extending the range of the collections in the British Museum; the great Lion of Cnidus, that today sits so imposingly on its plinth in the Museum's Great Court, was lowered like some huge marble from its Turkish cliff-face and finally arrived in Great Russell Street at the end of that decade. Heinrich Schliemann's 'discovery' of Troy and Agamemnon's putative golden mask in the 1870s indicated that, in British cultural terms, the Augustan resonances of the classics were as powerful as ever. Indeed, Schliemann was almost more admired in Britain than he was in Germany, and when he gave a talk at the Society of Antiquaries in Burlington House in March 1877, it was packed out.[113] But Schliemann was essentially an amateur – if a lucky one – pushing against the main tendency towards a newly professional and naturally sceptical world of scholarship for whom romancing the imagination was much less important than engaging with the truth – sometimes brutal – of a past world. Newton himself was closely connected with the emergence of an institutional network in Britain based on this belief: the Society for the Promotion of Hellenic Studies in 1879; the Egypt Exploration Fund in 1882; and the British School of Archaeology at Athens in 1886 (the latter having first been mooted by Oscar Wilde's tutor, W. H. Muhaffy, when the British Association had met at Trinity College, Dublin in 1878).[114] The School in Athens, coming decades after the foundation of its distinguished French equivalent, was based on the supposition that the truth about the ancient Mediterranean world could no longer come so much from the almost exhausted classic texts but henceforth had to be *dug out* and examined in

The British School at Athens, 1892

all its complex, pedestrian and possibly disturbing reality.[115] Yet the old Wildean regret was never to completely dissipate. In 1953 Rose Macaulay, in evoking *The Pleasure of Ruins*, in a world still with plenty of recent ruins around it, could speak of 'the familiar tragedy of archaeology – the sacrifice of beauty to knowledge'.[116]

If ancient Greece was thereby falling into something of a greyer zone in British mentalities, modern Greece was as always mired in ambiguous sentiments. When Greece's Bavarian king, Otto, was deposed by a revolution in 1862, the British government was pleased to see the back of a regime that had proved unreliable during the Crimean War.[117] The Greeks themselves during the ensuing hiatus considered all sorts of eligible people to rule over their struggling and fragile new state, including Bulwer Lytton and Gladstone, even on one unavailing occasion electing Prince Alfred, Queen Victoria's second son, to the office (the queen would have none of it). It was not, after all, a very desirable or indeed safe job. In the event Otto's successor, seventeen-year-old Prince George of Denmark, a member of the Glücksberg branch, was picked out for the role when he attended the marriage of his sister, Alexandra, to the Prince of Wales in London in March 1863. It was to ease this foreign monarch's bumpy path to popularity in the country he was to reign over – as it happens for over sixty years till he was assassinated in Thessaloniki in November 1912 –

that Britain finally ceded its Ionian protectorate to the Kingdom of Greece.

The British departure from Corfu and the other Ionian Islands, climaxing in June 1864, however, was a brittle affair, underlining yet again the gaps in Anglo-Greek understanding. Edward Lear was a civilian resident throughout. Keenly conscious of the twilight setting over British rule, he toured the scattered protectorate producing the lovely watercolours that constituted his *Views in the Seven Ionian Islands*, arguably his most defining work in art (it was dedicated to the protectorate's last Lord High Commissioner, Sir Henry Storks).[118] Feelings were running high on all sides. Although he felt that the partial destruction of the old fort in Corfu Town insisted on by the British government in London was unnecessary and small-minded, Lear was also infuriated by what he felt to be local Greek ingratitude for all that the British had done during their stay since 1817.[119] On leaving, Lear rowed sadly out in a little boat with the future proconsul of Egypt, Evelyn Baring, to a waiting British warship.[120] In the following few years British views of Greece retained a certain sourness, and when Swinburne wrote an 'Ode to Candia' in 1867, the object being to arouse sympathy for Greek ambitions to seize the island of Crete from the Ottoman Empire, it stirred very little interest, politically or poetically, in Britain. To this one qualification needs to be made. Princess Alexandra of Wales idolized her brother now on the Greek throne, and henceforth not only the Wales household in London but Queen Victoria herself – always very protective of dynastic connections on shaky European thrones – took a close interest in Athenian affairs. This royal prism to Anglo-Greek relations was to continue, giving a certain patina to high society Hellenism in Britain.[121]

The political tensions surrounding Greece go some way towards explaining why throughout the nineteenth century the flow of visitors to that country remained slack. Actually getting there was still by no means straightforward. By the end of the 1860s it could be recalled of the country that 'in fact there was little communication with western Europe, except through the [French] *Messagerie* steamer, which stood off Piraeus during their fortnightly voyages between Marseille and Constantinople'.[122] Moving about Greece outside towns still held dangers, as a shocking event in April 1870 showed. Four tourists, three of them British, had set out from the Hôtel d'Angleterre in Athens for a tour of the battle site of Marathon.[123] They were abducted by

The trial of the alleged murderers of British tourists at Dilessi in Greece,
1870

brigands, and after a harrowing experience and botched rescue attempt, brutally murdered at the village of Dilessi. This led to a diplomatic crisis, and uproar in the British press during which the Greeks were lambasted as worse than the Ottomans. Even very respectable traders from the Greek diaspora in London had to keep a low profile for a few weeks. As it happens, Thomas Cook, the entrepreneur of organized British tourism to the Continent, had been staying at the Hôtel d'Angleterre at the same time as the fated travellers. He had been planning to extend his successful Alpine and Italian excursions to Greece, but quickly put the idea on hold after the tragedy.[124]

What became known as 'the Dilessi murders' constituted a low point in British perceptions of contemporary Greece, but Athens in particular in this period was generally seen as a problematical destination. To Edward Lear it had 'a queer analytical dryness of soul', too redolent of tedious guidebooks.[125] One British aristocrat cruising the Aegean, with a disdain that was a commonplace of the period, said that Athens was 'the best place to dis-Hellenize one'.[126] Oscar Wilde was rare in going to Greece before he ever went to Italy, visiting with his tutor from Trinity College, Dublin in March 1877. He woke at five in the morning to witness, as he wrote excitedly, 'the outposts of Hellas. No more sleep for me.'[127] But his experiences thereafter were a bit mixed. He found seeing the real Mount Olympus 'truly disenchanting', and various archaeological excavations he passed were to him rather ugly. He never visited Greece again. One visit was enough also for A. J. Symonds, a passionate philosophical and emotional Hellenist, who found Athenian drainage hard to take, however.[128] He considered going again, but rejected the idea. The Greece of the imagination sufficed, and fundamentally that was the case with many amongst the itinerant Anglo-American intelligentsia. Henry James was arguably the least classically inclined of all the great nineteenth-century writers in English: to him Italy (and really just northern Italy) was 'the subtlest daughter of History'.[129] Although tempted to see both Sicily and Greece, he never did. For James the latter country remained just beyond the realm of actuality or, indeed, in his hierarchy of the senses, of beauty itself.

Spain and Spanish influences as a presence in High Victorianism also remained enclosed within its old constraints. Yet a subtle process in which these elements had begun to infiltrate British cultural life, starting in the 1840s and 1850s, still continued and slowly assumed more concrete shape. At the start Spain as a culture was still hard for even the most cultivated and receptive English minds to get a grip on. George Eliot's experience indicated the continuing obstacles, social and psychological. After finishing *Romola*, drenched as it was in Florentine history, she started looking to Spain for inspiration, itself suggestive of her own internal quest for experiment. By 1866 she was, in her own words, 'swimming in Spanish history and literature', adding that the country 'is the one I long to go to'.[130] Her husband, George Lewes, the author of *The Spanish Drama: Lope de Vega and Calderon* (1846), initially shared all her enthusiasm. They made a great loop through the east and centre of the country. Eliot described to a correspondent at home 'a monochrome landscape, far stretching brown plains, with brown sheep-folds, brown towns and villages, and far-off walls of brown hills'.[131] But they were, like so many foreign visitors, also cocooned in almost total social isolation. 'They were spectators,' one writer observes, 'and Spain was the spectacle', but by the end they were, as Eliot's emphasis on the unyielding *brownness* of the country suggests, happy to leave Andalusia behind them.[132] The long poem Eliot subsequently wrought from this experience, 'The Spanish Gypsy', was a tragedy of human and political idealism destroyed by the sheer weight of events. But it remained the case that it was much harder to turn Spanish themes to British purposes with the same effect or clarity that had for so long been feasible where Italy was concerned. The critics were not much interested in Eliot's Spanish story. Henry James, who felt that it lacked 'a central quickening flame',[133] was himself never attracted to Spanish subject matter. He visited the country once, but only briefly, and after attending a bullfight said he preferred the bulls to the people.[134] Such condescension yet remained typical of outsiders.

The underlying problem was, essentially, not one of 'understanding' Spain externally. Who could ever *really* do that? Rather it was one of how to relate Spain, with all its inherent distinctiveness, to recognizably British experiences and preoccupations. The vacuum was too easily filled by the old 'Black Legend' of an alien, hostile, papist country and the prejudices attached to it. The lingering anti-Catholicism in Britain underpinned this, and influenced one of the first modern and sweeping national histories of the English nation. This was J. H. Froude's *History of England from the Fall of Wolsey to the Death of Elizabeth*, appearing in stages from 1858 to 1870. The climax of Froude's narrative was the defeat of the Armada, and the massive work has been described as an 'anti-Catholic polemic', reasserting all things Spanish as inherently opposed to a British Protestant identity still very much alive in Victorian Britain.[135] An Armada Memorial on Plymouth Hoe was erected in 1888 to celebrate the tercentenary of the Spanish fleet's inglorious debacle. The statue of conquering Britannia on top of this granite structure simply added a very contemporary imperial flourish to the lucky escape once enjoyed by Elizabethan England thanks to providential storms in Scottish and Irish waters.

Underneath these hoary old verities, however, something was stirring, as the glimmerings of awareness in Britain that Spanish art was distinctive and collectable as something now entirely separate from the revered Italian schools testify.[136] An earlier episode in the career of Austen Layard provides a telling sidelight. In late 1869, famous for his discoveries in Near Eastern archaeology, he had successfully lobbied to be sent to Madrid as ambassador, though only because no senior diplomat was interested in the job.[137] Unusually for such a post, Layard continued as a Trustee of the British Museum, and he set out to concentrate on cultural activities, if only because the British government was determined to take no part in rivalry over the Spanish royal succession (the issue that finally led to the Franco-Prussian War in 1870–1). Layard launched a campaign to bring the artistic riches of Spain not only to the attention of the British Museum and, by extension, to the National Gallery in London, but to the wider public at home.[138] He even got Giovanni Morelli, Sir Charles Eastlake's old trusted adviser, to come to Madrid to see what glories were there, travelling together to Seville, Granada and other cities.

In Madrid Layard and Morelli rummaged through the storerooms of the Prado Museum, to which Layard had privileged access, looking particularly for art of the old Spanish Netherlandish school that had been neglected. It was under Layard's urging that the Prado authorities for the first time since its opening in 1819 dedicated display rooms to this branch of Spanish art history.[139] Lady Layard was, perhaps, even more unusual whilst in Madrid in that she became a frequent visitor, and encourager, in the studios of younger Spanish artists.[140] The Layards went off in 1877 for what proved a dramatic diplomatic posting in Constantinople – including a Russo-Turkish war in the backwash of which Cyprus was occupied by British-Indian troops – but meanwhile they had played a part in widening the conduit for Anglo-Spanish cultural flows.

At the same time a distinctive Spanish influence entered into the actual *practice* of British art for the first time. It did so in ways that touched on basic fault lines within the art world itself. This operated initially through admiration for the paintings of Velázquez but, crucially, involved mediation via Paris as the forcing ground for radical artistic change. Hispanicism in art appreciation was far more developed in France than in Britain, and this was particularly so during the era of Emperor Napoleon III. The empress, Eugenie de Montijo, was herself Spanish. Montmartre and the city's boulevards and theatres were crowded with Spanish dancers, singers and guitarists in the middle decades of the nineteenth century. This was the milieu in which the opera *Carmen* by the French composer Georges Bizet was to be such a storming popular success.

In the visual arts, Velázquez and his *Spanishness* in particular touched a contemporary chord. There were two factors at work. Firstly, he was thought to have 'painted facts', not classical and romantic inventions.[141] Secondly, his technique, appearing as a kind of proto-Impressionism, with its swift, broad brushwork, was considered more up to date than the laborious exactitude of conveying figurative or literary settings. John Singer Sargent, of American birth but brought up in the Anglo-Florentine world, went to

Paris in 1874 to train in the atelier of Charles Carolus-Duran, who initially had three words of advice for him: 'Velázquez, Velázquez, Velázquez.'[142] Sargent spent time in Madrid in 1879 copying in the Prado, afterwards travelling to Andalusia. The main product of the latter visit was his *El Jaleo*, said to be the most evocative image ever painted of Spanish flamenco.[143] It was one of the sensations of the 1882 salon in Paris.[144] Subsequently Sargent spent several years in the English countryside before his crucial move to London in 1886. But he took a preoccupation with Velázquez with him. It was to mark his later Anglo-American society portraits, just as Spain was to figure in the landscapes that were to be an essential part of his legacy.

Equally important in this context is again the figure of J. A. M. Whistler, also trained partly in Paris. He visited Spain in 1862, though he only briefly crossed the Franco-Spanish border before turning back. But the effects of admiration for Velázquez fed into what became his atmospheric 'arrangements' and 'harmonies', especially his portrait of Thomas Carlyle, *Arrangement in Grey and Black* (1872). David Howarth observes that Whistler was the first painter working primarily in a British context who had his vision transformed by a Spanish master.[145] The main point, however, is that it was crucially through the prism of Velázquez – before long almost a cult among a generation for whom even the Pre-Raphaelites now seemed old-fashioned – that there was from the 1870s a discovery of the principles of progressive *French* art in Britain, since the processes involved had become so entwined.[146] It still did so, however, against an ingrained opposition. In 1889 Frederic Leighton devoted a significant part of his annual address to the students of the Royal Academy to the perceived shortcomings of the Spanish school.[147] But that he did so was suggestive that the latter – considered now as a 'school' – was trenching on contemporary and highly contested issues in British art.

Alongside this development in the visual arts were the first signs of British interest in Spanish literature as a genre, going far beyond the old Augustan admiration for *Don Quixote*. Clara Bell, a noted translator, started to add recent Spanish novels to her list of works alongside staple French and German texts. Perez (or 'Percy', as he was styled to be more accessible to Anglophones) Galdos acquired a specialized readership in Britain, with three English translations of his *Doña Perfecta* in the 1870s and 1880s. Glasgow-born James Fitzmaurice-Kelly, who went to Spain in

1885 as a tutor and started making connections in Spanish literary and cultural circles, on returning to live in London became a regular reviewer of Spanish material in organs like *The Spectator*, *The Athenaeum* and *Pall Mall Gazette*.[148] This was a time too when Anglo-Spanish trade was growing rapidly. After the *Exposición Internacional de Barcelona* was mounted in 1888, the decision was taken to transfer a Spanish exhibition to London the following year, the aim being to advertise 'the forward-looking and progressive state of Spain . . . in arts, sciences, industries and the goodness and wealth of its natural products'. This met with mixed success: a young Gertrude Bell, later a celebrated traveller in the Middle East, complained there was little of interest to see. The printed guide to the museum felt bound to play on stereotypical British anxieties, so that it carried a large advertisement for Keatings's Insecticide Powder for those thinking of going to Spain, or perhaps joining one of the Cook's Tours to the peninsula getting under way. But all these initiatives suggested, however erratically, that the old Tudor stereotype of Spain refracted through Victorian sensibilities, compounded by the bloody confusions of more recent Spanish events, was yielding to an appreciation of a society nonetheless clawing its way towards some kind of modernity.

The High Victorian aesthetic was often characterized in literature and art by gloom, obsessed with fogs, damp and a symbolically charged darkness.[149] It was part of the suppleness in the role ascribed to the ancient and modern Mediterranean that it provided a counter-therapy in visions of warm sunlit vistas – yet also not without its own versions of the sinister and forbidding. The latter were defined above all by death in the Mediterranean. There was something about this phenomenon that always caused a frisson in the northern European consciousness, a disjunction or sense of aberration brought about by contradictions deeply embedded in an idealized Mediterranean vision. Thomas Mann was to provide the classic expression in *Death in Venice* (1912). We shall end this chapter with the deaths in Italy of two very different English writers because their lives were so bound up with that nostalgic, piercing sadness which the Mediterranean generated in the British cultural imagination. The deaths are those of Edward Lear and Robert Browning.

Lear's life had been a long history of indecision,[150] and it was only with much changing of mind that, after so ruefully leaving Corfu and wishing to reside neither in Britain or in Greece, he had settled for the last time in San Remo, the summers being spent in Swiss mountains (an Alpine idyll remained powerful throughout the fag end of Victorianism). It was in San Remo that Lear wrote his last work, *Laughable Lyrics*, with such verses uniquely blending laughter and sorrowfulness as 'The Dong with the Luminous Nose'. Lear's most faithful companion, to whom he was devoted, was his cat, Foss.[151] Foss died in September 1877, and Lear followed four months later. He was buried in San Remo with lines from Alfred Tennyson on his tombstone (Tennyson's wife, Emily, had been the human being whom in adult life he had been closest to). Lear in his final years in the town had drawn apart from the local English community – 'the Colony', he called it – and perhaps it was not surprising that very few people attended the funeral (Italian regulations anyway required, as they had in the case of John Keats, a rapid burial).[152] '[S]o sad, so lonely,' one resident who was there summed up the scene.[153] Jenny Uglow writes that Lear's final resting place was away from other English graves which had their own special space: 'He is just round a corner, on a separate path. Slightly apart.'[154] Many of the figures explored in this book, shaped by their immensely varied Mediterranean experiences, were indeed just like that – slightly apart. Perhaps it was what had brought them there in the first place.

The case of Robert Browning was very different, though he too was always at a certain awkward tangent in his life. If Elizabeth Barrett Browning's death marked the ebb of mid-Victorianism, curiously it was Robert's that can be said to have embodied a rite of passage for the High Victorian era in its broad literary and cultural form.[155] In September 1888 he went with his sister from London to Italy, stopping first at Asolo, where he had conceived some of his earliest poetry. Here he completed his last collection of poems, *Asolando*, exuding a sense of exhaustion and disappointment in art itself; the 'once-burning bush', he admitted to himself, was now bare. They went on to Venice, where his son with Elizabeth, Pen, lived in Baroque but largely aimless splendour at the Palazzo Rezzonico. Robert and his sister were contemplating a visit to Greece, but had, once again, been putting such a daring venture off. He took a relaxing walk one day on the Lido, caught a bronchial infection and died on 12 December.

Browning had always intended to be buried alongside his wife in Florence's Protestant Cemetery – the natural return to that place which

Edward Lear

otherwise he had always avoided. The local municipality, however, refused permission. Instead there took place an impressive funeral service in the Palazzo Rezzonico, and afterwards a cortège of funeral gondolas down the Grand Canal out to the island of San Michele for temporary interment.[156] The body was then swiftly returned to London. Edward Burne-Jones was one who thought it would have been truer to Browning's life if the remains had stayed on the Venetian island. Listening to the service inside Westminster Abbey, when Browning duly received a place of honour in Poets' Corner, Burne-Jones found something banal in the whole thing.[157] 'How flat these English are,' he wrote afterwards.

Perhaps there was indeed something appropriate, beyond the curiosities of Lear's own life, in the poignant solitariness and lack of pomp of his own final burial in San Remo. Still, these two passings from the Victorian scene caught various aspects of the Anglo-Mediterranean engagement. As the *fin de siècle* loomed, that engagement was to go on, but in ways that reflected intensifying political and social transformations.

Chapter Six

THE CULT OF BEAUTY

THE MEDITERRANEAN AND BRITISH MODERNISM, 1890–1918

Italy makes one lose one's nerve – a malarious infection of humility creeps over one's soul.

Roger Fry, 1896

[T]he world of Hellas has perished; is dead, buried . . . such a country does not exist.

Vernon Lee (the pseudonym for Violet Page), 1910

Vernon Lee, the Anglo-Florentine historian of eighteenth-century Italy and art theorist, and the painter and critic Roger Fry observed the British cultural world of the early twentieth century from vantage points of different generations and contrasting intellects. But in both their statements above there is a transparently despairing note. It has been argued that cultural despair was the distinguishing mark of modernism in the British compared to their European and North American counterparts, where a generally upbeat tone was more evident.[1] A pathology deeply marked by Mediterranean influences had characterized British culture since the age of the Grand Tour. It was only logical that this remained true entering the twentieth century, and that despair and a sense of national fragility remained part of the mix.

That hallmark characteristic had various roots, but critical to it was a continuing apprehension that the British remained unique as a leading European power in lacking an authentic, mature civilization of their own. Rudyard Kipling expressed this when he compared Britain with Japan. Of the latter's much superior range of arts and crafts, indeed of artistic consciousness all round, there was no doubt, he stated, but went on that Japan 'has been denied the last touch of firmness in her character which would enable her to play with the whole round world. We possess that – we, the nation of the glass flower shade, the pink worsted mat, the red and green china puppy-dog, and the poisonous Brussels carpet. It is our compensation.'[2]

For Kipling the compensation of greatness as a nation, however sardonically framed, might have been enough to fill such an aesthetic void.[3] But for many others it was not. Looking in 1902 around the annual Royal Academy Exhibition, that mirror of Britain's artistic condition, Roger Fry assumed the role of spokesman for the younger generation in commenting that it brought into sharp relief 'the poverty of their emotional and intellectual condition . . . it is their misfortune to have come at a dead point in the revolution of our culture'.[4] Perhaps not coincidentally, at about the same time, and in a much older cultural condescension, a German critic, Oscar Schmitz, described Britain as still being 'a land without music' (*Das Land ohne Musik*).[5] A dead-end feeling was also, however, being experienced by a mostly older British cohort stemming not, in their view, from excessive timidity in embracing the future, but rather because they feared losing touch altogether with a past steeped in a beauty that could all too easily be effaced. It was said of both Edward Burne-Jones and George Frederic Watts, who died in 1898 and 1904 respectively, and whose lives had been permeated by a deep, if sorrowful, love of Italy, that they did so 'with despair in their hearts . . . no ray of light on the horizon, nothing but a sea of mud, no thought, no beauty . . . nothing but sensationalism of a degrading kind'.[6] Yet to critics – Fry thought Watts's pictures now 'quite childlike' – both men were stuck irretrievably in the past, 'stranded in a Romantic dream of the Parthenon Marbles'.[7] Inherent in this yawning gulf was the fundamental battleground staked out in British cultural life. This is why, as Stefania Arcara has written, the Mediterranean provided the location – or rather the point of dramatic tension – for the staging of the modern subject in Britain.[8]

The broad chronological development of modernism in Britain is usually presented as a pattern having had its roots in the Aestheticism of the 1870s and 1880s, assuming a tentative outline of modernity with *fin-de-siècle* decadence in the years after 1890, pausing and at times regressing in the decade after 1895, but surging again in the years before 1914. It was thereafter overwhelmed by the catastrophe of the great conflict that followed. This version privileges the visibility of those individuals whom a later generation identifies as in some incipient sense post-Victorian. In practice things were more fluid. Richard Ellman argues that the publication of Oscar Wilde's novel *The Picture of Dorian Gray* in 1890 operated as a hinge between the medley of movements and moods pointing ahead.[9] But public opinion, whipped up by conservative reviewers in the press, also led to a reaction against any challenge to Victorian norms, for which sexuality became a natural benchmark. Oscar Wilde, once the darling of high society for the success of his socially ironic plays on the London stage, functioned as a kind of tripwire. His trial in April 1895 for gross indecency and his conviction and subsequent imprisonment offered – as did Aubrey Beardsley, whose salacious black-and-white drawings were the quintessence of 1890s decadence – a convenient embodiment of all those high emotions surrounding a transition not only from one social milieu to another 'but from one morality to another, one culture to another'.[10]

There was, inevitably, a Mediterranean current running through these cultural and psychological eddies, often expressed in small but telling ways. When Wilde was finally allowed a few books in gaol, he chose Liddell and Scott's Greek–English lexicon, Dante's *La Divina Commedia* and an Italian dictionary.[11] On release from prison in May 1897 he went first to France before reuniting with his lover Lord Alfred Douglas ('Bosie') and going on to Naples where he finally completed *The Ballad of Reading Gaol*, but was cold-shouldered by the English community. When Wilde and Douglas entered the dining room of a hotel on Capri, the English clientele rose from their seats in protest.[12] The two men then travelled to Taormina in Sicily, where they met the German photographer Baron Wilhelm von Gloeden, whose lubricious images of young boys, sometimes splayed against Ionic columns, had once been much praised in Britain, including by the Royal Photographic Society. In April 1900 Wilde was in Rome to

Oscar Wilde

receive the blessing of Pope Leo XIII. After that he drifted further, without ever returning to Britain, dying a broken man in Paris the following 30 November. By then Beardsley was already dead, brought down amidst the public reaction in the wake of Wilde's own debacle, dragging his young but wracked body, desperately in need of warmth, to the south of France (he was only twenty-five). In March 1897 Beardsley was buried in the public cemetery on the hillside at Menton, though not before – like Wilde to come – a last-minute conversion to Roman Catholicism, pleading with friends at home to destroy his earlier succulent illustrations to Aristophanes' *Lysistrata*.

The tragedies of Beardsley and Wilde fitted into a familiar pattern of the warm South as the default zone – psychologically as well as climatically – for Britons who had rebelled in one way or another against the stifling conventions of their home country. Wilde, who always believed that in some deep place of the heart the Irish were 'the greatest Hellenes since the Greeks',[13] in that sense belonged alongside Shelley and Byron. As the critic Holbrook Jackson remarked in 1913, Beardsley himself was too uniquely a construct of *fin-de-siècle* decadence to fit into any other era, though his

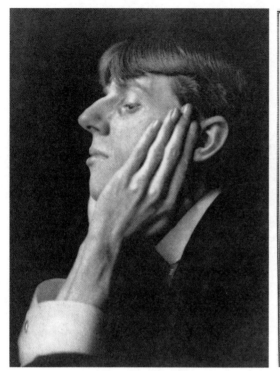

Aubrey Beardsley

Lysistrata refusing her favours
Illustration by Aubrey Beardsley (1896)

belief in the evanescence of beauty linked him to Keats, whose death in Rome from tuberculosis bore similarities to his. The imponderables of beauty – its nature and relevance to art – were to reverberate in cultural debates for the years remaining before the war of 1914–18.

Samuel Butler also shared something in common with Oscar Wilde. They were not proto-post-Victorians, because they were themselves much too Victorian for that. But they kicked and screamed against the things in Victorianism that maimed their lives, though the method of protest they adopted necessarily varied. But while Wilde was writing *The Picture of Dorian Gray*, Butler was changing tack to a close reading of Homer. Debates about the ancient Greek poet had always been central to the Victorian intelligentsia, and in entering that field Butler was taking issue with key tenets in his own society's culture at its 'highest' pinnacle. What was more, he did so in an outrageous way: he concluded that Homer of the *Odyssey* had actually been a woman. As he read the text, all the most convincing portraits were of women, whilst the human pathos rendered was essentially *womanly*. Only a female could have written it.[14]

Butler's iconoclasm, however, went further. With the help of an Admiralty chart from the British Museum, he moved the site of the *Odyssey*'s climax from the Greek waters of Ithaca to the Sicilian port of Trapani. Invited to the latter by local scholars, he proceeded to immerse himself in the topography and society of the island, conveniently finding that local myths substantiated his thesis. This argument he put forward in a series of articles arousing scorn in Hellenic circles in Britain both political and academic. A scathing early review that appeared in *The Athenaeum* was rumoured to be by the aged Gladstone himself. By the time Butler published his definitive *The Authoress of the Odyssey* (1897), Gladstone was dead, which perhaps was just as well because, as a biographer states, it was calculated to explode the whole Gladstonian assertion that the Homeric virtues should define the moral character of contemporary Britain.[15] To cap it all, Butler's accompanying translation of Homer's text was in simple, matter-of-fact English – 'Tottenham Court Road English', it was said – and quite different to the portentousness of earlier efforts. Years later James Joyce was to say that Butler's writings shaped his own *Ulysses* (1922), 'reducing the Authoress's journey round Sicily to Bloom's day in Dublin'.[16]

After this Butler moved on to take potshots at Shakespeare as a Victorian icon, though he continued to visit Trapani regularly. But falling ill in London, in the spring of 1901 he set out with his close friend, Henry Festing Jones, determined to 'go to Sicily if it cost him his life'.[17] He got as far as Palermo, where his friends from Trapani, understandably enjoying their own brief spot in the literary limelight, came to see him. Butler returned to London and died there on 18 June 1902. In the spring of the following year Festing Jones went to Varollo and Trapani, those little capitals of Butler's Italian obsessions, leaving photographs and mementoes from Butler's papers with his old local acquaintances.[18] Shortly afterwards there appeared Butler's posthumous semi-autobiographical novel, *The Way of All Flesh*, which became a bible to many in a new generation as a ringing condemnation of Victorian values. Meanwhile his idea of using Homer as a symbolic way of cocking a snook at pompous elitism has never gone away: one later Italian writer has claimed to prove that the poet of the *Iliad* was actually Swedish and what has been taken to be the Mediterranean was the Baltic.[19] Not even Butler went that far.

In fact the elements that made up a progressive or what some called a 'critical' attitude within British cultural practices as the old century came to an end were by no means a coherent body, rather more a rag-bag of dislikes and inclinations. In writing, as with Butler's Greek translations, there was an antipathy to Mayfair English and that heavy scholasticism, often about the Mediterranean, that had been a passport to respectability in Victorian society. In painting, a dissident faction was concentrated for a time around the New English Art Club as a polar opposite to the now much-derided Royal Academy, after 1896 headed by Sir Edward John Poynter, who in the eyes of a younger generation symbolized the bank-ruptcy of the 'Victorian Olympian' school (Poynter clung on to his post, despite mounting ill-health, until 1918).[20] In radically inclined art circles, anything overtly 'pretty' was now suspect, and a general sympathy prevailed for anything Parisian – 'To Paris! To Paris!' Gwen John, then a twenty-two-year-old student at the Slade School of Art, chanted ecstatically when her first chance to go there became real.[21] Beauty as a principle invited sarcasm, as did what the painter Walter Sickert identified as the 'august site' motif, whereby a painting derived immediate reputational gloss simply by virtue of where it was painted, or what it purported to represent.[22] Perhaps the most telling reaction was against anything that included any kind of moral exhortation; that is, anything that had echoes of Ruskin, who now became a target for younger spirits. All these elements had implications for the place of the Mediterranean in British culture one way or another.[23]

What is suggestive about the ambivalence surrounding this process, however, so that any *proclamation* of modernism is really too clear-cut to convey what actually happened, is that old preferences were modified or experimented with rather than completely abandoned. It did not mean, for example, that an artist necessarily avoided painting Venice. But it did mean that there was advantage in the presentation of some new angle or odd perspective to suggest novelty. This was not itself wholly new. Whistler, whose Aestheticism also became rather old-fashioned, had done the same. But what could introduce a whole new mood into an accustomed location was an element of the sinister (in this visual artists were perhaps only catching up with what Robert Browning had already done in literature years before). Sickert, a pupil of Whistler, escaping the public backlash against anything experimental in Britain following the Wilde trial, spent two protracted periods in Venice in 1895–6 and 1903–4. On his first trip, still true to Whistler in mood and composition, Sickert depicted grand edifices such as St Mark's 'massily pinioned to the insecure earth on which it is built' (something at odds with the elegant lightness of Canaletto).[24] But in the city again during the winter of 1903–4 he went further and began using prostitutes – 'obliging little models,' Sickert explained acidly, 'to amuse me with smutty talk while posing like angels' – to produce works of nudes in gloomy Venetian interiors with cheap furnishings and plain washstands.[25] He left Venice and did not return for twenty-five years, but the turn his art had taken crucially affected a generation of younger British artists.[26] Back in London, Sickert carried the theme of creepy mystery much further in his controversial *Camden Town Murder* series of 1908–9, with their sordid evocation of low-life London. Such a relocation of exper-imental Mediterranean images into British settings had long had a role to play, but the ploy now became more meaningful in relation to debates about the true role of art in British society. Sickert even gave one of his canvases at this time two interchangeable titles – *Summer in Naples* and *Dawn, Camden Town*.[27]

Another tendency in these years was for artists and writers to continue to seek inspiration in Mediterranean settings, but ones that hitherto had not found such a prominent place in the British cultural atlas. The so-called Glasgow Boys were a group of painters, again influenced by Whistler, who dealt in contemporary Scottish scenes, but were increasingly drawn to Spain and North Africa (Algeria had also featured amongst Oscar Wilde's final wanderings). This fitted with their taste for strong colours, dazzling sunlight and bold shapes, not the dappled Italian mellowness enshrined in much visual Victoriana. Arthur Melville's *A Mediterranean Port* (1892) and *A Barber's Shop, Spain* (1895), the latter with a pronounced modernist formlessness, were in this style, though Melville's career was cut short when he contracted fever in Spain and died in 1904.

Meanwhile Queen Victoria's holidays in the south of France in the 1880s and 1890s, taking her Scotch gillie, John Brown, and Indian servants with her, had brought to that region a new glamour and an influx of thousands of British tourists. The queen's last visit was in 1899, and she allegedly remarked when close to death in January 1901, 'If only I were at Nice, I would recover.'[28] Artists began to drift in the same general direction. One was the Welsh painter James Dickson Innes, also trained at the Slade and a member of the New English Art Club, but who, rather more traditionally, carried around with him a copy of Turner's *Liber Studiorum*. Setting off, as a close friend remarked, in search of 'the reflection of some promised land', Innes went to the small town of Collioure and was captivated by the transparency of the light, capturing in his work 'a Saracenic church and a gem-like bay', with red-roofed houses, dark pines and indigo-blue water.[29] Echoing Thomas Jones well over a century before, he brought back a taste for impacted, flatter colours, including bright pinks and yellow-greens, rendering Welsh scenes like his beloved mountain-summit of Arenig in their sublimity; he buried on the latter peak a casket of letters from his one-time lover with whom he spent time in Collioure, the famously promiscuous Euphemia Lamb.[30] Innes died from tuberculosis, aged twenty-seven, in August 1914.

At the other end of the Mediterranean, Cyprus, so often passed over by earlier British travellers, offered even more searing visual qualities. (In retrospect, the most well-known cultural celebrity to visit Cyprus in the nineteenth century, unlikely though it seems, was the French symbolist poet Arthur Rimbaud, though not in a literary capacity – he worked in 1879 first as a stone quarryman and later as a foreman constructing the Troodos summer retreat of the British high commissioner.) Hercules Brabazon Brabazon's watercolours of the island – for instance of the medieval ruins of Famagusta, viewed through a thick blue haze – featured in a series of one-man displays in the progressive Goupil Gallery in the 1890s. In the *Spectator* Brabazon was hailed as the best watercolourist since Turner.[31] This revival of Turner as a benchmark, especially in the use of colour and palette, indicated how changing times could also reignite older Romantic modes of feeling that were by no means defunct.

In this way, indeed, there was around 1900 a recrudescence of spirits that in their richness had been rather spurned of late. The European-based American writer Edith Wharton was deeply influenced by Vernon Lee's recreations of the rococo style of eighteenth-century Italy, even carrying a copy of Lee's *Belcaro* (1881) around in her pocket.[32] Wharton, after her own Italian novel *The Valley of Decision* was published in 1902, turned to the theme of garden design, and especially to the revivalist cause of the Italian formal Renaissance tradition. In her *Italian Villas and Their Gardens* (1905) she rhapsodized the Villa Medici with its 'deep ilex wood, a haunt for fauns and dryads'.[33] This was hardly very modern. In the realm of ancient Greece, it was on 5 April 1900 that the archaeologist Arthur Evans, impervious to Nietzschean gloom and bent on substantiating the folklore and earliest myths of Greece, unearthed in Crete the first human representations that were to make the palace complex of Knossos world famous, and to reveal a new Minoan civilization, pushing back the vision of a flowering art and culture – the values of Hellenism – into the Bronze Age. Excavations and restorations with Evans's polychromatic imagination were to take many years, but already in 1904 the assorted statuary and other objects attracted fascinated crowds at a London exhibition. Evans's much younger sister, Joan, recalled how at Knossos he set about creating a world of his own, 'exactly to his taste, set in a beautiful Mediterranean country, aristocratic and humane in feeling . . . a world which served to isolate him from a present in which he had no place'[34] – an antidote to the pessimism and disturbing change otherwise pressing down from so many directions. Such a pushback against grim and perplexing modernity was to be manifested on many fronts. Certainly in archaeology the Minoan myth – subject to much later academic revision – was to resonate in twentieth-century cultural memory.

These widely divergent forces provide the context for the career of Roger Fry, who constitutes an important reference point for the next three decades, not least because of their contradictions and fluctuations. If Britain had, in artistic terms at least, a true apostle of modernism, it is usually assumed to have been Fry; he was to become a focal point of what became known as the Bloomsbury Group. Yet his first visits to Italy in the early 1890s had been characterized by overt Ruskinian enthusiasms. 'But Raphael's "Galatea"! Isn't it divine!' was one of Fry's expressions of delight about the old Venetian school, as recorded by Virginia Woolf in her biography.[35] In fact Fry had difficulty, and never succeeded, in wrenching his own painting out of this classical groove. An image like *The Pool* (1899) in its balance and harmony was reminiscent of Italian models, something noticed not only by critics like Osbert Sitwell, but of which Fry was also conscious himself.[36] Perhaps the frustrations of his own work as an artist seeking some original slant underpinned the virulent radicalism of his art criticism once that became his central role. Meanwhile his taste at this stage had a certain primness. In an article in the *Athenaeum* in 1904 he dismissed Aubrey Beardsley as 'the Fra Angelico of Satanism'.[37] The pull of an older, more serene Romanticism remained powerful even for somebody who at the same time thirsted for new directions.

John Singer Sargent – who once described himself as Vernon Lee's twin because their families were so familiar with each other when he was growing up in the Rome of the 1870s[38] – is particularly significant here because his life and tastes conjure up an Anglicized Mediterranean idyll which with all its limitations in a modernist perspective was simply still too powerful to fade away. After 1900 he gave up the portraiture for which he is mostly remembered today for Mediterranean landscapes and scenes, a conscious retreat into an older Southern tradition. Richard Ormond evokes Sargent's rustic, timeless vision, adding that 'He applied all his painterly powers to subjects that were deliberately not of the modern world, bringing them vividly to life: Renaissance fountains, gardens of aristocratic villas, white swine and oxen, groves of olives, traditional sailing ships, men weaving and mending nets.'[39]

In addition to Majorca, where he spent time at a villa in Valldemossa where George Sand and Frédéric Chopin had carried out a famous tryst many years before,[40] Sargent also loved Corfu, with the luxuriant orchards that had so enchanted Edward Lear. He painted *In a Garden, Corfu* (1909) while periodically reading aloud to his companion from G. M. Trevelyan's *Garibaldi* trilogy, a combination that in itself made a statement of emotional as well as artistic loyalties. One of Sargent's most favoured locations to paint was Villa Torlonia at Frascati, and on one occasion after finishing work on a canvas he told the friends with him that there was a danger that the outcome would look like 'an idyll in a P & O liner'. As they headed off to the villa for refreshment, this recollection continued, Sargent suggesting that 'we all take strychnine. This morning he said there was nothing left but hari-kari.'[41] For Sargent this was the point: the sheer satiation of beauty in such a setting was so blissful that nothing worthwhile could possibly lie beyond – all that was left was to die without more ado. After 1911–12 Sargent's days of Mediterranean travel and art were behind him, and his

Graveyard in the Tyrol (1914), with its imagery of falling crosses and newly muted colours, presaged sadder times ahead. It might be said that Sargent did not have his 'artistic footing in the new century'.[42] But then, who in the English-speaking aesthetic world at this time really did? For Roger Fry, Sargent's work became a symbol of an artistic order that was a burden on the evolution of British culture as a whole, but a preoccupation with certain ingrained principles of 'the beautiful' – always at their most narcotic when set in Mediterranean contexts – was ultimately to possess a final hold even over Fry himself.

In the emergent hybrid of British modernism, literature and the visual arts were worked upon by the same forces but moved in far from identical trajectories. In the English novel from the end of the 1880s one impulse was to write about urban poverty, not just as part of a general social background replete with Dickensian pathos, but as a brutal social reality. If decadence was to be the expression of a new age lusting for new sensations, social realism was integral to its public consciousness.[43] Yet there were strict limits to how far this could be taken; and those writers who took the risk often displayed a habit of falling back on 'safer' Mediterranean themes more likely to consolidate a personal readership and win favour with middle-class reviewers. One example was George Gissing, who described the High Victorian working class in *The Nether World*, published in 1889 – the year of the great London strikes in the docks and the matchstick factories of the East End. But Gissing used his earnings to finance the travel in Italy he had long hankered after, out of which came *The Emancipated* (1890), mixing issues of moral and social redemption in the mill towns of Yorkshire and in Naples – a kind of post-Ruskinian duality. Thereafter he interlarded gritty social critique of *fin-de-siècle* London – *New Grub Street* (1891) was his classic – with gentle travel memoirs such as his final book, *By the Ionian Sea* (1901).[44]

One person who reviewed *By the Ionian Sea* was the young W. Somerset Maugham. Maugham praised how Gissing had evoked the capacity of the Mediterranean South to allow people to 'seize more vigorously all that experience has to offer . . . every experience, every pleasure and pain, seems so much more intense'.[45] Maugham had already followed something of the same path. His own first book, *Liza of Lambeth* (1897), had conjured up the harsh social and personal world of a young woman in a poor London borough, based on his experience as a trainee doctor at St Thomas's Hospital. It had some modest success, but was also denounced in the *Daily Mail* because 'it reeks of the pot-house'. This sort of criticism was potentially dangerous for the future prospects of any aspiring writer, and he later recalled how he had fended off pressure from his publisher to write another book about slums.[46] Instead he went off to live in Seville. While there he wrote the first draft of a novel, eventually titled *Of Human Bondage*, which was to set him on the road to massive success. But more immediately he published *The Land of the Blessed Virgin* (1905) in which Andalusia is portrayed as an antidote to the stresses and strains of English life. For all of Maugham's later writing about a variety of exotic and tropical settings, Spain remained a recurring passion; and thirty years later in another book about that country, *Don Fernando*, he described how his early experience in Andalusia had made him what he was.[47] Gissing and Maugham illustrate a dialectical relationship between writing about the internal ills of British society itself and explorations of the purely personal discovery that individuals could still, in the early 1900s, find in 'the South'.

Gissing and Maugham were yet small names set beside that of 'The Master' himself, Henry James. It was a literary mastery that could hardly be separated from a certain Anglo-American Victorianism integrated with a vision of Italy. In fact most of James's novels set in that country were completed before 1890. These were grounded in the 'old, eternal Italy' – that 'raw state of the imagination', as he had once said of Rome[48] – and it was difficult to sustain this against the realities that had since come into existence. When the British diplomat Rennell Rodd arrived to be ambassador in 1902 he found only 'an afterglow of the old stately life', with just a few noble and aged ladies now holding the celebrated weekly receptions for Roman high society and expatriate cognoscenti (in the same vein, and indeed the same year, the last of the castrati employed in the choir of the Sistine Chapel finally retired).[49] James once said that he had been lucky to be just in time to be 'present at the feast' of that world, but the feast had really ended.[50] Increasingly he turned far more to French culture, with which he was anyway much more closely acquainted, and after 1905 he pressed Edith Wharton to go in the same direction; his influence on Wharton's development in this regard was to be critical for her career and indeed life.[51] This reflected a general, if not always consistent, drift of Italy further away from the epicentre of Anglophone cultural consciousness.

James, however, towards the end of his own writing career *did* come back to Italy as a setting, albeit transiently. In *The Wings of the Dove* (1902) he recreated the atmosphere of the Villa Barbaro, long a focus of expatriate Venetian life. But what one writer calls the 'basically hallucinatory', or trance-like, effects of this farewell suggested that the country itself had slipped from James; this was reflected also in the very obliqueness of his late Italian fiction.[52] It was because Venice was, for James, so redolent of a lost world that this was the most painful farewell of all. 'I don't care, frankly,' he told Edith Wharton of his last visit to Italy in 1907, 'if I don't see the vulgarized Rome or Florence again, but Venice never seemed to me more loveable.'[53] But did Venetians – or Italians generally – at this stage want the sort of love that James or any other Anglo-American could give, with all the condescension of a colonizing sensibility?[54] The first Biennale festival of modern arts had been held in the city in 1895, and in the early years of the twentieth century it became increasingly international and diverse in its coverage. The first British Pavilion in 1909 was tellingly described as 'fashionable' rather than avant-garde (by contrast, already in 1905 a work by Pablo Picasso had been taken out of the Spanish Pavilion because it was too shocking).[55] Somewhere in amongst this flux the Jamesian world of post-Risorgimento cosmopolitan Italy, with its impeccable (perhaps too impeccable) cultural polish, exhaled its final delicate breath.

Yet almost exactly when James was having his last exquisite glimpses of Venice, E. M. Forster was completing *A Room with a View*, with its defining sections depicting the characteristic routines of British visitors in their Florentine *pensione*. Italy clearly still had uses for the English literary imagination, but from a different generational, social and emotional viewpoint from that represented by Henry James (in fact Forster did once visit James at Lamb House in Rye and found the experience 'stuffy and precious').[56] Forster's chief literary and emotional hero was Samuel Butler, whose old Piedmontese haunts Forster on one occasion made a considerable detour to visit. For our purposes Forster is especially interesting because whilst a quintessentially Edwardian author – that is, an observer of contemporary life from a liberal humanist perspective, steeped in a Victorian inheritance, rather than an experimentalist as such – he was only to die in 1970, and became a defining figure in later twentieth-century English literary culture.[57] He represents a key continuity with the future.

Forster's first instinct as an aspiring writer had been to repulse the whole idea of Italy as a literary medium. After spending five weeks with his mother in Florence in 1901 he wrote home to his old tutor at Cambridge that 'though I do love Italy . . . she has no . . . awakening power on me'.[58] But he had already started shaping an Italian story that finally became, after multiple versions, *A Room with a View*, though it was in Naples, not Florence, that Forster's conception of the story actually got put down on paper.[59] In practice this still half-formed plot was put aside while Forster published his first two novels, *Where Angels Fear to Tread* (1905, also with an Italian theme) and *The Longest Journey* (1907). But it was the appearance in October the following year of *A Room with a View* that made his name and clarified themes that were, and remained, the essence of his outlook on the human lot.

The narrative hinges on Lucy Honeychurch, who with her rather brittle female cousin, Miss Bartlett, 'takes the plunge' and visits Italy (that in 1908 the travel involved could still be discussed in such terms is striking). They arrive at the Pensione Bertolini in Florence, expecting to enjoy south-facing rooms overlooking the Arno, only to be given accommodation with a northern aspect – 'It might be London,' Lucy complains archly. The drawing room was like a Bloomsbury boarding house, with not much Italian about it at all. But Lucy falls into the company of a clever, independent soul, Miss Lavish, who encourages her to leave behind her constricting Baedeker guidebook and *drift* with her towards the great church of Santa Croce. 'One does not come to Italy for niceness,' Miss Lavish states when talk at the Bertolini turns to the vexed matter of smells, 'one comes for life.' It is in drifting and getting lost in the buzzing city that Lucy witnesses not only life but the violence it can bring: in a quiet piazza she sees a man knifed to death in an air of trivial unreality.

Lucy is escorted back to the pensione on this occasion by young George Emerson, who with his father insists on giving up their south-facing bedrooms for the enjoyment of Lucy and her relative. George's character – his kindness 'like sunlight touching a vast landscape' – is scarcely developed, but it crystallizes a fundamental message. George himself, like Italy, constitutes a 'euphemism for Fate', or rather a fundamental choice for Lucy, as for everyone, between negation and saying yes – 'a transitory Yes, if you like, but a Yes' – to life and all its possibilities and risks (the shades here of Madame de Staël's *Corinne* must surely have been on Forster's mind). Lucy evades the choice suddenly put before her, symbolized by George's stolen kiss on an outing to the hills of Fiesole, and returns to the family home perched on the Surrey hills of the Weald: 'Ah, how beautiful the Weald looked! The hills stood out above its radiance, as Fiesole stands above the Tuscan plain, and the South Downs, if one chose, were the mountains of Carrara. She [Lucy] might be forgetting Italy, but she was noticing more things in her England. One could play a new game with the view.'

This was the critical thrust of Forster's story. Italy, or what Italy could symbolize as a choice facing those paralysed by frigid Northern moralism, was capable of opening a whole new world of experience and fulfilment. Yet *England* could do this just as well if one only chose to see the liberating vista stretching to the horizon, wherever you were. In the end Lucy is saved from her fatal engagement to the priggish Cecil Vyse, an old family friend with whom she and her cousin had stayed in Rome, and the novel ends happily, but perhaps somewhat banally, with Lucy and George enjoying their honeymoon back in the Pensione Bertolini, with of course those south-facing rooms and a view over the graceful Arno. Lucy, unlike Madame de Staël's Oswald, had been redeemed from the backslidings that crippling parochialism so easily induced. But whilst the two young people sit on the balcony with that tranquil vista and revel in their shared passion, Forster concludes, 'they were conscious of a love more mysterious than this. The song died away; they heard the river, bearing down the snows of winter into the Mediterranean.' This was a larger 'mystery' central to the bind of Forster's cultural homeland, including (though Forster shrank from saying this directly) its sexual hypocrisies.

Forster later worried that this whole tale was really a bit of 'tosh'.[60] His own personal uncertainties, including a homosexuality that could never quite 'come out', in later terms, inclined him to ponder darker matters, less susceptible to apparently easy resolutions. In *A Passage to India* (1924) another stolen kiss leads to an agonizing portrayal of the subject of colonialism and race. But the actual *meaning* of that discussion in its context remained, perhaps inevitably at the time, more ambiguous and veiled. As Malcolm Bradbury writes, it is in *A Room with a View* – celebrating a life of instinct, transcendence and naturalness – that we find the spirit of E. M. Forster in its most accessible form. Italy might have lost some of its traction in British cultural debates by 1908, but the Mediterranean still offered an effective means of dissecting painful dilemmas, because this warm Southern world presented a polar opposite to 'home', with all its demons and thwarted fulfilments, but was also sufficiently alike for any transposition of issues to be credible and plain.

Suggestively, given the essentially modest middle-class world Forster constructed in *A Room with a View*, several of the characters had contemplated a further trip to Greece but speedily cast aside any such prospect as being what one describes as 'absolutely out of our suburban focus', adding that 'Italy is as much as we can manage'. But for those with higher cultural preoccupations and associated social status, Greece still remained an indispensable means of identification – not at all 'silly Greece', as the slightly naïve, if sensitive, Lucy Honeychurch at one point utters (what she had really meant was the silliness of somebody like her aspiring to go there). British art galleries in the 1890s remained full of the neo-Hellenic paintings of Frederic Leighton, Lawrence Alma-Tadema and their fellow 'Olympians'.[61]

Yet shifts in perceptions of ancient Greece and their utility in clarifying novel forms of discussion had entered a fresh phase from the end of the 1880s. In 1890 Glasgow-born James George Frazer, a Fellow of Trinity College, Cambridge, published his two volumes of *The Golden Bough*. The title came from an illustration by J. M. W. Turner of a sacred grove in the *Aeneid*, with a tree in constant growth set in a transfigured landscape. The book's basic thesis was that classical religion, as the stem of all other religions, consisted of fertility cults hinging on the sacrifice of a sacred king, dying at the harvest and being reborn in the spring. 'For Frazer,' Frank Turner writes, 'savagery, cruelty and irrationality had survived well into the classical age of Greece, not only in the stories of the myths but in the religious life of the people.'[62] Frazer's book was to be transformative as a new kind of social anthropology, but also in more profound ways.

In fact Frazer's ultimate thrust was never intended to be primitivist as such (say, like D. H. Lawrence later). Its message was that human civilization could claw its way from magical roots through bloody ritual to a scientific basis for the here and now. Unlike the old Dilettanti of the eighteenth century, who had also been fascinated by ritual, Frazer – reared in the Free Church of Scotland – was not titillated by the sexual aspects of mythology; his comments on this were couched in late Victorian soberness or, as one writer puts it, 'veiled in polysyllabic descriptions'.[63] In his memoirs Frazer said that when he had started writing his book he had 'no idea of the voyage on which I was embarking; I thought only to explain . . . an ancient Italian priesthood'.[64] Here 'Italian' and 'Greek' really meant the same thing. Still, a biographer writes that Frazer was 'engaged all the time in a covert campaign against religion in general and Christianity in particular, and may perhaps be seen as the most important exponent of secularism in the twentieth century'.[65]

This is a big claim. But even at the time the implications of discussing the Christian story of Jesus and the Resurrection alongside the origins of pagan myth were clear enough. Many British readers were scandalized, whilst others were relieved that their agnosticism, dating from the aftershock of Darwin's *Origin of Species*, had been given a basis in understanding beyond simply biological or zoological determinism. *The Golden Bough* had a second edition in 1900 and sold in its thousands. Its influence thereafter was to be pervasive both in the academy and in literature. The pioneering anthropologist at the London School of Economics Bronisław Malinowski was, he said, 'enslaved' by Frazer's insights, applying them to New Guinea and Melanesia before and after the Great War. Later still, Robert Graves's *The White Goddess* (1948), written at his house in the Majorcan village of Deyá, was said by its author to be 'a historical grammar of poetic myth' that only made explicit what Frazer had earlier politely hinted at.

It is not easy to disentangle these developments from that of the contemporaneous classical scholar Jane Harrison, but she is particularly relevant for us because she brings together various threads in this book, including gender. In 1870 Harrison obtained an honours degree in the London University external studies programme, the first to make degree-level work available to females.[66] She set about studying archaeology and classics more professionally, lecturing widely and travelling in both Italy and Greece. At the end of the 1880s Harrison visited what she described as the 'inconceivably primitive and savage' Peloponnese, and from this revelation of the Greece of today began a slow-burning interest in the realities of ancient

Greek society that were not then reflected in the common rendering.[67] In one small but suggestive way Harrison makes a link between generations spanning this book: at different junctures in her life she met and discussed Greek aspects of modern civilization with George Eliot and Virginia Woolf (indeed Harrison makes an appearance in *A Room of One's Own*).[68]

Up to the point when Harrison became a Fellow of Newnham College, Cambridge in 1898 her stance had remained mostly in the mould of establishment Hellenism. Her early *Introductory Studies in Greek Art* (1885) had rocked no boats. She had been a critic of Samuel Butler, and if it was not Gladstone who had attacked Butler's solecisms about Homer in the *Athenaeum*, the other rumoured author was her. But after 1899 she began publishing a series of articles in the *Journal of Hellenic Studies* exploring ritual and myth, not on the basis of classical texts, as so often, but on artefacts and what they indicated as to the nature of cultic religion and the 'shadowy powers' behind them.[69] These insights were gathered together in her major *Prolegomena to the Study of Greek Religion* (1903). The basic message, as Mary Beard has summarized it, was that 'somewhere underneath the calm, shining, rational exterior of the classical world is a mass of weird, seething irrationality'.[70]

But rather more remarkable, and indicative that, for all the hesitations, undercurrents in cultural debates in Britain were tugging powerfully in uncharted directions, was the way that Harrison was subsequently drawn towards Continental sociological theorizing, especially as represented by the work of Henri Bergson and Émile Durkheim. This radical phase in her own thinking – rather striking for a sixty-year-old – was expressed in Harrison's book *Themis* (1912), where Greek gods were mainly interpreted as fertility spirits. *Themis* was to influence at various points T. S. Eliot, W. B. Yeats and D. H. Lawrence, testimony to the fact that Harrison 'struck a responsive chord with one of the major impulses of early twentieth-century intellectual life'.[71] By this time she was more interested in religion than in anything specifically Greek, and thereafter she dedicated herself to the study of Russian mysticism and during the war of 1914–18 to the sufferings of the Russian people. But her life embodied the unusual capacity of Greece as a presence in British intellectual and cultural life not only to reflect what was fresh in the surrounding environment, but also to affect the environment itself.

It was, however, where the Hellenic theme went beyond strictly intellectual or academic debate and trenched on matters with more public attention, such as the visual arts, that the sensitivities became still greater. The
nub here was the idealized encapsulation of beauty in the Greek world of
around 500 BC as a building block of visual aesthetics in British culture.
This principle had held broadly steady since incorporation in the discourses
of Sir Joshua Reynolds in the later eighteenth century. But in the early
1900s even this came under open attack. Roger Fry called for a 'frank
attempt to dethrone Greek art altogether' (the 'frank' in particular suggesting
Fry's consciousness that at stake were not merely artistic values but widespread social conventions).[72] Inevitably, there was a strong reaction. Percy
Gardner, the Lincoln and Merton Professor of Classical Archaeology and
Art at Oxford, rose on behalf of beauty in its most classicized form in his *A
Grammar of Greek Art* (1905), in which he stated that Greek sculpture was
'a mighty cultural weapon for the defence of art and morality, against the
assault of the modern, the relative and the chaotic'. In framing this counter-
statement, Gardner, a committed Christian, was all too conscious for his
own times of just what the old Greeks had understood by the word *chaos*.[73]

Gardner did not by any means exaggerate the issues being fought out.
The degree to which these became more overt in the next few years gained
expression in a contribution by Walter Sickert in the radical art journal
New Age in June 1910, at a time when the political and constitutional
structure of Britain was itself under threat. A ferocious battle was raging
over the ability of the House of Lords to block the previous year's radical
budget presided over by David Lloyd George as chancellor of the Exchequer,
including social welfare provisions. These assorted tensions were as always
mutually reinforcing. Inveighing against the 'tasteful artificiality' blocking
the development of British art as a whole, Sickert posited a notional artist's
model to whom he gave the name, with its double entendre, Tilly Pullen.
Instead of dressing her to the nines, he suggested,

> let us strip Tilly Pullen of her lendings and tell her to put her own
> things on again. Let her leave the studio and climb the first dirty little
> staircase in the first shabby little house. Tilly Pullen becomes inter-
> esting at once. She is in surroundings that mean something. She
> becomes the stuff for a picture. Follow her into the kitchen or, better

still . . . into the bedroom; and now Tilly Pullen is become the stuff of which the Parthenon is made.[74]

That Tilly Pullen, with her lendings and progressing up her own shabby stairs, could be put in the same written sentence as the Parthenon said it all. Percy Gardner's earlier fears over how far the relativity of things could slide were real enough. But Sickert's meaning was compelling. It was only by aligning the life of Tilly Pullen, along with what Sickert called the 'gross material facts' that her imaginary existence was meant to embody, with the true spirit of the Elgin Marbles, those exemplars of human creativity, that British art in the world of 1910 could renew itself. This was not so much to dethrone the place of Greece in the confrontational style of Roger Fry, but to make its spirit for British purposes truly contemporary.

Nevertheless, there were some for whom the dethronement of old classical certainties seemed all too real, and the resulting bereftness stood for something much larger. Vernon Lee conjures up this sentiment in the most acute way for us because her life had been so quintessentially Anglo-Mediterranean. Her *Studies of the Eighteenth Century in Italy* (1880), published when she was twenty-three, breathed new life into discussion of a subject that had hitherto been overshadowed by other periods. Apart from a few not altogether successful years in London, Lee lived in Italy, mainly in Florence, and was soaked in its atmosphere. T. S. Eliot made the comparison between Henry James, who, for all his love of Italy and of Europe, remained an outsider, and Vernon Lee who by contrast 'did not "become" a European; she was European'.[75] Her happiest times were spent cohabiting with her lover, Clementina ('Kit') Anstruther-Thomson, researching psychological and physiological responses to art, that 'sensation of harmony and increased vitality' that came from simply looking at a canvas like Titian's *Sacred and Profane Love*.[76] But perhaps Lee's most important literary legacy lay in her travel writing and its experimentation with the notion of the *genius loci*, the sensitivity to, and ability to convey in words, the inherent quality of a particular place that in the mass age of travel and tourism too often got lost. Edith Wharton dedicated her *Italian Villas and Their Gardens* to Lee, saying that no one else better interpreted 'the garden-magic of Italy'.[77] The later tradition of British travel writing – a line that runs through names like Robert Byron, Patrick Leigh-Fermor,

Lawrence Durrell and more recently Bruce Chatwin and Paul Theroux – really consists in evoking Vernon Lee's *genius loci* according to the language and style of their own generations.

For Lee, as an Anglo-Italian, there was one place in particular, however, that remained an unspoken but absent presence, one deeply bound up with Italy itself, but often, perhaps usually, remaining just over the horizon: Greece. She eventually made it there in January 1910. Like Oscar Wilde some twenty years before, she was immensely excited on arrival. 'Greece at Last' was the essay she wrote soon afterwards, describing how after her first night in Olympia she woke to the goats on the hillsides and 'knew by that sound, that scent, that this real Greece was the one I had loved, recognizing, I scarce knew how, its every vestige in other places'. On finally leaving from Piraeus harbour at the end of March on the Naples-bound steamer she was overwhelmed by sadness, but the sadness, her biographer writes, was both for Greece and for herself.[78] Yet it was also for something larger still: for the landmarks, the contours of a familiar and humane European civilization, decaying before one's eyes. Lee expressed the poignancy as 'The sadness of understanding, what I seem never to have guessed before, that the world of Hellas has perished; is dead, buried, its very grave devastated . . . And now I knew that such a country does not exist; that these museums, all the world over, hold for the greater amount . . . the wreckage of that world: broken things, headless and armless.'[79]

That devastation, its headlessness and armlessness, was a premonition of some cavernous hole opening up before the world of cultivated sensibility in which Lee had lived her life, garden-magic and all. Hellas itself was a symbol of the illusions of permanence on which it had been based. What one was left with, Lee concluded, in Greece, Sicily and southernmost Italy above all, with their contemporary poverty and ills, but also by implication elsewhere, and even in Britain itself, was a grim reality being stripped of its dreams and aspirations – 'the smell,' as she put it shortly in another context, 'of dead leaves and of charnel'.[80] Lee was to spend the years remaining before the war mainly in England writing to promote women's equality and a fairer distribution of wealth, and against militarism. Frustrated at being away from her beloved Italy once war had erupted, in 1915 she was to write *The Ballet of the Nations*, described by one later writer as 'the most thorough literary analysis of war neurosis'.[81]

Glimmerings of that neurosis could be apprehended from aboard the ship from Piraeus to Naples in late March 1910, a time when the Greece of the day was about to be sucked into first Balkan and then European wars lasting, in Greece's case, until 1922, leaving that country indeed broken and devastated.

As always, Anglo-Spanish cultural interaction operated rather more obliquely. That relationship carried a particular burden of the past and the occluded sympathies that went with it. Yet gradually the Spain of the day and its relevance for Britain gained still sharper focus. This process now became more systemic. A historian of modern Anglo-Hispanic interchange argues that it was in the Edwardian years after 1901 that British knowledge about Spain was transformed,[82] and with such knowledge automatically went a susceptibility to be influenced by it. During an age when professional academia was assuming a critical role in cultural affairs generally, Hispanic topics were gaining a foothold in the universities. James Fitzmaurice-Kelly, whose experience of the world of letters and journalism in Madrid we noted back in the later 1880s, became professor of Spanish Studies in Liverpool in 1909 (he was to move to King's College, London in the same role in 1916).[83] He edited the English translation of the complete works of Cervantes in 1901–3, and in the next few years Spanish literature acquired for the first time an academic and intellectual focus in Britain.

In painting we saw how it was through the medium of Velázquez that a Spanish school started to affect the practice of visual art in Britain. That thread continued, and R. A. M. Stevenson, the cousin of the writer Robert Louis Stevenson,[84] published the first major study of Velázquez in English in 1895; this was to be a bible among art students of the day. But admiration of the Spanish master was still often framed in proto-Impressionist principles, so that Stevenson saw Velázquez as 'the great Spanish Impressionist'.[85] Yet at about the same time, awareness of Spanish painting as a distinctive and deep-rooted genre, one not dependent on a single great name, took root. In 1892 the Bowes Museum, after years of preparation, finally opened at Barnard Castle in Teesdale, its collection that of John Bowes and his first wife Josephine, both of whose tastes had been shaped by the Spanish flavours surrounding the Paris theatre world of the 1850s and 1860s in which they had been closely involved. The collection at the museum was the largest private collection of Spanish art in Britain, including not only canvases by Velázquez, Goya and El Greco but also by many less noted Spanish painters.[86] Not to be outdone by the provinces, the National Gallery in London acquired its first painting by Goya in 1896, having recently bought its first El Greco. Younger British artists started to take note. When in 1902 Wyndham Lewis and Spencer Gore visited Madrid, they did so mainly to study the holdings of indigenous Spanish art in the Prado.[87] Both these artists went on to become active in 'rebellious' circles such as the Fitzroy Street Group. One contemporary Spanish painter was not yet quite in focus in London, though he was increasingly so in Paris: Pablo Picasso. In fact when the war broke out in July 1914 over half the Picassos in Britain were allegedly hanging on the walls of the German embassy.[88] To one English writer later close to Picasso himself this was a 'shameful' testimony to the timidity of the British avant-garde.[89] This is too prejudicial. What it rather reflects is that, whilst modernism took root in Britain, it did so in a peculiarly British way, without the brusque discontinuity and intellectual elan of the Continent, and still obstinately attached to established ways of seeing and, even more importantly perhaps, of *feeling*.

Meanwhile Picasso personified a more general truth: insofar as Spanish culture, famously introverted, had an external reference point, it remained instinctively Parisian. But just as Spanishness was becoming more salient in Britain, so in Spain there was an enhanced openness towards British influences. Admittedly, this was not always, perhaps not mostly, for strictly cultural reasons. Recreativo de Huelva, the oldest football club in Spain, was originally formed in this period by two local Scots as 'Huelva Recreation Club'. (Football was a massive purveyor of British cultural habits in and around much of the Mediterranean, as illustrated by the founding by two Englishmen in 1899 of the Milan Foot-Ball and Cricket Club, soon to become the great A. C. Milan.) On 31 May 1906 Spain even acquired a British queen – Queen Ena as she was widely known – when Queen Victoria's granddaughter Victoria Eugenie married King Alfonso XIII. It was not a happy day – a bomb was thrown at the royal carriage, killing one of the escort – and indeed it was not to be a happy marriage, because for one thing the new queen was very unpopular in highly conservative court circles.[90] Yet this was the point. British influences (which Queen Ena did something to promote in matters of style and fashion) were associated with exactly the sort of change that residues of old Bourbonism detested. As Spain sought to recover – 'regenerate' was the term of the day – from the 'Disaster' of 1898, when it had lost its remaining overseas empire in a war with the United States, Reformist Republicans looked to British political models as Italian patriotic radicals had done earlier in the century. In fact it has been said of the ensuing period that this was when Spain, with all its inner dislocations, set about 'discovering itself for the first time' (and if so, it was hardly surprising that the British, other than in clichéd form, had not 'discovered' a real Spain before for themselves).[91]

Britain and Spain, indeed, had something fundamental in common: modernism came to them in skewed and qualified ways because of the complexities of their circumstances. (So, in Spain, *Modernisme*, or art nouveau, was an almost exclusively Catalan phenomenon, focused in the architectural vision of Antoni Gaudí, and for some, in a way fused with medieval Gothic.)[92] During the years leading up to 1914 any deepening of the linkage between the two countries stalled because of political turbulence and subsequent Spanish neutrality in the coming war.[93] Here were the roots, however, of a distinct Anglo-Spanish interaction to take shape, albeit temporarily and very partially, when that conflict finally ended. Already by 1914 the old 'Black Legend' of Spain, the country of darkened Catholicism and an ominous Inquisition, so vivid in the Victorian imagination, had lost much of its force in the age of modern secularism. But there remained a shadow in the continuing idea of Spain as the embodiment of passions unbridled, the wild flamenco Spain that John Singer Sargent had captured in his portrait of *El Jaleo* (1882). This interpretation of Spain was never to disappear entirely.[94]

'On or about December 1910 human nature changed . . . All human relationships shifted'. So Virginia Woolf – whose sister, Vanessa Bell, was the friend and for a while lover of Roger Fry – famously asserted about the effect of Fry's exhibition at London's Grafton Gallery on 'Manet and the Post-Impressionists'.[95] The exhibition, which opened on 8 November 1910, featured works previously very little known in Britain by such artists, in addition to Manet himself, as Seurat, Van Gogh and above all Cézanne. Woolf's description of its effect mingled serious observation with an element of the sardonic, and as such contained an unspoken truth about the modernist urge in her own country. But it conveyed also the powerful churning of the ripples caused by the rock thrown by Fry into London's cultural pool.

Why had Fry – and British modernism – become so preoccupied with progressive French art as a model and inspiration? It was a measure of how embedded the Mediterranean remained in the country's cultural makeup that the reason lay not only in progressive French art itself, but rather in what Fry and those associated with him felt they were reacting *against*. Virginia Woolf explained in her 1940 study of Fry (who had died six years earlier) why France came to mean more to him than any other country, and tellingly something different from Italy. She explained Fry's view that Italy 'was a place where one worked hard all day seeing old masters; where one settled down at night in some little [Italian] pub to sample strange dishes and to argue with other English travellers about art. But it was not a place with a living art and a living civilization that one could share with the Italians themselves. France was to be that country.'[96]

To see things in these terms was of course to aim a direct hit against the whole engagement with Italian art that went back decades to the Dilettanti era of the Enlightenment, indeed the very spirit surrounding the Grand Tour, down to the meals in little pubs – or really *trattorie* – dotted around the Piazza di Spagna in Rome. The despised 'hard work' was all that copying that British artists had done during their sojourns, which had reached its climax with Ruskin, spreadeagled on the floor of some Venetian church to get a better perspective on a fabulous ceiling. It was to stamp on Ruskin's grave as an art theorist, just as Samuel Butler's posthumous *The Way of All Flesh* had quite recently stamped on Victorian patriarchal society. That aspiring British 'Post-Impressionists' subsequently proved wavering in their own progressivism has an explanation in that what they were reacting *against* from the start was actually more powerful than what they were espousing to move *towards*, about which anyway they were necessarily vague. This was all the more compelling given that the thing that was so detested – a quest for a form of Mediterranean beauty that made Fry feel helpless and paralysed – was in fact *so* embedded, so ineradicable, in British consciousness that it could not be gouged out of one's own being, try as one might.

Italy did not, of course, represent a dead art or a dead civilization; rather it represented something that Fry felt was dead in himself and in his country, and which he resented. Post-Impressionism was just an incantation to get rid of it: 'Oh, let's just call them Post-Impressionists; at any rate they came after the impressionists,' Fry had said when discussing what the label for the contents of the Grafton Gallery exhibition should be.[97] It did not really matter what they were called so long as they had a certain cleansing effect. The irony was that just as Fry wanted to repudiate Italy, some Italian counterparts wanted to repudiate the legacy of England and the shadow of the 'milords' who constituted a deadweight on their own national culture. It was a Milanese – though Alexandrian-born – intellectual, Filippo Marinetti, who on 20 February 1909 launched a Futurist Manifesto in the Parisian newspaper *Le Figaro*. 'Except in struggle,' Marinetti declared, 'there is no more beauty' – which was as big a put-down of Ruskin as any Roger Fry had to offer, topped off by denigration of foreign-dominated Venice with its crumbling palaces and gondolas, 'those rocking chairs for cretins'.[98] Later, on a visit to London, Marinetti was to denounce England as a nation of sycophants and snobs, enslaved by worm-eaten traditions, social conventions and Romanticism. English art and artists, he said, now meant nothing to him, the latter fixated 'on a nostalgic feeling, longing for a past that is beyond recall, imagining that they live in a pastoral age'.[99] The National Gallery's collection of Turners and Pre-Raphaelites, Marinetti suggested, should be dragged into Trafalgar Square and burnt. There was something logical in the fact that such self-appointed spokespeople for the cultural futures of their own countries as Fry and Marinetti should denounce their mutual legacies more or less simultaneously and in similar terms.

Marinetti's very ferocity of language, however, arose from the fact that he knew all too well that there were countervailing forces to his own harsh ideals. The British School at Rome had been set up in 1901 to expand advanced studies in the art, history and culture of Italy (its first director, Thomas Ashby, set about amassing a unique photographic collection of the Roman Campagna, with all its traces of Grand Tour days).[100] In 1909, the year of Marinetti's Futurist Manifesto, after a long campaign raising British, American and Italian financial support, the house where Keats had died in Rome was dedicated and opened as the Keats-Shelley Memorial House.[101] It was to be a site of literary tourism for generations for whom an Anglo-Italian Romantic spirit still breathed life. The first of a three-volume study of Garibaldi by the Cambridge historian G. M.

The Spanish Steps in Rome, with the house where John Keats died on the right

Trevelyan (already mentioned accompanying Sargent at work on a painting in Corfu) had been published in 1907, incorporating a view resonant in British liberalism of the Risorgimento as 'a latter-day morality tale, a battle between good and evil, in which virtue eventually triumphed'.[102] The last of this vivid trilogy was published in 1911, in time for the fiftieth anniversary of the founding of the Italian state. By then, for a liberal optimist like Trevelyan the contemporary relevance of the moral lessons of the Risorgimento was as compelling as ever. But even his optimism wilted when Italy invaded Tripolitania a few months later – the trigger for the Balkan wars that proved the geopolitical prelude to August 1914. This Italian move towards an overseas empire of its own, so enthralling for a nationalist like Marinetti, was galling for Trevelyan precisely because it was 'its would-be imitation of *us* [Great Britain] – to appear to be a great power – that has misled them'.[103] The fact that the warship inaugurating the bombardment of Tripoli was called the *Garibaldi* only drove the shaft home with exquisite irony.

The focus of this chapter cannot embrace the parting of the ways that lay ahead on so many fronts. Yet in a profound sense, beauty – be it the aesthetic beauty that Marinetti found so supine for Italy, the artistic beauty that aroused in Fry a sense of inferiority as a British artist, or the political beauty personified in the story of the Risorgimento that G. M. Trevelyan felt to be endangered internationally – provided one common point of contention buried amidst all the hubbub. The most impassioned critics of the original Post-Impressionist exhibition in London had instinctively risen to defend what they saw not only as a central doctrine of art, but as a precondition for all civilized discourse. The critic J. Comyns Carr wrote that Fry's display of pictures in the Grafton Gallery 'seems to me to indicate a wave of disease, even of absolute madness ... [a] combined endeavour to degrade and discredit all forms of feminine beauty'.[104]

The feminist slant was hardly accidental since the campaign of the Suffragettes, focusing, as the name indicated, on votes for women in Britain, was steadily mounting – an important part of an interlocking crisis later described in George Dangerfield's influential book *The Strange Death of Liberal England* (1935). Indeed, when Marinetti visited England for a Futurist exhibition in 1912, he made a point of attending several Suffragette demonstrations, partly because he luxuriated in the physical encounters when the police took protesting women into custody.[105] Beauty, art and politics seemed to be colliding from all sorts of angles. On 10 March 1914, the day after the arrest of the Suffragette leader Mrs Emmeline Pankhurst in Glasgow, one angry activist, Mary Richardson, walked into the National Gallery in London and made seven wide slashes with a meat-cleaver in Velázquez's *Rokeby Venus* (the marks can still just be made out on the restored canvas). The choice of target said a great deal. Richardson was convicted and given six months' imprisonment, the maximum possible for damaging an artwork. 'I have tried to destroy the picture of the most beautiful woman in mythological history as a protest against the Government for destroying Mrs. Pankhurst, who is the most beautiful character in modern history,' she told the Women's Social and Political Union after her release, adding, 'Justice is an element of beauty as much as colour or an outline on canvas.'[106]

The nature of the beautiful, then, was itself part of the contestation. Only a few weeks after Mary Richardson raised her meat-cleaver just off Trafalgar Square, Vanessa Bell had visited Picasso's studio in Paris. Duncan Grant, later to be her lifelong partner, was in Tunis at the time, and she wrote to him about the occasion and the works she had found deposited around Picasso's room. 'Some of the newest ones,' Bell remarked, 'are very lovely . . . [they] do give me great satisfaction . . . I came to the conclusion that he is probably one of the greatest geniuses that ever lived.'[107] Yet there was a slightly evasive tone in this commendation, a sense that Picasso may indeed be a genius and that some of his work was undoubtedly lovely, but was it *beautiful*? When she returned to London, Bell found a large bouquet of flowers from Duncan Grant. In her thank-you note sent quickly to Tunis she gently mocked the progressive art theory of Roger Fry and the radical formalism of her own husband, Clive Bell; but it is hard to imagine that she did not also have Picasso in mind. Her note, with some self-irony, went on with regard to the flowers that had made up Duncan Grant's bouquet, 'They are so lovely that against all modern theories I stuck some into my yellow Italian pot and at once began to paint them. I mean one isn't supposed to paint what one thinks beautiful. But the colour was so exciting that I couldn't resist it.'[108] The result was *Oranges and Lemons* (1914), with all its sunny yellow and citrine one of Vanessa Bell's most charming naturalist images. It was as if, by instinctively turning to the beauty of still life, the accelerating turmoil in European diplomacy might itself be imaginatively stilled for a passing moment. Henri Matisse's delicately pale *Lilacs* in the same fateful year is another example.

For some, charm had died once and for all. In the same period Ezra Pound lamented in the radical journal *Egoist* 'this pothering about the Greeks' and the ideal of 'caressable' beauty they had brought into British art, including, he would have said, when presented in a delightful Italian pot.[109] Yet there was something in the mood of despair in the prelude to war that made a surrender to beauty, a renewed desire to go in search of its *caressing*, all the more tempting, however much it was at odds with up-to-date trends in art. And by some homing instinct, such a search still led South, either imaginatively or even literally by going to, or at least towards, the Mediterranean. This was true no less for practitioners in France than in Britain, two countries that, for all their differences, were now being shunted into a military alliance by the sheer force of the surrounding diplomatic crisis.[110] 'Artists today are being drawn to the Midi,' Guillaume Apollinaire, the French poet, himself later to be badly wounded on the Western Front, reported on 12 June 1914. He went on to list those at that very moment heading to Provence, including André Derain, Georges Braque and Henri Matisse.[111] Picasso was due to go two days later.

This movement marked an instinctive turn against the grim stringencies of the old Gothic North wrapping itself in the shroud of war preparations. Here was a pre-echo of that Provençal-cum-Mediterranean setting for expressions of a 'return to order' (the phrase was to be coined by the French art critic Jean Cocteau in 1926), including a revival of neoclassicism destined to be a prominent aspect of post-war European art and literature responding to contemporary collapse. Inevitably there was a *sui generis* British variant. Such a mode of coming to terms after August 1914 with what Henry James, still corresponding with Edith Wharton close to his own death, called 'this crash of our civilization . . . the utter extinction of everything', accelerated as the scale of the disaster became clear.[112] In the spring of 1915 Roger Fry, shaken by the ending of his relationship with Vanessa Bell, travelled to the Meuse region in France to see his sister, who was working with Quaker War Relief. For a short period he helped with building temporary huts, distributing agricultural seed and repairing farm equipment, but concluded he was not suited to the tasks.[113] He, like others, was drawn ineluctably southwards and discovered as he passed through the Midi that it now felt like a spiritual home. Heading to stay with friends at Roquebrun in the Upper Languedoc, he stumbled upon the town of Cassis, later to play a part in his life (another visitor to the town at this time was the writer Katherine Mansfield, also looking for a refuge from grim wartime England, along with her partner, the literary critic John Middleton Murry).[114] Fry painted Cassis harbour, and from the hotel on the quayside he wrote to a friend in England, 'I know quite well whenever I get to this Mediterranean country that I ought never to leave it. It all seems just right, the right kinds of colours and shapes everywhere.'[115]

Fry's intense satisfaction in Mediterranean colours and shapes – the evocation of which by John Singer Sargent he had dismissed as essentially journalistic just a few years before – was to become more intense in the years ahead. There was something in the now darkened world that gave them heightened resonance. To grasp just how acute this became as the war unfolded it is enough to quote from a letter by Paul Nash, a young official war artist who saw the Battle of Passchendaele up close. He wrote home on 16 November 1917 that he had witnessed 'the most frightful nightmare of a country . . . unspeakable, utterly indescribable . . . no glimmer of God's hand is seen anywhere. Sunset and sunrise are blasphemies, they are mockeries to man, only the black rain out of the bruised and broken clouds through the bitter black of night is fit atmosphere in such a land.'[116] Black rain, black sunrises and sunsets, a black land – this was a nightmare, conveyed in his *The Menin Road* (1919) that, as Nash expressed it, could only make beauty itself more poignant.[117] One side effect was that the luminescence and *rightness* of what Fry called so generically 'Mediterranean country' was underscored anew in the British imagination. An aching desire for indefinable qualities of vividness and openness to life of which contemporary circumstances were such a travesty affected Fry's own approach, so that when in 1918 he came to decorate a spinet by Arnold Dolmetsch, the French-born musician who played a leading role in the revival of early music in Britain, the lid displayed a monumental reclining nude, set, Renaissance-style, in an idyllic Tuscan scene.

All this helps to explain the continuing hybrid and qualified character of the modernist phenomenon in its British dimension. It has been said that 'ultimately the nativist line predominated' in the British arts even when more radical currents triumphed elsewhere,[118] and it is the case that British modernism is generally seen as lurking in the shadows of French progressivism.[119] But this cannot mean that British practitioners were immune to those currents, and still less – though it is sometimes implied – that there was something wholly antithetical between British culture and the modernist impulse itself. Nearer the truth is John Steegman's observation that in the arts, as in politics and religion, the British had over time always kicked against the pricks of any extraneous authority, resulting in a process in which foreign influence was invariably absorbed into the indigenous structure rather than vice versa.[120] This was what the eminent art historian Kenneth Clark was surely getting at when he quipped in his grand survey of civilization, with his trademark social swish, that 'Rococo . . . spread to England, although the native good sense of a fox-hunting society prevented its more extravagant flights.'[121]

If a tussle along these lines had much earlier swirled around rococo, the contest surrounding how latter-day modernism fitted with British instincts and prejudices was conducted with greater intensity. During that struggle British sensibilities were peculiarly subject to a backward tug, to what in the case of Augustus John, that *enfant terrible* of British art in the years before 1914, has been described as 'a strange, troubled feeling for beauty', keeping him, as it kept many British contemporaries, at a tangent to those movements pulsing through the adjoining Continent.[122] Ineradicably lodged in aesthetic awareness and identity, such an instinctive tendency to default towards the beautiful over many decades had been framed within an overarching Anglo-Mediterranean tradition. That ideal, distinctive but also authentically European in its own right, has been at the heart of this book. Far from ebbing, the horrors of 1914–18 served only to make it even more enduring in its appeal. How it evolved in a world left grey and exhausted when peace came we shall see.

Chapter Seven

THAT SPLENDID ENCLOSURE

MEANINGS OF THE MEDITERRANEAN FROM RUPERT
BROOKE TO DAMIEN HIRST

The Rock had dropped below the horizon and there was no land
in sight. The sea might have been any sea by the look of it, but
he knew it was the Mediterranean, that splendid enclosure
which held all the world's history and half the happiest memories of his own life; of work and rest and battle, of aesthetic
adventure and of young love.

Evelyn Waugh, *The Ordeal of Gilbert Pinfold*, 1957

The grave of Rupert Brooke, the first English poet to die on military
service since Sir Philip Sidney fighting the Spanish in 1586, lies in a
remote spot near the south-west coast of the Greek island of Skyros.
Brooke passed away on a French hospital ship on the late afternoon of 23
April 1915. Early that evening a digging party went ashore to prepare a
suitable spot in an olive grove. The coffin, draped in a Union Jack and the
French Tricolore, was taken ashore and up a dry watercourse by a party of
twelve Australian petty officers to the place selected. One of those present
wrote to Brooke's mother the following day to convey as soothing an
impression of this sad event as possible. Her son's body, this description
stated, had been interred in 'one of the loveliest places on this earth, with
grey-green olives round him . . . the ground covered with flowering sage,
bluish-grey and smelling more delicious than any other flower I knew . . .

Think of it under a clouded moon, with the three mountains around and behind us and those divine scents everywhere. We lined his grave with all the flowers we could find.'[1] It was hardly unintentional that this evocation had all the flavour of the burial of a glorious Trojan warrior taken from Homer's *Iliad*, a modern Hector. Whether such warm classicism took any edge off this contemporary bereavement we can hardly know, but Brooke's mother did come to worry afterwards that the reality of the burial place could in such circumstances be little more than a loose pile of boulders around a simple stone cairn. Shortly after the end of the war she had replaced what was already there with a more substantial tomb by a Greek sculptor on which is inscribed Brooke's poem, 'The Soldier', with its famous opening lines: 'If I should die, think only this of me: / That there's some corner of a foreign field / That is for ever England.'

Virginia Woolf, like some other old friends of Brooke, felt uneasy about the irony of his rapid canonization thereafter, given the 'neo-Paganism' of his young adulthood – one of Brooke's party tricks when bathing nude in the river outside Cambridge had been 'jumping in the water at Byron's Pool and emerging with an instant erection'.[2] But it was not surprising in the circumstances of a death in uniform under war conditions. Unlike the case of that other pagan, Shelley, the canonization came about almost instantaneously rather than stretching over decades. It perhaps helped the strength of his appeal that Brooke died early enough in the war for his verses to retain a vein of chivalry – infused with the antique spirit of what had been called 'the Constantinople expedition' against the Ottomans – and lacking the empty disillusion of Siegfried Sassoon's poetry later in the conflict. To this day a regular trickle of Brooke admirers make their way to the rural grave site, with a Greek military base just down the road.

After the Great War ended on 11 November 1918, the corner of a foreign field where the vast majority of the British war dead remained was, of course, in Belgium and northern France. It may be true, as John Pemble observes, that the resulting necropolis in northern Europe 'reconfigured the Western world's geography of mourning and remembrance' away from those antique Mediterranean ruins which hitherto had encapsulated a Romantic sensibility of irrecoverable loss.[3] But the spirit of commemoration of those killed in the Great War that became such a hallmark of national culture in the years ahead – and which continues, compounded by later conflicts – always remained overwhelmingly Southern and Greek. The art historian Ana Carden-Coyne explains: 'In the aftermath of the First World War, a classical imagery was rehabilitated, not just as a familiar cultural vocabulary or retreat to a safe past, but as a relevant set of values regarding beauty, symmetry, and civilization. Since classicism was a universal aesthetic aimed at resolving paradoxes harmoniously, it offered a special understanding of a world in violent conflict.'[4]

What was involved here was not just aesthetic in a purely artistic sense. The legacy of physical disfigurement from war service was one prime reason why consciousness of beauty was habitual in society at large. Simplicity, minimalism and the whiteness of marble were inherent in this rejuvenation of classical principles.[5] The bare austerity of Edwin Lutyens's Cenotaph in Whitehall, erected in 1920, drew upon ancient Greek tombs at Xanthos, and was attacked in the *Catholic Herald* as 'nothing more or less than a pagan monument, insulting to Christianity'.[6] This recycled issues that went back to the eighteenth century in British cultural debates. In addition to municipal and village memorials up and down the country, the memory of the recent war on all its fronts was rendered into Greek shapes in countless ways. Examples came from the eventually abortive plan for a national Hall of Remembrance for which commissions were given to a range of well-known artists. Out of this project came Stanley Spencer's portrayal of the wounded arriving at a dressing station in Macedonia in September 1916, with horses' heads straight out of Homer's tales, and John Singer Sargent's *Gassed* (1919), like a frieze from the Parthenon, a sequence of wounded soldiers limping across a landscape lit up by a noxious yellow light.[7] It was a far cry indeed from the same painter's lyrical evocations of Tuscan villa life in the Edwardian years that had so irritated Roger Fry; but yet again the Mediterranean tradition was reworked in new ways to fit an altered reality.

In her 1925 volume of essays, *The Common Reader*, Virginia Woolf captured essential elements in this national mood during the first years after the war by relating the British condition to the ancient Greek mind. The very closeness of that society to the natural world, she argued powerfully in one of those pieces, had made its people 'even more aware than we are of a ruthless fate' – though, by implication, the war had taught contemporary Britons, too, a good deal on that score. Such awareness underpinned 'a sadness at the back of life' in classical culture, but a sadness that did not so much paralyse the spirit as harden it to survive; and because of that resilience it remained more than ever true, Woolf concluded, that 'it is to the Greeks that we turn when we are sick of the vagueness, of the confusion, of the Christianity and its consolations, of our own age'.[8]

Turning to the Greeks always came naturally to Woolf. This was not just because the classics had provided one focus in an otherwise rather muddled girlhood education conducted mostly at home. The instinct also came from the traumatic aftermath of a family visit to Greece in 1906, when her brother Thoby had died from an infection. Images of Thoby frequently lingered in her consciousness in later life, and with them memories of the Greece she had seen alongside him, captivated as she had been by the curious mingling of ancient and modern represented by a railway station, of all things, bearing the name of Olympus.[9] It was entirely in keeping that Woolf's first full-length experiment in modernist fiction, *Jacob's Room* (1922), tracing the oblique, fleeting impressions on the surface of life left by a young Englishman seemingly destined for anonymous extinction on the battle front, features a prolonged visit to Athens.

In this sequence the disconnected stream of Jacob's thoughts, the married Englishwoman for whom the loveliness of a sultry evening merges seamlessly into idle self-obsession with her own beauty, the half-sad, half-careless attitude of the husband to the transient affair he sees unfolding between Jacob and his wife, all so indefinite and inconsequent, have as their backdrop the exactly opposite qualities in the ancient fabric. There they stand with extreme definiteness, Woolf writes of the pillars, the pediment, the Temple of Victory and the Erechtheum crowning the Acropolis, with shifting shades of brilliant white, yellow and sometimes red. They convey a sense of durability, of the emergence through the earth of spiritual energy uncontaminated by all those everyday trifles which continue to tumble random and uninvited into the mind of the viewer even of such a formidable spectacle. Woolf goes on,

But this durability exists quite independently of our admiration. Although the beauty is sufficiently humane to weaken us, to stir the deep deposit of mud – memories, abandonments, regrets, sentimental devotions – the Parthenon is separate from all that; and if you consider how it has stood out all night, for centuries, you begin to connect the blaze (at midday the glare is dazzling and the frieze almost invisible) with the idea that perhaps it is beauty alone that is immortal.

Wrapped in silent composure, the Parthenon, to Woolf, seemed likely to outlast the world itself. And for somebody of her class and late-Victorian provenance, that is precisely what, amidst the confusions and uprooted expectations of the present, the classical Greek inheritance might do: drive a stake into the ground, something lasting and unshakeable, around which the post-war generation – though not, alas, poor Jacob – might organize new certainties as the basis for a recuperating civilization.

But if Woolf looked for healing continuity, the 'Post-War' in Britain was also a time of acute dissonance. Nothing summed up that jarring change more in popular culture than the imported syncopated rhythms of African American jazz. The Scottish painter John Bulloch Souter explored the relationship of this shift to a classical Mediterranean inheritance in *The Breakdown* (1926), in which a black saxophonist in evening dress sits on a shattered Roman column while a naked white female figure, with elements of the androgynous, dances close by, clapping her hands ecstatically. This image was displayed at that year's Summer Exhibition at the Royal Academy only to be removed after five days following complaints from the Colonial Office for being racially 'obnoxious'.[10] But as a younger generation got on with living their lives, classicism soon proved entirely adaptable to new moods and styles. Allusions to idealized Greek beauty became commonplace in the worlds of advertising, film, fashion and portraiture in the later 1920s and 1930s, with stock images of the 'Modern Venus' and the 'Modern Diana' reproduced in such journals as *Vogue*.[11] Meredith Frampton was one painter who exploited such sources of inspiration, most notably in his 1928 portrait of the model Marguerite Kelsey, described as the epitome of modern classicism in its 'qualities of restrained simplicity, formal clarity, elegance and idealized beauty'.[12] Yet there was still something ethereal, otherworldly, indeed *deadly* white about this image that remained frozen in the shadow of a lost world. It was a million miles from the classical attitudes of an Emma Hamilton or Ellen Terry, alive with passion, movement, possibility. It was only gradually that such traits became feasible, even perhaps *seemly*, in a society where deep channels of grief ran through so many lives.

This supple post-war classical impulse had a relevance also for general political culture in Britain. Shifts in wartime strategy provided part of the background. After David Lloyd George had become prime minister of the coalition government in December 1916 the focus of the British war effort had shifted perceptibly towards the eastern Mediterranean. Whatever few tangible gains the British made in the war were to be in that region, not elsewhere. Greece had loomed large in this readjustment, and from 1917 onwards the British premier formed a particularly close bond with the Greek leader, Eleuthérios Venizélos, who later played a prominent role at the Paris Peace Conference.

For many, particularly in the British Army, this dilution of a commitment to the Western Front had been a cause of much bitterness and underpinned the domestic battle lines of 'Westerners' versus 'Easterners' swirling around Lloyd George himself, continuing into peacetime. In the end it was a Greek debacle – the collapse of the Greek forces still fighting the Turks in western Anatolia after the summer of 1922, the burning of Smyrna (September 1922) and its aftermath – that shaped the ending of Lloyd George's years in power.[13] But on a larger plane the post-war reaction against militarism associated with a commitment to Continental European security, and a return instead to an essentially naval strategy of limited liability overseas, were bound up with an enhanced British focus on the Mediterranean generally in the 1920s. In essence, this represented a desire, if possible, to return to a British orthodoxy of a nineteenth-century kind.[14] If there was, then, from a British vantage point a 'return to order' in art and aesthetics with a Mediterranean typology, so there was in the realm of geopolitics.

One figure responsible for crafting yet another version of Hellenism to fit British and indeed European public purposes was Gilbert Murray, who again helps to provide a connecting thread through generations. Australian-born, but of Irish family descent, Murray's educational brilliance in Latin and Greek was steeped in a liberal Victorian tradition.[15] First as Richard Jebb's successor as professor of Greek at Glasgow University and after 1908 elected to the Regius Chair of Greek at Oxford, Murray pressed the case that 'Greece, not Greek, is the real subject of our study'. By this he meant that it was what Greece meant in the widest possible sense for life now, not any narrow preoccupation with a past language and literature, that gave it continuing relevance in Britain. His most basic conviction was that Hellenism was a phenomenon with a capacity that could be endlessly reinterpreted to express today's issues. Although he flirted with the cultic and anthropological approaches of his friend Jane Harrison, he recognized that in the end such primitivism could not sustain real contemporary purposes. Only the shining ideal of the most classical of Greeces, the one of Pericles and, because of his sceptical dissent, his own favourite Euripides could do that.

Murray subsequently viewed the Great War as a modern version of the Peloponnesian conflict that had brought down the glory that was Greece – that is, a fault line across the advance of civilization itself. While employed in the publicity operations of the wartime government in London he had been involved in private discussions among those looking towards a peace deal to end the fighting, and was a key figure in the League of Nations Society set up in 1915. He was prominent in the work leading to the foundation of the League of Nations itself in 1920, and in 1928 became chairman of the League's committee of intellectual cooperation based in Geneva. Murray was never a party politician, and the drift towards irrelevance of the League as the 1930s proceeded was reflected in his own flailing purposiveness. But for the post-war years his form of internationalist liberalism, set in a Hellenic framework, defined a certain type of cultivated British radicalism and continued optimism.

Still, there were some who now began to feel that they had had enough of ancient Greeks, and that it was time to move on, if only chronologically. One of these was the writer Robert Byron (*the* Byron was a family ancestor). Robert Byron had travelled through Greece in the wake of the recent catastrophic defeat to Turkey and as the great population exchanges agreed under the Treaty of Lausanne were taking shape. He had intended to write a book about the modern Greek tragedy of the years between 1919 and 1923, but instead decided to concentrate on the Byzantines and their legacy.[16] In Byron's mind, these were *real* Greeks, with a clear, not bogus, connection with the Greeks of today.

The result was *The Station* (1928), focusing on the monastic haven of Mount Athos, whose monks may be rogues in everyday matters – cheating visiting pilgrims could sometimes be par for the course – but whose spiritual devotion impressed Byron. *The Station* above all contrasted this with the 'aimlessness and incoherence of life in England'.[17] Shortly afterwards he produced a more strictly historical work, *The Byzantine Achievement* (1929), which Rebecca West described as a wholesome corrective to the long-standing prejudice against the old Eastern Roman Empire.[18] Robert Byron's work was popular and often acerbic – not least about the classics – but it marked another stage towards reasserting studies of medieval Byzantium as a critical aspect of European cultural development; the young Steven Runciman was just then starting a writing career dedicated to the same goal.[19] But less academically, and more to do with the whole body of English travel writing, there was also a fresh engagement with Greeks and Greece in recognizable form, warts and all, not clad in ancient drapes. This was to become a prominent literary genre. Robert Byron later died on his way to the Mediterranean as a war correspondent when the troop ship taking him to Egypt was torpedoed in 1941.

'Byzantium is to Mr. Byron,' D. H. Lawrence remarked of *The Station*, 'what Baroque is to the Sitwells',[20] referring to the remarkable triumvirate of Sacheverell, Osbert and Edith Sitwell who hunted as a family pack in the post-war literary chase. To them the Baroque was synonymous with the true spirit of southern Europe, and after travels to the Mediterranean in the first few years of peace they evoked this in highly enriched form. Osbert's *Discursions on Travel, Art and Life* (1925) found a symbol in the orange trees that he saw dotting the Sicilian countryside as he travelled through by train from Palermo. The orange growth was, he wrote, 'indelibly a beautiful object', and it followed logically that where you found its sweet wood, clusters of golden globes and dark, glossy leaves, you also found the best architecture and art.[21] By implication you also found the most natural, spontaneous form of human possibilities.

This, as it happens, was also the message of D. H. Lawrence's story 'Sun', written in the same year, about a neurotic New York woman who visits Sicily in search of therapy. Nervously, tentatively, she lies naked under the cypress trees, is gradually transformed and redeemed by light, and a free spirit is coaxed into being. On returning home she is shocked by those around her: 'They were so un-elemental. So un-sunned.'[22] This story was one fragment – his *Sea and Sardinia* (1921) was another – in Lawrence's romantic primitivist revolt against a modern mechanical world of which the war had been the most brutalized expression.[23] For Lawrence, who spent two years living with his wife close to Taormina, Sicily always lay at the heart of his writing and his concern with the equilibrium of spirit and senses. Even when he tried to evoke the same theme elsewhere, as he did in *Mornings in Mexico* (1927), he came back in the book's closing sentences to Sicily and what it stood for: 'the Mediterranean, so eternally young, the very symbol of youth!' It is striking that 'the warm South' and its meanings for a British writer could not simply be spliced onto other settings without losing something indefinable but absolutely essential.

Of more lasting importance in art historical terms than his brother's Mediterranean travelogue was Sacheverell Sitwell's *Southern Baroque Art* (1924). This was not so much an architectural description, Sarah Bradford writes, 'as an interpretation of the spirit of the Baroque', and inherent in his technique was 'a capacity to shed every vestige of the twentieth century and to experience the past in a visual time machine'.[24] Perhaps only somebody who had experienced the Western Front – Sacheverell had served there in the Grenadier Guards – could be driven enough to expel the recent from surface consciousness quite so effectively. In *Southern Baroque Art* he invites the reader to put aside current obsessions with the likes of Henri Matisse and André Derain. Instead, he whisks their imagination off on a tour towards the old Bourbon palace at Caserta, where Sir William Hamilton's country villa had once been close by. It is, Sitwell describes, six o'clock in the morning – he disdains to state the year, but it is now the seventeenth century – with the Neapolitan heat already bearing down, latticed shutters thrown open to allow a fluttering music to be already heard, a foaming geyser in the square in front of the church of San Domenico Maggiore 'blowing out its lava like fine glass'.[25] We proceed to a Jesuit convent where the artist Solimena is busily engaged on a fresco – we meet him stuck on a staircase as *The Expulsion of Heliodorus from the Temple* emerges in glorious colour. The overall effect, in Bradford's words, was 'a dizzying interchange of imagination and reality' as the author unfolds a brilliant tapestry of southern heat and excess.[26] To many post-war British readers, soaked in the greyness of war memories and the aftermath of austerity, the effect can only have been luscious and invigorating.

Whether it be revivalism of the classical or Southern Baroque kinds, secreted within these phenomena was a very powerful current of cultural nostalgia.[27] This was reflected in a new enthusiasm for almost anything eighteenth century. 'Why is it that the eighteenth century so particularly delights us?' asked Lytton Strachey, and one answer was that one had to go back that far to reach a society that had no possible discernible responsibility for the road to 1914, and thus could be pictured in a state of blissful innocence. The complaisant husband pictured by Virginia Woolf in Athens in *Jacob's Room* spends much of his time comparing the age of Chatham and Pitt with the current day, never to the latter's advantage, and it was not coincidental that the 1920s witnessed the start of what became a golden age for eighteenth-century British historiography. Lewis Namier's mind-numbingly factual *The Structure of Politics at the Accession of George III*, the precursor of a veritable 'school' of rather narrow political history, appeared in 1929.

In the British society world, however, the reverence for the eighteenth century had a distinctly Mediterranean flavour. In furniture and design Robert Adam's Roman creations came back into fashion. The foundation of scholarships to the British School at Rome exposed a new generation of British artists to the great cycles of Italian murals from the Renaissance through to the age of rococo.[28] Winifred Knights trained at the School between 1920 and 1923 having won the Prix de Rome with an unfinished version of *The Deluge*, today widely regarded as one of the great British paintings of the twentieth century. It was in Rome that Knights married the painter Walter (later Sir Walter) Monnington, whose realist images were also to bear the mark of this formative post-war Italian influence.[29] In Monnington's *The Wine Press* (*c.* 1923), Rachel Spence writes, 'the pristine spinal curve of the man bending to trample grapes echoes that of the figure shedding his shirt in the Baptism of Christ by Quattrocento master Piero della Francesca';[30] and indeed it was in this period that the fifteenth-century Tuscan painter, hitherto largely ignored, was being inscribed in the Anglo-American canon of art.[31] Another artist influenced by his time at the British School at Rome in the later 1920s was Rex Whistler, for whom the eighteenth century became a special inspiration. He belonged to a group – which also included the young composer and Sitwellian protégé William Walton – who at country-house weekends dressed up and were photographed in poses looking like court pages in Bourbon Naples. The epitome of Whistler's work, apart from the dining room in the Tate Gallery that is still admired by visitors, was his design for the interior of Lord

Anglesey's house at Plas Newydd in 1936. 'Sitting at the table in the dining room,' Alexandra Harris remarks, 'one could look out in one direction across the Menai Straits to Snowdonia, and in the other direction across a sunny Mediterranean port to ethereal mountains beyond.'[32] Rex Whistler was later killed serving in a tank regiment after the Normandy landings in June 1944.

The travel writer Jan Morris has remarked that Spain, having limped into modern times, had become so inessential in the larger European picture that the First World War 'contemptuously passed her by'.[33] Yet after 1918 aloofness from the recent war was widely taken as a tribute to good sense, and affording some special significance. One couple, Jan and Cora Gordon, escaped from London after 1919 to the Iberian Peninsula and wrote about their experiences in *Poor Folk in Spain* (1922). 'I think we went,' they explained, 'to look for something that had been taken from us.' Ernest Hemingway chose the country to frame his modernist exploration of themes of post-war death and renewal in *The Sun Also Rises* (1926) because, he wrote, it 'hasn't been shot to pieces' and was untainted by the madness of the recent war.[34] A biographer writes of Hemingway's tortured personality that 'Spain was a healing country for him.'[35]

In Hemingway's novel the authenticity of the country symbolized by the bullfight is set off against the faux bohemianism of its Anglo-American protagonists. J. B. Trend, James Fitzmaurice-Kelly's successor as the main British commentator on Spain's cultural life, expressed the same idea of the country's contemporary uniqueness in his *A Picture of Modern Spain* (1921): 'The Spanish of today have done a special service to Europe. By remaining neutral they not only saved their country, but they have preserved the European spirit – or what we used to believe was the European spirit – more than any of the belligerent peoples of Europe.'[36] The conclusion Trend drew was that Spain had something distinctive to say to the British themselves as they sought to recover from the recent conflict. Virginia Woolf went there in 1923 to stay with the writer and decorated young war veteran Gerald Brenan, who had gone to live in a remote village high up in the Alpujarra mountains, later recorded in his *South from Granada* (1957). Woolf was impressed with the zest and high spiritedness even in a small community, and went home thinking that English children should be brought up as Roman Catholics because it seemed to induce 'warmth of heart'[37] – an indication of how in British minds exposure to the Mediterranean still almost instantly took on a religious tinge, even with those who professed no faith of their own. A whole stream of British artists and writers found their way to Brenan's village of Yegen in the following years, including Lytton Strachey, Dora Carrington, Bertrand Russell, Roger Fry, David Garnett and the young V. S. Pritchett, often accompanied by others.[38] On her way there Carrington visited art galleries in Madrid and Toledo and found herself so overwhelmed by Spanish art as to fear losing her own self-control. After viewing one El Greco, and perhaps anticipating her destabilizing involvement with Brenan himself then taking shape, Carrington wrote that 'one has to keep it all inside'.[39]

It was this kind of excitement, and the resulting collaboration of intellectuals like Trend, T. S. Eliot and José Ortega y Gasset, that suggested for a while that Britain and Spain might form a cultural bridge of their own, or what one historian refers to as 'an Anglo-Spanish vanguard' in the post-war formation of a modernist network.[40] The exhibition *Ancient and Modern Spanish Art* in 1920–1 was the first dedicated overview of the country to be held at the Royal Academy. But the experiences of individual artists suggested that the interaction nonetheless remained tentative and apt to run into the sand. One example was David Bomberg. Like some of his English counterparts he had toyed with radical tendencies before 1914 – in his case, Cubist – and later retreated into more orthodox representational practices. Jewish, but not Zionist, Bomberg had gone to Palestine in 1920 and, with the encouragement of the military governor, Sir Ronald Storrs, then restoring to Jerusalem some much-needed civic polish, had produced striking views of the holy city with its pearlescent light and warm limestone. But Bomberg's work in this immediate post-war period was restricted in its mainly topographical approach.[41] When his canvases of Palestine failed to arouse much interest after his return home, he next went to Spain and sought to find a way of translating his admiration for El Greco into a distinctly contemporary style, developing a fresher and more free-flowing manner – his vision of *The River Tajo and the Road up to the City, Toledo* (1929) with its inferno of colour summed this up.

Bomberg moved to Andalusia and painted Ronda, one critic writes, as 'a living force' in a way that earlier portrayals, such as that of David Roberts

A Spanish Good Friday (Ronda)
Muirhead Bone (1925)

in 1834, had failed to do.[42] In such a way the rest of the time Bomberg spent in Spain exemplified the tension felt by many British artists between expressing a post-war thirst for a return to older values, of which the country was an embodiment, yet wishing to find something new to say visually. Bomberg left Spain with his family in 1935, now fearful of the civil commotions already under way, as did another more ostensibly experimental British painter, Edward Burra, whose pictorial Spanish cast of 'fanciful prostitutes, spivs and performers' were replaced by ominous hooded figures.[43]

Overall, there was a new density in Anglo-Spanish cultural relationships, but one also hedged around by practical and mental limitations. Bomberg, for example, had little to do with any Spanish artists while he was in the country. An ingrained ambivalence was reflected in a comment made by Kenneth Clark soon after his appointment as director of the National Gallery was announced in 1933, at the strikingly young age of thirty. 'I really cannot direct the National Gallery unless I have seen the Prado,' he wrote to the then very aged Edith Wharton, at whose home in the south of France he had become an occasional visitor. But he went on that although he was about to leave for Madrid, 'I shan't attempt to see Spain – I shall simply go straight to the Prado, and [come] back, after one large orgy.'[44] A flippant semi-regard and subliminal connotation of art and eroticism, redolent of Victorian ideas about Spain, were still alive.

'Bloomsbury was killed by the War,' Vanessa Bell said in 1931 of that loose bond of writers and artists originally designated by a world of leafy London squares and flexible relationships.[45] But insofar as the tie had continued through the 1920s, it was also defined by time spent together in France, especially in sunny Provence. The 'intensely visual consciousness' characterizing this connection found in the Provençal landscape a mirror for its own senses and emotions.[46] Apart from old 'Bloomsburyites', the French Mediterranean – perhaps because it was relatively untouched by war – now attracted other stray figures, such as Charles Rennie Mackintosh, the Glasgow-based art nouveau architect and designer who lived in Port Vendres, close to the Spanish border, for five years, painting images evoking the blend of surrounding hills, buildings and water reflections. (After his death in 1928 his wife scattered his ashes from the mole in the harbour.) Augustus John and his cohort of assorted lovers and their offspring had been spending extended periods in Martigues, the 'Provençal Venice', since pre-war days, and it was here, around the Villa Sainte Anne, that in the 1920s he produced some of his finest pictures before his career petered out into the mediocrity of his portraiture. As John's biographer Michael Holroyd points out, the very fact that Provence was not burdened by an 'accumulated glory of the past' like Italy, and did not carry all the over-heated expectations and intellectual baggage of Paris, made it more conducive to the creativity of visiting British artists.[47] Nobody eulogized Provence more vividly than Roger Fry. 'Oh the joy of the Mediterranean,' Roger Fry wrote of being once more in Cassis in 1925. 'It's irresistible – life seems to have twice the value.'[48]

What is telling, however, is that Fry framed this sentiment in terms of the broad Mediterranean, and not just a narrow preoccupation with France and its art, for which he came to be criticized at the time and later for its allegedly constricting effects. For him, as he noted in his critical compilation

Transformations (1926), Provence was inherently pagan and also 'decidedly Greek'.[49] At the same time Fry summed up in a private letter what he conceived as a decisive cultural struggle, one that clearly showed the influence of D. H. Lawrence's ideas: 'It seems to me that nearly the whole Anglo-Saxon race . . . have lost the power to be individuals. They have become social insects like bees and ants. They are just lost to humanity, and the question of the future is whether that will spread or will be repulsed by the people who still exist, namely the people round the Mediterranean.'[50]

To this generality there were some exceptions. Whereas Aix was 'a holy place' to him, Fry disliked what he called the violent egoism of Marseilles (seemingly for the reason that John Ruskin and Henry James had earlier been appalled by Naples – that is, its welter of primal forces beyond control, artistic or otherwise).[51] But what stands out is Fry's attribution to the Mediterranean of an integral quality promising salvation to those, however few, prepared to open themselves fully to it. This played a not

Leonard Woolf, Virginia Woolf, Roger Fry and Joan Fry in Athens, May 1932

insignificant part in the remaining years of his life. Fry might once have called for the dethroning of Greek art, but when he visited Greece with Virginia and Leonard Woolf in 1932 his enthusiasm was infectious, and he picked up Greek information everywhere – 'far and away the best admirer of life and art I've ever travelled with,' Virginia wrote in her diary.[52] The passion for Italian Renaissance art that had fired Fry's early career also came back strongly at the end – he was to die in 1934 – despite those malarious effects he had once denounced in his radical prime.

Indeed, Fry had been one of the instigators on the British side of the great exhibition *Italian Art, 1200–1900* held at Burlington House in early 1930, though the original suggestion had in fact come from the Italian dictator Benito Mussolini, who intended it as an exercise in Italian cultural propaganda: one critic called this striking venture 'Botticelli in the service of Fascism' (since classical-Renaissance echoes became emblematic of the post-1922 regime in Rome).[53] A remarkable assemblage of invaluable treasures including Masaccio's *Crucifixion*, Botticelli's *The Birth of Venus* and Titian's *Portrait of a Young Englishman* were all consigned on one vessel, the fittingly named *Leonardo da Vinci*, and sailed to London; concern about the ship's safety explains its being personally greeted by the Italophile Sir Austen Chamberlain and his art-loving wife, as well as by many sight-seers, on its arrival into Portsmouth.[54] More than half a million people subsequently passed through the Burlington Gallery to see what was still then a rare concentration of Italian master paintings outside their home setting. Art, politics and diplomacy were combining once again to under-line Mediterranean elements in British public consciousness.

Those elements, however, could as ever be combined and reconfigured in freshly experimental ways, as was now being done by a figure about whom both Virginia Woolf and Roger Fry harboured a somewhat wry attitude. This was the American-born poet T. S. Eliot, whose publication of *The Waste Land* (1922), with its evocation of the parched interior land-scapes of the modern personality, had made him seem the epitome of a fresh poetic voice. A seemingly contradictory element in the coldness of that voice, however, was its hard-edged, persistent classicism. The American poet E. E. Cummings once complained about Eliot that he 'couldn't write his own lines instead of borrowing from dead [Mediterranean] poets'.[55] But this was to fail to grasp that for Eliot they were not dead at all, but very much alive and shifting in their significance all the time. On this Eliot never changed his mind. In 1951, commending a new translation of *Oedipus Rex*, he wrote to a correspondent, 'The reader who knows the masterpieces of Greek tragedy only in the translation of an older generation, is astonished to find how living, how contemporary they become when translated by a modern poet and the meters of modern verse.'[56]

Eliot's fundamental goal, in a life that was fragmented at many personal levels, including sexual,[57] was to assert the authenticity of an English literary tradition, and it was obvious to him that it was not least defined by a Mediterranean legacy filtered through English letters. Apart from ancient Greek poets and tragedians, Virgil was central to his vision, but at least equally so was Dante, who embodied simplicity, lucidity and medieval European continuity with the present.[58] A specifically Italian Catholicism gelled with this, and on a visit to Rome in 1926 Eliot surprised those with him when he fell to his knees in front of Michelangelo's *Pietà*.[59] When he adopted Christian belief the next year his strict sense of Englishness ensured that this was into the Anglican communion, but even so he always liked his church services to be as 'high' as possible, short of actual Romanism (in this he resembled Gladstone, and indeed it was said of Eliot that he was at heart an American Victorian).

Not long afterwards Eliot took British citizenship. His religious transformation appalled some contemporaries and put him at odds with more radical circles, and it was arguably to bait the latter, with whom he was increasingly disenchanted, that he described himself in *For Lancelot Andrewes* (1928) as a 'classicist in literature, royalist in politics and anglo-catholic in religion'. Adding in Virgilian classicism and a good dose of Dante, there was here a highly complex mix that drew thirstily on Mediterranean currents in Anglo-American culture as a whole. It must be said that Eliot, like J. A. M. Whistler and William Morris years before, was never fully a 'man of the south' in the vein of many in this book. Of Goethe he once said, 'I never liked his stuff', whilst he dismissed Byron – whose hedonism went against every grain of Eliot's being – as nothing more than 'a touring tragedian'.[60] Later in life Eliot liked travelling to the West Indies rather than to Italy or Spain; and although he once spent a month in Granada he felt uncomfortable and seems to have been unmoved by the Alhambra.[61] But Eliot's role as a dominant figure in

English letters still bore the markers of the warm South, albeit, as always, in its infinite permutation of ways.

The process of Mediterraneanization infusing British culture over decades was therefore still running strongly as the 1930s got under way. But there were always contrary currents, and another surge in the Northern impulse within British culture was also making itself felt. 'North was the inevitable destination of the 1930s,' Peter Davidson writes,[62] and certainly at some profound level notions of greyness were melded with a pessimism bred by economic depression and the beginnings of a new international disintegration. George Orwell's *The Road to Wigan Pier* (1937) documented the social deprivation in what, referring to Lancashire and Yorkshire, he called 'a strange country'.[63] In the same year W. H. Auden and the radically inclined Irish poet Louis MacNeice, seeking an expression of a bleak comedy that defined their mentality at the time, published *Letters from Iceland*, replete with all the afflatus of oilskin trousers, sou'westers and the need to wear flannel under-trousers at all times.[64] Yet it is telling that in the verses making up these *Letters* from a cold climate, the authors' imagination drifted inexorably to the warm South. Selecting a famous figure to whom to address his words, Auden settled on Lord Byron, perhaps because the latter's moral contempt for the Britain of his own day mirrored that of Auden under contemporary conditions. Auden poured gentle irony on Britain's reduced circumstances and vulnerability as it then appeared, and accused the country's social and political leadership of helping to make a desolation and to call it peace. In the view of both Auden and MacNeice, the governing classes of the 1930s – like the Athenian plutocracy that judicially murdered Socrates to eliminate his dissent – had stamped on the poor and underprivileged in the age of depression. (Louis MacNeice's classicism, including a much-praised translation of Aeschylus' *Agamemnon*, later made him a suitable appointment as the director of the British Institute in Athens.) Here again was the revolving dialectic where shifting pulls of North and South, along with the cultural baggage each carried, repeatedly alternated, but always finally cut across each other, and for one compelling reason: ultimately they represented the same thing, a melancholic, nostalgic, but always yearning search for the palliation of present-day discontents. In the 1930s those discontents were increasingly all too real.

The other characteristic cultural tendency of the 1930s was a turning *into* Britain. It was as if in reaction to compulsive innovation a desire arose to rediscover some distinctive English tradition. This was to some degree a cultural reflection of the political phenomenon of appeasement, which in its deepest origins had little to do with policy towards fascist Germany or Italy as such, and more with an urge to discover an authentic and insular interest inherent in Britain itself.[65] Virginia Woolf's posthumously published last novel, *Between the Acts*, centred on a village pageant, expresses what one cultural critic calls a 'turn towards an impure, inclusive and very English eye'.[66] The same instinct was tangible in the art world. John Piper, a young painter with modernist pretensions, turned to English topography as a special theme, but as time went on became a champion of what he called 'British Romantic Artists', 'praising', a biographer states, 'the use of line and of particularity of observation as national characteristics'.[67] Nor could such British Romanticism, with its pastoral nostalgia, be disconnected from Mediterranean roots, ruins and all. Duncan Grant reflected the same entanglement. In the late 1930s he painted lush scenes of the Sussex countryside close to the house, Charleston, which he shared with Vanessa Bell. But he also painted a canvas like *The Italian Handkerchief* (1937), Cubist in shape but suffused with Southern colour and warmth. Englishness, modernism, Romanticism and the spirit of the Mediterranean superimposed on each other – the combination implicitly defined the essence of a large part of twentieth-century British culture.

There is one English writer who was just coming to the fore in the 1930s, however, who does not fit into any general pattern, but who was to greatly affect how the Mediterranean was refracted through the British popular imagination. This was Robert Graves. Although his early poetry had failed to win any real appreciation and he had then endured a rather dismal period teaching in Cairo, his autobiography of the war (having served in the Royal Welch Fusiliers in France), *Goodbye to All That* (1929), proved a sudden success. The fact that the account in many respects bore little resemblance to Graves's real life and relationships scarcely mattered.[68] In the year of publication Graves and his partner, the mercurial American poetess Laura Riding, moved to the Majorcan village of Deyá. Graves needed money quickly and he had become well aware that he lacked the inventiveness for pure fiction.[69] As a dedicated classicist, it made sense to lift some readymade plot from the ancient world. He would have preferred doing so from the Hellenistic canon – he worshipped the Greeks. But despite later admitting that he 'did not like Rome or the Romans, and Nero is a bore', he thought Rome had the most readily accessible stories for a mass public. Graves found a neat twist in taking as his subject not some well-known Roman figure, but the idiot-emperor, Claudius, who had allegedly written an autobiography of his own, since lost, but which Graves could now re-supply as supposed 'history' – a bit like *Goodbye to All That*.

In fact the Claudian saga, which Graves began writing in 1932, gelled with various aspects of his own feelings and experience. Behind the seemingly bumbling emperor could be made to appear a clear-eyed observer of the vicious power struggles in Rome, the puerilities of Caesarism and the concentrated evil of ambitious women of whom the archetype was Livia Drusilla, wife of the dead Augustus. Graves carried out punctilious research on the sociology, customs, institutions and even geography of Rome in the confused aftermath of the Augustan era, and the library he accumulated and the desk at which he sat scribbling away can still be seen in the house, Canellün, that he and Laura Riding had built in Deyá. They did so despite their exploding relationship, not helped by Riding's contempt for what she saw as Graves's potboiler-in-the-making. Indeed, for Graves, the figures of Laura Riding and Livia Drusilla seem to have overlapped. 'All I can say,' Riding commented in the taxi when the draft of the book was finally taken to Palma for dispatch to London, 'it's a very boring book.'[70]

Boring or not, it was published as *I, Claudius* in May 1934, followed by *Claudius the God* in November 1936 (subsequently the two invariably appeared as a single volume). The sales in both Britain and the United States were huge from the start, with multiple impressions within the first two years. There was something about this version of a political society in moral dissolution that fitted the Europe of the mid-1930s, and perhaps to some degree also Depression-time America. Graves later could never be persuaded by any publisher to return to the Romans he disliked – preferring, as we shall see, his revered, if often imaginary, Greeks – but ironically his Claudius came to fix in the Anglo-American mind a picture of Rome, one drenched in revenge, ambition and perversion, very different from that once entertained by the Victorians. Alma Tadema this was most certainly not.

Graves and Riding's time in Deyá came to an abrupt end in November 1936 when they took the last chance to get out of Spain on a British destroyer. By then the ravages of the civil war in that country were reaching into Majorcan hill towns; Palma was bombed soon afterwards by General Franco's Nationalists. These events brought the Mediterranean painfully into the foreground of British public life in the second half of the 1930s. The British government's convoluted efforts to remain aloof from the bloody Spanish conflict – the suitably slippery term was 'non-intervention' – is not important here.[71] For British intellectuals, writers and artists it was almost impossible not to take some position, but these varied across a wide range. For the Sitwells, General Franco represented the best chance for Spain's future.[72] William Russell Flint, the painter of an old-fashioned and often titillating version of Iberia, was openly Nationalist in sympathy. When asked to respond to a questionnaire eliciting the views of authors, T. S. Eliot prevaricated, saying that he was 'naturally sympathetic' to the plight of Spanish people, but went on that it was right on some matters to maintain a tactful – some might say revealing – silence.[73] George Orwell, after his long walk to Wigan, left to fight for the Spanish Republican cause in July 1937, but his witnessing in beleaguered Barcelona of the vicious splits on the left generated an anti-communism given full vent in *Homage to Catalonia* (1938). Virginia Woolf summed up her strategy with the terse principle that 'thinking is my fighting', but it was a principle not least determined by the family effort to persuade her nephew, the poet Julian Bell, not to carry out his intention to actually go and fight with the International Brigade against the Spanish fascists. He went, only to be killed outside Madrid in July 1937. It was a loss from which his mother, Vanessa Bell, never fully recovered. What is most striking for us, however, is that of all the crises and internalized conflicts across Europe presaging some larger catastrophe, it was the civil war in Spain that cut deepest and aroused emotions across an ideological and moral spectrum; as if it was only in the Mediterranean – not, say, in that faraway country of Czechoslovakia – that the British found their passions and sympathies sufficiently stirred, one way or the other.[74]

Amidst the plethora of responses in the British cultural milieu, however, there was one general issue that was a test of authenticity: was it possible for the English amalgam of Romantic modernism to find an effective expression of feeling over these Spanish events? A 'Spain and Culture' symposium was held in London in June 1937 where the black American singer Paul Robeson spoke, exhorting that 'the artist must take sides'. Stanley Hayter's *Paysage Anthropophage* (*Man-Eating Landscape*, 1937) evoked the searing heat and the brown, barren setting for the dark emotions of Spanish society, and as such reflected the long-standing and deeply embedded British understanding of the country.[75] To one critic, it was 'one of the most forceful canvases of pre-war [British] surrealism'. The causes and character of the Spanish tragedy were soon given their most insightful contemporary portrayal in Gerald Brenan's work *The Spanish Labyrinth* (1943).

One frightening new reality was mass vulnerability to air attack. For the British public, this risk came vividly alive with Pablo Picasso's painting of the bombardment by German warplanes of the town of Guernica, with its desperate women and animals and broken-up frames – an extremity of terror. *Guernica* (1937) was taken on tour to raise funds for the Republican side, and, after first being on view in the New Burlington Galleries in London, was displayed in an exhibition at the Whitechapel Art Gallery, opened by the Labour Party leader Clement Attlee, for several weeks after 30 September 1938 (ironically, the same day as Neville Chamberlain and Adolf Hitler signed the Munich Agreement). During the first week alone 15,000 people visited the gallery to see the painting, and it has remained a 'recurring point of reference for human beings in fear of their lives'.[76]

A vital aspect of the struggle to come was that, after the fall of France in May 1940 and the securing of Britain from invasion, the United Kingdom's war would be one fought principally *in* the Mediterranean itself. As first lord of the Admiralty Winston Churchill had predicted that the British would be most comfortable fighting the next war in that theatre, above all because it would not then be one that consumed lives on the frightful scale of the Western Front after 1914. Subsequently, as wartime prime minister one of his key aims was to ensure that it was indeed in the Mediterranean that the British should concentrate most of their efforts beyond the homeland itself. The main set-piece actions of this strategy, by no means uniformly successful, included the intervention in Greece and the retreat from Crete in spring 1941, the siege of Malta, the fighting in North Africa, the long slog of the Italian campaign after the invasion of

Sicily in July 1943 (a slice of it captured in arguably the most atmospheric of British memoirs of the conflict, Norman Lewis's *Naples '44*), and thereafter the return to the Greek mainland. 'The image of Britain and "Britishness" moulded by the experience and stereotypes of 1939–45,' one historian writes, 'retains an indelible Mediterranean imprint.'[77]

This inevitably had lasting cultural as well as political effects, something that the Jewish refugee scholars Fritz Saxl and Rudolf Wittkower reflected in their 1941 exhibition on the centrality of southern Europe to British artistic development over successive centuries. Perceptions of the war and its meanings among British writers and artists were instinctively worked out in Mediterranean contexts because that was what came naturally, whilst in relation to anywhere else – say, to the northern European Continent, from which the British were absent after Dunkirk until the Normandy landings in June 1944 – it was difficult to frame any coherent British engagement. Of course those contemporary Mediterranean meanings could be very different. For Evelyn Waugh the retreat from Crete in 1941, which he experienced and which gave him a jaundiced view of the whole military caste, became in his *Officers and Gentlemen* (1955) a metaphor for the implosion of the British Empire. A sense of moral disintegration, Waugh's biographer writes, 'seeps like a stain' through the novel.[78] In another cultural form, and contrasting spirit, the 1953 film *Malta Story*, featuring Jack Hawkins, Alec Guinness and Flora Robson, evoked the wartime account of the island's siege and relief against enormous odds, with a contrasting message of endurance and ultimate redemption.

So firmly embedded in British experience, a classical Mediterranean turn asserted itself in many aspects of wartime culture. The sculptor Henry Moore, who had previously been more engaged with non-Western art as his inspiration, suddenly realized that his drawings of people taking shelter in the London Underground during the Blitz 'were essentially reclining figures under drapery'. This awareness fed into his later large-scale bronzes in the 1950s, described by art historian Simon Martin as 'the apotheosis of modern classicism in Britain', such as *Falling Warrior* and *Draped Reclining Woman* (this Southern tendency in Moore's work being strengthened by a visit to Greece in 1951).[79] The Mediterranean repeatedly shaped how the British digested the war experience in a way that no other part of the world could equal, other, that is, than the United Kingdom itself; and as Henry Moore's insight on the London Tube indicated, these two contexts could not be separated out because at a deep level they were part of each other.

Inevitably, the war in the Mediterranean had contradictory effects on much of the phenomenon we have been concerned with. British expatriate life in Italy, especially in its emblematic Florentine setting, had clung on through the 1930s despite mounting difficulties, its members by no means wholly hostile to the dictatorship of Benito Mussolini.[80] Furthermore, British opinion at home had not viewed the latter dictator, with all his tomfoolery, in quite the same light as Adolf Hitler. When Italy, a country whose modern unification had echoed so powerfully in Britain's Victorian ethos, became a belligerent after June 1940 it went against the grain to perceive her as an 'enemy'. Consequently the portrayal of Italy in terms of outright hostility usually carried a certain nuance, as if it was a distortion of the natural order, and this subtle distinction has been integrated into British popular memory of the war.[81]

A revealing sidelight on the deep roots of this came when, after the National Gallery's great collection was evacuated for safety to Wales at the outset of the conflict, a scheme was hatched whereby one of the paintings should be brought back each month for display in the Trafalgar Square building. This was something that helped to satisfy a hunger for culture that, paradoxically, but also perhaps perfectly logically, soon emerged as a feature of public mentality during wartime. But when the Gallery's director, Kenneth Clark, allowed members of the public to write in on a postcard to recommend their favourites, he found that by far the majority of the choices were Italian, something he put down to 'a longing for the sense of order and the noble types of humanity which the great Renaissance painters show'.[82] Certainly 'Picture of the Month', duly more often than not an Italian painting, helped to constitute the legend of the National Gallery as a bastion of Britain's wartime spirit, compounded by the weekly, and hugely attended, concerts in Trafalgar Square spearheaded by the pianist Myra Hess.

Nevertheless, from early in the war many long-standing Italian residents were taken into custody in Britain, and such institutions as the Italian Hospital in London's Queen Square, as well as the premises of the old Mazzini-Garibaldi Club in Clerkenwell, were requisitioned. Many

Holborn-born Italians were among the more than 800 who drowned in July 1940 when the SS *Arandora Star*, taking them to internment in Canada, was torpedoed by a German U-boat; many of the Italians who survived the disaster finally returned to their London homes.[83] Thousands of Italian prisoners of war were also brought to Britain. A large contingent, fresh from the North African theatre, was taken to Orkney in 1942 where the prisoners laboured on the Churchill Barriers controlling access to the grey waters of Scapa Flow. In their spare time the prisoners set about building a Catholic chapel on the uninhabited island of Lamb Holm, using whatever suitable material might come to hand. Peter Davidson writes that 'Unpromising salvaged materials were transformed into a very fair simulacrum of a modest Italian village church . . . [it was] an incongruous place: a Mediterranean village church in exile on a bare island on the sea route to the Arctic.'[84] Light-holders for this chapel were made from used corned beef tins. The very un-magnificence of this expression of Italian Catholicism testified more than anything else could have done to the continuing possibilities of what Sir Henry Wotton recognized 300 years earlier: the cultural transplantation of the Mediterranean into a Northern land, driven by a thirst for colour, vibrancy and imagination. After the war one ex-prisoner stayed on for a while to finish the job before the chapel's consecration, and the Italian Chapel, Orkney, now a Category A listed historic building, still stands in all its unexpectedness. In a unique way it embodies an essential principle of this book's theme.

After peace came in 1945, just as after 1815 and 1918, there was an instinctive urge among many Britons to escape the cultural deadness that inevitably had become associated with war conditions at home. The Mediterranean was the natural destination for those with any means (though sheer devastation in Europe and practical matters like obtaining foreign currency meant that such opportunities developed only slowly). David Bomberg again provides an illustration. During the war he had applied to be an official war artist, but was refused, receiving only a few isolated commissions to paint a number of bomb stores. This led to some of his most experimental work but when peace came he remained dependent on his job as an art teacher at the Borough Polytechnic in London (Frank Auerbach was one of his students). In 1948 he was, however, invited to Cyprus by Austen Harrison, an old patron in Jerusalem and currently an architect based in Limassol.[85] On the island Bomberg reverted to the visual effervescence of his years in Spain, only turned up an extra notch, reflecting, perhaps, all the frustrations of the intervening period – a palette 'never more tropical', his biographer Richard Cork states, 'in its insistent use of brilliant ochre, scarlet, yellow and rose madder'. Bomberg, Cork writes, 'emerged from the subterranean world of his "Bomb-Scare" pictures and blitzed London cityscapes into the dazzling sunlight of the Mediterranean', producing a series of Cypriot landscapes in a burst of sustained exhilaration.[86] Most remarkable was an image of the crusader castle of St Hilarion overlooking Kyrenia from its airy peak, evoked as if it were growing out of the very rocks themselves. On returning to England, Bomberg yet again failed to find new openings and his final years were spent trying to set up an art school in a villa in his old Andalusian haunt of Ronda, though with little success. He suffered from depression and then severe illness. Hospitalized in Gibraltar, he got back to Britain in 1957, only to die within weeks. Such a sequence captured not only the way that the Mediterranean met a thirst for vividness and variety after all the monochrome grey of the war, but also the curtailments and pathos that could all too quickly blunt any such fulfilment.

Another example of how in the early years after the Second World War the Mediterranean vitalized British art is provided by Joan Eardley. She was a Scottish painter who had trained at the Glasgow School of Art. Helped by a scholarship from the Royal Scottish Academy, she travelled to Italy in 1948–9 where, influenced by the old masters Giotto and Masaccio, she painted pictures of ragged children, of which her *Beggars in Venice* was typical with its Giotto-like blue colouring. Back in Glasgow she set about recording the street kids of the city's tenements, with the same sympathetic rendering of intense cheerfulness amidst acute material deprivation.[87] Thereafter she concentrated on painting the seaside life of Catterline, a small fishing village on the Kincardineshire coast. She died in 1963, aged forty-two. Above all a painter of rustic Scottish life, in its early phase her career had nonetheless been moved in a particular direction by Italy, poverty and the spareness of people's circumstances being a critical theme.

Not at all surprisingly writers resembled visual artists in aching to leave behind drained and exhausted post-war Britain and feel some warmth on their backs. In 1953 Lawrence Durrell published *Reflections on a Marine Venus*, the very title of which struck a yearning desire; as Raymond Mortimer noted in *The Sunday Times*, Durrell's sensuous description 'excites a longing to leave for Rhodes at once'. The fact that for most Britons there was absolutely no possibility of doing so only intensified the effect. Rose Macaulay's *Fabled Shore* (1949) did the same for the Spanish coastline from Catalonia southwards to Malaga, driving down it in her battered old Morris, parts of which fell off as she went, including the steering axle. A highlight was her arrival in Torremolinos. Lara Feigel records, 'For Rose the beauty of the place and of the hour – the smooth opal morning sea, the spread of the bay, the colourful garden – was like "the returning memory of a dream long forgotten".'[88]

But given the constant ability of the Mediterranean, as an idea and setting, to touch polar aspects of experience, this post-war rediscovery of Southern travel could also trigger darker insights. This was evoked in the 1954 film *Journey to Italy*, and although strictly an Italian production (the director was Roberto Rossellini) it was to have a much broader influence on cinematic taste and fitted into an Anglo-Italian tradition of long standing. The film portrayed a middle-aged English couple, played by Ingrid Bergman and George Sanders, who travel by car to a villa near Naples. Little actually happens, but as they tour the ancient statues of the old royal museum in the city, and visit the volcanic forms of the Phlegraean Fields and the ruins of Pompeii, their marriage totters and they discuss divorce. Shortly afterwards they are caught up in the exotic procession of St Gennaro, with its marching children, sacred banners and the image of the Virgin carried aloft. Sucked into the surging crowd of a transformative ritual that had fascinated outsiders going back to the Grand Tour, the fractious couple are suddenly pulled in different directions and a recognition of what love really is, warts and all, powerfully revives, though the ending is left suitably ambiguous. The film was not an immediate box-office success, but its themes of ennui, sterility and possible renewal made it iconic for New Wave filmmakers in the later 1950s and 1960s.[89]

In a lighter vein, there was one aspect of everyday life in Britain that over time came to be massively altered by renewed interaction with the Mediterranean: eating. In cookery Elizabeth David revived deadened British taste buds through the art of Mediterranean gastronomy. Having set out to sail to Greece in early 1939, and then having spent most of the war in Egypt, David returned to Britain in 1946 only to be shocked at the food that was being consumed. She started a cookery column in *Harper's Bazaar* and in 1950 published *A Book of Mediterranean Food*, richly illustrated by the painter John Minton. This came 'just at the right moment: the British middle class, exhausted by austerity, were longing for the taste of sunshine'.[90] The fact that few of the ingredients that David used in the recipes were then available did not matter; it was the *idea* of the food that was important. Her *French Country Cooking* (1951) followed, but David spent 1952 in Italy, leading to *Italian Food* (1954), her own favourite publication. Before long ordinary Britons could not only start cooking Italian, but by the 1960s they could also start 'going for an Italian'. The phrase itself summoned that sense of 'you've never had it so good' which, as an election slogan in 1959, underpinned Harold Macmillan's great appeal as Conservative prime minister in these years.

Greece, past and present, had a special resonance in this renewal of British alertness to the textures and possibilities of a wider world. Perhaps this was in part because that country in 1940–1 had been almost the lone ally of the British Empire in fighting Germany. (With tragic aptness the first British ship to be sunk by the German Navy in the Second World War had been the SS *Athenia*.)[91] The memory of that special tie lingered even if the events of the spring of 1941 – including a disorderly British withdrawal from Greece – had complicated repercussions. The dire Greek experience of the later phases of war, including famine, inevitably increased these effects. Indeed, when the later distinguished film critic Dilys Powell, whose adult life had been deeply marked by time in Greece, returned to Athens in 1945 amidst a renewed British intervention she found that her old Greek friends were no longer so well disposed, and that the feeling was indeed mutual. It was, she feared, 'the end of an affair'.[92]

Yet paradoxically this proved not at all to be the case. The idea of Greece, still framed in its classical purity, came to resonate in a British mentality seeking to reconnect with old certainties after so much upheaval, just as it had after 1919. When the *Exhibition of Greek Art* was held at the Royal Academy in London in 1946, seen by 72,000 visitors, the organizers stated in the accompanying publication, 'It might be asked why such an exhibition should be held at this time, and the answer . . . [is] that Greek art was the symbol of everything that we stood for, and everything we were fighting for, and everything the Nazis and Fascists were seeking to crush.'[93] Indeed, in the next few years a new era in Anglo-Greek mutuality ('love affair' would be too exaggerated) got under way. That at the high point of the Greek Civil War (1946–9) the local influence of the United States eclipsed that of the older British patron only assisted this process, because it made once perennial suspicions between contemporary Greeks and Britons less central to modern Athenian political culture.[94]

Certainly Athens at the end of the war and during the years immediately following attracted a considerable galaxy of British talents. The writer who had first made a mark before 1939 for his mixing of experimentalism with classical legend, Rex Warner, was director of the British Institute in Athens in 1944–6. The cultural attaché at the British embassy was then Osbert Lancaster, who recorded his experiences in *Classical Landscape with Figures* (1947). Lawrence Durrell, already mentioned in this context, was part of this scene, as was the poet Louis MacNeice, the Byzantine historian Stephen Runciman and Patrick Leigh Fermor, who succeeded Rex Warner at the British Institute, but who proved far from suited to any position that required aptitude for administrative detail.[95] What was novel was a more open, intimate interaction with an Athenian intelligentsia such as the painter Nikos Ghika and writers such as George Seferis and George Katsimbalis, though the ensuing troubles surrounding the end of British rule in Cyprus were to leave much sourness.[96] Ostensibly, George Katsimbalis was the titular character of Henry Miller's *The Colossus of Maroussi* (1941), which the critics and Miller himself considered his best work.[97] However, the real Colossus eulogized by Miller was the warmth, friendship and freedom that a Mediterranean spirit was capable of offering alienated modern man, a feeling Miller admitted he had first imbibed from D. H. Lawrence.

This subsequently provided the background to a golden age in British writing, especially fiction, on Greek themes. Mary Renault, turning her back on her previous attempts at a contemporary comedy of manners, proceeded to write a mature series of historical novels on ancient Hellenic life. The distinctly modern *The Last of the Wine* (1956) – a story of two male lovers in the Peloponnesian War, reflecting something of the author's own same-sex feelings – *The King Must Die* (1958) and *The Bull from the*

Sea (1962) had a stunning effect on a coming generation of readers, myself included.[98] The poetic imagination of the day drew on Robert Graves's *The White Goddess* (1948) and more lastingly on his version of *The Greek Myths* (1955), with its moon goddesses, muses and matriarchal worship. The anthropology, with nods to James George Frazer's late-Victorian *Golden Bough*, was widely seen as nonsense in any scientific sense, but that was not the point; it was, one writer says, 'a gigantic metaphor' that hit the spot for the times, especially at the start of the 1960s when Graves became professor of poetry at Oxford.[99] The fact that, after living on Majorca for much of the time since the 1920s, Graves had never previously been to Greece himself did not matter, though it was something he tried to keep quiet about when interviewed on television (he finally did visit Greece for the only time in his life shortly afterwards).[100]

But increasingly it was the Greece of now – not of Robert Graves's murdering old gods and goddesses or the glories of Periclean Athens,[101] but of cheerful local farmers and unchanging village life – that exerted special attraction in a Britain at last emerged from the 'post-war'. This was perhaps one aspect of a desire amongst British people to find a counter to the brutalist urbanism of a new society at home, reflected in the preserva-tionist campaign of activists like the poet John Betjeman, who saved St Pancras railway station in London from demolition (echoes here of Ruskin 'saving' Venice in the 1870s and 1880s, and indeed Ruskin became something of a reference point for 1960s social-environmental radicalism). Patrick Leigh Fermor's accounts of his wanderings on the mainland of Greece, first *Mani* (1958), with a cover designed by the artist John Craxton,[102] and then *Roumeli* (1966), met this need for a vision of rustic authenticity perfectly. These gentle descriptions of a Greece still recovering from bitter internal conflict stressed not so much urbane, sophisticated Hellenism, but rather a conservative, sorrowful but resilient tradition, more Byzantine than classical in spirit.[103]

The same unbending vitality was evoked in the 1964 film *Zorba the Greek* with Anthony Quinn and Alan Bates, its raw romantic emotion climaxing in the dancing of the *sirtaki* on the beach at Chania in Crete. In a simpler, happier spirit, it was at this time, too, that the film *Summer Holiday* (1963) saw Cliff Richard setting off from London with his youthful mates in a red double decker bound for sun-splashed Athens,

The painter, John Craxton, and the star of the Royal Ballet, Margot Fonteyn, on the islet of
Bourtzi, Bay of Nafplio, Greece, 1951

picking up a few winsome female friends on the way. The theme song's
lyric conveys the freshness and virginal excitement that could still surround
going to the Mediterranean in the early and middle 1960s, above all for
those in their teens and twenties. Something of that excitement could be
simulated at home. The 'mods', one wing of the sometimes fractious 1960s
British youth culture, were characterized by a love of African American
music and suede shoes but primarily embraced Italian motor scooters,
especially the Vespa, as their distinguishing marker, ideally kitted out with
chrome frames, footrests and lots of wing mirrors.[104] The mods on their
Vespas had lost traction as a phenomenon by the latter part of the decade,
but the cachet of the sleek Italian machine as a British style category has
persisted.

Inevitably, too, such Mediterranean undercurrents running through
British life, always liable to trigger deep-laid remembrances and understandings, seeped into politics. Harold Macmillan, in seeking to reconstruct
Britain's self-confidence after the diplomatic debacle following the disastrous Suez incident in late 1956, tried to promote the idea that henceforth,
vis-à-vis America, the British would 'play the Greeks to their Romans' – in
other words, the United States might wield the real force within the Western
Alliance, but it would be the British who would ensure the necessary
subtlety and guile. This was never likely to mean much at all in practice, but
it sounded good.

Ironically, as the British successively lost the rest of their empire in the coming years, it was distant but somehow intensely contemporary echoes of Roman decline that seemed to pre-echo Britain's current plight most aptly. It was no accident that arguably the best-known speech given by any British politician in the whole of the post-war period was that by Enoch Powell in Birmingham's Midland Hotel on 20 April 1968.[105] In it, the erstwhile professor of Greek at the University of Sydney instinctively fell back on classical Mediterranean allusion to attack non-white immigration from the Commonwealth occurring under Harold Wilson's Labour government. In this address to Conservative activists – known as the 'rivers of blood' speech, though that exact formulation was not in fact used – Powell quoted from Virgil's *Aeneid*: 'As I look ahead,' Powell ominously predicted, 'I am filled with foreboding; like the Roman, I seem to see the River Tiber foaming with much blood.'[106] This grim and, as it proved, utterly baseless vision caused uproar, though it has often been said that by tapping into a populist constituency Powell helped win the 1970 election for the Tories.

The cultural uncertainties still bedevilling a country whose angst was now being played out over the vexed matter of whether to join the European Economic Community fed into the intense public engagement with the BBC Television series entitled *Civilisation*, first broadcast in thirteen programmes after February 1969. The original idea had been David Attenborough's, then controller of BBC2, who had been tasked with introducing colour broadcasting to the United Kingdom.[107] He sensed that nothing could do this better than the luscious visuality offered by a focus on the riches of Mediterranean painting and culture generally. For Kenneth Clark, the distinguished personal narrator and guide on screen, *Civilisation* was a largely Mediterranean story, and this was embedded in the structure of what proved one of the BBC's seminal productions (it was also a big hit across the Atlantic). Michelangelo, Raphael and da Vinci emerged as the dazzling but all too brief summit of human achievement.

This did not mean northern European culture was ignored by Clark, but it occupied a distinctly secondary role. Indeed, as his biographer James Stourton notes, Clark seemed to find it extraordinarily difficult to deal with the art of Germany and the North in general, encapsulated in the contrast between his respective treatments of portraits by Raphael and his contemporary and archetypal figure of the Northern Renaissance, Albrecht Dürer.[108]

Whereas the one was seen as embodying qualities of balance, harmony and serenity, the other was characterized by alleged nervousness and ill-suppressed hysteria. In the book of the series, bourgeois Dutch art of the seventeenth century was similarly dismissed as having 'a defensive smugness and senti-mentality'.[109] To Stourton, whilst the series was very important in reasserting a broad civilizational perspective amidst all the cultural flux of the late 1960s, these elements in Clark's interpretation left it hopelessly flawed. If so, however, it was a bias that arose perfectly naturally from the British aesthetic psyche that had shaped Clark's own awareness. He was, fundamentally, somebody whose values, as Alastair Sooke has said, were defined by Renaissance – one might say Florentine – humanism:[110] a champion of Southern light and beauty in the vein that we have pursued throughout this book. George Eliot, fresh from *Romola*, would have entirely approved.

There was, however, another striking feature of the *Civilisation* series: it excluded Spain. This was Kenneth Clark's personal decision. The reason given is telling. Had the purpose been simply to present the history of art, he explained, then Spain would surely have needed to be there (with, by implication, lots of Velázquez and some Goya to boot). But, Clark went on in his book, 'When one asks what Spain has done to enlarge the human mind and pull mankind a few steps up the hill, the answer is less clear . . . she has simply remained Spain.'[111]

In this rationalization, Spain was ignored as a stationary, even stagnant, factor in the progress of Western culture in its broadest sense. This exclusion aroused acute resentment not only in Spain itself but also in South America, since it could be seen as a slur on Hispanicism generally. It also led to accusations that the programmes had provided a sectarian Protestant interpretation (this at a time when new troubles in Ulster were brewing). Clark had been equivocal about Spain even during his time at the helm of the National Gallery in the 1930s.[112] The continuance of such hesitation well into the 1960s undoubtedly had something to do with the post-war longevity of the authoritarian regime of General Franco. But underneath this strictly political antipathy, those ambivalent feelings we have seen over many decades towards the cultural meaning of Spain for both Britain and the larger European canon – a grudging recognition of the country's achievements, yet also an underlying fear of some shadowy factor – were evidently still there in 1969.[113] Nor, when just a few years later the Franco regime gave way to a democratic transition, did the larger conundrum necessarily disappear entirely.

For Clark himself, the most essential purpose of presenting an accessible, even popular, overview of a Mediterranean-centric civilization, however, was because it constituted, in Stourton's words, 'an eloquent defence of everything he stood for'.[114] That it *did* need defending at that time, in a Cold War world subject to disintegration at every level, is important. But even in responding to those pressures, and their special application to a United Kingdom entering a period of grave uncertainty, an instinctively Southern reflex still operated. The perceived ungovernability of Britain in the 1970s, its industrial and political sickness (the 'sick man of Europe'), had about it an air of foetid intrigue and paralysis characterizing Rome after the death of the great Augustus. Robert Graves had written *I, Claudius* as some kind of metaphor for the malady of Britain and Europe in the early 1930s, but when it was finally televised as a BBC series in 1976 it caught the spirit of new discord, with an average audience of 2.5 million viewers per episode. The snake that slithered between the letters of the *I, Claudius* headline at the outset of each programme insidiously captured a venomous mood in the country. Here, too, there was a transatlantic transmission belt, so that the BBC version of Graves's reconstruction of divided, treacherous Rome enjoyed even bigger audiences on public service television in the United States, which had its own troubles in the Watergate era. In 2007 *Time* magazine rated *I, Claudius* among the 'Top 100 TV programmes of all time'.

The point about the Mediterranean tradition in British culture, nevertheless, was that it was one for all seasons and constantly changing circumstances. By the 1980s the fear of being ungovernable had passed and been replaced, in the era of Margaret Thatcher's premiership, by anxiety as to which groups and classes might prove the beneficiaries of unregulated markets. As Britain became a wealthier and more consumer-driven society, now embedded, seemingly permanently, in Europe's institutions as well as wider culture, a sense of enhanced *material* appetites became mixed up with a magnetic Southern pull that had always been signified in part by sheer luxuriousness (Latin *luxus*, after all, meant sumptuous enjoyment). Owning your own home in a desirable suburb or in the English countryside became almost pedestrian; the dream was now one of acquiring a patch on some Mediterranean hillside, or gazing over an azure sea, with other consumables to match. The turning point here was Peter Mayle's *A Year in Provence* (1989), the story of a fifty-something couple moving to the south of France and their travails with dodgy builders and other eccentric locals while converting a derelict farmhouse into their idealized escape (again, really all very Victorian). Mayle's book sold a million copies in the UK, and 6 million worldwide, and gave rise to a whole new genre of travel writing, much of it about southern Europe, hitherto the preserve of relatively highbrow writers such as Freya Stark and more recently Jan Morris.[115] Vernon Lee would have turned in her grave – not much real *genius loci* here, more the spirit of Surbiton transposed onto the Mediterranean and its hinterlands. Still, before long a whole flood of British retirees were on the move southwards, creating de facto communities, transforming corners of Tuscany into Chiantishire, the somewhat less affluent making do with cramped apartments on Spanish coasts; though it is in line with the paradoxes of our subject that academic research presented to the British Sociological Association in 2014 discovered that Brits who moved to the Mediterranean, like other northern Europeans, were less happy than their peers who stayed at home.[116]

This phenomenon, not so much translating the Mediterranean into England, as Sir Henry Wotton had envisioned in the seventeenth century, but translating Britain into the Mediterranean at the end of the twentieth century, takes our argument full circle: that a Mediterranean tradition in British life and culture, endlessly replicated and spread across a spectrum from the refined arts to the most parochial activities, had evolved into an instinct riveted into national experience, though interwoven with an abundance of other elements in an increasingly globalized culture. In February 1915 the poet Ezra Pound had suggested that, just as in the nineteenth century British civilization had discovered the Middle Ages, so 'this [twentieth] century may find a new Greece in China';[117] or he might have said a new Mediterranean in the Orient. But no such aesthetic discovery, or cultural replacement, was ever found. Nothing could replicate the warm South as a benchmark and inspiration, because of the relentless pull exerted from the Graeco-Roman past, and the range and power of its more modern manifestations. So it was, too, that in expressing the most acute sadness, a genuine *lamentation*, the British continued to draw on the depths of a profoundly Greek spirit when John Tavener's 'Song for Athene' caught the public mood so powerfully during the funeral service for Princess Diana in

Westminster Abbey on 6 September 1997 – for many British people of that generation, not even necessarily royalist by disposition, the most emotional public event in their lifetimes.

A very different and parting illustration, however, comes from the work of Damien Hirst, the arch-entrepreneur of brazen, sod-the-past BritArt that shook up much of the cultural scene from the 1990s. After years of relative quiescence, in 2017 Hirst put on a new show in Italy called *Treasures from the Wreck of the Unbelievable,* the event housed in the Punta della Dogana, the old customs house in Venice facing the sea, and the nearby and ornately classical Palazzo Grassi. But what is telling here is not so much where it took place but what was in it. Jan Dalley reviewed the show and its essential method: '[W]e're invited to take part in a game. Or rather a convoluted shaggy-dog story that plays with truth and lies, fantasy and fiction, origi- nality and copying, that unwinds into a self-referencing web.'[118] In other words, yet another form of Homeric odyssey, and indeed Hirst's installa- tions laid out amidst Venetian splendour included underwater formations, allegorical figures, bronzes, Cyclopean skulls and a few 'jokes' such as the face of the celebrity supermodel Kate Moss tacked onto the front of a winged Egyptian goddess. 'If the narrative has a presiding deity,' Dalley wrote of the overall effect, 'it would be Medusa, the blood from whose severed head . . . was believed to have turned into coral.' The palaces, the gods and goddesses, the preoccupation with death and yet also with being completely up to date, surrounded by Mediterranean presences and interlocking references, is entirely in keeping with the thread this book has followed from the age of the Grand Tour onwards. The pull of the Mediterranean that has so deeply affected the successive movements charting the flux of British cultural change since the making of the Union in 1707 shows no sign of abating.

At the dawn of the twentieth century the Victorian artist Edward Burne- Jones said this about his understanding of the role of art: 'I mean by a picture a beautiful romantic dream of something that never was, never will be – in a light better than any light that ever shone – in a land no one can define or remember, only desire – and the forms divinely beautiful.'[119] Burne-Jones's definition of the artistic imagination was essentially the same as that sense of a Magick Land overwhelming ordinary consciousness – 'Every scene . . . anticipated in some dream' – or a 'fairy precinct' firmly embedded through Mediterranean experience in the English-speaking sensibility.[120] This imagery had proved so resilient precisely because it could be endlessly made and remade to fit all sorts of purposes, which might ultimately be unreal but which bore some conceivable relation to reality. It incorporated an ideal beauty constantly reinterpreted and possessing an intensity which, refracted through a Tuscan villa on a summer day, could make John Singer Sargent just want to lie down and die. Yet simultaneously the elusive nature of such idealization underpinned a 'continued unsatisfied desire' which the historian of aesthetics, A. J. Symonds, felt Italy signified in his own life, and which in the early twentieth century set a number of British painters and critics, including Augustus John and Roger Fry, off in search of a reflection of some promised land in Provence.[121] The pathology of the Mediterranean in the British cultural makeup arose from this fusion of beauty and disillusion, yearning and the constantly receding dream of fulfilment. Nothing else, and no other 'sense of place', came to embody these poignant human impulses – and most exquisitely, sensual self-discovery – in the epic geography of British minds; and far from being lost amid successive waves of modernism and postmodernism, the Mediterranean instinct in British tradition intermingled and blended as always with fresh circumstances and preoccupations.

But what of British culture as a coherent *national* entity and the role of the Mediterranean in it? The Grand Tour was a series of disconnected personal narratives. Yet it also served as a metaphor for an emerging British polity notching up successes in material, military and imperial advances, while still searching for a credible cultural identity manifestly possessed by more refined European societies. This also was a kind of yearning. The Grand Tour came and went, but the goal of self-definition, and a nagging sense of failure in grafting the finer arts onto a rough, homespun British stem, remained. There was no doubting the subsequent achievements of Victorian civilization in those practical improvements, cities and things lauded in our own times by the distinguished social historian – and in David Cannadine's description, 'quintessential Victorian' – Asa Briggs.[122] But that there remained a cultural weakness even amidst this apotheosis of British imperial and industrial greatness was something embedded in those allegations – by no means entirely fair – of crippling philistinism made by the Victorians' immediate successors.

Two world wars in the twentieth century only intensified the dilemmas surrounding how the British saw themselves and were seen by others. In the soul-searching following the vote to leave the European Union in the referendum of June 2016, a political historian has argued that the strenuous efforts of the British to portray themselves as victors in both of those twentieth-century global conflicts became a decided liability in defining Britishness under contemporary conditions: a liability reflected in the continuing lack of a metanarrative with a clear relevance to peacetime needs.[123] Perhaps, too, this had something to do, deep down, with the strain of pessimism running through Kenneth Clark's synoptic view of world civilization already discussed: that cultures fail and ultimately disappear above all through a lack of direction and *confidence* in themselves (it was hard to think that a similarly distinguished member of the cultural establishments in France or Germany would have ended on such a fragile and wavering world view). An unresolved confusion as to what, in cultural as well as political terms, Britain as a nation actually consists of, and how it relates to a larger whole, has also never gone away and still bedevils underlying psychology, though sometimes masked by an insecure bravado.

But, just as in geopolitics, so in the cultural sphere the British turning and returning to the Mediterranean have over a long period been critical in offsetting this persisting weakness, even sense of inadequacy, felt in relation to European peers whose equilibrium has seemed so much more assured. By mixing and fusing indigenous elements with a whole repertoire of aesthetic, classical and Romantic themes drawn from a warm Southern world, an Anglo-Mediterranean phenomenon – a translation of Latinate freedom and richness into a core compound of parochial Britishness – helped underpin an evolving hybrid culture. That hybridity drew on Northern as well as Southern rimlands; and although this book has been concerned with the latter, it has also stressed that these two forms of inflection were by no means mutually at odds. Both were pervaded by nostalgia, loss and an indestructible hope of reaching some undefined goal. This was, perhaps, a peripheral, indirect and oblique way of being European, and the condescension shown towards it by others has never quite disappeared. Still, that it *is* European cannot be seriously questioned; and any retreat from it, either towards a disembodied material globalism or into some hermetically sealed nativist vision, can only end in the most dismal of dead ends.

NOTES

1 Shelley Burning

1. This description is taken from Edward Trelawny, *Recollections of the Last Days of Byron and Shelley* (1952; first published 1858).
2. Ibid., 132.
3. For another such occasion, see p. 91.
4. Kim Wheatley, 'Attracted by the Body: Accounts of Shelley's Cremation', *Keats-Shelley Journal*, Vol. XLIX (2000), 163.
5. Getting permission for the interment meant that for many months the remains were kept in a cellar in Rome. Intervention was required by the British consul to expedite the process. For the cemetery, the name of which changed in later times, see Nicholas Stanley-Price, *The Non-Catholic Cemetery in Rome: Its History, Its People and Its Survival for 300 Years* (2014).
6. Sylva Norman, *Flight of the Skylark: The Development of Shelley's Reputation* (1954), 29.
7. Ibid., 263.
8. Ibid., 254–6.
9. Ibid., 251.
10. Mandy Swann, 'Shelley's Utopian Seascapes', *Studies in Romanticism*, Vol. LII (2013), 3. Byron shared this fascination with the sea.
11. David Crane, *Lord Byron's Jackal: The Life of Edward John Trelawny* (1986), 50.
12. See p. 93.
13. See Marilyn Butler, *Romantics, Rebels and Reactionaries: English Literature and its Background, 1760–1830* (1982).
14. J. Christopher Herold, *Mistress to an Age: A Life of Madame de Staël* (1959), 303.
15. The classic statement is Vincent Harlow, *The Founding of the Second British Empire, 1763–1793, Vol. II* (1964).
16. Linda Colley, *Britons: Forging the Nation 1707–1837* (1992), 145.
17. J. C. D. Clark, *English Society, 1688–1832: Ideology, Social Structure and Political Practice during the Ancien Regime* (1985), 7.
18. See Clare Haynes, *Pictures and Popery: Art and Religion in England, 1660–1760* (2006). Brian Dolan, *Ladies of the Grand Tour* (2007), provides a good account of those British females who did travel, mainly to Italy, during that era.

19. Suggestively, the respective French and German terms for the intellectual sea-change of the eighteenth century, the *Lumières* and *Aufklärung*, had for decades no distinctive English analogue. Victorian writers conventionally referred to 'the Illumination', following the French usage. 'The Enlightenment' was an invention of twentieth-century English-speaking discourse. See John Pemble, *The Rome We Have Lost* (2017), 65–6.

20. Lawrence Lipking, *The Ordering of the Arts in Eighteenth Century England* (1970).

21. Christoph Becker, Axel Burkarth and Francis Russell (eds), 'The International Taste for Venetian Art', in Jane Martineau and Andrew Robison (eds), *The Glory of Venice: Art in the Eighteenth Century* (1994), 56.

22. Marie Peters, 'Early Hanoverian Consciousness: Empire or Europe?', *English Historical Review*, Vol. CXXII, 497 (June 2007), 638.

23. Douglas Sladen, *In Sicily, Vol. I* (1901), ix.

24. Robert Holland, *Blue-Water Empire: The British in the Mediterranean since 1800* (2012), 228

25. Fritz Saxl and Rudolf Wittkower, *British Art and the Mediterranean* (1948), 1.

26. In Cyprus, however, the British retained two very small Sovereign Base Areas which remain today. In independent Malta, Queen Elizabeth II remained head of state until the island became a republic in 1974.

27. Nathaniel Hawthorne, *The Marble Faun* (1900; first published 1860), ix.

28. Nigel Townson (ed.), *Is Spain Different? A Comparative Look at the Nineteenth and Twentieth Centuries* (2015); commentary by Sasha Pack in the *English Historical Review*, Vol. CXXXII, 558 (October 2017).

29. For E. M. Forster's *A Room with a View* see pp. 206–8.

30. John Pemble, *The Mediterranean Passion: Victorians and Edwardians in the South* (1987). This is an important book for the overall theme.

31. See p. 114.

32. Roy McMullen, *Victorian Outsider: A Biography of J. A. M. Whistler* (1974), 263.

33. Fiona MacCarthy, *The Last Pre-Raphaelite: Edward Burne-Jones and the Victorian Imagination* (2011), 236.

34. See Gerard Carruthers and Alan Rawes (eds), *English Romanticism and the Celtic World* (2003).

35. Francis Spufford, *I May Be Some Time: Ice and the English Imagination* (1996), 187.

36. Peter Davidson, *The Idea of North* (2005), 8.

37. See Jeffrey Wilson, *The German Forest: Nature, Identity, and the Contestation of a National Symbol, 1871–1914* (2012).

38. Hawthorne, *The Marble Faun*, 259.

39. Jenny Uglow, *Mr Lear: A Life of Art and Nonsense* (2017), 129. Also see John Pemble (ed.), *John Addington Symonds: Culture and the Demon Desire* (2000).

40. Claire Tomalin, *Charles Dickens: A Life* (2011), 159–66. The book Dickens wrote about his journey was *Pictures of Italy* (1846).

41. James Buzard, *The Beaten Track: European Tourism, Literature, and the Ways to 'Culture', 1800–1914* (1993), 103–4.

42. For a fuller discussion of the theme see the chapter on 'Destabilized Travel' in Chloe Chard, *Pleasure and Guilt on the Grand Tour: Travel Writing and Imaginative Geography, 1600–1830* (1999), 173–208.

43. Patricia Alleridge, 'Richard Dadd', *New Oxford Dictionary of National Biography* (hereafter *Oxford DNB*).

44. Arthur Symons, *Confessions: A Study in Pathology* (1930), 6.

45. Mathew Sturgis, *Passionate Attitudes: The English Decadence of the 1890s* (1995), 278.

46. Michael Llewellyn Smith, 'The Substance and the Shadows: Reflections on British-Greek Relations over Two Centuries', in Anastasia Yiangou and Antigone Heraclidou (eds), *Cyprus from Colonialism to the Present: Visions and Realities. Essays in Honour of Robert Holland* (2018), 200. For the same episode and psychological currents in Anglo-Greek relations see

Robert Holland, 'Patterns of Anglo-Hellenism: A "Colonial" Connection?', *Journal of Imperial and Commonwealth History*, Vol. XXXVI, 3 (2008), 383–96.

47. See James Boswell, *Boswell on the Grand Tour: Italy, Corsica and France, 1765–6*, ed. Frank Brady and Frederick A. Pottle (1955), 37.

48. Ellis Cornelia Knight, *The Autobiography of Miss Cornelia Knight, Lady Companion to Princess Charlotte of Wales* (1861). Knight spent several years living in Naples.

49. Phyllis Grosskurth, *John Addington Symonds* (1964), 236–7.

50. Ibid., 313–14.

51. See pp. 124–6.

52. Fiona Becket, 'Strangeness in D. H. Lawrence', in George Donaldson and Mara Kalnins (eds), *D. H. Lawrence in Italy and England* (1999), 38–9.

53. See Michael Haag, *The Durrells of Corfu* (2017).

54. Stefania Arcara, 'Constructing the South: Sicily, Southern Italy and the Mediterranean in British Culture, 1773–1926', PhD thesis, University of Warwick (1998), 11. This thesis is significant for the subject as a whole.

55. Robert Halsband, *The Life of Lady Mary Wortley Montagu* (1956), 75, 173, 279.

56. See Alexander Bevilacqua, *The Republic of Arabic Letters: Islam and the European Enlightenment* (2017).

57. D. H. Lawrence, *Sea and Sardinia* (1997; first published 1927), 8–9.

58. Neil Roberts, *D. H. Lawrence, Travel and Cultural Difference* (2004), 44.

59. Other examples of the fetish for donning Arab regalia on their travels might include Lord Curzon and T. E. Lawrence.

60. See Robert Irwin, *For Lust of Knowing: The Orientalists and their Enemies* (2006), and by the same author, *The Alhambra* (2004).

61. Byron's praise for Leigh Hunt's *Story of Rimini* (1816), that it had 'two excellent points . . . originality and Italianism', reflects his growing interest in an authenticity derived from exploiting southern European literary styles. Elizabeth French Boyd, *Byron's Don Juan: A Critical Study* (1945), 50.

62. Claudia Heide, 'The Spanish Picturesque', in David Howarth et al. (eds), *The Discovery of Spain: British Artists and Collectors. From Goya to Picasso* (2009), 49.

63. See pp. 35–6.

64. John Matteson, *The Lives of Margaret Fuller* (2012), 307. Fuller wrote for the *New York Tribune*, which published her impressions of Italy in the later 1840s. From an American perspective, what became the Italian Risorgimento, a collection of disparate states coming together despite oppression, had clear echoes in their own experience. See Axel Körner, *America in Italy: The United States in the Political Thought and Imagination of the Risorgimento, 1763–1865* (2017).

65. Pemble, *The Rome We Have Lost*, 73; also see Randall Stewart, *Nathaniel Hawthorne: A Biography* (1948).

66. Quoted in Van Wyck Brooks, *The Dream of Arcadia: American Writers and Artists in Italy, 1760–1915* (1959), 47. Also on this theme see Paul Baker, *The Fortunate Pilgrims: Americans in Italy, 1800–1860* (1964).

67. Stewart, *Nathaniel Hawthorne*, 424.

68. Leon Edel, *Henry James: A Life* (1987), 397.

69. This was Hemingway's novel *The Sun Also Rises* (1926), later reissued under the title *Fiesta* and usually regarded as his most 'modernist' and often as his finest work.

70. Peter Ackroyd, *T. S. Eliot* (1984), 289.

71. 'Stunning Roman Mosaic Unearthed by Amateur Archaeologists', *The Times*, 4 September 2017.

72. Michael Pye, *The Edge of the World: How the North Sea Made Us Who We Are* (2014), 50.

73. Saxl and Wittkower, *British Art and the Mediterranean*, 42.

74. Ibid., 44. Wotton was Francis Bacon's cousin, and for many years after his diplomatic career ended was provost at Eton College.

2 The Antique, the Noble and the Stupendous

1. The Kingdom of the Two Sicilies was a union of Naples and Sicily. It was a Spanish possession after 1734, but in 1759 passed to a Bourbon branch under King Ferdinand IV.
2. Outstanding examples are in Room 1 of the Museum.
3. Brian Fothergill, *Sir William Hamilton: Envoy Extraordinary* (1969), 229–31.
4. Friedrich Rehberg, *Drawings Faithfully Copied from Nature at Naples* (1794).
5. Elizabeth Prettejohn, *Beauty and Art, 1750–2000* (2005), 36–9. A recreation of the 'Attitudes' formed the centrepiece of the exhibition *Emma Hamilton: Seduction and Celebrity* at the National Maritime Museum in Greenwich in 2016–17.
6. *Illustrated Sporting and Dramatic News*, 29 January 1881.
7. Judith R. Walkowitz, 'The "Vision of Salome": Cosmopolitanism and Erotic Dancing in Central London, 1908–1918', *American Historical Review*, Vol. CVIII (April 2003), 337–76.
8. Fothergill, *Hamilton*, 419.
9. P. J. Marshall and Glyndwr Williams, *The Great Map of Mankind: British Perceptions of the World in the Age of Enlightenment* (1982), 9.
10. John Buxton, *The Grecian Taste: Literature in the Age of Neo-Classicism, 1740–1820* (1978), 2.
11. One writer who has examined the Italian backgrounds in Shakespeare's plays and matched them to the actual locations, however, does believe that the author of the plays must have been there. See Richard Paul Roe, *The Shakespeare Guide to Italy* (2011). Thomas Cromwell, Henry VIII's principal secretary, visited Italy twice as a young man, first in 1504, when he stayed with a rich Florentine banking family, and again in 1514.
12. Voltaire once visited Pope's residence in Twickenham, and it has been suggested by some scholars that its garden suggested to him the idea for *Candide*. Kim Wilkie, 'Rooted to the Plot: What Can Voltaire's *Candide* Teach Gardeners?', *Financial Times*, 24 March 2016.
13. Edward Chaney, *The Grand Tour and the Great Rebellion: Richard Lassels and 'The Voyage of Italy' in the Seventeenth Century* (1985); also see Bruce Redford, *Venice and the Grand Tour* (1996), 125.
14. See Jeremy Black, *France and the Grand Tour* (2003).
15. Isobel Grundy, *Lady Mary Wortley Montagu: Comet of the Enlightenment* (1999), 456.
16. Frank Salmon, *Building on Ruins: The Rediscovery of Rome and English Architecture* (2000), 20.
17. The venue became the King's Theatre on George III's accession.
18. Jenny Uglow, *Hogarth: A Life and a World* (1997), 489. The London opera had become so dominated by Italian singers that Catharine Tofts, the leading female English soprano of the day, lost her place and went to pursue her own career in Venice, where she died in 1756. She married Joseph Smith, the great collector of Venetian treasures. See p. 59.
19. Martin Postle, 'Boswell Redivivus: Northcote, Hazlitt and the British School', *Hazlitt Review*, Vol. VIII (2015), 6. Hogarth was himself by no means immune to influences from abroad. Cervantes's *Don Quixote* significantly affected the way he saw the world, as it did many English writers and artists in the eighteenth century. Although Lord Byron hugely admired the works of Pope, Smollett and Richardson, he put *Don Quixote* at the very top of the list (Boyd, *Byron's Don Juan*, 108).
20. Alexander Bevilacqua and Helen Pfeiffer, 'Turquerie: Culture in Motion, 1650–1750', *Past and Present*, Vol. 221 (November 2013), 96.
21. Alexandra Harris, *Weatherland: Writers and Artists under English Skies* (2015), 176.
22. See pp. 80–3.
23. Redford, *Venice*, 14.
24. Salmon, *Building on Ruins*, 27.
25. Giberne Sieveking, *The Memoir of Sir Horace Mann* (1912), 6.
26. Halsband, *The Life of Lady Mary Wortley Montagu*, 251.
27. Louise Lippincott, 'Arthur Pond', *Oxford DNB*.

28. Bruce Redford, *Dilettanti: The Antic and the Antique in Eighteenth-Century England* (2008), 2. Also see Jason Kelly, *The Society of Dilettanti: Archaeology and Identity in the British Enlightenment* (2009).

29. Patrick Woodland, 'Francis Dashwood', *Oxford DNB*. For a biography see Betty Kemp, *Sir Francis Dashwood: An Eighteenth-Century Independent* (1967).

30. Uglow, *Hogarth*, 104–5; Evelyn Lord, *The Hell-Fire Clubs: Sex, Satanism and Secret Societies* (2008), 97–113.

31. Woodland, 'Francis Dashwood'.

32. James Worsdale's portrait of this Club held in the National Gallery of Ireland has a tell-tale Italian landscape sketched in the background.

33. Redford, *Dilettanti*, 1, 12.

34. John Fleming, *Robert Adam and His Circle in Edinburgh and Rome* (1962), 168.

35. Ann Sumner and Greg Smith (eds), *Thomas Jones (1742–1803): An Artist Rediscovered* (2003), 38.

36. Fleming, *Robert Adam*, 165–6, 217.

37. A. A. Tait, 'Robert Adam', *Oxford DNB*.

38. Lord Charlemont was a prime example of the link between the growth of Anglo-Irish institutions and Mediterranean travel. He spent the best part of nine years in Italy, and was one of the few who also travelled to Greece. Back in Dublin he built a much admired classical mansion in Rutland Square, and was the founding president of the Royal Irish Academy. See Michael McCarthy, *Lord Charlemont and His Circle* (2001).

39. Christopher Johns, 'Visual Culture and the Triumph of Cosmopolitanism in Eighteenth-Century Rome', in David Marshall et al. (eds), *Roma Britannica: Art Patronage and Cultural Exchange in Eighteenth-Century Rome* (2011), 14.

40. James Steven Curl, *Georgian Architecture in the British Isles, 1714–1859* (2011, 2nd edn), 169.

41. James Lees-Milne, *The Age of Adam* (1947), 145, 169.

42. Roderick Graham, *Arbiter of Elegance: A Biography of Robert Adam* (2009), 103.

43. Alain Schnapp, 'The Antiquarian Culture of Eighteenth-Century Naples as a Laboratory of New Ideas', in Carol C. Mattusch (ed), *Rediscovering the Ancient World on the Bay of Naples, 1710–1890* (2013), 179.

44. Rose Macaulay, *The Pleasure of Ruins* (1953), 157.

45. David Watkin, *Athenian Stuart, Pioneer of the Greek Revival* (1982), 16–18.

46. Julia Williams, 'Gavin Hamilton', *Oxford DNB*.

47. David Watkin, 'James Stuart', *Oxford DNB*.

48. Curl, *Georgian Architecture*, 142.

49. That the appreciation of ancient Greek (and Roman) female nudes, or what Robert Adam termed 'to feast on marble ladies', was driven by the heterosexuality of many supposedly impassive critics, goes almost without saying. See Fleming, *Robert Adam*, 135.

50. Humphrey Trevelyan, *Goethe and the Greeks* (1941), 46.

51. Ibid., 85.

52. Perhaps most famously Adolf Hitler – who saw the modern Germans as the spiritual and aesthetic descendants of ancient Greeks – was fascinated with the *Discobolus Palombara*, a Roman copy of a famous lost Greek sculpture capturing the athletic power of a discus thrower. After finally acquiring it from the Italian state in 1938, the German dictator had it installed in Munich's Glyptothek. It was returned to Italy in 1948. A second copy of the *Discobolus* was purchased by the leading English art collector in Rome, Thomas Jenkins, in 1790 and passed to the British Museum in 1805. It can be seen in Room 1 of the Museum alongside one of Sir William Hamilton's vases.

53. Robert Adam, *Ruins of the Palace of the Emperor Diocletian at Spalatro in Dalmatia* (1764). The remains at Spalatro were especially appropriate for Adam's purposes because they constituted an example of a luxurious private Roman residence, not a building with public functions, and so offered stylistic guidelines for the requirements of noble customers at home.

54. Fleming, *Robert Adam*, 294.

55. Countess Evelyn Martingo Cesarese, *Glimpses of Italian Society in the Eighteenth Century* (1892), 202.

56. Peter (or Pietro) Fabris's *Raccolta* (1773) consisted of etchings of assorted figures and groups depicting street life in Naples. It was dedicated to Sir William Hamilton. See Melissa Calaresu, 'Collecting Neapolitans: The Representation of Street Life in Late Eighteenth-Century Naples', in Melissa Calaresu and Helen Hills (eds), *New Approaches to Naples, c. 1500–c. 1800: The Power of Place* (2013), 177–90.

57. Rosemary Sweet, *Cities of the Grand Tour: The British in Italy, c. 1690–1820* (2012), 192–3.

58. Michael Kelly, *Reminiscences* (1826). Michael Kelly, the great Irish singer, was the first male performer from the British Isles to sing professionally in Italy.

59. Ian McIntyre, *Garrick* (1999), 341.

60. Jeremy Black, *The British Abroad: The Grand Tour in the Eighteenth Century* (1992), 230. Lady Craven's home, Villa Craven, was in Posillipo on the Bay of Naples. Craven Cottage by the Thames, today the grounds of Fulham Football Club, was part of the estate of her first husband.

61. Trevelyan, *Goethe and the Greeks*, 124.

62. See p. 114.

63. Bevilacqua and Pfeiffer, 'Turquerie: Culture in Motion', 107.

64. See Schnapp, 'The Antiquarian Culture of Eighteenth-Century Naples'.

65. E. Schenk, *Mozart and His Times* (1960), 133. Catherine died from an infection in August 1783. Near the end of her life she told her husband, 'I would have preferred begging with you to a kingdom without you.'

66. Fothergill, *Hamilton*, 108–9.

67. Ibid., 114.

68. Geoffrey M. Morson, 'Sir William Hamilton', *Oxford DNB*.

69. Tim Blanning, *The Pursuit of Glory: Europe 1648–1815* (2007), 487.

70. Sacheverell Sitwell, *Southern Baroque Art: A Study of Painting, Architecture and Music in Italy and Spain of the 17th and 18th Centuries* (1924), 19.

71. Arcara, 'Constructing the South', 69–71.

72. The modern American writer and activist Susan Sontag wrote the novel *The Volcano Lover* on Hamilton in this context. The book had a distinctly contemporary 'take', but the interesting thing is that a feminist and modernist of the later twentieth century should feel so drawn to the topic. Sontag – who died in 2004 – once said 'to enter a larger life, that is the zone of freedom', and that is indeed what Neapolitan art and raw nature meant to Hamilton.

73. Fothergill, *Hamilton*, 184.

74. C. Stumpf-Condry and S. J. Skedd, 'Richard Payne Knight', *Oxford DNB*.

75. Michael Clarke and Nicholas Penny, *The Arrogant Connoisseur: Richard Payne Knight, 1751–1824* (1982), 97.

76. Mattusch, *Rediscovering the Ancient World*, 24–6; James Moore and Ian Macgregor Morris, 'History in Revolution? Approaches to the Ancient World in the Long Eighteenth Century', in James Moore et al., *Reinventing History: The Enlightenment Origins of Ancient History* (2008), 3–29.

77. See *Museo Paestum Nei Percorsi del Grand Tour: Dipinti, acquerelli e stampe* (Fondazione Giambattista Vico), 2007.

78. Fleming, *Robert Adam*, 293.

79. Sweet, *Cities of the Grand Tour*, 54.

80. Kathleen Turner, 'Patrick Brydone', *Oxford DNB*.

81. Henry Swinburne's widely read *Travels in Two Sicilies*, first published in two volumes in 1785, had by the 1790 edition expanded to four volumes. The Victorian poet, Algernon Swinburne, was a descendant of the author.

82. Arcara, 'Constructing the South', 77.

83. Trevelyan, *Goethe and the Greeks*, 124.

84. See Robert Miles, *Ann Radcliffe: The Great Enchantress* (1995).

85. Roderick Marshall, *Italy in English Literature, 1775–1815: Origins of the Romantic Intellect* (1934), 196–7.

86. Robert Miles, 'Ann Radcliffe', *Oxford DNB*.

87. This condescension never did disappear. One of Oscar Wilde's characteristic statements at the end of the next century was, 'When I look at a landscape, I cannot help seeing all its defects.' Less cryptically, Pablo Picasso once told a friend that for him landscape was always foreign, adding, 'I never see any . . . I've always lived inside myself', which had really been William Blake's point.

88. Martin Postle and Robin Simon, *Richard Wilson and the Transformation of European Landscape Painting* (2014), 11.

89. Ibid., 24.

90. Judy Egerton, 'Thomas Jones', *Oxford DNB*.

91. Sir William Hamilton once let Jones use the billiard room in the Palazzo Sessa for painting during one of the periods when the artist was struggling to find accommodation.

92. Christopher Riopello, 'Thomas Jones in Italy', in Sumner and Smith (eds), *Thomas Jones*, 56.

93. Towne was in Italy in 1780–1, but was one who felt unsettled and came home early. Yet in that time he produced a striking series of watercolours later bequeathed to the British Museum. In 2016 Towne's works were displayed together for the first time since 1805 in the Museum's exhibition *Light, Time, Legacy: Francis Towne's Watercolours of Rome*. For Towne's influence on Ravilious, see Andy Friend, *Ravilious & Co.: The Pattern of Friendship* (2017), 37.

94. Blanning, *The Pursuit of Glory*, 524.

95. Frances Gerard, *Angelica Kauffmann: A Biography* (1982), 36.

96. An example of the social mobility that Grand Touring encouraged was Richard Dalton, apprenticed to a coach painter in Clerkenwell, who scraped together the resources for two visits to Italy in 1741 and 1747. He became librarian to the Prince of Wales and eventually surveyor of the King's Pictures.

97. Salmon, *Building on Ruins*, 28. The original design for Mylne's bridge – called upon opening the 'William Pitt Bridge' – can be seen reproduced on the attractive tiling in the short underpass along the South Bank just by Blackfriars (or 'Blackfryers', as it was then). The bridge was demolished in 1860 and replaced by the current construction.

98. Martin Postle, 'Sir Joshua Reynolds', *Oxford DNB*.

99. This deprecation towards contemporary Italian achievements applied chiefly in the arts. In philosophy and the sciences a different attitude sometimes prevailed. John Strange, British resident minister in Venice 1771–89, himself a natural scientist, saw it as his role to keep both the Royal Society and the Society of Antiquaries in London regularly informed of Italian scientific research. See Robert Sharp, 'John Strange', *Oxford DNB*.

100. David Howarth, *The Invention of Spain: Cultural Relations between Britain and Spain, 1770–1870* (2007), 120. Sir Robert Walpole's canvases by Velázquez were sold with the rest of the collection to Empress Catherine of Russia in 1779, and ended up in the Hermitage Museum. However, they returned temporarily to Houghton Hall, hung in the selfsame spots, for an exhibition in 2013.

101. Nigel Glendinning et al. (eds), *Spanish Art in Britain and Ireland, 1750–1920* (2010), 51.

102. Adeline Hartcup, *Angelica: The Portrait of an Eighteenth-Century Artist* (1954), 126. Marat was living in London in these years and met Kauffmann through Antonio Zucchi.

103. The allegation that Kauffmann made drawings from male nudes touched one of the sensitivities surrounding any professional female artist. Years later one of Kauffmann's male models, then aged eighty, was asked about this. His reply was that only his arms, shoulders and a leg had been exposed, and that Kauffmann's father had always been present (Hartcup, *Angelica*, 10). Even in the 1890s at the Slade School of Art there were separate life classes for males and females, and in the latter case 'nude' male models were never completely naked.

104. Steffi Roettegen, 'German Painters in Naples and Their Contribution to the Revival of Antiquity', in Mattusch, *Rediscovering the Ancient World*, 130.

105. Wendy Wassyng Roworth, 'Angelica Kauffman', *Oxford DNB*; Hartcup, *Angelica*, 96, 113.

106. Hartcup, *Angelica*, 134–5.

107. Wendy Roworth, 'Between "Old Tiber" and "Envious Thames": The Angelica Kauffmann Connection', in Marshall et al. (eds), *Roma Britannica*, 296.

108. Wendy Roworth, 'The Residence of the Arts: Angelica Kauffmann's Place in Rome', in Paula Findlass et al. (eds), *Italy's Eighteenth Century: Gender and Culture in the Age of the Grand Tour* (2009), 169.

109. Hartcup, *Angelica*, 172.

110. The other female founding member of the Royal Academy in London was Mary Moser. Women members were not expected to attend meetings, but could vote on the award of annual prizes and the selection of new members. Memorials to Kauffmann can be found in several European cities. In Naples the Via Angelica Kauffmann leads into one of the city's liveliest street markets.

111. Carol Burnell, *Divided Affections. The Extraordinary Life of Maria Cosway: Celebrity Artist and Thomas Jefferson's Impossible Love* (2007), 120. The film *Jefferson in Love* was made in 1995 about this incident. Jefferson in fact never married.

112. Stephen Lloyd, 'Maria Cosway', *Oxford DNB*.

113. Peter Tomory, *The Life and Art of Henry Fuseli* (1972), 180.

114. Kevin Salatino, 'Fuseli's Phallus: Art and Erotic Imagination in Eighteenth-Century Rome', in Marshall et al. (eds), *Roma Britannica*, 303–14, and Frederick Antal, *Fuseli Studies* (1956), 31. William Blake said of Fuseli, 'This country [England] must advance two centuries in civilization before it can appreciate him.'

115. Exhibitions of Maria Cosway's works were held at the Scottish National Portrait Gallery in Edinburgh and the National Portrait Gallery in London in 1995–6.

116. For a biography see Vernon Lee, *The Countess of Albany* (1884).

117. A threat from Italy to an English dynasty had historical resonance. During Henry VIII's dispute with Rome one of the most influential centres of opposition was the household of Reginald Pole, son of a Plantagenet mother, who lived in various Italian cities before becoming a Roman cardinal in 1536. To Henry's supporters Pole was 'an *inglese Italianato*, an Englishman seduced by effeminate, rhetorical and, worst of all, papist Italians'. He later became Archbishop of Canterbury under Queen Mary. See T. F. Mayer, 'Reginald Pole', *Oxford DNB*.

118. Boswell, *Boswell on the Grand Tour*, xix.

119. Clothilde Prunier, 'Peter Grant', *Oxford DNB*. Also see Edward Corp, 'The Stuart Court and the Patronage of Portrait Painters in Rome, 1717–1757', in Marshall et al. (eds), *Roma Britannica*, 39–54.

120. The only place in London to attend a Catholic service was at the chapel of the Sardinian embassy. This was notable for such fine music that even some Protestants attended.

121. Marshall, *Italy in English Literature*, 81.

122. Ibid., 104.

123. Blanning, *The Pursuit of Glory*, 363, 389–91.

124. Black, *The British Abroad*, 241.

125. Richard Holmes, *Shelley: The Pursuit* (1974), 485.

126. Pemble, *The Rome We Have Lost*, 14.

127. Blanning, *The Pursuit of Glory*, 372.

128. Glendinning et al. (eds), *Spanish Art in Britain and Ireland*, 137.

129. A. M. Broadley and Lewis Melville (eds), *The Beautiful Lady Craven* (1914), lxi.

130. Quoted in Sitwell, *Southern Baroque Art*, 62.

131. Henry Kamen, *The Disinherited: The Exiles Who Created Spanish Culture* (2007), 151.

132. Edith Wharton, *The Valley of Decision* (1902), 64.

133. John Eglin, *Venice Transfigured: The Myth of Venice in British Culture, 1660–1797* (2001), 140.

134. Alessandro Bettagno, 'Rococo Artists', in Martineau and Robison (eds), *The Glory of Venice*, 122.

135. Michael Levey, 'Introduction to Eighteenth-Century Venetian Art', in Martineau and Robison (eds), *The Glory of Venice*, 32.

136. Redford, *Dilettanti*, 25.

137. Eglin, *Venice Transfigured*, 81. The musicologist Dr Burney, however, found that in his case Venetian institutions proved very accessible, perhaps due to his own reputation across Europe. He was particularly moved by the Conservatorios, which were in effect female orphanages, where the singing seemed to Burney that of 'absolute nightingales' (Percy Scholes, *The Great Dr. Burney, Vol. 1* (1948), 166–70).

138. Eglin, *Venice Transfigured*, 56.

139. Sweet, *Cities of the Grand Tour*, 214.

140. Today it is the Palazzo Mangili-Valmarana.

141. By 1762 Joseph Smith, whose commercial dealings were always somewhat suspect, was in financial difficulty and sold much of his collection to George III for £20,000. George IV later donated the books to the British Library. Today they are the centrepiece of the striking internal glass tower in the British Library at Euston. Smith's original paintings and drawings remain in the Royal Collection. See Stuart Morrison, 'Joseph Smith', *Oxford DNB*.

142. Andrew Graham-Dixon, 'A Tale of Two Cities', *Independent*, 16 November 1993; Redford, *Venice and the Grand Tour*, 130.

143. Eglin, *Venice Transfigured*, 117.

144. J. G. Links, 'Canaletto', in Martineau and Robison (eds), *The Glory of Venice*, 240.

145. Robert Colville's remark was as an introduction to the 2017 exhibition *Canaletto and the Art of Venice* at the Queen's Gallery, Buckingham Palace.

146. George B. McClellan, *Venice and Bonaparte* (1931). The bronzes were returned to St Mark's in 1815. Today the originals can be seen just inside the basilica.

147. Tiffany Jenkins, 'Mad for Marble', *Literary Review*, July 2016.

148. Eglin, *Venice Transfigured*, 8, 203.

149. John Pemble, *Venice Rediscovered* (1995), 86, 141.

150. Francis Russell, 'The International Taste for Venetian Art', in Martineau and Robison (eds), *The Glory of Venice*, 48.

151. See Introduction to Edith Clay (ed.), *Sir William Gell in Italy: Letters to the Dilettanti, 1831–1835* (1976), 20–1.

152. Ilaria Bignamini and Clare Hornsby, *Digging and Dealing in Eighteenth-Century Rome* (2010), 209–10.

153. Admiral Nelson had gone to Naples directly after his victory over the French fleet at the Battle of the Nile. In the long term this battle secured a British primacy in Mediterranean waters but it did not do much to affect matters on the surrounding landmass at the time.

154. Fothergill, *Hamilton*, 351.

155. Ibid., 382–3.

156. Ibid., 398.

157. Ibid., 423.

158. Redford, *Dilettanti*, 125.

159. But Gillray himself was not untouched by Italian influences. He had studied engraving in London under Francesco Bartolozzi, who had himself once worked in Rome for Giovanni Piranesi.

160. Clarke and Penny, *The Arrogant Connoisseur*, 61.

161. See Amanda Goodrich, *Debating England's Aristocracy in the 1790s: Pamphlets, Polemics and Political Ideas* (2005), 172.

162. Stanley Jones, *Hazlitt: A Life* (1989), 47. Also see Maureen McCue, *British Romanticism and the Reception of Italian Old Master Art* (2014). The Orléans collection was also put on

restricted display in 1803 at what is today known as Bridgewater House in Westminster, where sections of it remain; some parts – the Sutherland Collection – rotate between the National Galleries in London and Edinburgh.
163. Blanning, *The Pursuit of Glory*, 521.

3 The Distorted Mirror

1. Ambrogio Caiani, 'Ornamentalism in a European Context? Napoleon's Italian Coronation, 26 May 1805', *English Historical Review*, Vol. CXXXII, 554 (February 2017), 41–72.
2. See Fernand Beaucour et al., *The Discovery of Egypt: Artists, Travellers and Scientists* (1990).
3. Pemble, *The Rome We Have Lost*, 22.
4. John Steegman, *The Rule of Taste: From George I to George IV* (1936), 156.
5. Jonathan Bate, 'William Hazlitt', *Oxford DNB*.
6. Boyd, *Byron's Don Juan*, 105.
7. E. M. Butler, *Byron and Goethe: Analysis of a Passion* (1956), vii.
8. Fiona MacCarthy, *Byron: Life and Legend* (2002), 165.
9. Martin Aske, *Keats and Hellenism: An Essay* (1985), 19.
10. An example was the so-called Della Cruscan group of English and Italian (mainly Florentine) poets whose gentle, rather elaborate verses were sometimes ridiculed at the time, most savagely by the satirist William Gifford in *The Baviad* (1791). The Della Cruscans nevertheless played a part in shaping a Mediterranean poetic in British literary styles.
11. Nicholas Roe, 'John Tweddell', *Oxford DNB*.
12. R. R. Madden, *The Life and Correspondence of the Countess of Blessington* (1855), 427.
13. Yolanda Foote, 'Edward Dodwell', *Oxford DNB*.
14. David Roessel, *In Byron's Shadow: Modern Greece in the English and American Imagination* (2002), 88–9. Survivors of the Suliote capitulation ended up taking refuge in the coastal enclave of Parga, only to suffer again at British hands, this time directly, when the latter gave their new homes away to Ali Pasha in 1815. The refugees moved on to Corfu, where their community was to be a thorn in the side of the ensuing British protectorate in the Ionian Islands.
15. Leake did not, however, make the topographical sketches in Cyprus that he made elsewhere, probably because the purpose of his visit was simply to reconnoitre the utility of Larnaca harbour. See Rita C. Severis, *Travelling Artists in Cyprus 1700–1960* (2000), 73–4.
16. Clay (ed.), *Sir William Gell in Italy*, 59. Gell was knighted in 1814.
17. Richard Riddell, 'Sir Robert Smirke', *Oxford DNB*.
18. William St Clair, *Lord Elgin and the Marbles* (1967), 95.
19. The most famous example is the Rosetta Stone, the inscriptions on which later provided the key to the meaning of Egyptian hieroglyphics. Originally 'discovered' by a French soldier in Memphis in 1799, the British took possession of the slab during their invasion of 1801. The Stone has been on almost continuous display in the British Museum since 1802.
20. St Clair, *Elgin and the Marbles*, 139. However, Smirke's revulsion did not extend to refraining from acquiring some marbles of his own while in Athens.
21. Edward Dodwell, *A Classical and Topographical Tour through Greece, Vol. I* (1819), 322.
22. MacCarthy, *Byron*, 112, 162.
23. As a result, Gregson became something of an icon bringing together popular fame and aesthetic 'quality'. He was painted by Sir Thomas Lawrence and his bust was erected in the Royal Academy.
24. This was the essential argument levied against the much later campaign to return the Elgin Marbles to Greece. When the British Museum held an exhibition on *Rodin and the Art of Ancient Greece* in 2018 the director of the Museum stated in the publicity, 'The message this museum can give is that seeing them [the Parthenon Marbles] in a world culture context makes you realize things you can only realize here.' Validation for this view was

found in the fact that whilst Auguste Rodin visited the British Museum fifteen times between 1881 and 1917 for inspiration, he never went to Greece. See 'Rodin's Case for Elgin Marbles to Remain at British Museum', *The Times*, 12 January 2018.

25. St Clair, *Elgin and the Marbles*, 172.
26. Pemble, *The Rome We Have Lost*, 90–2.
27. This is the style worn by so many female figures in the novels of Jane Austen as reproduced in modern film and television. In France it evolved into the 'Empire' style of dress.
28. Harris, *Weatherland*, 176.
29. Linda Dowling, *Hellenism and Homosexuality in Victorian Oxford* (1994), 20.
30. Tomory, *The Life and Art of Henry Fuseli*, 42.
31. Elizabeth Jenkins, *Lady Caroline Lamb* (1932), 56.
32. David Watkin, *Thomas Hope 1769–1831 and the Neo-Classical Idea* (1968), xx.
33. Phidias was the ancient Greek sculptor and painter usually taken as the originator of classical design, though in fact no original works by him have been identified with certainty.
34. John Orbell, 'Thomas Hope', *Oxford DNB*.
35. Elizabeth Bartman, 'Egypt, Rome and the Concept of Universal History', in Marshall et al. (eds), *Roma Britannica*, 171; Sumner and Smith (eds), *Thomas Jones*, 38. The great collector Hans Sloane, though never a Grand Tourist, had sometimes bulk-bought ancient Egyptian artefacts available on the London market. See James Delbourgo, *Collecting the World: The Life and Curiosity of Hans Sloane* (2017), 208.
36. Watkin, *Thomas Hope*, 4.
37. Boyd, *Byron's Don Juan*, 132–4.
38. Spufford, *I May Be Some Time*, 46.
39. Donald Sultana, *Samuel Taylor Coleridge in Malta and Italy* (1969), 71.
40. Ibid., 142–3.
41. Holmes, *Coleridge: Darker Reflections*, 143.
42. Richard Holmes, *Coleridge: Darker Reflections* (1998), 20, 71.
43. See Desmond Gregory, *Sicily: The Insecure Base. A History of the British Occupation of Sicily, 1806–1815* (1988).
44. Holmes, *Coleridge: Darker Reflections*, 23–4.
45. Ibid., 43.
46. This aspect is fully covered in Barry Hough and Howard Davis, *Coleridge's Laws: A Study of Coleridge in Malta* (2010).
47. This was not by any means how all Neapolitans saw the recent history of their city. See Holland, *Blue-Water Empire*, 24–5.
48. A handsome memorial, paid for by Maltese as well as British subscriptions, was erected in Lower Barakka Gardens and still stands overlooking Valletta's Grand Harbour.
49. Sultana, *Samuel Taylor Coleridge*, 243. De Quincey was the author of *Confessions of an English Opium-Eater* (1821).
50. Madame de Staël was the daughter of Jacques Necker, the minister of finance whose dismissal from office was part of the sequence of events leading to the storming of the Bastille in July 1789. For Anglomania as an element in European culture see Ian Buruma, *Voltaire's Coconuts, or Anglomania in Europe* (1999).
51. Herold, *Mistress to an Age*, 309. The French artist Élisabeth Vigée Le Brun, indeed, painted a canvas entitled *Madame de Staël as Corinne* in 1807–8.
52. Germaine de Staël, *On Corinne, Or Italy* (1807), Book XI, Chapter III.
53. Madelyn Gutwirth, *Madame de Staël, Novelist: The Emergence of the Artist as a Woman* (1978), 217–18.
54. Ibid., 308.
55. Herold, *Mistress to an Age*, 197.
56. Joanne Wilkes, *Lord Byron and Madame de Staël: Born to Opposition* (1999), 47.
57. Herold, *Mistress to an Age*, 336.
58. Mark Storey, *Robert Southey: A Life* (1977), 192. The British military engagement in the Iberian Peninsula was the largest overseas in British history before 1914.

59. Butler, *Romantics, Rebels and Reactionaries*, 117.
60. David Howarth, 'The Quest for Spain', in Baker et al. (eds), *The Discovery of Spain: Goya to Picasso* (2009), 16.
61. However, at the Battle of Vitoria in 1813 a number of Spanish master paintings originally from the Bourbon royal collection were seized by British troops from the baggage train of Joseph Bonaparte, the Napoleonic ruler of Spain, including Diego Velázquez's *The Waterseller of Seville*. Passing into the personal ownership of the Duke of Wellington, this collection was installed in the Duke's London home, Apsley House. After 1852 these Spanish canvases could be viewed by private appointment, but were not accessible to a wider public for another century.
62. Norman Gash, 'Arthur Wellesley', *Oxford DNB*.
63. Howarth, 'The Quest for Spain', 16–17.
64. John Prest, *Lord John Russell* (1972), 11.
65. F. Rosen, *Bentham, Byron, and Greece: Constitutionalism, Nationalism, and Early Liberal Political Thought* (1982), 292.
66. Lord Byron, *Childe Harold's Pilgrimage* (1812), Canto 1, stanza LVIII.
67. MacCarthy, *Byron*, 163.
68. John Buxton, *Byron and Shelley: The History of a Friendship* (1968), 79.
69. For Byron's homosexuality see Louis Crompton, *Byron and Greek Love: Homophobia in 19th-Century England* (1985).
70. David Reiman, 'Byron in Italy: The Return of Augustus', in Andrew Rutherford (ed.), *Byron: Augustan and Romantic* (1990), 185.
71. MacCarthy, *Byron*, 149. About the only leading contemporary writer Byron admired was Walter Scott.
72. Jerome McGann, 'George Gordon Noel Byron', *Oxford DNB*.
73. M. C. Curthoys, 'Frederick North', *Oxford DNB*. North had converted to Greek Orthodoxy when visiting Corfu, then under Venetian rule, in 1791.
74. See Michael Cook, 'Byron, Pope and the Grand Tour', in Rutherford (ed.), *Byron*.
75. Butler, *Byron and Goethe*, 6.
76. MacCarthy, *Byron*, 131.
77. Stephen Minto, *On a Voiceless Shore: Byron in Greece* (1998), 5.
78. For a discussion of this theme's ambiguity in the poetry of John Keats, usually taken as the epitome of Romantic Hellenism, see Aske, *Keats and Hellenism*.
79. MacCarthy, *Byron*, 158.
80. Pemble, *The Rome We Have Lost*, 43.
81. One of many later examples was John Ruskin's pursuit of the adolescent Rose La Touche.
82. MacCarthy, *Byron*, 114.
83. Ibid., 341–5.
84. McGann, 'George Gordon Noel Byron'.
85. MacCarthy, *Byron*, 285; Wilkes, *Lord Byron and Madame de Staël*, 21.
86. Peter Quennell, *Byron in Italy* (1941), 140.
87. Roderick Cavaliero, *Italia Romantica: English Romantics and Italian Freedom* (2005), 7.
88. McGann, 'George Gordon Noel Byron'.
89. Spufford, *I May Be Some Time*, 86.
90. Buxton, *Byron and Shelley*, 67.
91. Quennell, *Byron in Italy*, 85–6.
92. MacCarthy, *Byron*, 313–14.
93. Butler, *Romantics, Rebels and Reactionaries*, 121.
94. Ibid., 137.
95. Boyd, *Byron's Don Juan*, 159.
96. The 'Massacre' occurred during August 1819 when British cavalry were ordered by the local authorities to charge into a large crowd demanding reform on St Peter's Field in Manchester. About fifteen were killed and hundreds wounded.

97. Caroline had travelled very widely, from Italy (including a visit to Napoleon's former prison at Elba) to Athens, Corinth, Constantinople, Jerusalem and even Tunis in North Africa, where her presence as the guest of the local bey on one occasion saved the city from bombardment by a British warship. She increasingly relied on Italian servants along the way as less likely than British ones to betray her for a profit.

98. E. A. Smith, 'Queen Caroline', *Oxford DNB*. For a full account see Jane Robins, *Rebel Queen: The Trial of Queen Caroline* (2006).

99. The Carbonari was a network of secret revolutionary societies in Italy providing the model for subversive organizations in Europe throughout the nineteenth century, including in Tsarist Russia.

100. Quennell, *Byron in Italy*, 258.

101. MacCarthy, *Byron*, 387.

102. Buxton, *Byron and Shelley*, 147.

103. Maria Schoina, *Romantic 'Anglo-Italians': Configurations of Identity in Byron, the Shelleys, and the Pisan Circle* (2009).

104. Holmes, *Shelley*, 685.

105. Crane, *Lord Byron's Jackal*, 108.

106. Cavaliero, *Italia Romantica*, 38.

107. In fact, when the grave of the Shelleys' child had been investigated prior to Percy's interment, no bones were found. Norman, *Flight of the Skylark*, 35, 246.

108. Timothy Webb, 'Mia Bella Italia: Mary Shelley's Italies', *Journal of Anglo-Italian Studies*, Vol. XII (2013).

109. MacCarthy, *Byron*, 133.

110. Buxton, *Byron and Shelley*, 159.

111. Roderick Beaton, *Byron's War: Romantic Rebellion, Greek Revolution* (2013), 136.

112. Buzard, *The Beaten Track*. 114.

113. Beaton, *Byron's War*, 214.

114. Ibid., 28.

115. Holmes, *Coleridge: Darker Reflections*, 542.

116. Leslie Mitchell, *Bulwer Lytton: The Rise and Fall of a Victorian Man of Letters* (2003), 94.

117. Butler, *Byron and Goethe*, 103.

118. Matthew Arnold, 'Stanzas from the Grande Chartreuse' (1850), stanza 23.

119. Buzard, *The Beaten Track*, 114.

120. William St Clair, 'The Impact of Byron's Writing: An Evaluative Approach', in Rutherford (ed.), *Byron: Augustan and Romantic*. Suggestively, Charlotte Brontë, Elizabeth Barrett Browning and George Eliot all found Byron's poetry hard to stomach.

121. Timothy Hilton, *Keats and his World* (1971), 32.

122. Boyd, *Byron's Don Juan*, 98.

123. MacCarthy, *Byron*, 366.

124. Kelvin Everest, 'John Keats', *Oxford DNB*.

125. Scathing attacks on Keats's poetry had been made in Tory literary journals, such as the Edinburgh *Blackwood's Magazine*, tarring him with the brush of the denigrated 'cockney school' of art and literature.

126. This was Keats's 'Ode to a Nightingale' (1819).

127. Nicholas Roe, *John Keats: A New Life* (2012), 387-8.

128. Sue Brown, *Joseph Severn, A Life: The Rewards of Friendship* (2009), 64.

129. Hilton, *Keats*, 94-7.

130. Roe, *Keats*, 392.

131. Brown, *Joseph Severn*, 95.

132. Ibid., 206.

133. Everest, 'John Keats'. Also see George F. Ford, *Keats and the Victorians: A Study of His Influence and Rise to Fame, 1821-1895* (1945).

134. Crane, *Lord Byron's Jackal*, 47. In Pisa Shelley had written a poem after Keats's death, 'Adonais', in which past sarcasm in private about the poet now slid into commemoration of a pale but beautiful flower.
135. The house in Missolonghi where Byron died was pulled down in the nineteenth century. There is today a Byron research centre in the town.
136. Richard Mullen and James Munson, *'The Smell of the Continent': The British Discover Europe, 1814–1914* (2009), 1.
137. Constantine Normanby, *The English in Italy* (1825), 118.
138. Jonathan Keates, *Stendhal* (1994), 184, 209–10.
139. Cecilia Powell, *Turner in the South: Rome, Naples, Florence* (1987), 71.
140. The Nazarenes constituted a movement in German art which rejected neoclassicism and sought to return to the artistic ideals of the Middle Ages and early Renaissance. Concentrated in Rome, its members led a semi-monastic life there dedicated to religious themes. In Britain the later Pre-Raphaelite Brotherhood was influenced by the Nazarenes – as usual, cycles in British art proceeded a few steps in arrears.
141. Suzanne Avery-Quash and Julie Sheldon, *Art for the Nation: The Eastlakes and the Victorian Art World* (2011), 33.
142. Buzard, *The Beaten Track*, 19.
143. H. Cox, *A Picture of Italy* (1815).
144. Kathleen Wells, 'The Return of British Artists to Rome after 1815', PhD thesis, University of Leicester (1974), 75–6.
145. James Boswell once said Goldsmith *disputed* his way across Europe, but as a biographer says, this is inadequate to describe quite how Goldsmith relied on hospitality from friars and convents, sleeping in barns, and playing his flute to earn much-needed cash. Byron was one of Goldsmith's greatest admirers. See Stephen Gwynn, *Oliver Goldsmith* (1935), 78–81.
146. Avery-Quash and Sheldon, *Art for the Nation*, 17.
147. See Aubrey S. Garsington, *Society, Culture and Opera in Florence, 1814–1830* (2005).
148. David Robertson, 'Sir Charles Lock Eastlake', *Oxford DNB*.
149. Harris, *Weatherland*, 230–1. Wordsworth's *Guide to the Lakes* had first been published in 1810 as an accompaniment to a book of engravings, but in 1822 it appeared as a separate volume subsequently celebrated as a hymn to English Romanticism.
150. See Jonah Siegel, *Desire and Excess: The Nineteenth-Century Culture of Art* (2000), and Pemble, *The Rome We Have Lost*, 26. Lord Castlereagh's post-war diplomacy had included an emphasis on the restoration of looted art treasures to former owners. In practice, however, about half the booty remained in France.
151. Brown, *Joseph Severn*, 166.
152. Avery-Quash and Sheldon, *Art for the Nation*, 18
153. C. P. Brand, *Italy and the English Romantics: The Italianate Fashion in Early Nineteenth-Century England* (1957), 152.
154. Raymond Lister, 'Samuel Palmer', *Oxford DNB*.
155. Geoffrey Grigson, *Samuel Palmer: The Visionary Years* (1947); Michael Prodger, 'Sage of Shoreham', *Literary Review* (August 2015).
156. Steegman, *The Rule of Taste*, 179–82.
157. Anthony Bailey, *Standing in the Sun: A Life of J. M. W. Turner* (1997), 247.
158. Ibid., 242.
159. Powell, *Turner in the South*, 38.
160. Ibid., 188.
161. Ibid., 17.
162. Pemble, *Venice Rediscovered*, 117.
163. Bailey, *Standing in the Sun*, 204.
164. Harris, *Weatherland*, 272.
165. Timothy Webb, 'The Journal of Samuel Rogers: An Alternative Vision of Italy', *Journal of Anglo-Italian Studies*, Vols XIII–XIV (2014), 36–9.

166. Quennell, *Byron in Italy*, 131. Rogers had a pernickety aspect that some people thought provided a model for Grandfather Smallweed in Charles Dickens's *Bleak House* (1852). But Rogers's London breakfasts were almost a cultural institution and many artists and writers in difficulty received his charity. See Richard Garnett, 'Samuel Rogers', *Oxford DNB*.

167. Clara Thomas, *Love and Work Enough: The Life of Anna Jameson* (1967), 34. See p. 150.

168. Ibid., 48.

169. Pemble, *Venice Rediscovered*, 4; Dennis Farr, *William Etty* (1958), 31.

170. Brand, *Italy and the English Romantics*, 150.

171. Ibid., 155–65; M. H. Port, 'Sir Charles Barry', *Oxford DNB*.

172. Frank Turner, *The Greek Heritage in Victorian Britain* (1981), 78.

173. See p. 86.

174. G. P. Henderson, *The Ionian Academy* (1988), ix.

175. Z. D. Ferriman, *Lord Guilford* (1919), 94–5. North had a long-standing taste for donning 'native' dress abroad. As early as 1788, when he was in Madrid, the British ambassador had come across him dressed up as a Spanish mule driver. See Curthoys, 'Frederick North'.

176. Alexander Grammatikos, 'Childe Harold's Pilgrimage: British Travellers to Greece and the Idea of Europe', in Roderick Beaton and Christine Kenyon-Jones (eds), *Byron: The Poetry of Politics and the Politics of Poetry* (2016), 226.

177. Holland, *Blue-Water Empire*, 49.

178. Agustin Coletes-Blanco, 'Byron and the Spanish Patriots: The Poetry and Politics of the Peninsular War', in Beaton and Kenyon-Jones (eds), *Byron*, 226–7.

179. Robert Boyd, 'The Execution of General Torrijos and Robert Boyd, 1831', *English Historical Review*, Vol. XX (October 1905), 763–7.

180. Michael S. Stevens, 'Spanish Orientalism: Washington Irving and the Romance of the Moor', PhD thesis, Georgia State University (2007), 4.

181. Michael Barry, 'The Alhambra's Irish Connection', *Irish Times*, 8 May 2017.

182. Today this portrait hangs in O'Connell's old family home of Derrynane House in County Kerry.

183. Glendinning et al. (eds), *Spanish Art in Britain and Ireland*, 166.

184. Brian Fothergill, *Nicholas Wiseman* (1963), 41

185. Robert Blake, *Disraeli's Grand Tour: Benjamin Disraeli and the Holy Land, 1830–31* (1981), 14.

186. Ibid.

187. Ibid., 30.

188. MacCarthy, *Byron*, 559. Disraeli's *Contarini Fleming* (1832) is an example.

189. Buzard, *The Beaten Track*, 123.

190. MacCarthy, *Byron*, 560.

191. Blake, *Disraeli's Grand Tour*, 105.

4 Blue Solitudes

1. Steegman, *The Rule of Taste*, 10.

2. Ibid., 228.

3. Hiram Powers was born in Vermont in 1805 but from 1837 lived permanently in Florence apart from trips to Britain. *The Greek Slave* toured America in 1847 and was seen by over 100,000 people, and was already famous when it became a centrepiece of the Great Exhibition at Crystal Palace. The image was widely used afterwards by the abolitionist cause in the United States.

4. John Stuart Mill, *An Autobiography* (1989; first published 1873), 182–3.

5. Andrew Thompson, *George Eliot and Italy: Literary, Cultural and Political Influences from Dante to the Risorgimento* (1998), 43. George Eliot's real name was Mary Ann Evans.

6. Paul Young, *Globalization and the Great Exhibition: The Victorian New World Order* (2009), 151.

7. Antonia Fraser, *Perilous Question: The Drama of the Great Reform Bill, 1832* (2013), 159.
8. Ibid., 76.
9. Rosemary Ashton, *Victorian Bloomsbury* (2012), 137.
10. Holger Hoock, 'Reforming Culture: National Art Institutions in the Age of Reform', in Arthur Burns and Joanna Innes (eds), *Rethinking the Age of Reform, 1780–1850* (2003), 260.
11. Quoted Fraser, *Perilous Question*, 271.
12. Hoock, 'Reforming Culture', 264.
13. Gordon Ray, *Thackeray: The Uses of Adversity, 1811–1846* (1955), 11.
14. Goodrich, *Debating England's Aristocracy in the 1790s*, 177–8.
15. Allan Conrad Christiansen (ed.), *The Subverting Vision of Bulwer Lytton: Bicentenary Reflections* (2004), 116.
16. Mitchell, *Bulwer Lytton*, 45.
17. Ibid., 62.
18. Marc Mulvey-Roberts, 'Writing for Revenge: The Battle of the Books between Edward and Rosina Bulwer Lytton', in Christiansen (ed.), *The Subverting Vision of Bulwer Lytton*, 170.
19. Richard Jenkyns, *The Victorians and Ancient Greece* (1980), 344–5.
20. G. K. Chesterton, *The Victorian Age in Literature* (1926), 136.
21. Mitchell, *Bulwer Lytton*, 197.
22. See Kate Flint, *The Victorians and the Visual Imagination* (2000).
23. Mitchell, *Bulwer Lytton*, 90.
24. Ibid., 99.
25. Ian Ker, *John Henry Newman: A Biography* (1988), 42–3.
26. Ibid., 58.
27. Geoffrey Faber, *Oxford Apostles: A Character Study of the Oxford Movement* (1936), 267–7, 286–7, 333.
28. Ker, *John Henry Newman*, 61. Suggestively, 'animal' as a qualifying adjective in reference to Naples became quite frequently used at this time. When Richard Cobden visited in 1848 he reckoned that the concerns of Neapolitans rarely went beyond 'animal enjoyments': Anthony Howe, *The Letters of Richard Cobden, Vol. II: 1848–1855* (2010), 311–12.
29. Ker, *John Henry Newman*, 61.
30. Buzard, *The Beaten Track*, 102.
31. Frank Turner, *John Henry Newman: The Challenge to Evangelical Religion* (2002), 146.
32. Fothergill, *Nicholas Wiseman*, 26.
33. Ker, *John Henry Newman*, 71.
34. Ibid., 78
35. Faber, *Oxford Apostles*, 320–2.
36. Tim Hilton, *John Ruskin: The Early Years* (1985), 160.
37. John Unrau, *Ruskin and St Mark's* (1984), 193.
38. Pemble, *The Mediterranean Passion*, 10.
39. Glendinning et al. (eds), *Spanish Art in Britain and Ireland*, 210.
40. Kamen, *The Disinherited*, 203.
41. Maurizio Isabella, *Risorgimento in Exile: Italian Émigrés and the Liberal International in the Post-Napoleonic Era* (2009), 114–15. The milieu is conjured up in Giuseppe Pecchio's *Semi-Serious Observations of an Italian Exile, during his Residence in England* (1833).
42. See Margaret Wicks, *The Italian Exiles in London, 1816–1848* (1937).
43. Denis Mack Smith, 'Britain and the Italian Risorgimento', in Martin McLaughlin (ed.), *Britain and Italy from Romanticism to Modernism* (2000), 20–1.
44. Brand, *Italy and the English Romantics*, 39–40.
45. Ibid., 34, 66.
46. In 1871 Foscolo's remains were taken by the Italian government back to Florence and buried with much pomp in the church of Santa Croce alongside Machiavelli, Michelangelo and Galileo.
47. Brand, *Italy and the English Romantics*, 32.

48. Constance Brooks, *Antonio Panizzi: Scholar and Patriot* (1931), 49–50.
49. Ashton, *Victorian Bloomsbury*, 144.
50. Brooks, *Antonio Panizzi*, 161.
51. John Morley, *Life of Gladstone, Vol. I* (1903), 308.
52. Joseph Leach, *Bright Particular Star: The Life and Times of Charlotte Cushman* (1970), 191. Cushman, the great American actress, had been at the same occasion. She was devoted to Jane Carlyle, and kept a portrait of her in her bedroom when living for some years in Rome.
53. Matteson, *The Lives of Margaret Fuller*, 321.
54. See p. 19.
55. See John Zucchi, *The Little Slaves of the Harp: Italian Child Street Musicians in Nineteenth-Century Paris, London and New York* (1992).
56. Tudor Allen, *Little Italy: The Story of London's Italian Quarter* (2008). This is an excellent study by the Camden Local Studies and Archives Centre.
57. Toni Cerutti, *Antonio Gallenga: An Italian Writer in Victorian England* (1974), 39.
58. However, there had been a well-established tradition of the malevolent Italian, often an assassin, in Elizabethan and Jacobean drama.
59. Brown, *Joseph Severn*, 194.
60. Brand, *Italy and the English Romantics*, 177–82.
61. See p. 30.
62. David Kimball, 'The Performance of Italian Opera in Early Victorian England', in McLaughlin (ed.), *Britain and Italy from Romanticism to Modernism*, 50–4.
63. Brand, *Italy and the English Romantics*, 231.
64. G. K. Chesterton, *Robert Browning* (2001; first published 1903), 47–8.
65. Sue Brown, 'The Burning Bush: Browning's First Visit to Asolo, June 1838', *Journal of Anglo-Italian Studies*, Vol. X (2013), 89–95.
66. Donald Thomas, *Robert Browning: A Life Within a Life* (1982), 161.
67. Clyde de Ryals, 'Robert Browning', *Oxford DNB*.
68. See Sutherland Orr, *Life and Letters of Robert Browning* (1891).
69. Brown, 'The Burning Bush', 89–90.
70. Ernest Fontana, 'Sexual Tourism and Browning's "The Englishman in Italy"', *Victorian Poetry*, Vol. XXXVI, 3 (1998).
71. Thomas, *Robert Browning*, 110.
72. Marjorie Stone, 'Elizabeth Barrett Browning', *Oxford DNB*.
73. Leach, *Bright Particular Star*, 250.
74. Stone, 'Elizabeth Barrett Browning'.
75. Alison Chapman, *Networking the Nation: British and American Women's Poetry and Italy, 1840–1870* (2015), xxviii.
76. Margaret Forster, *Elizabeth Barrett Browning* (1988), 214.
77. Ibid., 235.
78. Chapman, *Networking the Nation*, 64.
79. Matteson, *The Lives of Margaret Fuller*, 408.
80. Marianne Camus, 'Elizabeth Barrett Browning in Italy', in Alessandro Vecovi et al. (eds), *The Victorians in Italy: Literature, Travel, Politics and Art* (2009), 233.
81. Ibid., 227.
82. Forster, *Elizabeth Barrett Browning*, 216.
83. When Nathaniel Hawthorne visited the Brownings at Casa Guidi he felt worried about young Pen, who appeared 'not in ill-health but as if he had little or nothing to do with human flesh and blood . . . I should not want to be the father of such a boy . . . [and] wonder what is to become of him' (Stewart, *Nathaniel Hawthorne*, 200). Something of Hawthorne's foreboding was borne out by Pen Browning's later life.
84. The villa, in the Piazza dell'Indipendenza, stayed in the Trollope family until 1872.
85. Pamela Neville-Sington, 'Mrs. Frances [Fanny] Trollope', *Oxford DNB*.
86. Wilfrid Blunt, *England's Michelangelo: A Biography of G. F. Watts* (1975), 33–47.

87. Thomas Trollope was one of the first English writers to use 'Renaissance' as a historical term in this context (see Pamela Neville-Sington, 'Thomas Trollope', *Oxford DNB*). The most influential 'discoverer' of the Renaissance as a pillar in European historiography, however, was the Swiss Jacob Burckhardt, whose *The Civilization of the Renaissance in Italy* was first published in 1860.

88. Hilary Fraser, *The Victorians and Renaissance Italy* (1992), 1, 38–9.

89. Chapman, *Networking the Nation*, 285.

90. James L. Clifford, *Hester Lynch Piozzi* (1952), 248.

91. Mitchell, *Bulwer Lytton*, 40.

92. 'If Mr. Casaubon read German,' George Eliot's Will Ladislaw remarks when he first meets Dorothea in Rome, 'he would save himself a great deal of trouble.'

93. Uglow, *Mr Lear*, 110.

94. Baker, *The Fortunate Pilgrims*, 8.

95. Giuliana Artom Treves, *The Golden Ring: The Anglo-Florentines, 1847–1862* (1956), 172.

96. Quoted in Stewart, *Nathaniel Hawthorne*, 197. Hawthorne worked such themes – above all, the nature of sinfulness under Italian moral conditions as he saw it – in his romantic fable of Rome, *The Marble Faun* (1860).

97. Wayne Franklin, 'James Fenimore Cooper and American Artists in Europe', in Andrew Hemingway (ed.), *Transatlantic Romanticism: British and American Art and Literature, 1790–1860* (2015), 151–2.

98. Baker, *The Fortunate Pilgrims*, 57.

99. Thomas, *Robert Browning*, 237.

100. Treves, *The Golden Ring*, 28–32.

101. Chapman, *Networking the Nation*, 20.

102. Treves, *The Golden Ring*, 42–6; Adam Roberts, *Landor's Cleanness: A Study of Walter Savage Landor* (2014), 41.

103. Neville-Sington, 'Thomas Trollope'.

104. Lady Morgan, *Italy, Vol. II* (1821), 374. Lady Morgan's biography echoes various aspects in this book. Dublin-born, many of her novels railed against English prejudices against all things Irish. Sir William Gell encouraged her to write about Greece, despite never having been there, and her *Woman: Or, Ida of Athens* (1809) was 'an attempt to delineate perfected feminine character in its natural state and Greece as the perfect setting for doing so' (Dennis Dean, 'Sydney Morgan', *Oxford DNB*). Morgan travelled widely in Europe after 1815, but settled in London between 1837 and her death in 1859. The neoclassicist sculptor Richard Westmacott designed her tomb in Brompton Cemetery.

105. Waterloo Bridge was widely considered a symbolic site for the suicides of poor Londoners, especially women, and used as such by various artists in the Victorian era.

106. Nicholas Tromans, *The Art of G. F. Watts* (2017), 17–19.

107. See pp. 166–7.

108. Fothergill, *Nicholas Wiseman*, 167.

109. See D. G. Pas, *Popular Anti-Catholicism in Mid-Victorian England* (1992).

110. John Steegman, *Victorian Taste: A Study of the Arts and Architecture from 1830 to 1870* (1970), 227–8.

111. Ibid.

112. Virginia Hoselitz, *Imagining Roman Britain: Victorian Responses to the Roman Past* (2007), 34–44. One measure was the growth of interest in King Alfred as a founder of the English nation. See Joanne Parker, *'England's Darling': The Victorian Cult of Alfred the Great* (2007).

113. Richard Jenkyns, 'Distilled', *Times Literary Supplement*, 11 December 2015.

114. Kenneth Clark, *The Gothic Revival: An Essay in the History of Taste* (1928), 148. See James Stourton, *Kenneth Clark: Life, Art and Civilisation* (2016), 62–6.

115. Avery-Quash and Sheldon, *Art for the Nation*, 41.

116. Such an attempt was made in the 1920s when southern European Baroque enjoyed a revival in Britain. See p. 234.

117. Andrew Wawn, *The Vikings and the Victorians: Inventing the Old North in Nineteenth-Century Britain* (2000), 5.
118. Ibid., 31.
119. For the theme see William Vaughan, *German Romanticism and English Art* (1979), and Mathew C. Potter, *The Inspirational Genius of Germany: British Art and Germanism, 1850–1939* (2012)
120. Ray, *Thackeray*, 146.
121. Fred Kaplan, 'Thomas Carlyle', *Oxford DNB*.
122. John Monro, *Thomas Carlyle* (2000), 36, 45.
123. Ian Campbell, 'Carlyle on Italy', in Martin McLaughlin (ed.), *Britain and Italy from Romanticism to Modernism*, 110.
124. Mitchell, *Bulwer Lytton*, 10.
125. Thomas, *Love and Work Enough*, 76.
126. Hilton, *John Ruskin: The Early Years*, x.
127. MacCarthy, *The Last Pre-Raphaelite*, 105.
128. See Darren Bevin, *Cultural Climbs: John Ruskin, Albert Smith and the Alpine Aesthetic* (2010).
129. Robert Hewison, 'John Ruskin', *Oxford DNB*.
130. Hilton, *John Ruskin: The Early Years*, 85, 238.
131. Ibid.
132. Ibid., 143–5.
133. Clark, *The Gothic Revival*, 190, 267.
134. John Ruskin, *The Stones of Venice, Vol. I* (1898), vi.
135. Clark, *The Gothic Revival*, 278.
136. Hilton, *John Ruskin: The Early Years*, 149.
137. Bevin, *Cultural Climbs*, 76, 126–36.
138. Ibid., 138.
139. Prettejohn, *Beauty and Art*, 115–16.
140. Hilton, *John Ruskin: The Early Years*, 118; Hewison, 'John Ruskin'.
141. Hilton, *John Ruskin: The Early Years*, 259.
142. Hilary Fraser, 'Ruskin, Italy and the Past', in McLaughlin (ed.), *Britain and Italy from Romanticism to Modernism*, 89–90.
143. Hilton, *John Ruskin: The Early Years*, 93.
144. Oswald Doughty, *A Victorian Romantic: Dante Gabriel Rossetti* (1949), 51.
145. Powell, *Turner in the South*, 187.
146. John Rignall, *George Eliot and Europe* (1997), 188.
147. Ray, *Thackeray*, 352.
148. Ibid.
149. Edith Hall, 'Making It New: Dickens versus the Classics', in Edith Hall and Henry Stead (eds), *Greek and Roman Classics in the British Struggle for Social Reform* (2015), 110–12.
150. Ibid.
151. Roberts, *Landor*, 42.
152. Dorothy Mermin, *Godiva's Ride: Women of Letters in England, 1830–1860* (1993), 51.
153. Ibid.
154. See Isobel Hurst, *Victorian Women Writers and the Classics: The Feminine of Homer* (2006).
155. See 'Why the Greeks and Not the Romans in Victorian Britain?', in G. W. Clarke (ed.), *Rediscovering Hellenism: The Hellenic Inheritance and the English Imagination* (1989), 61–83. For the view that in fact Roman history always remained more resonant see Norman Vance, *The Victorians and Ancient Rome* (1997). The truth is probably that the two pasts cannot be effectively separated in British cultural contexts, any more than they can be in terms of pure aesthetics.
156. Turner, *The Greek Heritage in Victorian Britain*, 8.
157. Ibid., 213.
158. The main target here was William Mitford's *History of Greece* published between 1784 and 1810.

159. Joseph Hamburger, 'George Grote', *Oxford DNB*.
160. Ibid.
161. Jenkyns, *The Victorians and Ancient Greece*, 199.
162. Turner, *The Greek Heritage in Victorian Britain*, 149.
163. Jenkyns, *The Victorians and Ancient Greece*, 203.
164. Holland, *Blue-Water Empire*, 52.
165. H. C. G. Matthew (ed.), *The Gladstone Diaries, Vol. V: 1855–60* (1978), 359.
166. Ibid., 346.
167. Robert Holland and Diana Markides, *The British and the Hellenes: Struggles for Mastery in the Eastern Mediterranean, 1850–1960* (2006), 42.
168. Viscount Kirkwall, *Four Years in the Ionian Islands* (1864), 245.
169. Lawrence Durrell, *Prospero's Cell: A Guide to the Landscape and Manners of Corfu* (1945), 91.
170. Edward Noakes, *Edward Lear: The Life of a Wanderer* (1968), 119.
171. Peter Levi, *Edward Lear: A Biography* (1995), 145–6.
172. Peter Sherrard, *Edward Lear: The Corfu Years* (1988).
173. The architect Sir George Whitmore played the key role in redesigning – again in modern classical mode – the heart of Corfu Town. He also designed Villa Bighi, one of the most outstanding buildings in Valletta. See Athanasios Gekas, *Xenocracy: State, Class and Colonialism in the Ionian Islands, 1815–1864* (2016).
174. J. M. Hussey, 'George Finlay', *Oxford DNB*.
175. Anthony Howe, *The Letters of Richard Cobden, Vol. I: 1815–1847* (2007), 98–9.
176. See James Auchmuty, *Sir Thomas Wyse, 1791–1862: The Life and Career of an Educator and Diplomat* (1939). In his political and parliamentary career Wyse was a notable figure in Irish education.
177. Holland, *Blue-Water Empire*, 78. 'Civis Romanus sum' means 'I am a Roman subject'.
178. B. Kingsley Martin, *The Triumph of Lord Palmerston* (1924), 51–68.
179. The episode of *The West Wing* was 'A Proportional Force', series 1, no. 3. The original bent of the criticisms of Lord Palmerston's conduct towards Greece had precisely been that it was *disproportionate* to the circumstances.
180. For a near-contemporary description see Major Francis Duncan, *The English in Spain* (1877); for the art see Glendinning et al. (eds), *Spanish Art in Britain and Ireland*, 20.
181. Villiers, later the Earl of Clarendon, was unusual in that the Madrid posting proved a route towards high office in Britain, including foreign secretary. He spoke Spanish and while in Spain mixed successfully in high society. When his close friend the Countess of Montijo was asked if her daughter Eugénie, later Empress of the French, had been fathered by Villiers, she merely replied, 'Les dates ne correspondent pas.' See David Steele, 'George William Villiers', *Oxford DNB*.
182. Holland, *Blue-Water Empire*, 60.
183. Howe, *The Letters of Richard Cobden*, I, 60.
184. See David Williams, *A World of His Own: The Double Life of George Borrow* (1982).
185. Ibid., 103.
186. Ibid., 108.
187. John Palache, *Gautier and the Romantics* (1927), 75. A series of 'filters' separating Spain from the Europe to the north was to persist in all sorts of ways. Claude Debussy in his musical composition 'La Soirée dans Grenade' (1903) evoked, through its Arabic scale and guitar strummings, a languid atmosphere of Andalusia without his ever having been near the place. This did not stop the noted Spanish composer Manuel de Falla saying that Debussy's work 'in its most minute details conveys Spain admirably'. But then Debussy would have heard many Spanish gypsy players in Paris (see Jonathan Bellman (ed.), *The Exotic in Western Music* (1995), 172).
188. Ian Robertson, *Richard Ford, 1796–1858: Hispanophile, Connoisseur and Critic* (2004), 158. Gerald Brennan, the twentieth-century writer on Spain, considered Ford's *Handbook* 'the pre-eminent account of a foreign country in the English language'.

189. Howarth, *The Invention of Spain*, 204.
190. Hilary Macartney, 'Sir William Maxwell Stirling', *Oxford DNB*.
191. William Stirling, *Annals of the Art of Spain* (1848), 49.
192. Powell, *Turner in the South*, 65.
193. Avery-Quash and Sheldon, *Art for the Nation*, 55; Elizabeth A. Pergam, *The Manchester Art Treasures Exhibition* (2011), 95.
194. Hilary Macartney, 'The British "Discovery" of Spanish Golden Age Art', in Howarth et al (eds), *The Discovery of Spain*, 82.
195. Ibid., 84.
196. I am grateful to one of the anonymous readers of the original manuscript of this book for pointing this out.
197. Giardini di Luce (ed.), *Sorolla: Gardens of Light* (2013), 3.
198. Lee Fontanella, 'Charles Clifford', *Oxford DNB*.
199. Rachel Bullough Ainscough, '"A Photographic Scramble through Spain": An Image of Spain in Charles Clifford's Book', *Index.Comunicación*, Vol. III (2013), 187–228.
200. Claudia Heide, 'The Spanish Picturesque', in Howarth et al. (eds), *The Discovery of Spain*, 50.
201. Holland, *Blue-Water Empire*, 87.
202. David Cannadine, *G. M. Trevelyan: A Life in History* (1992), 31–2.
203. H. C. G. Matthew, 'William Ewart Gladstone', *Oxford DNB*.
204. Denis Mack Smith, 'Britain and the Italian Risorgimento', in McLaughlin (ed.), *Britain and Italy from Romanticism to Modernism*, 20.
205. O. J. Wright, 'The Risorgimento and "Persecutions" in the Grand Duchy of Tuscany and British Sympathy for Italian Nationalism', *History*, Vol. CII, 35 (July 2017).
206. Patrick Waddington, 'Jessie White Mario', *Oxford DNB*.
207. Treves, *The Golden Ring*, 207.
208. Thomas, *Robert Browning*, 191.
209. Avery-Quash and Sheldon, *Art for the Nation*, 117–20.
210. Rosemary Ashton, *George Eliot: A Life* (1996), 57.
211. Tom Winnifrith, 'Renaissance and Risorgimento in *Romola*', in Rignall (ed.), *George Eliot and Europe*.
212. Margaret Harris and Judith Johnston (eds), *The Journals of George Eliot* (1998), 336.
213. Thompson, *George Eliot and Italy*, 39, 46.
214. Gordon S. Haight, *George Eliot: A Biography* (1968), 326–7; Lawrence Hutton, *Literary Landmarks of Florence* (1895), 75.
215. Felicia Bonaparte, *The Triptych and the Cross: The Central Myths of George Eliot's Poetic Imagination* (1979), 76.
216. Thomas, *Robert Browning*, 208.
217. Ibid., 210.

5 An Enchanted Garden

1. Andrew Graham Dixon, *The Art of France: There Will Be Blood*, BBC4 television documentary, 12 February 2017. Ingres's idea of portraying a large number of languid female nudes in a harem was drawn from the description of such a scene in Lady Mary Wortley Montagu's *Turkish Embassy Letters*.
2. Steegman, *Victorian Taste*, 294–5.
3. Edel, *Henry James*, 397.
4. Thomas, *Robert Browning*, 237.
5. See p. 202.
6. Treves, *The Golden Ring*, 184.
7. See Caroline Dakers, *The Holland Park Circle: Artists and Victorian Society* (1999).
8. Grosskurth, *John Addington Symonds*, 201.
9. See Francis Toye, *Truly Thankful* (1957), 126.
10. See E. A. Daniels, *Jessie White Mario: Risorgimento Revolutionary* (1971).

11. Danilo Raponi, *Religion and Politics in the Risorgimento: Britain and the New Italy, 1861–1877* (2014), 139.
12. The Prince Consort had died in December 1861.
13. In the wake of the visit a Mazzini-Garibaldi Club was set up in Clerkenwell. The organization, despite a hiatus in the Second World War, survived to celebrate the 150th anniversary of Garibaldi's coming to London at a theatre in Islington.
14. Gordon Waterfield, *Layard of Nineveh* (1963), 307.
15. Rikky Rooksby, 'Algernon Charles Swinburne', *Oxford DNB*.
16. Rikky Rooksby, *A. C. Swinburne: A Poet's Life* (1997), 186.
17. Philip Henderson, *Swinburne: The Portrait of a Poet* (1974), 134.
18. Rooksby, *A. C. Swinburne*, 164.
19. Mollie Panter-Downes, *At the Pines: Swinburne, Watts-Dunton and Putney* (1971), 76.
20. Ibid., 139, 189. Like Robert Browning, whatever liberal views Swinburne previously held on Italy, he saw no contradiction in being fiercely hostile to Home Rule for Ireland.
21. Avery-Quash and Sheldon, *Art for the Nation*, 156–8, 177–82.
22. Antonio Gallenga, *Italy Revisited, Vol. I* (1875), 12–13.
23. James Jackson Jarves, *Italian Rambles: Studies of Life and Manners in New and Old Italy* (1885), 108.
24. Apparently Gladstone's natural prolixity meant that it took two proposals – the second and successful one on returning to London – to make his intentions fully clear and to be accepted. A visit at night to the Coliseum, viewed by the light of tapers, was a conventional highlight of the Victorian tourist experience in Rome. Nathaniel Hawthorne describes the experience in *The Marble Faun*.
25. Matthew, *Gladstone 1809–1874*, 166; Waterfield, *Layard of Nineveh*, 306.
26. For the reportage of Britain's representative in Rome, Odo Russell, steeped in papal affairs, see N. Blakiston (ed.), *The Roman Question: Extracts from the Despatches of Odo Russell from Rome, 1858–1870* (1962).
27. For Gladstone the sanctity of Christian practice in the Mediterranean acted as a measure of the perceived banality of much English Anglicanism. He also went against the grain of much English opinion, for example in having a great respect for Greek Orthodoxy. Once when visiting a monastery in Corfu, and seeing a case of extreme self-denial amongst the clergy, he commented on the spiritual intensity this indicated. See Holland and Markides, *The British and the Hellenes*, 30.
28. When in December 1869, following the withdrawal of French military protection, Italian troops occupied papal territory, clerical students in the English College wanted to go and fight but were refused permission by the rector. A few went anyway and some were wounded in a scrappy and forlorn encounter. For an account by an English observer in Rome at the time see David Hunter Blair, *In Victorian Days* (1939), 180–5.
29. Pemble, *The Rome We Have Lost*, 113.
30. Augustus Hare, *Walks in Rome* (1905).
31. In 1936 this was made into a film starring Rodney Colman and Claudia Colbert.
32. Sir James Rennell Rodd, *Social and Diplomatic Memories, 1884–1893* (1922), 13.
33. Lyn Pyket, 'Opinionated Ouida', in Jane Jordan and Andrew King (eds), *Ouida and Victorian Popular Culture* (2013), 148, 169–70.
34. Helen Killoran, 'Marie Louise de la Ramée', *Oxford DNB*.
35. A. H. Sayce, *Reminiscences* (1923), 150.
36. Raponi, *Religion and Politics in the Risorgimento*, 4.
37. Hilary Fraser, 'Ruskin, Italy and the Past', in McLaughlin (ed.), *Britain and Italy from Romanticism to Modernism*, 99–101.
38. Tim Hilton, *John Ruskin: The Later Years* (2000), 161.
39. Ibid., 340.
40. Robert Gale, 'Henry James and Italy', *Nineteenth-Century Fiction*, Vol. XIV (September 1959), 163.
41. Pemble, *Venice Rediscovered*, 142.

42. Unrau, *Ruskin and St Mark's*, 192.

43. Jarves, *Italian Rambles*, 217.

44. Pemble, *Venice Rediscovered*, 35–6.

45. Unrau, *Ruskin and St Mark's*, 198; Carl Maves, *Sensuous Pessimism: Italy in the Works of Henry James* (1973), 57.

46. For a snapshot of Anglo-Italian relations at this time see C. J. Lowe, *Salisbury and the Mediterranean, 1886–1896* (1972).

47. Sir James Rennell Rodd, *Social and Diplomatic Memories, 1902–1919* (1922), 3.

48. MacCarthy, *The Last Pre-Raphaelite*, 109.

49. See Elizabeth Prettejohn, *Modern Painters, Old Masters: The Art of Imitation from Pre-Raphaelites to the First World War* (2018).

50. Burne-Jones's friendship with Ruskin was later bruised when the latter attacked Michelangelo in an Oxford lecture in 1871 for his 'dark carnality', a view Burne-Jones could not share. This was a cover for more personal tensions that never entirely dissipated.

51. MacCarthy, *The Last Pre-Raphaelite*, 147.

52. Ibid., 211. Also see Jan Marsh, *Pre-Raphaelite Sisterhood* (1985), 273.

53. Thomas, *Robert Browning*, 270. This passing comment was perhaps meant to encompass attempted suicides. In 1869 George Eliot was in Venice having recently married her second husband, John Cross, when the latter seemingly jumped from a hotel balcony (he survived and long outlived Eliot).

54. MacCarthy, *The Last Pre-Raphaelite*, 248.

55. Harris, *Weatherland*, 306.

56. MacCarthy, *The Last Pre-Raphaelite*, 397.

57. Robin Spencer, 'James Abbott McNeill Whistler', *Oxford DNB*.

58. McMullen, *Victorian Outsider*, 199–200.

59. Elinor Shaffer, 'Samuel Butler', *Oxford DNB*.

60. Peter Raby, *Samuel Butler: A Life* (1991), 200–3. For Butler's photography see Elinor Shaffer, *Erewhons of the Eye: Samuel Butler as Painter, Photographer, and Art Critic* (1988).

61. Raby, *Samuel Butler*, 179.

62. Simon Heffer, *High Minds: The Victorians and the Birth of Modern Britain* (2013), 414. The critique of British economic performance in Martin J. Wiener's *English Culture and the Decline of the Industrial Spirit, 1850–1980* (1981) reflects various strands, including the classicism of the British ruling class, shaping the ideology of Thatcherism after the mid-1970s.

63. Richard Jenkyns, 'Hellenism in Victorian Painting', in Clarke (ed.), *Rediscovering Hellenism*, 66.

64. Ibid., 107.

65. Keren Rosa Hammerschlag, 'Frederic Leighton's Paintings of the Female Nude', *Victorian Studies*, Vol. LVI, 3 (Spring 2014).

66. Farr, *William Etty*, 4.

67. Ibid., 31.

68. Susan Chitty, *Gwen John, 1876–1939* (1981), 36.

69. For a full discussion see Alison Smith, *The Victorian Nude: Sexuality, Morality and Art* (1996).

70. Keren Rosa Hammerschlag, *Frederic Leighton: Death, Mortality, Resurrection* (2015), 115.

71. Tim Barringer and Elizabeth Prettejohn (eds), *Frederic Leighton: Antiquity, Renaissance, Modernity* (1999), xx.

72. *Pall Mall Gazette*, 11 May 1867.

73. Jenkyns, *The Victorians and Ancient Greece*, 135. For a fuller discussion of these themes see Caroline Vout, *Sex on Show: Seeing the Erotic in Greece and Rome* (2013).

74. Simon Goldhill, *Victorian Culture and Classical Antiquity: Art, Opera, Fiction, and the Proclamation of Modernity* (2010), 36.

75. Ibid., 63.

76. Jenkyns, *The Victorians and Ancient Greece*, 136.

77. Christopher Newall, 'Frederic Leighton', *Oxford DNB*.
78. Potter, *The Inspirational Genius of Germany*, 6.
79. Newall, 'Frederic Leighton'.
80. J. Comyns Carr, *Coasting Bohemia* (1914), 114.
81. Jenkyns, 'Hellenism in Victorian Painting', 101.
82. The Fine Arts Institute in Glasgow, for example, remained firmly grounded in the Greek tradition.
83. Jenkyns, 'Hellenism in Victorian Painting', 89.
84. There was nothing particularly new or, indeed, British in this. From the sixteenth century onwards visions of ancient villa life had been evocations of cultivated contemporary existence simply read back in time. See Victor Tschudi, *Baroque Antiquity: Archaeological Imagination in Early Modern Europe* (2016).
85. For a full discussion see Elizabeth Prettejohn and Peter Trippi (eds), *Lawrence Alma-Tadema: At Home in Antiquity* (2016). This was published in association with an exhibition of his work held at Leighton House in London in 2017, the first full retrospective since 1913.
86. Cecil B. DeMille had first produced a silent film on this theme in 1923.
87. Rachel Campbell-Johnson, 'Not the Worst Painter of the Nineteenth Century After All', *The Times*, 24 June 2017.
88. Prettejohn, *Beauty and Art*, 134.
89. Jenkyns, 'Hellenism in Victorian Painting', 99.
90. There was nothing original about an interest in Eastern art as such, since in the eighteenth-century wallpapers with Chinese design had been very popular, though their luxurious quality limited social diffusion. See Emile de Bruijn, *Chinese Wallpapers in Britain and Ireland* (2017).
91. Jenkyns, *The Victorians and Ancient Greece*, 301.
92. David Brownlee, 'George Street', *Oxford DNB*. Another figure in this context was the 3rd Marquess of Bute, whose medieval mania had a strong Greek bent. He was rare in travelling widely in Greece. But when his family mansion, Mount Stuart, was rebuilt after a fire in 1877, it was still done with largely Florentine, not Greek, flourishes. See Gavin Stamp, *Robert Weir Schultz, Architect, and his Work for the Marquess of Bute* (1981).
93. Kate Nichols, *Greece and Rome at the Crystal Palace: Classical Sculpture and Modern Britain, 1854–1936* (2015), 103.
94. François Crouzet, *De la supériorité de l'Angleterre sur la France: L'économique et l'imaginaire XVI–XX siècles* (1985), 545–65.
95. Edel, *Henry James*, 207.
96. Richard Ellman, *Oscar Wilde* (1987), 256.
97. James personified Leighton in the character of Lord Mellifont in his short story 'The Private Life' (1892).
98. Ian Ross, *Oscar Wilde and Ancient Greece* (2013), 18.
99. Rictor Norton, 'John Addington Symonds', *Oxford DNB*.
100. Pemble (ed.), *John Addington Symonds*, 4–5.
101. See p. 12.
102. Herbert Schoeller and Robert Peters (eds), *The Letters of John Addington Symonds: Vol. III* (1969), 53.
103. Pemble (ed.), *John Addington Symonds*, 9.
104. See p. 15.
105. Pemble (ed.), *John Addington Symonds*, 12.
106. Debbie Challis, 'Fashioning Archaeology into Art', *Journal of Literature and Science*, 5 (2012), 62. The idea of Greek dress as inherently 'free' and liberating for the modern woman stretched into the twentieth century. The wife of the painter David Bomberg adopted Greek costume in this spirit for his *Greek Dance Movement* (1914), when Bomberg was in his most radical phase as an artist. For Bomberg see pp. 236–7, 249–50.
107. Ellman, *Oscar Wilde*, 109.

108. Challis, 'Fashioning Archaeology into Art', 59–60.
109. Hurst, *Victorian Women Writers and the Classics*, 171.
110. Nietzsche, however, found his own salvation from northern Wagnerian gloom in a different version of the South distilled during his first visit to Sorrento. 'When for the first time I saw the evening with its red and grey softened in the Naples sky, it was like a shiver,' he wrote, 'and the feeling of having been saved at the very last second.' See Paolo D'Iorio, *Nietzsche's Journey to Sorrento: Genesis of the Free Spirit* (2016). This was pure Byronism feeding into the later nineteenth century.
111. Suzanne L. Marchand, *Down from Olympus: Archaeology and Philhellenism in Germany, 1750–1970* (1996), 16.
112. Ellman, *Oscar Wilde*, 245.
113. See David Traill, *Schliemann of Troy: Treasure and Deceit* (1995).
114. Sayce, *Reminiscences*, 151.
115. See Helen Waterhouse, *The British School at Athens: The First Hundred Years* (1986), and Michael Llewellyn Smith et al. (eds), *Scholars, Travels, Archives: Greek History and Culture through the British School at Athens* (2009).
116. Macaulay, *The Pleasure of Ruins*, 147.
117. In 1854, with Turkey distracted by war with Russia, King Otto of Greece had overseen an attempt to seize a part of Thessaly, then still under Ottoman rule. To punish this ill-timed adventurism, Britain and France had sent troops to occupy Piraeus. They were not withdrawn until 1858.
118. Uglow, *Mr Lear*, 323–7.
119. Levi, *Edward Lear*, 213.
120. Holland and Markides, *The British and the Hellenes*, 77.
121. Charilaos Trikoupis, one of the two dominant politicians of Greece in the later nineteenth century, had been raised in London among the affluent Anglo-Greek merchant community. Members, especially the Ionides family, were significant patrons of the arts in London, including the Pre-Raphaelite set. The Greek Orthodox Cathedral on Moscow Road, another example of the neo-Byzantine revival, celebrated its first liturgy in 1879, and has since remained a focus for London Greek life.
122. Sayce, *Reminiscences*, 76.
123. Today it is the Hotel Grande Bretagne.
124. Romilly Jenkins, *The Dilessi Murders: Greek Brigands and English Hostages* (1998), 29. The first 'Cook's Tour' to Italy occurred in 1863, and by the end of the 1860s had taken in Rome and Pompeii. It was not until after the first modern Olympic Games in Athens during 1896, also attended by Thomas Cook himself, however, that Greece featured in the programme. By then the whole phenomenon of the 'organized tour' (what E. M. Forster in *A Room with a View* was to parody as 'the coupons of Cook') had become somewhat déclassé, though of course the phenomenon was to take many future forms.
125. Noakes, *Edward Lear*, 200.
126. Earl of Carlisle, *Cruising in Turkish and Greek Waters* (1854), 286.
127. Ross, *Oscar Wilde and Ancient Greece*, 44.
128. Grosskurth, *John Addington Symonds*, 159.
129. Maves, *Sensuous Pessimism*, x.
130. Rignall, *George Eliot and Europe*, 123.
131. Ibid., 131.
132. Ibid., 129.
133. Ashton, *George Eliot*, 63.
134. Edel, *Henry James*, 201.
135. Howarth, 'The Quest for Spain', 25. However, it was significant that Froude, a great linguist, in 1861 went to carry out research in the Spanish archives at Simancas, one of the first English scholars to do so. This was to treat Spanish history seriously as a phenomenon requiring close documentary attention rather than remaining based on purely inherited suppositions.

136. See p. 149.
137. Waterfield, *Layard of Nineveh*, 313.
138. Howarth, *The Invention of Spain*, 143–6; Jonathan Parry, 'Sir Henry Austen Layard', *Oxford DNB*.
139. Howarth, *The Invention of Spain*, 143–6.
140. Glendinning et al. (eds), *Spanish Art in Britain and Ireland*, 28.
141. McMullen, *Victorian Outsider*, 69.
142. Hilary Macartney, 'The British "Discovery" of Spanish Golden Age Art', 108.
143. Michael Jacobs, 'Colour and Light: From Sargent to Bomberg', in Howarth et al (eds), The Discovery of Spain, 119.
144. Elaine Kilmurray and Richard Ormond, 'John Singer Sargent', *Oxford DNB*.
145. Howarth, *The Invention of Spain*, 193.
146. Jacobs, 'Colour and Light: From Sargent to Bomberg',109–13.
147. Macartney, 'The British "Discovery" of Spanish Golden Age Art', 109.
148. James Beechey, 'James Fitzmaurice Kelly', *Oxford DNB*.
149. Harris, *Weatherland*, 302.
150. Levi, *Edward Lear*, 196.
151. Noakes, *Edward Lear*, 311.
152. Uglow, *Mr Lear*, 515.
153. Noakes, *Edward Lear*, 312.
154. Uglow, *Mr Lear*, 521.
155. Malcolm Bradbury and James McFarlane, *Modernism: A Guide to European Literature 1890–1930* (1976), 178.
156. Ryals, 'Robert Browning'. The cemetery of San Michele is where Horatio Brown, the late Victorian historian of the Venetian State Papers who described the world of Venetian gondoliers and fishermen in his popular *Life on the Lagoons* (1884), was buried in 1926. Ezra Pound was interred there in 1972.
157. MacCarthy, *The Last Pre-Raphaelite*, 350.

6 The Cult of Beauty

1. See chapter on 'The Name and Nature of Modernism' in Bradbury and McFarlane, *Modernism*, 182.
2. Charles Carrington, *Rudyard Kipling: His Life and Work* (1978), 123–4.
3. This sentiment was quintessentially late Victorian. John Addington Symonds similarly wrote, 'A great and puissant nation does not live by sensitivity and knowledge but by the formation of character.' It was clear to him what was England's strongest suit. See John Addington Symonds, *In the Key of Blue* (1893), 196.
4. Virginia Woolf, *Roger Fry: A Biography* (1940), 109.
5. For a much later rejoinder to Schmitz's allegation, proudly pointing to the fact that at that very moment British music was about to enjoy a renaissance, see Boris Johnson, 'A Land Without Music? Parry, Holst and Elgar to You, Schmitz', *Daily Telegraph*, 19 October 2006. What Boris Johnson fails to point out was that Hubert Parry was a great admirer of German *Kultur*, not least Wagner, and despaired when the two nations went to war against each other in August 1914.
6. Blunt, *England's Michelangelo*, 220.
7. Tromans, *The Art of G. F. Watts*, 115.
8. Arcara, 'Constructing the South', 200.
9. Ellman, *Oscar Wilde*, 288.
10. Holbrook Jackson, *The Eighteen-Nineties: A Review of Art and Ideas at the Close of the Nineteenth Century* (1913), 34.
11. Ellman, *Oscar Wilde*, 465.
12. For this phase of Wilde's life, including his Mediterranean passages, see Nicholas Frankel, *Oscar Wilde: The Unrepentant Years* (2017).

13. Ellman, *Oscar Wilde*, 284.
14. Raby, *Samuel Butler*, 243.
15. Shaffer, 'Samuel Butler'. Gladstone died in 1896.
16. Ibid.
17. Raby, *Samuel Butler*, 285.
18. Ibid., 297.
19. Adam Nicolson, *The Mighty Dead: Why Homer Still Matters* (2014), 47.
20. Alison Inglis, 'Sir Edward John Poynter', *Oxford DNB*.
21. Chitty, *Gwen John*, 46.
22. Charles Harrison, *English Art and Modernism, 1900–1939* (1981), 35.
23. Ibid., 17, 20.
24. Wendy Baron, *Sickert* (1973), 50–1; Michael Glover, 'Don't Look Back: Walter Sickert's Venice', *Independent*, March 2009.
25. Wendy Baron, 'Walter Richard Sickert', *Oxford DNB*; Lucy David, 'Sickert in Venice', *Daily Telegraph*, 27 February 2009.
26. Baron, *Sickert*, 80.
27. Baron, 'Walter Richard Sickert'.
28. See Michael Nelson, *Queen Victoria and the Discovery of the Riviera* (2001); 'The Queen on Tour', *Guardian*, 1 September 2001. A special British connection with Nice and Cannes went back further. The Whig-Radical politician Henry Brougham, who had defended Queen Caroline in court against the charges laid against her in 1820, and who was lord chancellor at the time of the 1832 Reform Act, lived in Cannes for long periods of his life, dying there in 1869. His statue is a striking feature in the Cimetière du Grand Jas. In Nice the Camin des Anglés was renamed during the 1860s the Promenades des Anglais, as it remains today.
29. Michael Holroyd, *Augustus John* (1999), 353. Also see Averil King, 'The Work of James Dickson Innes', *Country Life*, 4 February 2006, and Mathew Sturgis, 'James Dickson Innes', *Oxford DNB*.
30. Innes had become infatuated with Euphemia Lamb when he met her at a café on the Boulevard du Montparnasse in Paris, and they were in Collioure during the early stages of Innes's tuberculosis. But Euphemia had many relationships – she was later a regular among the louche penumbra of the Café Royal in London – and the one with Innes quite quickly foundered.
31. Severis, *Travelling Artists in Cyprus*, 89–90. Brabazon's works dated from the 1860s and 1870s, but only attracted attention much later. John Singer Sargent was an admirer, and acted as a pall bearer when Brabazon died in 1906.
32. Hermione Lee, *Edith Wharton* (2007), 97.
33. Ibid., 112.
34. J. Alexander MacGillivray, *Minotaur: Sir Arthur Evans and the Archaeology of the Minoan Myth* (2000), 6.
35. Woolf, *Roger Fry*, 68.
36. Frances Spalding, *Roger Fry: Art and Life* (1980), 74–6.
37. Philip Walsh, *Brill's Companion to the Reception of Aristophanes* (2016), 233.
38. Kilmurray and Ormond, 'John Singer Sargent'.
39. Richard Ormond, 'Around the Mediterranean', in Warren Adelson (ed.), *Sargent Abroad: Figures and Landscapes* (1997), 115.
40. George Sand recorded this time in *A Winter in Majorca* (1842), which first put the island on the map for travellers from northern Europe.
41. Ormond, 'Around the Mediterranean', 123.
42. Ibid., 214.
43. Holbrook Jackson, *The Eighteen Nineties*, 50–1.
44. Pierre Coustillas, 'George Gissing', *Oxford DNB*.
45. Robert Calder, *Willie: The Life of W. Somerset Maugham* (1989), 60.
46. W. Somerset Maugham, *The Summing Up* (1935), 168.
47. Calder, *Willie*, 94.

48. Maves, *Sensuous Pessimism*, 122.
49. Rodd, *Social and Diplomatic Memories, 1902–1919*, 7–8, and Pemble, *The Rome We Have Lost*, 4. Rodd, as an aspiring young artist, had once been part of that world himself.
50. Maves, *Sensuous Pessimism*, 120.
51. Lee, *Edith Wharton*, 217–19. James was fluent in French, but much less so in Italian.
52. This applies perhaps above all to *The Golden Bowl* (1904). It was one of the first books to be reviewed by Virginia Woolf, when she was twenty-three, and she found it hard going – 'the toughest job I have had', she wrote privately. Hermione Lee, *Virginia Woolf* (1996), 217.
53. Edel, *Henry James*, 633.
54. Pemble, *The Rome We Have Lost*, 5.
55. Pemble, *Venice Rediscovered*, 26.
56. P. N. Furbank, *E. M. Forster, A Life: Vol. I. The Growth of the Novelist (1879–1949)* (1977), 104.
57. Malcolm Bradbury, 'Introduction', in E. M. Forster, *A Room with a View* (2000; first published 1908), vii. In this summary Forster's early visits to Italy are discussed as being his own 'Grand Tour', but in truth by 1901 the whole concept of a 'Tour' in the eighteenth-century vein had long since disappeared.
58. Furbank, *E. M. Forster, A Life*, 89.
59. Bradbury, 'Introduction', xiii.
60. Ibid., xxiii.
61. Goldhill, *Victorian Culture and Classical Antiquity*, 23.
62. Turner, *The Greek Heritage in Victorian Britain*, 119–20.
63. Ibid., 81.
64. James George Frazer, *Aftermath: A Supplement to the Golden Bough* (1936), vi.
65. Robert Ackerman, 'Sir James Frazer', *Oxford DNB*.
66. See Christine Kenyon-Jones, *The People's University: 150 Years of the University of London and its External Students* (2008), 23–30.
67. Mary Beard, *The Invention of Jane Harrison* (2000), 73.
68. Ibid., 8.
69. Hugh Lloyd Jones, 'Jane Harrison', *Oxford DNB*.
70. Beard, *The Invention of Jane Harrison*, 7.
71. Turner, *The Greek Heritage in Victorian Britain*, 127–8.
72. Jenkyns, *The Victorians and Ancient Greece*, 344.
73. Ibid., 57–8.
74. Walter Sickert, 'The Study of Drawing', *New Age*, 16 June 1910.
75. Vineta Colby, *Vernon Lee: A Literary Biography* (2003), 251.
76. Ibid., 155.
77. Phyllis F. Mannocchi, 'Violet Paget', *Oxford DNB*.
78. Colby, *Vernon Lee*, 157.
79. Ibid.
80. Ibid., 256.
81. Mannocchi, 'Violet Paget'.
82. Kirsty Hooper, ' "Moorish Splendour" in the British Provinces, 1886–1906: The Spanish Bazaar, from Dundee to Southampton', paper for Contact and Connection Symposium, University of Warwick, June 2013.
83. In 1916 a committee at King's College, London was also at work raising the money for what was finally established in 1919 as the Koraes Chair of Modern Greek. These professorships in Spanish and Greek Studies were part of a drive in London in the early years of the war to tap a more professionalized and reliable knowledge of current conditions in southern Europe.
84. R. M. Stevenson was his cousin's companion on the canoe trip through various rivers in France recorded in R. L. Stevenson, *Inland Voyage* (1878).

85. Sidney Colvin (revised Kate Flint), 'Robert Mowbray Stevenson', *Oxford DNB*.

86. John Bowes, a coal industrialist, had bought a Paris theatre in 1847. Helped by connections with art dealers in the city, in 1862 he acquired the Madrid collection of the courtier Conte de Quinto, including El Greco's *The Tears of St Peter*. In 2017 the Wallace Collection in London hosted the exhibition *Spanish Masterpieces from The Bowes Museum*.

87. Matthew Sturgis, 'Spencer Gore', *Oxford DNB*. The increased flow of painters went in both directions. Joaquín Sorolla had an exhibition at London's Grafton Gallery in 1908 but found England gloomy and never returned.

88. Lady Lichnowsky, the wife of the German ambassador, had fallen in love with Picasso's images on first sight, and became an avid collector.

89. John Richardson, *A Life of Picasso, Vol. II, 1907–1917: The Painter of Modern Life* (2009), 310–11.

90. Queen Ena's position was seriously undermined when it emerged that she was a carrier of haemophilia, prevalent in Queen Victoria's line. In fact two of the four surviving Spanish princes from this marriage proved to be haemophiliacs. For a study see Gerard Noel, *Ena: Spain's English Queen* (1984).

91. Kamen, *The Disinherited*, 219.

92. Gabrielle Fahr-Becker, *Art Nouveau* (1997), 197–9.

93. Holland, *Blue-Water Empire*, 170–1.

94. The critique of a 'deep Spain' behind an alluring front never goes away. 'Atavistic forces are coming to the surface,' one British journalist wrote about the crisis sparked by Catalonian separatism in October 2017, 'exposing a deeper Spain that was always just beneath the surface, but disguised in good times by the EU veneer': 'Spain on the Brink of Full-blown Crisis', *Daily Telegraph*, 24 October 2017. Here was a belief that Spain was 'different' in a profounder and inherently darker way that went beyond the mere elusiveness of Italy or the natural chaos of Greece, an analysis that particularly resonated with a certain type of English Toryism.

95. Bradbury and MacFarlane, 'The Name and Nature of Modernism', 33.

96. Woolf, *Roger Fry*, 80.

97. Spalding, *Roger Fry*, 133.

98. Peter Nicholls, *Modernisms: A Literary Guide* (2008), 87–9.

99. David Boyd Haycock, *A Crisis of Brilliance: Five Young British Artists and the Great War* (2009), 139.

100. In 1916 the British School at Rome was to move to its present site on what is now the Via Antonio Gramsci, the building itself a classical design by Edwin Lutyens.

101. Keats and Shelley, however, still had their detractors. When Rennell Rodd, then the British ambassador, invited Britain's serving poet laureate Alfred Austin, who happened to be staying in Albano, to the opening ceremony at the Keats-Shelley Memorial House, he refused, saying too much attention was paid to those two poets. 'For my part,' Austin said rather stuffily, 'I must remain with Shakespeare and with Milton.' See Rodd, *Social and Diplomatic Memories, 1902–1919*, 145.

102. Cannadine, *G. M. Trevelyan*, 66.

103. Ibid.

104. Spalding, *Roger Fry*, 139.

105. Haycock, *A Crisis of Brilliance*, 139.

106. June Purvis, *Emmeline Pankhurst: A Biography* (2003), 255. Mary Richardson later joined the British Union of Fascists.

107. Richardson, *A Life of Picasso, Vol. II*, 256.

108. Ian Dejardin and Sarah Milroy (eds), *Vanessa Bell* (2017), 111.

109. Ezra Pound, 'The Caressability of the Greeks', *Egoist*, 16 March 1914.

110. For a brief summary of the Mediterranean in the run-up to war, and specifically its part in the nascent Franco-British alliance, see Holland, *Blue-Water Empire*, 140–8.

111. Ibid., 327. Apollinaire was later wounded serving in the French Army and never fully recovered. He was of Polish descent, but had been born in Rome.

112. Lee, *Edith Wharton*, 258. James died in February 1916. Wharton was by then living in France, and was very active in charities dealing with French casualties during the fighting, including visits to the front.
113. Spalding, *Roger Fry*, 196–7.
114. Mansfield and Murry subsequently lived for some time in Bandol. 'Life at the Villa Pauline was good,' Murry recalled, 'the best we were ever to know.' They returned to live in south Cornwall, but it was in Bandol during January 1918 that Mansfield had the first haemorrhage foreshadowing her early death. John Middleton Murry, *Between Two Worlds* (1935), 372–94.
115. Spalding, *Roger Fry*, 197–9.
116. Haycock, *A Crisis of Brilliance*, 277.
117. Anja Foerschner, '"In the Midst of this Strange Country": Paul Nash's War Landscapes', in Gordon Hughes and Philipp Blom, *Nothing But the Clouds Unchanged: Artists in World War I* (2014), 82.
118. Bradbury and MacFarlane, 'The Name and Nature of Modernism', 31.
119. See David Solkin, *Towards a Modern Art World* (1995).
120. Steegman, *The Rule of Taste*, 189.
121. Kenneth Clark, *Civilisation: A Personal View* (2018; first published 1969), xi.
122. Holroyd, *Augustus John*, 107, 240.

7 That Splendid Enclosure

1. Geoffrey Keynes (ed.), *The Letters of Rupert Brooke* (1968), 676.
2. Lee, *Virginia Woolf*, 295.
3. Pemble, *The Rome We Have Lost*, 101.
4. Ana Carden-Coyne, *Reconstructing the Body: Classicism, Modernism, and the First World War* (2009), 2.
5. Ibid., 128.
6. Simon Martin, *The Mythic Method: Classicism in British Art, 1920–1950* (2016), 12.
7. Ibid.
8. Virginia Woolf, 'On Not Knowing Greek', in *The Common Reader* (1929; first published 1925), 58–9.
9. Lee, *Virginia Woolf*, 227.
10. 'Racist Undertones of Britain's Jazz Age Exposed in Exhibition', *Guardian*, 24 January 2018. The exhibition was *Rhythm and Reaction: The Age of Jazz in Britain* held at London's Two Temple Place, January–April 2018. Souter destroyed the offending canvas in 1926, but towards the end of his life made a new copy displayed at the exhibition.
11. Martin, *The Mythic Method*, 16.
12. Ibid., 86.
13. See Michael Llewellyn Smith, *The Ionian Vision: Greece in Asia Minor, 1919–1922* (1973). This passage of Graeco-Turkish history casts a long shadow even today. A recent evocation in English fiction is Louis de Bernières, *Birds Without Wings* (2004). One infant taken off on a British warship from the flaming Smyrna harbour was Alec Issigonis, the designer of the Austin Mini, which revolutionized the British car industry.
14. Holland, *Blue-Water Empire*, 189–90.
15. Christopher Stray, 'Gilbert Murray', *Oxford DNB*.
16. Paul Fussell, *Abroad: British Literary Travelling between the Wars* (1980), 87.
17. Ibid., 85.
18. Ibid.
19. See Minoo Dinshaw, *Outlandish Knight: The Byzantine Life of Steven Runciman* (2017).
20. Fussell, *Abroad*, 87.
21. Osbert Sitwell, *Discursions on Travel, Art and Life* (1925), 191–3.
22. Harris, *Weatherland*, 337.
23. Arcara, 'Constructing the South', 187–91.

24. Sarah Bradford, *Sacheverell Sitwell: Splendour and Miseries* (1993), 121.
25. Sitwell, *Southern Baroque Art*, 15.
26. Bradford, *Sacheverell Sitwell*, 122–5.
27. Carden-Coyne, *Reconstructing the Body*, 28.
28. Martin, *The Mythic Method*, 18.
29. Judy Egerton, 'Sir Walter Monnington', *Oxford DNB*.
30. Rachel Spence, 'Real Britannia', *Financial Times*, 20 August 2017.
31. Caroline Elam, *Roger Fry and the Re-evaluation of Piero della Francesca* (2004).
32. Alexandra Harris, *Romantic Moderns: English Writers, Artists and the Imagination from Virginia Woolf to John Piper* (2010), 80.
33. Jan Morris, *The Presence of Spain* (1964), 35.
34. William Balssi, 'Hemingway's Greatest Iceberg: The Composition of *The Sun Also Rises*', in James Barbour and Tom Quirk (eds), *Writing the American Classics* (1990), 127.
35. Edward Stanton, *Hemingway and Spain: A Pursuit* (1989), xv.
36. J. B. Trend, *A Picture of Modern Spain: Men and Music* (1921), 1.
37. Lee, *Virginia Woolf*, 465.
38. Frances Partridge, 'Edward [Gerald] Brenan', *Oxford DNB*. Lytton Strachey, however, found the isolation of a Spanish mountain village too much and warned the Woolfs from making the same trip because 'it was death'. They went anyway, and seem to have enjoyed their time, but Virginia quizzed Brenan closely as to why he chose to live in such a remote place. See Gerald Brenan, *South from Granada* (1988; first published 1957), 39,139–45.
39. Glendinning et al. (eds), *Spanish Art in Britain and Ireland*, 33.
40. Gayle Rogers, *Modernism and the New Spain: Britain, Cosmopolitan Europe and Literary History* (2012), 28–63.
41. Richard Cork, *David Bomberg* (1987), 165.
42. Ibid., 211.
43. Paul Stirton, 'British Artists and the Spanish Civil War', in Howarth et al. (eds), *The Discovery of Spain*, 133.
44. Stourton, *Kenneth Clark*, 91.
45. Spalding, *Roger Fry*, 163.
46. Mary Caw and Sarah Wright, *Bloomsbury and France: Art and Friends* (2000), 10.
47. Holroyd, *Augustus John*, 312.
48. Spalding, *Roger Fry*, 251.
49. Roger Fry, *Transformations* (1926), 173.
50. Quoted in Woolf, *Roger Fry*, 271–2.
51. Caw and Wright, *Bloomsbury and France*, 180.
52. Lee, *Virginia Woolf*, 631.
53. See Francis Haskell, *The Ephemeral Museum: Old Master Paintings and the Rise of the Art Exhibition* (2000).
54. Stourton, *Kenneth Clark*, 69–70.
55. Malcolm Cowley, *Exile's Return* (1994), 114.
56. Valerie Eliot and John Haffenden (eds), *The Letters of T. S. Eliot, Vol. VI: 1932–33* (2016), 162.
57. Ackroyd notes that Eliot was 'both disturbed and disgusted by female sexuality, particularly as it was embodied in his [first] wife', though he adds that this by no means logically implied homosexuality, as is sometimes deduced. The parallel with Ruskin seems clear. See Ackroyd, *T. S. Eliot*, 309–10, but also Carole Seymour-Jones, *Painted Shadow: A Life of Vivienne Eliot* (2001).
58. Ackroyd, *T. S. Eliot*, 155–6, 179.
59. Ibid., 159.
60. See p. 93.
61. Ackroyd, *T. S. Eliot*, 305.
62. Davidson, *The Idea of North*, 84.

63. Katharine Cockin, 'Locating the Literary North', in Katharine Cockin (ed.), *The Literary North* (2012).

64. Harris, *Weatherland*, 332.

65. Robert Holland, *The Pursuit of Greatness: Britain and the World Role, 1900–1970* (1991), 148–50.

66. Harris, *Romantic Moderns*, 109.

67. David Fraser Jenkins, 'John Piper', *Oxford DNB*.

68. Richard Perceval Graves, 'Robert Graves', *Oxford DNB*.

69. Martin Seymour-Smith, *Robert Graves: His Life and Work* (1982), 230.

70. Richard Perceval Graves, *Robert Graves: The Years with Laura Riding, 1926–40* (1990), 207.

71. See Jill Edwards, *The British Government and the Spanish Civil War, 1936–1939* (1979).

72. Philip Ziegler, *Osbert Sitwell* (1998), 129.

73. There is a good deal of persuasiveness, however, in Peter Ackroyd's suggestion that the main reason for Eliot's reaction lay in his constant scepticism and his aversion to 'the idea of poets "cashing in" on other people's misery'. See Ackroyd, *T. S. Eliot*, 243.

74. Fussell, *Abroad*, 132. There are several war memorials in London to Britons who fought and died in the International Brigade. One is close to the Craven Cottage ground of Fulham Football Club by the Thames, commemorating the sizeable group who came from Fulham and Hammersmith. Another is adjacent to the London Eye.

75. See Simon Martin, *Conscience and Conflict: British Artists and the Spanish Civil War* (2014).

76. T. J. Clark, 'Picasso and Tragedy', *London Review of Books*, Vol. XXXIX, 6 (17 August 2017); Stirton, 'British Artists and the Spanish Civil War', 137.

77. Holland, *Blue-Water Empire*, 231.

78. Selina Hastings, *Evelyn Waugh: A Biography* (1994), 425–30.

79. Martin, *The Mythic Method*, 21.

80. This ambience was conjured up in the 1999 film *Tea with Mussolini* directed by the producer Franco Zeffirelli. The film tells the story of a set of cultured Anglo-American women whose life in Florence disintegrates during the 1930s. A codex to the film identifies the figure of Luca, embodying an Anglo-Italian blend of art and sensibility, with the young Franco Zeffirelli himself.

81. The evergreen BBC comedy *Dad's Army* features an episode, first broadcast in 1970, entitled 'Don't Fence Me In' about the visit of Captain Mainwaring's platoon to an Italian prisoner-of-war camp. 'But we are enemies,' Mainwaring tells an Italian general when the latter expresses strongly British affections. 'No, Capitano, we are friends,' the general asserts, and indeed Mainwaring and his unit are then drawn into covering up the Italian prisoners' shambolic but harmless shortcomings from inspection by a stern British Army regular officer.

82. Stourton, *Kenneth Clark*, 170–1.

83. The bodies of some of those who went down with the *Arandora Star* were washed up on the Irish coastline. Their memorial is included in the Glencree German War Cemetery in the Wicklow Mountains.

84. Davidson, *The Idea of North*, 142; for Wotton see pp. 21–2.

85. Harrison had trained in the office of Sir Edwin Lutyens, the architect of the British viceroy's house in New Delhi, and he brought the style of the Raj, modified by a touch of modernity, to the Mediterranean. He also later designed the buildings of Nuffield College, Oxford. Costas Georghiou, *British Colonial Architecture in Cyprus: The Architecture of the British Colonial Administration, 1878–1960* (2013), 188–95.

86. See Cork, *David Bomberg*, 277; also Severis, *Travelling Artists in Cyprus*, 230.

87. Cordelia Oliver, 'Joan Eardley', *Oxford DNB*. Also see Frances Spalding, 'Joan Eardley: The Forgotten Artist Who Captured Scotland's Life and Soul', *Guardian*, 10 February 2017.

88. Lara Feigel, *The Love-Charm of Bombs: Restless Lives in the Second World War* (2013), 366.

89. Laura Mulvey, 'Vesuvian Topographies', in David Forgacs et al. (eds), *Roberto Rossellini: Magician of the Real* (2000), 95–112.

90. Rachel Cooke, 'The Enduring Legacy of Elizabeth David, Britain's First Lady of Food', *Guardian*, 8 December 2013. See Artemis Cooper, *Writing at the Kitchen Table: The Authorized Biography of Elizabeth David* (2011).
91. The *Athenia*, setting out from Liverpool, had been sunk within hours of Prime Minister Chamberlain's broadcast on 3 September 1939 announcing war with Germany. Some hundred people drowned. The remains of the *Athenia* were finally located off Rockall Point in Irish waters in September 2017.
92. See Dilys Powell, *An Affair of the Heart* (1957). Dilys Powell had first married Humphrey Payne, the director of the British School at Athens, who died suddenly in 1936. Perhaps the most evocative expression of an Anglo-Hellenic experience for that generation was evoked in Powell's remembrances, *The Villa Ariadne* (1973), an account pivoting on the villa originally built by the archaeologist Sir Arthur Evans, very close to the Minoan palace at Knossos in Crete. The villa still stands, part of the Greek Archaeological Service.
93. See Caroline Vout, *Classical Art: A Life History from Antiquity to the Present* (2018), 233.
94. For the background see Robert Holland, 'The End of an Affair: Anglo-Greek Relations, 1939–55', in Peter Mackridge and David Ricks (eds), *The British Council and Anglo-Greek Literary Interactions, 1945–1955* (2018).
95. Artemis Cooper, *Patrick Leigh Fermor: An Adventure* (2012), 206.
96. This Athenian ambience is conjured up in Mackridge and Ricks (eds), *The British Council and Anglo-Greek Literary Interactions*.
97. Henry Miller had first come to Greece in 1939 as the guest of Lawrence Durrell in Corfu.
98. Mary Renault was a pseudonym. See Caroline Zilboorg, 'Mary Challens (pseud. Renault)', *Oxford DNB*. David Sweetman, *Mary Renault: A Biography* (1993) provides a full discussion.
99. Seymour-Smith, *Robert Graves*, 389.
100. Richard Perceval Graves, *Robert Graves*, 50.
101. The eminent archaeologist and effective popularizer Sir Mortimer Wheeler, however, presented a BBC series on *The Glory That Was Greece* in 1959. The string of Pan paperbacks on archaeology through the 1950s and 1960s, like Leonard Cottrell's *The Bull of Minos* mostly to do with the Mediterranean, also had a wide following amongst a general reading public.
102. John Craxton, dissatisfied in post-war England, had gone to live in Crete in the later 1940s. His subsequent images of the island were marked by geometric appreciation of its light, 'celebrating his release from the chiaroscuro of north London'. Craxton helped design sets for the Royal Ballet and in 1951 cruised in the Aegean on holiday with the choreographer Frederick Ashton and the prima ballerina Margot Fonteyn. 'Greece at that time was magical beyond belief', Craxton, who had a brief relationship with Fonteyn, later recalled. In 2010 Craxton's ashes were scattered over the waters of Chania harbour. See Ian Collins, *John Craxton* (2011); Magdalen Evans, 'John Craxton', *Oxford DNB*; and Meredith Daneman, *Margot Fonteyn* (2005).
103. Cooper, *Patrick Leigh Fermor*, 332–3.
104. The mods' contemporary rivals were the 'rockers' who detested Vespa-type Italianism and soft soul music, and who were devotees of sturdy British-made Triumph scooters. The competing cultural elements here went back a long way but are enduring.
105. In intellectual and moral terms, Enoch Powell was shaped by his training as a Cambridge classicist in the early 1930s, especially by the long-time professor of Latin there, A. E. Housman, better known as the author of *A Shropshire Lad*. A biographer notes that Powell's style of maverick Toryism reflected Housman's own contempt for 'the fashion of the present'. In his inaugural lecture as professor of Greek in Sydney in May 1938, Powell had presented Greek scholarship as 'a powerful antidote to the poisons of the modern world'. See Robert Shepherd, *Enoch Powell: A Biography* (1996), 21–2, 33.
106. It is striking that whilst the most famous speech by a British politician in the nineteenth century – that by Lord Palmerston during the Don Pacifico incident – had punchlines borrowed from Cicero, the most remembered in the twentieth century drew on Virgil.

Both addresses cultivated the 'old Roman spirit' to evoke a contemporary British – or English – mood. For the case of Palmerston, see p. 146.

107. Stourton, *Kenneth Clark*, 317–31.
108. Ibid., 349.
109. Clark, *Civilisation*, xi. This book sold 1.5 million copies, a remarkable figure for a work on the subject of art. It has never been out of print and arguably has been more influential in shaping English-speaking appreciations of its subject than the original television series.
110. See Alastair Sooke's Introduction in ibid.
111. Ibid., xvii.
112. See pp. 237–8.
113. It is notable that Clark, apart from a short opening sequence, also omitted indigenous Irish culture from his agenda for the BBC series on much the same grounds that he excluded Spain. Scotland did much better.
114. Stourton, *Kenneth Clark*, 308.
115. John Crace, 'A Year in Provence, 20 Years On', *Guardian*, 11 January 2010.
116. 'Those Who Move to the Mediterranean Unhappier than People in Britain', *Daily Telegraph*, 23 April 2014.
117. An analogy between the Mediterranean and China as alternative sources of inspiration enjoyed a brief fashion at this time. Bernard Berenson, the connoisseur par excellence of Tuscan old masters, once said that if he started out again, 'I would devote myself to China as I have to Italy.' But any such choice on his part seems highly unlikely. See Sylvia Sprigge, *Berenson: A Biography* (1960), 216.
118. Jan Dalley, 'Because He Can', *Financial Times*, 8 April 2017.
119. Cosmo Monkhouse, *Exhibition of Drawings and Studies by Sir Edward Burne-Jones* (1899), vii.
120. See p. 8.
121. Grosskurth, *John Addington Symonds*, 236.
122. David Cannadine, *Victorious Century: The United Kingdom, 1800–1906* (2017). Asa Briggs's successive volumes *The Age of Improvement, 1783–1867* (1959), *Victorian Cities* (1963) and *Victorian Things* (1988) defined a fresh sympathy for the Victorians and shaped the historical thinking of a generation of history students in Britain, both at school and university level.
123. David Reynolds, 'Britain, the Two World Wars and the Problem of Narrative', *Historical Journal*, Vol. LX (1 March 2017), 195–231. There is nothing, however, especially new about this argument. The chancellor of the Federal Republic of Germany, Helmut Schmidt, made the quip in the mid-1970s, 'The trouble with the British is that they think they won the war.'

SELECT BIBLIOGRAPHY

Abulafia, David, *The Great Sea: A Human History of the Mediterranean* (2011)

Ackroyd, Peter, *T. S. Eliot* (1984)

Adelson, W. (ed.), *Sargent Abroad: Figures and Landscapes* (1997)

Allen, Tudor, *Little Italy: The Story of the Italian Quarter* (2008)

Arapoglou, Eva (ed.), *Ghika, Craxton, Leigh Fermor: Charmed Lives in Greece* (2017)

Arcara, Stefania, 'Constructing the South: Southern Italy and the Mediterranean in British Culture, 1773–1926', PhD thesis, University of Warwick (1998)

Ashton, Rosemary, *G. H. Lewes: A Life* (1991)

—, *George Eliot: A Life* (1996)

—, *Victorian Bloomsbury* (2012)

Aske, Martin, *Keats and Hellenism: An Essay* (1985)

Auchmuty, James, *Sir Thomas Wyse, 1791–1862: The Life and Career of an Educator and Diplomat* (1939)

Avery-Quash, Suzanne, and Julie Sheldon, *Art for the Nation: The Eastlakes and the Victorian Art World* (2011)

Bailey, Anthony, *Standing in the Sun: A Life of J. M. W. Turner* (1997)

Baker, Paul, *The Fortunate Pilgrims: Americans in Italy, 1800–1860* (1964)

Barringer, Tim, and Elizabeth Prettejohn (eds), *Frederic Leighton: Antiquity, Renaissance, Modernity* (1999)

Barry, Michael, 'The Alhambra's Irish Connection', *Irish Times*, 8 May 2017

Beard, Mary, *The Invention of Jane Harrison* (2000)

Beaton, Roderick, *Byron's War: Romantic Rebellion, Greek Revolution* (2013)

Beaton, Roderick, and Christine Kenyon Jones (eds), *Byron: The Poetry of Politics and the Politics of Poetry* (2016)

Beaucour, Fernand et al., *The Discovery of Egypt: Artists, Travellers and Scientists* (1990)

Bernières, Louis de, *Birds Without Wings* (2004)

Bevilacqua, Alexander, and Helen Pfeiffer, 'Turquerie: Culture in Motion, 1650–1750', *Past and Present*, 221, November 2013

Bevin, Darren, *Cultural Climbs: John Ruskin, Albert Smith and the Alpine Aesthetic* (2010)

Black, Jeremy, *The British Abroad: The Grand Tour in the Eighteenth Century* (1992)

Blake, Robert, *Disraeli's Grand Tour: Benjamin Disraeli and the Holy Land, 1830–31* (1981)

Blanning, Tim, *The Pursuit of Glory: Europe 1648–1815* (2007)

Blunt, Wilfrid, *England's Michelangelo: A Biography of G. F. Watts* (1975)

Bonaparte, Felicia, *The Triptych and the Cross: The Central Myths of George Eliot's Poetic Imagination* (1979)

Boyd, Elizabeth French, *Byron's Don Juan: A Critical Study* (1945)

Bradbury, Malcolm, 'Introduction', in E. M. Forster, *A Room with a View* (2000; first published 1908)

Bradbury, Malcolm, and James McFarlane (eds), *Modernism: A Guide to European Literature 1890–1930* (1976)

Bradford, Sarah, *Sacheverell Sitwell: Splendour and Miseries* (1993)

Brand, C. P., *Italy and the English Romantics: The Italianate Fashion in Early Nineteenth-Century England* (1957)

Broadley, A. M., and Lewis Melville (eds), *The Beautiful Lady Craven* (1914)

Brooks, Constance, *Antonio Panizzi: Scholar and Patriot* (1931)

Brooks, Van Wyck, *The Dream of Arcadia: American Writers and Artists in Italy, 1760–1915* (1959)

Brown, Sue, 'The Burning Bush: Browning's First Visit to Asolo, June 1938', *Journal of Anglo-Italian Studies*, Vol. X (2013)

—, *Joseph Severn, A Life: The Rewards of Friendship* (2009)

Burden, Robert, *Travel, Modernism and Modernity* (2015)

Burnell, Carol, *Divided Affections: The Extraordinary Life of Maria Cosway* (2007)

Burns, Arthur, and Joanna Innes (eds), *Rethinking the Age of Reform, 1780–1850* (2003)

Butler, E. M., *Byron and Goethe: Analysis of a Passion* (1956)

Butler, Marilyn, *Romantics, Rebels and Reactionaries: English Literature and its Background, 1760–1830* (1982)

Buxton, John, *Byron and Shelley: The History of a Friendship* (1968)

—, *The Grecian Taste: Literature in the Age of Neo-Classicism, 1740–1820* (1978)

Buzard, James, *The Beaten Track: European Tourism, Literature, and the Ways to 'Culture', 1800–1914* (1993)

Byron, Robert, *Europe in the Looking Glass* (1926)

Caiani, Ambrogio, 'Ornamentalism in a European Context? Napoleon's Italian Coronation, 26 May 1805', *English Historical Review*, Vol. CXXXII, 554 (February 2017)

Calaresu, Melissa, and Helen Hills, *New Approaches to Naples, c. 1500–c. 1800: The Power of Place* (2013)

Cannadine, David, *G. M. Trevelyan: A Life in History* (1992)

—, *Victorious Century: The United Kingdom, 1800–1906* (2017)

Carden-Coyne, Ana, *Reconstructing the Body: Classicism, Modernism, and the First World War* (2009)

Carrington, Charles, *Rudyard Kipling: His Life and Work* (1978)

Carruthers, Gerard, and Alan Rawes, *English Romanticism and the Celtic World* (2003)

Cavaliero, Roderick, *Italia Romantica: English Romantics and Italian Freedom* (2005)

Caw, Mary, and Sarah Wright, *Bloomsbury and France: Art and Friends* (2000)

Cerruti, Toni, *Antonia Gallenga: An Italian Writer in Victorian England* (1974)

Challis, Debbie, 'Fashioning Archaeology into Art', *Journal of Literature and Science*, Vol. V (2012)

Chaney, Edward, *The Grand Tour and the Great Rebellion: Richard Lassels and 'The Voyage of Italy' in the Seventeenth Century* (1985)

Chapman, Alison, *Networking the Nation: British and American Women's Poetry and Italy, 1840–1870* (2015)

Chard, Chloe, *Pleasure and Guilt on the Grand Tour: Travel Writing and Imaginative Geography* (1999)

Chesterton, G. K., *The Victorian Age in Literature* (1926)

Chitty, Susan, *Gwen John, 1876–1939* (1981)

Christiansen, Allen Conrad (ed.), *The Subverting Vision of Bulwer Lytton: Bicentenary Reflections* (2004)

Clark, J. C. D., *English Society, 1660–1832: Ideology, Social Structure and Political Practice during the Ancien Regime* (1985)

Clark, Kenneth, *Civilisation: A Personal View* (2018; first published 1969)

—, *The Gothic Revival: An Essay in the History of Taste* (1928)

Clarke, G. W. (ed.), *Rediscovering Hellenism: The Hellenic Inheritance and the English Imagination* (1989)

Clarke, Michael, and Nicholas Penny, *The Arrogant Connoisseur: Richard Payne Knight, 1751–1824* (1982)

Clay, Edith (ed.), *Sir William Gell in Italy: Letters to the Dilettanti, 1831–1835* (1976)

Clifford, James L., *Hester Lynch Piozzi* (1952)

Colby, Vineta, *Vernon Lee: A Literary Biography* (2003)

Colley, Linda, *Britons: Forging the Nation, 1707–1837* (1992)

Collins, Ian, *John Craxton* (2011)

Constantini, Mariaconcetta, 'This Extraordinary Party: Wilkie Collins, Italy and the Controversies of the Risorgimento', *Journal of Anglo-Italian Studies*, Vol. XII (2013)

Cooper, Artemis, *Patrick Leigh Fermor: An Adventure* (2012)

Crane, David, *Lord Byron's Jackal: The Life of Edward John Trelawny* (1986)

Crompton, Louis, *Byron and Greek Love: Homophobia in 19th-Century England* (1985)

Curl, James Steven, *Georgian Architecture in the British Isles, 1714–1859* (2011)

Dalley, Jan, 'Because He Can', *Financial Times*, 8 April 2017

Daniels, Elizabeth Adams, *Jessie White Mario: Risorgimento Revolutionary* (1971)

Davidson, Peter, *The Idea of North* (2005)

Dejardin, Ian, and Sarah Milroy, *Vanessa Bell* (2017)

Delbourgo, James, *Collecting the World: The Life and Curiosity of Hans Sloane* (2017)

Dinshaw, Minoo, *Outlandish Knight: The Byzantine Life of Steven Runciman* (2017)

Donaldson, George, and Mara Kalnins, *D. H. Lawrence in Italy and England* (1999)

Doughty, Oswald, *A Victorian Romantic: Dante Gabriel Rossetti* (1949)

Dowling, Linda, *Hellenism and Homosexuality in Victorian Oxford* (1994)

Duncan, Major Francis, *The English in Spain* (1877)

Durrell, Lawrence, *Prospero's Cell: A Guide to the Landscape and Manners of Corfu* (1945)

Edel, Leon, *Henry James: A Life* (1987)

Eglin, John, *Venice Transfigured: The Myth of Venice in British Culture, 1660–1797* (2001)

Ellman, Richard, *Oscar Wilde* (1987)

Faber, Geoffrey, *Oxford Apostles: A Character Study of the Oxford Movement* (1936)

Fahr-Becker, Gabrielle, *Art Nouveau* (1997)

Farr, Dennis, *William Etty* (1958)

Feigel, Lara, *The Love-Charm of Bombs: Restless Lives in the Second World War* (2013)

Ferriman, Z. D., *Lord Guilford* (1919)

Findlass, Paula et al. (eds), *Italy's Eighteenth Century: Gender and Culture in the Age of the Grand Tour* (2009)

Fleming, John, *Robert Adam and his Circle in Edinburgh and Rome* (1962)

Flint, Kate, *The Victorians and the Visual Imagination* (2000)

Fontana, Ernest, 'Sexual Tourism and Browning's "The Englishman in Italy"', *Victorian Poetry*, Vol. XXXVI (1998)

Ford, George H., *Keats and the Victorians: A Study of His Influence and Rise to Fame, 1821–1895* (1945)

Forster, Margaret, *Elizabeth Barrett Browning* (1988)

Fothergill, Brian, *Nicholas Wiseman* (1963)

—, *Sir William Hamilton: Envoy Extraordinary* (1969)

Frankel, Nicholas, *Oscar Wilde: The Unrepentant Years* (2017)

Fraser, Antonia, *Perilous Question: The Drama of the Great Reform Bill, 1832* (2013)

Fraser, Hilary, *The Victorians and Renaissance Italy* (1992)

Frazer, James George, *Aftermath: A Supplement to the Golden Bough* (1936)

—, *The Golden Bough* (1890)

Fry, Roger, *Transformations* (1926)

Furbank, P. N., *E. M. Forster, A Life, Vol. I: The Growth of the Novelist (1879–1949)* (1977)

Fussell, Paul, *Abroad: British Literary Travelling between the Wars* (1980)

Gale, Robert, 'Henry James and Italy', *Nineteenth-Century Fiction*, Vol. XIV (1959)

Gallenga, Antonio, *Italy Revisited* (1875)

Garsington, Aubrey, *Society, Culture and Opera in Florence, 1814–1830* (2005)

Gekas, Athanasios, *Xenocracy: State, Class and Colonialism in the Ionian Islands, 1815–1864* (2016)

Georghiou, Costas, *British Colonial Architecture in Cyprus: The Architecture of the British Colonial Administration, 1878–1960* (2013)

Gerard, Frances, *Angelica Kauffmann: A Biography* (1982)

Glendinning, Nigel et al. (eds), *Spanish Art in Britain and Ireland, 1750–1920* (2010)

Goldhill, Simon, *Victorian Culture and Classical Antiquity: Art, Opera, Fiction and the Proclamation of Modernity* (2010)

Goodrich, Amanda, *Debating England's Aristocracy in the 1790s: Pamphlets, Polemics and Political Ideas* (2005)

Graham, Roderick, *Arbiter of Elegance: A Biography of Robert Adam* (2009)

Graham-Dixon, Andrew, 'A Tale of Two Cities', *Independent*, 16 November 1993

Gregory, Desmond, *Sicily: The Insecure Base. A History of the British Occupation of Sicily, 1806–1815* (1988)

Grigson, Geoffrey, *Samuel Palmer, The Visionary Years* (1947)

Grosskurth, Phyllis, *John Addington Symonds* (1964)

Grundy, Isobel, *Lady Mary Wortley Montagu: Comet of the Enlightenment* (1999)

Gwynn, Stephen, *Oliver Goldsmith* (1935)

Haag, Michael, *The Durrells of Corfu* (2017)

Haight, Gordon S., *George Eliot: A Biography* (1968)

Hale, J. R., *The Italian Journal of Samuel Rogers* (1956)

Hall, Edith, and Henry Stead (eds), *Greek and Roman Classics in the British Struggle for Social Reform* (2015)

Halsband, Robert, *The Life of Lady Mary Wortley Montagu* (1956)

Hammerschlag, Keren Rosa, *Frederic Leighton: Death, Mortality and Resurrection* (2015)

—, 'Frederic Leighton's Paintings of the Female Nude', *Victorian Studies*, Vol. LVI (Spring 2014)

Harlow, Vincent, *The Founding of the Second British Empire, 1763–1793, Vol. II* (1964)

Harris, Alexandra, *Romantic Moderns: English Writers, Artists and the Imagination from Virginia Woolf to John Piper* (2010)

—, *Weatherland: Writers and Artists under English Skies* (2015)

Harris, Margaret, and Judith Johnston (eds), *The Journals of George Eliot* (1998)

Harrison, Charles, *English Art and Modernism, 1900–1939* (1981)

Hartcup, Adeline, *Angelica: The Portrait of an Eighteenth-Century Artist* (1954)

Hastings, Selina, *Evelyn Waugh: A Biography* (1994)

Haycock, David Boyd, *A Crisis of Brilliance: Five Young British Artists and the Great War* (2009)

Haynes, Clare, *Pictures and Popery: Art and Religion in England, 1660–1760* (2006)

Heffer, Simon, *High Minds: The Victorians and the Birth of Modern Britain* (2013)

Hemingway, Andrew, *Transatlantic Romanticism: British and American Art and Literature, 1790–1860* (2015)

Henderson, G. P., *The Ionian Academy* (1988)

Henderson, Philip, *Swinburne: The Portrait of a Poet* (1974)

Herold, J. Christopher, *Mistress to an Age: A Life of Madame de Staël* (1959)

Hilton, Timothy, *John Ruskin: The Early Years* (1985)

—, *John Ruskin: The Later Years* (2000)

Holland, Robert, *Blue-Water Empire: The British in the Mediterranean since 1800* (2012)

—, *Britain and the Revolt in Cyprus, 1954–59* (1998)

—, *The Pursuit of Greatness: Britain and the World Role, 1900–1970* (1991)

Holland, Robert, and Diana Markides, *The British and the Hellenes: Struggles for Mastery in the Eastern Mediterranean, 1850–1960* (2006)

Holmes, Richard, *Coleridge: Darker Reflections* (1998)

—, *Coleridge: Early Visions* (1989)

—, *Shelley: The Pursuit* (1974)

Holmes, *Coleridge: Darker Reflections*, 143.

Hough, Barry, and Howard Davis, *Coleridge's Laws: A Study of Coleridge in Malta* (2010)

Howarth, David, *The Invention of Spain: Cultural Relations between Britain and Spain, 1770–1870* (2007)

Howarth, David et al. (eds), *The Discovery of Spain: British Artists and Collectors. From Goya to Picasso* (2009)

Howe, Anthony, *The Letters of Richard Cobden, Vol. I: 1815–1847* (2007)

—, *The Letters of Richard Cobden, Vol. II: 1848–1855* (2010)

Hughes, Gordon, and Philipp Blom, *Nothing But the Clouds Unchanged: Artists in World War I* (2014)

Hunter Blair, David, *In Victorian Days and Other Papers* (1939)

Hurst, Isobel, *Victorian Women Writers and the Classics: The Feminine of Homer* (2006)

Irwin, Robert, *The Alhambra* (2004)

—, *For Lust of Knowing: The Orientalists and their Enemies* (2006)

Isabella, Maurizio, *Risorgimento in Exile: Italian Émigrés and the Liberal International in the Post-Napoleonic Era* (2009)

Jarves, James Jackson, *Italian Rambles: Studies of Life and Manners in New and Old Italy* (1885)

Jenkins, Romilly, *The Dilessi Murders: Greek Brigands and English Hostages* (1998)

Jenkins, Tiffany, 'Mad for Marble', *Literary Review*, July 2016

Jenkyns, Richard, 'Distilled', *Times Literary Supplement*, 11 December 2015

—, *The Victorians and Ancient Greece* (1980)

Jones, Stanley, *Hazlitt: A Life* (1989)

Jordan, Jane, and Andrew King (eds), *Ouida and Victorian Popular Culture* (2013)

Kamen, Henry, *The Disinherited: The Exiles Who Created Spanish Culture* (2007)

Keates, Jonathan, *Stendhal* (1994)

Kelly, Jason, *The Society of Dilettanti: Archaeology and Identity in the British Enlightenment* (2009)

Kemp, Betty, *Sir Francis Dashwood: An Eighteenth-Century Independent* (1967)

Ker, Ian, *John Henry Newman: A Biography* (1988)

Keynes, G., *The Letters of Rupert Brooke* (1968)

King, Averil, 'The Work of James Dickson Innes', *Country Life*, 4 February 2006

Kirkwall, Viscount, *Four Years in the Ionian Islands* (1864)

Knight, Ellis Cornelia, *The Autobiography of Miss Cornelia Knight, Lady Companion to Princess Charlotte of Wales* (1861)

Körner, Axel, *America in Italy: The United States in the Political Thought and Imagination of the Risorgimento, 1763–1865* (2017)

Leach, Joseph, *Bright Particular Star: The Life and Times of Charlotte Cushman* (1970)

Lee, Hermione, *Edith Wharton* (2007)

—, *Virginia Woolf* (1996)

Lees-Milne, James, *The Age of Adam* (1947)

Levi, Peter, *Edward Lear: A Biography* (1995)

Lewis, Norman, *Naples '44* (1978)

Lipking, Lawrence, *The Ordering of the Arts in Eighteenth-Century England* (1970)

Llewellyn Smith, Michael, *The Ionian Vision: Greece in Asia Minor, 1919–1922* (1973)

Llewellyn Smith, Michael et al. (eds), *Scholars, Travels, Archives: Greek History and Culture through the British School at Athens* (2009)

Lowry, Elizabeth, 'Portrait of a Lady', *Guardian*, 19 July 2008

Macaulay, Rose, *The Pleasure of Ruins* (1953)

MacCarthy, Fiona, *Byron: Life and Legend* (2002)

—, *The Last Pre-Raphaelite: Edward Burne-Jones and the Victorian Imagination* (2011)

McCarthy, Michael, *Lord Charlemont and His Circle* (2001)

McClellan, George, *Venice and Bonaparte* (1931)

McCue, Maureen, *British Romanticism and the Reception of Italian Old Masters* (2014)

MacGillivray, J. Alexander, *Minotaur: Sir Arthur Evans and the Archaeology of the Minoan Myth* (2000)

McIntyre, Ian, *Garrick* (1999)

Mackridge, Peter, and David Ricks (eds), *The British Council and Anglo-Greek Literary Interactions, 1944–1955* (2018)

McLaughlin, Martin (ed.), *Britain and Italy from Romanticism to Modernism* (2000)

McMullen, Roy, *Victorian Outsider: A Biography of J. A. M. Whistler* (1974)

Marchand, Suzanne, *Down from Olympus: Archaeology and Philhellenism in Germany, 1750–1870* (1996)

Marshall, P. J., and Glyndwr Williams, *The Great Map of Mankind: British Perceptions of the World in the Age of Enlightenment* (1982)

Marshall, Roderick, *Italy in English Literature, 1775–1815: Origins of the Romantic Intellect* (1934)

Martin, Simon, *Consicience and Conflict: British Artists and the Spanish Civil War* (2014)

—, *The Mythic Method: Classicism in British Art, 1920–1950* (2016)

Martineau, Jane, and Andrew Robison (eds), *The Glory of Venice: Art in the Eighteenth Century* (1994)

Martinengo, Cesarese Evelyn, *Glimpses of Italian Society in the Eighteenth Century* (1892)

Matteson, John, *The Lives of Margaret Fuller* (2012)

Matthew, H. C. G., *Gladstone, 1808–1874* (1986)

Mattusch, Carol (ed.), *Rediscovering the Ancient World on the Bay of Naples, 1710–1890* (2013)

Maves, Carl, *Sensuous Pessimism: Italy in the Works of Henry James* (1973)

Middleton Murry, John, *Between Two Worlds* (1935)

Miles, Robert, *Ann Radcliffe: The Great Enchantress* (1995)

Mill, John Stuart, *An Autobiography* (1989; first published 1873)

Mitchell, Leslie, *Bulwer Lytton: The Rise and Fall of a Victorian Man of Letters* (2003)

Morley, John, *Life of Gladstone, Vol. I* (1903)

Moore, James et al., *Reinventing History: The Enlightenment Origins of Ancient History* (2008)

Morris, Jan, *The Presence of Spain* (1964)

Mullen, Richard, and James Munson, *'The Smell of the Continent': The British Discover Europe, 1814–1914* (2009)

Munro, John, *Thomas Carlyle* (2000)

Nelson, Michael, *Queen Victoria and the Discovery of the Riviera* (2001)

Nichols, Kate, *Greece and Rome at the Crystal Palace: Classical Sculpture and Modern Britain, 1854–1936* (2015)

Noakes, Edward, *Edward Lear: The Life of a Wanderer* (1968)

Noel, Gerard, *Ena: Spain's English Queen* (1984)

Norman, Sylva, *Flight of the Skylark: The Development of Shelley's Reputation* (1954)

Orr, Mrs Sutherland, *Life and Letters of Robert Browning* (1891)

Palache, John, *Gautier and the Romantics* (1927)

Panter-Downes, Mollie, *At the Pines: Swinburne, Watts-Dunton and Putney* (1971)

Pemble, John (ed.), *John Addington Symonds: Culture and the Demon Desire* (2000)

—, *The Mediterranean Passion: Victorians and Edwardians in the South* (1987)

—, *The Rome We Have Lost* (2017)

—, *Venice Rediscovered* (1995)

Peters, Marie, 'Early Hanoverian Consciousness: Empire or Europe?', *English Historical Review*, Vol. CXXII, 497 (2007)

Postle, Martin, 'Boswell Redivivus: Northcote, Hazlitt and the British School', *Hazlitt Review*, Vol. VIII (2015)

Postle, Martin, and Robin Simon, *Richard Wilson and the Transformation of European Landscape Painting* (2014)

Powell, Cecilia, *Turner in the South: Rome, Naples, Florence* (1987)

Powell, Dilys, *An Affair of the Heart* (1957)

—, *The Villa Ariadne* (1973)

Prest, John, *Lord John Russell* (1972)

Prettejohn, Elizabeth, *Beauty and Art, 1750–2000* (2005)

—, *Modern Painters, Old Masters: The Art of Imitation from the Pre-Raphaelites to the First World War* (2018)

Prodger, Michael, 'Sage of Shoreham', *Literary Review* (August 2015)

Pye, Michael, *The Edge of the World: How the North Sea Made Us What We Are* (2015)

Quennell, Peter, *Byron in Italy* (1941)

Raby, Peter, *Samuel Butler: A Life* (1991)

Raponi, Danilo, *Religion and Politics in the Risorgimento: Britain and the New Italy, 1861–1877* (2014)

Ray, Gordon, *Thackeray: The Uses of Advocacy, 1811–1846* (1955)

Redford, Bruce, *Dilettanti: The Antic and the Antique in Eighteenth-Century England* (2008)

—, *Venice and the Grand Tour* (1996)

Rial, Lucy, *Under the Volcano: Revolution in a Sicilian Town* (2013)

Richardson, John, *A Life of Picasso, Vol. II, 1907–1917: The Painter of Modern Life* (2009)

Rignall, John, *George Eliot and Europe* (1997)

Roberts, Neil, *D. H. Lawrence, Travel and Cultural Difference* (2004)

Robertson, Ian, *Richard Ford, 1796–1858: Hispanophile, Connoisseur and Critic* (2004)

Robins, Jane, *Rebel Queen: The Trial of Queen Caroline* (2006)

Rodd, Sir James Rennell, *Social and Diplomatic Memories, 1884–1893* (1922)

—, *Social and Diplomatic Memories, 1902–1919* (1925)

Roe, Nicholas, *John Keats: A New Life* (2012)

Roe, Richard Paul, *The Shakespeare Guide to Italy* (2011)

Roessel, David, *In Byron's Shadow: Modern Greece in the British and American Imagination* (2002)

Rogers, Gayle, *Modernism and the New Spain: Britain, Cosmopolitan Europe and Literary History* (2012)

Rooksby, Ricky, *A. C. Swinburne: A Poet's Life* (1997)

Rosen, F., *Bentham, Byron, and Greece: Constitutionalism, Nationalism, and Early Liberal Political Thought* (1982)

Ross, Ian, *Oscar Wilde and Ancient Greece* (2013)

Ruskin, John, *The Stones of Venice* (1898)

Rutherford, Andrew (ed.), *Byron: Augustan and Romantic* (1990)

St Clair, William, *Lord Elgin and the Marbles* (1967)

Salmon, Frank, *Building on Ruins: The Rediscovery of Rome and English Architecture* (2000)

Saxl, Fritz, and Rudolf Wittkower, *British Art and the Mediterranean* (1948)

Sayce, A. H., *Reminiscences* (1923)

Schenk, E., *Mozart and His Times* (1960)

Schoina, Maria, *Romantic 'Anglo-Italians': Configurations of Identity in Byron, the Shelleys, and the Pisan Circle* (2009)

Severis, Rita C., *Travelling Artists in Cyprus 1700–1960* (2000)

Seymour-Jones, Carole, *Painted Shadow: A Life of Vivienne Eliot* (2002)

Seymour-Smith, Martin, *Robert Graves: His Life and Work* (1995)

Sherrard, Peter, *Edward Lear: The Corfu Years* (1988)

Siegel, Jonah, *Desire and Excess: The Nineteenth-Century Culture of Art* (2000)

Sieveking, Giberne, *The Memoir of Sir Horace Mann* (1912)

Sitwell, Osbert, *Discussions on Travel, Art and Life* (1925)

Sitwell, Sacheverell, *Southern Baroque Art: A Study of Painting, Architecture and Music in Italy and Spain of the 17th and 18th Centuries* (1924)

Smith, Alison, *The Victorian Nude: Sexuality, Morality and Art* (1996)

Spalding, Frances, *Roger Fry: Art and Life* (1980)

Sprigge, Sylvia, *Berenson: A Biography* (1960)

Stanton, Edward, *Hemingway and Spain: A Pursuit* (1989)

Steegman, John, *The Rule of Taste: From George I to George IV* (1936)

—, *Victorian Taste: A Study of the Arts and Architecture from 1830 to 1870* (1970)

Stevens, Michael S., 'Spanish Orientalism: Washington Irving and the Romance of the Moor', PhD thesis, Georgia State University (2007)

Stewart, Randall, *Nathaniel Hawthorne: A Biography* (1958)

Storey, Mark, *Robert Southey: A Life* (1977)

Stourton, James, *Kenneth Clark: Life, Art and Civilisation* (2016)

Sturgis, Matthew, *Passionate Attitudes: The English Decadence of the 1890s* (1995)

Sultana, Donald, *Samuel Taylor Coleridge in Malta and Italy* (1969)

Sumner, Ann, and Greg Smith, *Thomas Jones (1742–1803): An Artist Rediscovered* (2003)

Swann, Mandy, 'Shelley's Utopian Seascapes', *Studies in Romanticism*, Vol. LII (2013)

Sweet, Rosemary, *Cities of the Grand Tour: The British in Italy*, c. *1690–1820* (2012)

Symons, Arthur, *Cities of Italy* (1907)

—, *Confessions: A Study in Pathology* (1930)

Thomas, Clara, *Love and Work Enough: The Life of Anna Jameson* (1967)

Thomas, Donald, *Robert Browning: A Life Within a Life* (1982)

Thompson, Andrew, *George Eliot and Italy: Literary, Cultural and Political Influences from Dante to the Risorgimento* (1998)

Tomalin, Claire, *Charles Dickens: A Life* (2011)

Tomory, Peter, *The Life and Art of Henry Fuseli* (1972)

Townson, Nigel (ed.), *Is Spain Different? A Comparative Look at the Nineteenth and Twentieth Centuries* (2015)

Trelawny, Edward, *Recollections of the Last Days of Byron and Shelley* (1952; first published 1858)

Trend, J. B., *A Picture of Modern Spain: Men and Music* (1921)

Trevelyan, Humphrey, *Goethe and the Greeks* (1941)

Treves, Giuliana, *The Golden Ring: The Anglo-Florentines, 1847–1862* (1956)

Tromans, Nicholas, *The Art of G. F. Watts* (2017)

Turner, Frank, *The Greek Heritage in Victorian Britain* (1981)

Uglow, Jenny, *Hogarth: A Life and a World* (1997)

—, *Mr Lear: A Life of Art and Nonsense* (2017)

Unrau, John, *Ruskin and St Mark's* (1984)

Vance, Norman, *The Victorians and Ancient Rome* (1997)

Vecovi, Alessandro (ed.), *The Victorians in Italy: Literature, Travel, Politics and Art* (2009)

Waterfield, Gordon, *Layard of Nineveh* (1963)

Waterhouse, Helen, *The British School at Athens: The First Hundred Years* (1986)

Watkin, David, *Athenian Stuart, Pioneer of the Greek Revival* (1982)

—, *Thomas Hope: 1769–1831 and the Neo-Classical Idea* (1968)

Wawn, Andrew, *The Vikings and the Victorians: Inventing the Old North in Nineteenth-Century Britain* (2000)

Webb, Timothy, 'The Journal of Samuel Rogers: An Alternative Vision of Italy', *Journal of Anglo-Italian Studies*, Vol. XIII (2014)

—, 'Mia Bella Italia: Mary Shelley's Italies', *Journal of Anglo-Italian Studies*, Vol. XII (2013)

Wells, Kathleen, 'The Return of British Artists to Rome after 1815', PhD thesis, University of Leicester (1974)

Wheatley, Kim, 'Attracted by the Body: Accounts of Shelley's Cremation', *Keats-Shelley Journal*, Vol. XLIX (2000)

Wicks, Margaret, *The Italian Exiles in London, 1816–1848* (1937)

Wiener, Martin J., *English Culture and the Decline of the Industrial Spirit, 1850–1960* (1981)

Williams, David, *A World of His Own: The Double Life of George Borrow* (1982)

Williams, Kate, *Emma Hamilton: Seduction and Celebrity* (2016)

Wilson, Jeffrey, *The German Forest: Nature, Identity and the Contestation of a National Symbol, 1871–1914*

Woolf, Virginia, *The Common Reader* (1929; first published 1925)

—, *Roger Fry: A Biography* (1940)

Yiangou, Anastasia, and Antigone Heraclidou (eds), *Cyprus from Colonialism to the Present: Visions and Realities. Essays in Honour of Robert Holland* (2018)

Young, Paul, *Globalization and the Great Exhibition: The Victorian New World Order* (2009)

Ziegler, Philip, *Osbert Sitwell* (1998)

Zucchi, John, *The Little Slaves of the Harp: Italian Child Street Musicians in Nineteenth-Century Paris, London and New York* (1992)

INDEX

Act of Union (1707), 4, 5, 29, 50
Act of Union (1800), 55
Adam, James, 46
Adam, Robert, 19, 34–6, 38, 39, 234
Aestheticism, 178, 194
African American jazz, 229
Agrigento (Girgenti), Sicily, 17, 47, *70*
Albani, Cardinal, 38
Albert, Prince, 132
Alexandra, Princess of Wales, 182, 183
Alfonso XIII, King, 215
Alfred, Prince, 182
Alhambra, Granada, 18, 104, *105*, 150
Ali Pasha, 68–9
Allan, Maud, 'Dance of the Seven Veils', 25
Alma-Tadema, Lawrence, 176, 208
Alpine Club, 137
Alps, British love of, 88–9, 135, 137, 179,
    190
American colonies, British loss of, 4, 5
Americans, in Europe, 19–20, 127
Ancient and Modern Spanish Art (exhibition,
    1920–1), 236
Angerstein, Sir John Julius, 112
Anglicanism, 150
Anglo-Florentine society, 98, 126–8, 155,
    159–60, 166, 187, 192
Anstruther-Thomson, Clementina ('Kit'),
    212
anthropology, 44, 208
Anti-Jacobin (journal), 63

Antiquities of Athens, The (1762), 37–8, 69
Apollinaire, Guillaume, 222
Arcara, Stefania, 193
archaeology, 180–2, 201, 209
architecture: absence of authentic British
    style, 158; Georgian, 36; Greek Revival,
    69–71; Moorish, 104–5; neo-Byzantine,
    177; Palladian, 27, 31, 34, 57; *see also*
    Adam, Robert
Armada Memorial, Plymouth, 186
Arnold, Matthew, 93, 95, 178; *Culture and
    Anarchy* (1869), 157, 158–9
art, British attitude to, 50–1, 112–13
Arundel Society, 167
Ashby, Thomas, 218
Ashton, Rosemary, 154
Athenaeum (journal), 197, 202
Athenaeum (London club), 69
Athens: *Antiquities of Athens, The* (1762),
    37–8; British ambivalence over, 39, 184;
    British School of Archaeology at, 181–2;
    Byron in, 87; in Grote's *History of Greece*,
    140–1; John Tweddell in, 67–8; Lord
    Elgin in, 71–3; modern rebuilding of,
    145; post-war, 253; Thackeray in, 139; in
    Virginia Woolf's *Jacob's Room*, 228–9
Athos, Mount, 69
Attenborough, David, 256
Attlee, Clement, 246
Auden, W. H., 242
Auerbach, Frank, 249

Augustus, Prince, 55
Austen, Alfred, 3
Austen, Jane, *Northanger Abbey* (1817), 48

Ball, Alexander, 78–9
banditti, 98
Banqueting House, Whitehall, 27
Baring, Evelyn, 183
Barry, Charles, 102
Batoni, Pompeo, 52
Battle of the Nile, 71
Baudelaire, Charles, 157
Beard, Mary, 210
Beardsley, Aubrey, 194–6
Beckford, William, 56
Bede, Venerable, 21
Bell, Clara, 188
Bell, Clive, 221
Bell, Gertrude, 189
Bell, Julian, 245
Bell, Vanessa, 216, 221, 238, 245
Bentham, Jeremy, 147
Bergson, Henri, 210
Bertozzi, Anna-Cecilia, 78
Betjeman, John, 254
Bizet, Georges, *Carmen* (1875), 187
'Black Legend' of Spain, 56, 216
Blackfriars Bridge, London, 51
Blagden, Isa, 159, 160
Blake, Robert, 107
Blake, William, 48, 99
Blessington, Countess of, 68, 92
Bloomsbury Group, 201, 238
Blunt, Wilfrid, 17
Bomberg, David, 236–7, 249–50
Bonaparte, Letizia, 145
Bone, Muirhead, *A Spanish Good Friday (Ronda)* (1925), *237*
Borrow, George, *The Bible in Spain* (1843), 147
Boswell, James, 14, 15, 33, 41, 55
Bouverie, John, 39
Bowes, John, 214
Bowes, Josephine, 214
Bowes Museum, Teesdale, 214–15
Boyd, Robert, 104
Brabazon, Hercules Brabazon, 200
Bradbury, Malcolm, 207
Bradford, Sarah, 233
Bradford Mechanics' Institute, 138
Braque, Georges, 222
Brawne, Fanny, 94–5
Brenan, Gerald, 235–6, 246
Briggs, Asa, 261

British Art and the Mediterranean (exhibition, 1941), 7
British landscape painting, 48–50
British Legion, in Spanish war, 146–7
British Liberal Party, 85, 119
British Museum, 62, 70, 74, 119, 186–7
British School at Rome, 218, 234
British School of Archaeology at Athens, 181, *182*
British 'School of Art', 50
British Sociological Association, 259
British Watercolour Society, 169
'Britishness', growing sense of, 19, 35–6, 63
Brooke, Rupert, 225–6
Broschi, Carlo *see* Farinelli
Brougham, Henry, 1st Baron Brougham, 119
Brown, Ford Madox, 89
Browning, Elizabeth Barrett, 15, 19, 96, 110, 124–6, 127, 153, 159; *Aurora Leigh* (1856), 125, 140; *Casa Guidi Windows* (1851), 124–5
Browning, Robert, 19, 121–4, 159–60, 169, 190–1; *The Ring and the Book* (1868), 9; 'A Toccata of Galuppi's' (1855), 9; 'The Englishman in Italy' (1845), 109, 122; *Pippa Passes* (1841), 123; *Sordello* (1840), 122
Browning, Robert Barrett ('Pen'), 124, 125, 159, 190
Bruce, James, interior view of a Doric temple at Paestum, *46*
Brydone, Patrick, *A Tour through Sicily and Malta* (1773), 23, 47, 55
Bulwer Lytton, Edward, 12, 93, 113–15, 127, 133, 142, 143, 182; *Godolphin* (1833), 10; *The Last Days of Pompeii* (1834), 114–15
Bulwer Lytton, Rosina, 113
Burghersh, Lord, 98
Burke, Edmund, 63
Burlington House, Piccadilly, 173, 181, 240
Burne-Jones, Edward, 11, 168–70, *170*, 191, 193, 260
Burra, Edward, 237
Bury St Edmunds, 165, 166
Butler, E. M., *The Tyranny of Greece over Germany* (1935), 39
Butler, Marilyn, 3, 84, 89
Butler, Samuel, 50, 171–2, 196–8, 205, 210; *The Way of All Flesh* (1903), 197, 217
Byng, Admiral, 33
Byron, Allegra, 92

INDEX

Byron, George, Lord: Calvinism of, 85, 89; death and funeral, 93; dismissal of Lake poets, 67; on Elgin marbles, 73; 'exaggerated times' of, 66; Grand Tour, 86; in Greece, 87–8, 92–3; and Italy, 12, 61, 89–92; and Madame de Staël's *Corinne*, 83; and opera, 78; and 'poetic geography', 47; risqué love poetry of, 76; on Samuel Rogers, 101; at Shelley's cremation, 1–2; and Spain, 104; status of, 94; in Switzerland, 88–9; on Thomas Hope's *Anastasius*, 76; *Beppo* (1818), 89; *The Bride of Abydos* (1813), 88; *Childe Harold's Pilgrimage* (1812), 85, 86–7, 88, 100, 106; *Don Juan* (1819–24), 18, 76, 89–90; *English Bards and Scotch Reviewers* (1809), 73, 86; *The Giaour* (1813), 88; *Manfred* (1817), 89; *The Siege of Corinth* (1816), 88
Byron, Robert, 212, 231–2

Campbell-Johnson, Rachel, 176
Canaletto (Giovanni Antonio Canal), 59–60, 171
Cannadine, David, 261
Canova, Antonio, 53, 61
'Captain Swing' riots, 111
Carden-Coyne, Ana, 227
Carlyle, Jane, 120
Carlyle, Thomas, 118, 120, 132–3, 188; *Sartor Resartus* (1836), 132
Caroline, Queen, trial for adultery, 90
Carolus-Duran, Charles, 188
Carr, J. Comyns, 220
Carriera, Rosalba, 58, 59
Carrington, Dora, 236
castrati, Italian, 29, 83, 204
Catholic emancipation, 106
Catholic Herald (newspaper), 227
Catholicism: British suspicion of, 10, 45, 54–6, 55–6, 129–30, 161, 186; Italian, 40, 164, 172, 241, 249; Neapolitan, 40; restoration of the episcopal hierarchy in Britain, 129; Spanish, 56, 88–9, 106, 148, 150; and T. S. Eliot, 241; *see also* Newman, John Henry
Cavour, Camillo Benso, Count of, 153
Cézanne, Paul, 216
Chamberlain, Neville, 246
Chamberlain, Sir Austen, 240
Charles I, King, 21
Chatwin, Bruce, 213
Chesterton, G. K., 114, 121
Chiswick House (1781), *27*

Chopin, Frédéric, 202
Churchill, Sir Winston, 246
Cintra, Convention of (1808), 83
Clark, J. C. D., 5
Clark, Kenneth, 131, 223, 237–8, 248; *Civilisation* (TV series), 256–8, 262
Clarke, Edward, 67–8
Clement XIV, Pope, 55
Clérisseau, Charles-Louis, 35
Clifford, Charles, *Photographic Scramble through Spain* (1861), 151
Cobden, Richard, 145, 147
Cocteau, Jean, 222
Coleridge, Samuel Taylor, 6, 77–80, 78–9, 83, 93
Colley, Linda, *Britons: Forging the Nation 1707–1837* (1992), 4
Colossus, HMS, 62
Constable, John, *The Hay Wain* (1824), 99
Cook, Thomas, 184, 189
Cooper, James Fenimore, 127
Corfu, 68, 142–4, 183, 202
Cork, Richard, 250
Cosway, Maria, 53–4
Cosway, Richard, 54
Cousin, Victor, 152
Craven, Lady, 41, 56
Craxton, John, 254, *255*
Cromwell, Oliver, 22
Crouzet, François, 177
Crystal Palace, 110, 161
Cubism, 236
Cummings, E. E., 240
Cunningham, Allan, *Lives of the Most Eminent British Painters* (1829–33), 113
Cyprus, 7, 69, 200, 249–50

Dadd, Maria, 149
Dadd, Richard, 13, 149
Dalley, Jan, 260
'Dance of Zalongo', 69
Dangerfield, George, *The Strange Death of Liberal England* (1935), 220
Dante, 118, 133, 164, 194, 241
Darwin, Charles, *On the Origin of Species* (1859), 159, 208
Dashwood, Sir Francis, 17, 33–4
David, Elizabeth, 251–2
Davidson, Peter, 242, 249
De Quincey, Thomas, 79
decadence, 194, 195, 203
DeMille, Cecil B., *The Ten Commandments*, 176
Derain, André, 222

Derby, Edward Smith-Stanley, 14th Earl of, 118, 141
Devonshire, Georgiana, Duchess of, 54
Dickens, Charles, 13, 123, 139; *Little Dorrit* (1855–7), 110; *Oliver Twist* (1837–9), 121
Dighton, Denis, 84
Dilettanti, Society of, 32–4, 37, 38, 45, 51, 63, 101
Disraeli, Benjamin, 111, 115, 141; *Coningsby* (1844), 76; *Sybil* (1845), 130
Disraeli, Isaac, 107
Dodwell, Edward: *A Classical and Topographical Tour through Greece* (1819), 68; on the Elgin Marbles, 73
Dodwell, Teresa, 68
Dolmetsch, Arnold, 223
Douglas, Lord Alfred, 194
Dryden, John, 30
Dulwich Picture Gallery, 52
Dürer, Albrecht, 256
Durkheim, Émile, 210
Durrell, Lawrence, 15, 213, 251, 253
Duty Free (TV series), 8

Eardley, Joan, 250
Eastlake, Charles Lock, 97, 98, 102, 149, 154, 163–4
Egoist (journal), 221
Egypt, 65, 76
Egypt Exploration Fund, 181
El Greco, 149, 215
Elgin, Lord, 71–5
Elgin Marbles, 71–5, *73*, 86, 102, 175, 212
Eliot, George, 110, 139, 140, 154–5, 180, 210, 257; on Spain, 185; 'The Spanish Gypsy' (1868), 185–6; *Middlemarch* (1871), 127, 137; *Romola* (1863), 155
Eliot, T. S., 20, 210, 212, 236, 240–2, 245; *The Waste Land* (1922), 240
Elizabeth I, Queen, 21
Ellman, Richard, 194
English Coffee House, Rome, 76
English College, Rome, 106, 116
'English Picturesque' style, 76
Etty, William, 173
Eugenie, Empress, 187
European Economic Community, 256
European Union, British referendum on membership of (2016), 262
Evans, Arthur, 201
Evans, Joan, 201
Exhibition of Greek Art (1946), 252
Eyck, Jacob van, *Arnolfini Portrait* (1434), 137

Fabris, Peter, 40
Falcieri, Tita, 107
Farinelli (Carlo Broschi), 29
Farington, Joseph, 70
Fauvel, Louis, 71, 73
Feigel, Lara, 251
Fergusson, James, *History of the Modern Styles of Architecture* (1891), 158
Festing Jones, Henry, 197
Fielding, Henry, 32
Finlay, George, *History of Greece* (1843–61), 145
First World War, 230–1, 235; memorials to, 226–7
Fitzmaurice-Kelly, James, 188, 214
Fitzwilliam Museum, Cambridge, 68
Flaubert, Gustave, *Madame Bovary* (1856), 157
Flaxman, John, 74, 76
Flint, William Russell, 245
Florence, Laurentian Library, 21
Florence, Italy: Brownings in, 124, 126, 153, 159; and Burne-Jones, 168; Duke of Tuscany's court in, 15; English community in, 19, 98, 126–8, 155, 159–60, 166, 248; in Forster's *A Room with a View*, 9, 20, 206–8; in George Eliot's *Romola*, 155; Henry James on, 157, 205; Protestant Cemetery, 159, 163
food, Mediterranean influence on British, 251–2
football, and British influence in Spain, 215
Ford, Richard, *Handbook for Travellers in Spain* (1839), 148
Forster, E. M., 9, 20, 160, 205–8
Foscolo, Ugo, 118, 119
Foundling Hospital, London, 33
Fournier, Louis Édouard, *The Cremation of Shelley* (1889), *2*
Frampton, Meredith, 229
France: cultural prestige of, 5, 66; July Revolution (1830), 111; Napoleonic Wars, 132; progressive art movement, 188, 217, 223; Revolutionary wars, 6, 60, 62, 83
Franco, General, 245, 257
Franco-Prussian War (1870–1), 158, 186
Franklin, Sir John, 11
Fraser, Antonia, 112
Frazer, James George, *The Golden Bough* (1890), 45, 208–9, 254
French realism, 157
Froude, James, 115, 116, 117, 186

Fry, Roger, 50, 192, 193, 236, 261; appeal of classicism, 201–2; in Athens, *239*, 240; attacks Greek art, 211; on John Singer Sargent, 203; Post-Impressionist exhibition (1910), 216–18, 220; in Provence, 222, 223, 238–9; *The Pool* (1899), 201

Fuller, Margaret, 19, 20, 120, 125

Fuseli, Henry, 54

Futurism, 218

Galdos, Perez, 188

Gallenga, Antonio, 164

Galuppi, Baldassare, 9

Gardner, Percy, *A Grammar of Greek Art* (1905), 211

Garibaldi, Giuseppe, 153, 160–2

Garnett, David, 236

Garrick, David, 41, 52

Gaskell, Elizabeth, *North and South* (1855), 130, 140

Gaudí, Antoni, 216

Gautier, Théophile, 147

Gell, William, 68, 69, 114

George, King of Greece (*formerly* Prince George of Denmark), 182

George IV, King, 90, 106

German culture, British interest in, 132–3

Ghika, Nikos, 253

Gibbon, Edward, 16, 53, 110, 136

Gilbert and Sullivan, *Patience* (1881), 180

Gillray, James, *Dido, in Despair!* (1801), 63

Gissing, George, 203

Gladstone, William: and Greece, 182; as lord high commissioner to the Ionian Islands, 142–3; and Italian unification, 119, 152, 164–5; Mediterranean influences on, 107; proficiency in Italian, 118; and Samuel Butler, 197; *Studies on Homer and the Homeric Age* (1858), 141–2

Glasgow Boys (group of painters), 199

Gloeden, Baron Wilhelm von, 194

Glorious Revolution (1688), 28, 57

Goethe, Johann Wolfgang von, 23–4, 38, 41, 47, 53, 62, 93, 132; *The Sorrows of Young Werther* (1774), 78, 86–7

Goethe, Ottilie von, 133

Goethe Society, 132

Goldhill, Simon, 174

Goldoni, Carlo, 59

Goldsmith, Oliver, 97

Gordon, Jan and Cora, *Poor Folk in Spain* (1922), 235

Gordon Riots (1780), 54

Gore, Spencer, 215

Gosse, Edmund, 155

Goya, Francisco, 84, 118, 149, 215

Grand Tour: acquisitions made during, 75, 76; decline of, 59, 61; evolution of, 5, 27–32, 261; and the fine arts, 50; and sense of dislocation, 12; and Spain, 56; and Venice, 57–9

Grant, Abbé, 55

Grant, Duncan, 221, 243

Graves, Robert, 209, 243–5, 254, 258

Gray, Effie, 135, 138

Great Exhibition (1851), 110, 124, 130, 150–1, 157

Grecian style, British craze for, 75–6

Greece, 14; British hesitation in visiting, 39–40, 183–5, 213–14; British travellers in, 36–7, 67–71, 102–3; and Byron, 92–3; Dilessi murders, 183–4; in the First World War, 230; modern kingdom of, 182–3; post-war, 254; rebellion against Ottoman rule, 92, 103; in the Second World War, 252–3; Victorian interest in, 140–6

Greek Civil War (1946–9), 253

Greek Revival, 38, 70, 112, 139

Greek tragedy, 180, 241

Gregson, Bob, 74

Grey, Charles, 2nd Earl, 111, 118

Grote, George, 111; *History of Greece* (1846–56), 140–1

Guiccioli, Countess Teresa, 90, 91

Guilford, Frederick North, 5th Earl of, 86, 102–3

Gunning, Isabel, 67

Hall, Edith, 139

Hamilton, Catherine, 42

Hamilton, Gavin, 36–8, 61

Hamilton, Lady Emma (*née* Hart), 61–2, 63; 'Attitudes' of, 24–6, 74

Hamilton, Sir William, 23–6, 42–5, 61–3, 76; *Campi Phlegraei* (1776), 43

Hancarville, 'Baron' d' (Pierre-François Hugues), 43

Handel, George Frideric: *Alexander's Feast* (1736), 30; *Giulio Cesare* (1724), *30*; *Rinaldo* (1711), 29

Hare, Augustus, 165

Harris, Alexandra, 75, 235

Harrison, Austen, 249

Harrison, Jane, 209–10, 231

Hawthorne, Nathaniel, 8, 19, 127; *The Marble Faun* (1860), 12

Hayter, Stanley, *Paysage Anthropophage* (1937), 246
Hazlitt, William, 13, 64, 66, 97, 100; 'English Students at Rome', 98–9
Head, Sir Edmund Walker, 148
Hellenism, 6, 38, 102–3, 141–3, 157, 159, 175, 178–84, 197, 201, 208–12, 227–31, 244, 253–4
Hellfire Club, 33
Hemingway, Ernest, 20; *The Sun Also Rises* (1926), 235
Henry III, King, 21
Henry VIII, King, 21
Herculaneum, 24, 32, 41–2
Herold, J. Christopher, 81
Hess, Myra, 248
Highsmith, Patricia, *The Talented Mr Ripley* (1955), 9–10
Hirst, Damien, *Treasures from the Wreck of the Unbelievable* (exhibition, 2017), 260
Hitler, Adolf, 246, 248
Hogarth, William, 30, 31
holidays, Mediterranean, 8
Holland, Elizabeth Fox, Baroness, 118, 126
Holland, Henry Vassall-Fox, 3rd Baron, 118, 126
'Holland House set', 118
Holman Hunt, William, 137
Holroyd, Michael, 238
Homer, 141–2, 196–8, 226
homosexuality, 178
Hope, Thomas, 76–7, 102
Houses of Parliament, destruction by fire (1834), 131
Howarth, David, 188
Hunt, Philip, 71, 72
Hutchinson, Sara, 77, 78
Huxley, Aldous, *These Barren Leaves* (1925), 160

Impressionism, 157, 170
industrialization, British
Ingres, Jean-Auguste-Dominique: *Turkish Baths* (1862), 157, 174
Innes, James Dickson, 200
Ionian Islands, 102, 142–3, 183
Irving, Washington, 20, 104–5
Islamic culture, 16–18, 104
Italian Art, 1200–1900 (exhibition, 1930), 240
Italian exiles in Britain, 118–21, 164
Italian language, British proficiency in, 118–19

Italian opera, in London, 29–30, 121
Italian prisoners of war, 249
Italy: Risorgimento, 152–5, 160–5, 219, 220; in the Second World War, 248–9; unification, 160, 163–6; uprisings against Austrian rule, 118, 120; *see also* Florence; Naples; Rome

Jackson, Holbrook, 195
Jacobite Rebellion (1745), 54
James, Henry: on Americans and the English, 20; on the 'crash of civilisation', 222; on Elizabeth Barrett Browning, 124; on English lack of aestheticism, 178; on Florence, 126, 157, 159, 160; and Greece, 185; Italian fiction of, 12, 204–5; on Naples, 167; and Spain, 185–6; T. S. Eliot on, 212; *The Wings of the Dove* (1902), 205
Jameson, Anna, 124, 150; *Diary of an Ennuyée* (1826), 101, 133; *Sacred and Legendary Art* (1848), 133
Japan, artistic consciousness of, 193
Japanese fashions, 1860s, 177
Jebb, Richard, 180
Jefferson, Thomas, 54
Jenkins, Thomas, 61
Jenkyns, Richard, 141, 174
John, Augustus, 224, 238, 261
John, Gwen, 198
'John Bull' stereotype, 29, 63
Johnson, Samuel, 28, 47, 50, 112, 126
Jones, Inigo, 27
Jones, Owen, 150–1
Jones, Thomas, 8, 49
Jordan, Mrs Dorothea, 75
Joseph II, Emperor of Austria, 42
Journey to Italy (film, 1954), 251
Joyce, James, *Ulysses* (1922), 197

Katsimbalis, George, 253
Kauffmann, Angelica, 52–4
Keats, John, 3, 14, 94–6
Keats-Shelley Memorial House, Rome, 95, 218, *219*
Kelsey, Marguerite, 229
Kemble, Fanny, 146
Kerr, Robert, *The Gentleman's House* (1864), 158
Kipling, Rudyard, 193
Knapton, George, 32–3
Knight, Richard Payne, 44, *45*, 75
Knights, Winifred, *The Deluge* (1920), 234
Knossos, Crete, 201

Lamb, Euphemia, 200
Lancaster, Osbert, 253
Landor, Walter, 128, 139
landscape painting, 48–50
Langtry, Lillie, 179–80
Lassels, Robert, *The Voyage of Italy* (1670), 27
Laurentian Library, 21
Lawrence, D. H., 17, 208, 210, 232–3, 239, 253; *Twilight in Italy* (1915), 15
Lawrence, Frieda, 17
Lawrence, Sir Thomas, 97, 99–101
Layard, Austen Henry, 167, 186
Layard, Lady Mary, 187
League of Nations, 231
Leake, William Martin, 69
Lear, Edward, 97, 127, 143–4, 184, 189–91, *191*; *Campagna of Rome from the Villa Mattei* (1841), *144*; *Laughable Lyrics* (1877), 190; *Views in the Seven Ionian Islands* (1863), 183
Lee, Vernon, 192, 200–1, 212–14, 259
Lees-Milne, James, 36
Leigh-Fermor, Patrick, 212, 253, 254
Leighton, Frederic, 16, 159, 174, 175–6, 178, 208
Leo XIII, Pope, 195
Levant Company, 31
Lewes, George, 154, 185
Lewis, John Frederick, *Sketches and Drawings of the Alhambra* (1835), 148
Lewis, Matthew, *The Monk* (1796), 56–7
Lewis, Norman, *Naples '44* (1978), 247
Lewis, Wyndham, 215
Liberty's department store, 177
Lion Gate, Mycenae, 72
literary topography, 69
Little Holland House, 160
Lloyd George, David, 211, 230
London 'clubland', 69
London Photographic Society, 151
Louise of Stolberg-Gedern, Princess, 54
Louis-Philippe, King, 111, 149
Louvre, Musée du, 65, 66; *see also* Musée Napoléon (Musée du Louvre)
Lucca, Italy, 167
Lushington, Franklin, 143
Lusieri, Giovanni Battista, 71
Lutyens, Edward, Cenotaph (1920), 227

Macaulay, Rose: *Fabled Shore* (1949), 251; *The Pleasure of Ruins* (1953), 182
MacCarthy, Fiona, 85, 107, 168
Mackintosh, Charles Rennie, 238

Macmillan, Harold, 252, 255
MacNeice, Louis, 242, 253
Macpherson, James, *Poems of Ossian*, 11
Macri, Teresa, 87
Madrid, 151–2
Magna Graecia, 37, 40
Major, Thomas, *The Ruins of Paestum* (1768), 47
Malinowski, Bronisław, 209
Malta, 6, 7, 72, 77–9, 165
Malta Story (film, 1953), 247
Manchester, Charles Montagu, 1st Duke of, 5
Manet, Édouard, 216
Mann, Horace, 32
Mann, Thomas, *Death in Venice* (1912), 189
Mansfield, Katherine, 222
Marat, Jean-Paul, 53
Marchi, Gisueppe, 51
Maria Caroline, Queen, 61
Marinetti, Filippo, 218, 219, 220
Mario, Alberto, 152–3
Mario, Jessie White, 152–3, 160–1, 165
Martin, Simon, 247
Matisse, Henri, 221, 222
Maugham, W. Somerset, 203–4
Maupassant, Guy de, 157
Mavrocordatos, Prince, 92
Mayle, Peter, *A Year in Provence* (1989), 259
Mazzini, Giuseppe, 119–21, 152
Medmenham, Buckinghamshire, 33
Melville, Arthur, 199
Michelangelo, *Pietà* (1498–9), 241
Mill, John Stuart, 110, 141
Millais, John Everett, 11, 137, 138
Miller, Henry, *The Colossus of Maroussi* (1941), 253
Minton, John, 252
Missolonghi, Greece, 92, 95–6
'mods', and Italian Vespas, 255
Monnington, Sir Walter, 234
Monte Cassino, Italy, 164
Montesquieu, 33, 80
Moore, Albert, 177
Moore, Henry, 247–8
Morelli, Giovanni, 187
Morgan, Lady, 128
Morley, John, 119
Morris, Jan, 235, 259
Morris, William, 11, 241
Mortimer, Raymond, 251
Mozart, Leopold, 42
Mozart, Wolfgang Amadeus, 42

Muhaffy, W. H., 181
Murat, Joachim, 41
Murillo, Bartolomé Esteban, 52
Murphy, James Cavanah, *The Arabian Antiquities of Spain* (1812–16), 104–5
Murray, Gilbert, 230–1
Murray, John, 76, 85, 88, 137
Murry, John Middleton, 222
Musée Napoléon (Musée du Louvre), 65, 74, 99; *see also* Louvre, Musée du
Mussolini, Benito, 240, 248
Mylne, Robert, 51

Namier, Lewis, 234
Naples: 18th century, 40–2; Bulwer Lytton and *The Last Days of Pompei*, 113–14; Coleridge in, 79; Gladstone on, 152; Greek origins of, 37, 40; Henry James on, 167; John Henry Newman in, 116; in Madame de Staël's *Corinne*, 81; as Parthenopean Republic, 61; Sir William Hamilton's home in, 23, 24, 42–3; and the unification of Italy, 153; Victorian dislike of, 127
Napoleon Bonaparte, 11, 71, 96; 'Continental System', 66, 68; and Madame de Staël, 80, 83; occupies Venice, 60–1; seizure of cultural artefacts, 65–6, 74
Napoleon III, Emperor, 187
Napoleonic Wars, 132
Nash, Paul, *The Menin Road* (1919), 223
Nation (newspaper), 165
National Gallery, London: acquires Jacob van Eyck's *Arnolfini Portrait* (1843), 137; collection evacuated to Wales during Second World War, 248; foundation and relocation to Trafalgar Square, 112; Kenneth Clark appointed director, 237; Marinetti denounces English collections of, 218; Mary Richardson attacks the *Rokeby Venus*, 220; and Spanish paintings, 149–50, 187, 215, 257
Navarino, Battle of (1827), 103
Nazarene community, 96–7, 175
Nelson, Admiral Horatio, 61, 62, 71
neoclassicism, 26, 53, 71, 76, 222; after the First World War, 227–9
New Age (journal), 211
New English Art Club, 198, 200
Newman, John Henry, 109, 115–17, 129, 141
Newstead, Nottinghamshire, 93
Newton, Charles, 181

Nietzsche, Friedrich, *The Birth of Tragedy* (1872), 180
Nightingale, Florence, 128
North, Frederick *see* Guilford, Frederick North, 5th Earl of
Northern cultures, 242; appeal of, 11, 67, 77, 100
North–South dichotomy, 11–12, 14, 21, 242, 262; and Byron, 85, 89, 107; and Coleridge, 77; and Madame de Staël's *Corinne*, 80–3; Sir William Hamilton's home in Naples, 26; in Victorian England, 130–5
nudes, artistic depiction of, 173–5

O'Connell, Daniel, 106
Old Slaughter's Coffee House, London, 31
'Olympian Painting' school, 173, 175, 198, 208
opera: and the British, 78; Italian opera in London, 29–30, 121
Orkney, Italian chapel, 249
Orléans, Duke of (aka Philippe Égalité), collections exhibited in London, 63–4, 66
Ormond, Richard, 202
Ortega y Gasset, José, 236
Orwell, George: *Homage to Catalonia* (1938), 245; *The Road to Wigan Pier* (1937), 242
Otto, King, of Greece, 145, 182
Ottoman Empire, 71
Otway, Thomas, *Venice Preserv'd* (1682), 57
Ouida (Marie Louise de la Ramée), 165–6
Oxford Movement, 117

Pacifico, Don, 145–6
Paestum, Doric temples, 46–7, 70, 98
Palladian school of architecture, 27, 31, 34, 57
Palladio, Andrea, 27
Palmer, Samuel, 99
Palmerston, Lady, 161
Palmerston, Lord, 103, 104, 118, 145–6
Panizzi, Antonio, 119
Pankhurst, Emmeline, 220
'Papal Aggression', 129–30, 137
Paris, 149, 157–8, 170, 173, 188, 198; *see also* Louvre, Musée du
Pars, William, 49
Parthenon, Athens, 71, 73; Virginia Woolf on, 228–9
patriotism, British, emergence of, 4
Paxton, Joseph, 110
Pecchio, Giuseppe, 118

Peel, Sir Robert, 105, 111–12, 139–40
Pelligrini, Giovanni, 5
Pemble, John, 19, 56, 87, 165, 167, 179, 226
Peninsular War (Spain), 83–5, 103–4
Pergami, Count, 90
Peterloo Massacre (1819), 90
Phillip, John, 148–9, 150
photography, 151
Picasso, Pablo, 205, 215, 221, 222; *Guernica* (1937), 246
Piper, John, 243
Piranesi, Giovanni, 35, 76
Pisa: Ruskin compares to Bradford, 138; Shelley's group in, 91, 92
Pius IX, Pope, 129, 164–5
Pomardi, Simone, *A Classical and Topographical Tour through Greece* (1819), 68
Pompeii, 24, 41–2, 114
Pond, Arthur, 32–3
Pope, Alexander, 27, 132
Post-Impressionist exhibition (1910), 216–18, 220
Pound, Ezra, 163, 221, 259
Powell, Dilys, 252
Powell, Enoch, 'rivers of blood' speech, 256
Powers, Hiram, *The Greek Slave*, 110
Poynter, Sir Edward John, 198
Prado Museum, Madrid, 187, 188, 215, 238
Pre-Raphaelites, 137, 139, 168–9, 173
Priapus, cult of, 44–5, 63
Pritchett, V. S., 236
Provence, France, 222, 238–9, 259, 261
psychology, early interest in, 43–4
Pugin, Augustus, 131
Punch (magazine), 110

Quarterly Review (journal), 84, 103
Queen's Theatre, Haymarket, 29

Radcliffe, Ann, *A Sicilian Romance* (1790), 47–8
Raeburn, Henry, *The Reverend Robert Walker Skating on Duddingston Loch* (*c.*1795), 150
railways, introduction of, 28, 117, 137, 167
Raphael, 112, 201, 256; *The School of Athens* (1509–11), 51
Ravilious, Eric, 50
Reform Acts: (1832), 109, 111–12; (1867), 162
Rehberg, Friedrich, Emma Hamilton as 'The Muse of Dance' (1794), 25

Renault, Mary, 253
Revett, Nicholas, 36–8, 69
Reynolds, Sir Joshua, 51–2, 57, 211; *Meeting of the Society of Dilettanti* (1778), *34*
Ricci, Mario, 5
Richard, Cliff, 254
Richardson, Mary, 220
Richardson, Samuel, 31, 94
Riding, Laura, 243–5
Rimbaud, Arthur, 200
Risorgimento, 152–5, 160–5, 165, 219, 220
Roberts, David, 18, 148, 150, 236
Robeson, Paul, 246
Rodd, Rennell, 168, 204
Rogers, Samuel, 116; *Italy* (1828), 100–1
Roman Club, 32
Romano-British culture, 20–1
Romanticism, 26; English, 3, 11
Rome: American Church in, 169; British artists in, 96–7; British presence in, 127; English Coffee House, 76; English College in, 106, 116; English suspicion of, 110; Jacobites in, 55; John Henry Newman in, 116–17; Protestant Cemetery, 2–3, 91, 95
Rosa, Salvator, 48
Rossellini, Roberto, 251
Rossetti, Dante Gabriel, 119, 137, 139, 163
Royal Academy, 51–2, 53, 70, 97, 173, 175, 193, 236
Royal Academy Schools, 69–70
Royal Irish Academy, 104
Royal Photographic Society, 194
Royal Society, London, 43
Runciman, Steven, 232, 253
Ruskin, John, 61, 89, 99, 118, 134–9, 150, 154, 198, 217, 254; on Praxitiles' *Aphrodite*, 174; and preservation of Italian art, 166–9; *Fors Clavigera* (1884), 166, 171; *Modern Painters* (1843–60), 135; *The Palazzo Contarini Fasan, Venice* (1841), *136*; *The Stones of Venice* (1851–3), 134
Russell, Bertrand, 236
Russell, Lord John, 84–5, 118, 141, 162, 163

Said, Edward, *Orientalism* (1978), 15–16, 18
San Remo, Italy, 190
Sand, George, 202
Sandby, Paul, *The Opening of the Carnival at Rome* (c. 1781), *58*

Sardinia, 17

Sargent, John Singer, 160, 187–8, 202–3, 222, 260; *Breakfast in the Loggia* (1910), 8–9; *El Jaleo* (1882), 216; *In a Garden, Corfu* (1909), 202; *Gassed* (1919), 227; *Graveyard in the Tyrol* (1914), 203

Sassoon, Siegfried, 226

satire, English, of Italian culture, 29–31

Saxl, Fritz, 7, 247

Schliemann, Heinrich, 181

Schmitz, Oscar, 193

Schumann, Robert, 89

Scott, Ridley, *Gladiator* (film, 2000), 176

Scott, Sir Walter, 132

Second World War, 6, 7, 246–9, 252

Sedgwick, Catharine, *Letters from Abroad* (1841), 20

Seferis, George, 253

Seurat, Georges, 216

Seven Years' War, 50, 60

Severn, Joseph, 94–5, 98

Shaffer, Elinor, 171

Shakespeare, William, 27

Shelley, Mary, 2–3, 55, 88, 91, 92

Shelley, Percy Bysshe: and Byron, 88; 'canonization' after death, 226; death and cremation, 1–3, 93; and Keats, 95; and opera, 78; in Pisa, 91; in Rome, 55; *Hellas* (1822), 92

Shirley Valentine (film, 1989), 8

Sicily, 6, 47, 78, 116, 117, 233

Sickert, Walter, 198, 199, 211–12

Siddons, Sarah, 74

Sidney, Sir Philip, 225

Sismondi, Jean-Charles-Léonard Simonde de, 96

Sitwell, Edith, 232, 245

Sitwell, Osbert, 202, 232, 245

Sitwell, Sacheverell, 43, 232, 233, 245

Skyros, Greece, 225

Slade School of Art, 173

Smirke, Robert, 69–71, 72; *Temple of Concordia, Girgenti, Sicily* (1802–4), *70*

Smith, Adam, 56

Smith, Joseph, 59–60

Smollett, Tobias, 55

social realism, 203

Society for the Promotion of Hellenic Studies, 181

Society of Antiquaries, 181

Sooke, Alastair, 257

Souliotes, Epirus, 69

Soult, Marshal, 84

Sounion temple, 88

Souter, John Bulloch, *The Breakdown* (1926), 229

Southey, Robert, 83

Spain: 'Black Legend', 56, 216; British artists in, 236–7; British relations with, 103–4, 146–7, 189, 214–16, 245–6, 257; Catholicism of, 10, 56, 148, 150; Disraeli in, 106–7; and Ernest Hemingway, 235; excluded from Kenneth Clark's *Civilisation*, 257; Islamic culture, 18, 104; limited contact with local people, 14; modernism in, 216; Peninsular War, 83–5, 103; unique history of, 8; Victorian attitudes to, 185–6

Spanish art, British appreciation of, 148–52, 186–9, 214–16

Spanish Civil War, 245–6

Spanish exhibition (1889), London, 189

Spanish literature, 188–9, 214

Speedwell, HMS, 77

Spencer, Stanley, 227

Spencer House, London, 38

St Pancras Church, London, 158

Staël, Germaine de, 4, 88; *Corinne, or Italy* (1807), 31, 80–3, 85, 207; *De l'Allemagne* (1810), 83

Stark, Freya, 259

Steegman, John, 109, 131, 158, 223

Stendhal (Marie-Henri Beyle), 96

Stephen, Leslie, 137

Stephen, Thoby, 228

Stevenson, R. A. M., 214

Stirling, William, 148, 148–9, 150

Storks, Sir Henry, 183

Storrs, Sir Ronald, 236

Stourton, James, 256–7, 258

Strachey, Lytton, 234, 236

Street, George, 177

Stuart, Charles Edward (the Young Pretender), 54

Stuart, James, 36, 69

Suffragettes, 220

Summer Holiday (film, 1963), 254–5

Swinburne, Algernon, 162–3; 'Dolores' (1866), 156; 'Ode to Candia' (1867), 183; 'A Song for Italy' (1867), 163; *Poems and Ballads* (1866), 162; *Songs before Sunrise* (1871), 163

Symonds, A. J., 12, 15, 178–9, 184–5, 261; *A Problem of Greek Ethics* (1883), 178

Symons, Arthur, 13–14

Syracuse, Sicily, 47

Taine, Charles, 177
Tavener, John, 'Song for Athene' (1997), 259
Tennyson, Alfred, Lord, 161, 190
Terry, Ellen, 25, 177
Thackeray, William, 121, 132, 139; *Vanity Fair* (1847–8), 113
Thatcher, Margaret, 258
Theatre Royal, Covent Garden, 70, 121
Theroux, Paul, 213
Thrale, Mrs, 126
Tischbein, Johann, 23–5
Titian: *Man with a Glove* (*c.* 1520), 66; portrait of Charles V, 21; *Sacred and Profane Love* (*c.* 1515), 212
Tooke, John Horne, 67
Torrijos, General, 104
Towne, Francis, 50
travel writing, 47, 212–13, 232, 235, 259
Travellers' Club, 69, 102
Treaty of Amiens (1802), 66
Treaty of Paris (1814), 96
Treaty of Utrecht (1713), 29
Trelawny, Edward, 1–2, 11–12
Trench, Robert Chevenix, 104
Trend, J. B., 235, 236
Trevelyan, G. M., 152, 202, 218–20; *Garibaldi* trilogy (1907–11), 218–19
Trollope, Anthony, 126
Trollope, Fanny, 126
Trollope, Thomas Adolphus, *Marietta* (1862), 128
Troy, site of, 69
Turner, Frank, 140, 208
Turner, J. M. W.: admires Elgin Marbles, 74; and English landscape painting, 48, 50, 66; in Italy, 99–101; revival of, 200; in Ruskin's *Modern Painters*, 135; and Victorian 'taste', 149; *The Golden Bough* illustration, 208; *Liber Studiorum* (1807–9), 200
Tweddell, John, 67, 75

Uglow, Jenny, 190

Van Gogh, Vincent, 216
Vatican, 55
Velázquez, Diego, 11, 52, 112, 150, 215; influence on British artists, 187–8, 214; *Rokeby Venus* (1647), 220
Venice: Biennale Festival, 205; British anti-restoration campaign, 167–8; Browning's death in, 190–1; Byron in, 89; and Canaletto, 59–60; compared with Britain, 134; on the Grand Tour, 57–9;

and Henry James, 205; J. A. M. Whistler in, 171; and J. M. W. Turner, 100; and John Ruskin, 134–7; occupation by Napoleon, 60–1; Ruskin's *The Stones of Venice*, 134; unified with Italy, 162; Venetian masques, 15; Walter Sickert in, 199
Venizélos, Eleuthérios, 230
Verona, Italy, 167
Vesuvius, Mount, 41, 43, 114
Viareggio, Italy, 1, 91
Victor Emmanuel, King, of Italy, 153, 162
Victoria, Queen, 110, 129, 149, 161, 182, 183, 199–200
Victoria Eugenie, Queen, of Spain ('Queen Ena'), 215
Viking culture, 132
Villiers, George, 146
Virgil, 241; *Aeneid*, 256
volcanoes and earthquakes, 43–4
Voltaire, 33

Walpole, Horace, 32–3
Walpole, Robert, 52
Walton, William, 234
War of Austrian Succession, 28, 59
War of Spanish Succession, 29
Warner, Rex, 253
Waterloo, Battle of (1815), 96, 98
Watts, George Frederic, 126, 128–9, 160, 177, 193
Waugh, Evelyn: *Officers and Gentlemen* (1955), 247; *The Ordeal of Gilbert Pinfold* (1957), 225
Wedgwood, Josiah, 43
Wellington, Arthur Wellesley, Duke of, 83, 84, 103
West, Rebecca, 232
West Wing (TV series), 146
Westminster Cathedral, 177
Westminster Review (journal), 96, 118
Westmorland, Countess of, 98
Wharton, Edith, 200–1, 204, 222; *Italian Villas and Their Gardens* (1905), 201, 212; *The Valley of Decision* (1902), 57, 201
Wheeler, Sir George, 37
Whistler, J. A. M., 11, 170, 177, 241; admiration for Velázquez, 188; on British art, 178; in Venice, 171, 198–9; *Arrangement in Grey and Black* (1872), 188
Whistler, Rex, 234–5
White, Jessie *see* Mario, Jessie White

Wilde, Oscar, 13, 178, *195*; on archaeology, 181; disappointment in Greece, 184–5; and Greek style of dress, 179–80; travels in France and Italy after his release, 194–5; trial and imprisonment, 194

Wilkes, John, 33

Wilkie, David, 104–6, 112, 150; *The Defence of Saragossa* (1828), 106

Wilkins, William, 112

William III, King, 29

William IV, King, 111

Wilson, Richard, 48–9

Winckelmann, Johann Joachim, 38–40, 65

Wiseman, Nicholas, 116, 129

Wittkower, Rudolf, 7, 247

women, British: dress reform, Victorian, 179–80; Mediterranean influences on, 83, 85, 113; Suffragettes, 220

Women's World (magazine), 179

Woolf, Leonard, *239*, 240

Woolf, Virginia: in Athens, *239*; on the classical revival after the First World War, 227–9; and Jane Harrison, 210; on the Post-Impressionist exhibition (1910), 216; on Roger Fry, 201, 217, 240; and Rupert Brooke, 226; in Spain, 235; *Between the Acts* (1941), 243; *Jacob's Room* (1922), 228–9, 234

Wordsworth, William, 77, 78, 83; *Guide to the Lakes* (1822), 10, 98; *Lyrical Ballads* (1798), 67

Wortley Montagu, Lady Mary, 28, 32; *Turkish Embassy Letters* (1763), 16

Wotton, Sir Henry, 21, 249, 259

Wyse, Sir Thomas, 145

Yannina, Greece, 69, 107

Yeats, W. B., 210

'Young Italy' (*La Giovaine Italia*), 120

Zambaco, Maria, 169

Zorba the Greek (film, 1964), 254

Zucchi, Antonio, 53

Zurbarán, Francisco de, 149